What's on the CD?

THE ACCOMPANYING CD contains several valuable tools to help you prepare for your MCSE exams:

- **CBT Systems'** *Windows NT 3.5x to 4.0: Upgrade courseware*: A computer-based training course, this program provides eight hours of interactive NT 4.0 training.

- **Microsoft's** *Roadmap to Education and Certification*: An online course catalog and exam preparation guide that provides an overview of the process of becoming an MCSE.

- **Microsoft's** *Personal Exam Prep*: An evaluation copy of Microsoft's official exam preparation software for testing your knowledge of NT Workstation. (CODE: 888-SYX-002)

- **Microsoft's** *TechNet Technical Information Network*: An evaluation copy of a vast database of information related to Microsoft products and technologies. It includes more than 100,000 pages of articles, technical notes, service packs, and Knowledge Bases.

- **Transcender Corporation's** *Certification Sampler*: Provides sample exam questions to give you a clear idea of the types of questions you'll see when you take your MCSE exams.

The CD also contains programs provided by the authors that are required for the exercises in various chapters of the book. Please consult the README *file located in the root directory of the CD for information on these files and for installation instructions for the programs listed above.*

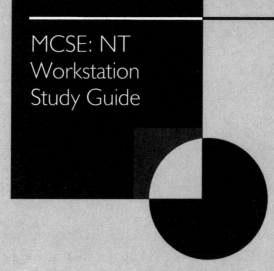

MCSE: NT
Workstation
Study Guide

GET THE BEST CONNECTIONS FROM
NETWORK PRESS™

You CAN judge a book by its cover.

This Network Press™ title is part of a new, expanded series replacing Sybex's acclaimed Novell Press® book series. With Network Press, you'll find the same dedication to quality from a truly independent and unbiased point of view. Our unique perspective guarantees you full coverage of Novell, Microsoft, and the other network environments.

Building on 20 years of technical and publishing excellence, Network Press provides you the broadest range of networking books published today. Our well-known commitment to quality, content, and timeliness continues to guarantee your satisfaction.

Network Press books offer you:

- winning certification test preparation strategies
- respected authors in the field of networking
- all new titles in a wide variety of topics
- up-to-date, revised editions of familiar best-sellers

Look for the distinctive black-and-white Network Press cover as your guarantee of quality. A comprehensive selection of Network Press books is available now at your local bookstore.

For more information about Network Press, please contact:

Network Press
1151 Marina Village Parkway
Alameda, CA 94501
Tel: (510)523-8233 Toll Free: (800)277-2346
Fax: (510)523-2373 E-mail: info@sybex.com

MCSE: NT® Workstation Study Guide

Charles Perkins
and Matthew Strebe
with James Chellis

San Francisco ■ Paris ■ Düsseldorf ■ Soest

Associate Publisher: Steve Sayre
Acquisitions Manager: Kristine Plachy
Associate Developmental Editor: Neil Edde
Editor: June Waldman
Project Editor: Kim Wimpsett
Technical Editor: John Schroeder
Book Design Director:Cătălin Dulfu
Book Designer: Seventeenth Street Studio
Graphic Illustrator: Patrick Dintino
Desktop Publisher: Susan Glinert Stevens
Production Coordinator: Nathan Johanson
Indexer: Matthew Spence
Cover Designer: Archer Design

Library of Congress Card Number: 96-70209
ISBN: 0-7821-1973-5

Manufactured in the United States of America

10 9 8

Software License Agreement: Terms and Conditions

The media accompanying this book contains software ("the Software") to be used in connection with the book. SYBEX hereby grants to you a license to use the Software, subject to the terms that follow. Your purchase, acceptance, or use of the Software will constitute your acceptance of such terms.

The Software compilation is the property of SYBEX unless otherwise indicated and is protected by copyright to SYBEX or other copyright owner(s) as indicated in the media files (the "Owner(s)"). You are hereby granted a single-user license to use the Software for your personal, noncommercial use only. You may not reproduce, sell, distribute, publish, circulate, or commercially exploit the Software, or any portion thereof, without the written consent of SYBEX and the specific copyright owner(s) of any component software included on this media.

Software Support

Components of the supplemental software and any offers associated with them may be supported by the specific Owner(s) of that material but they are not supported by SYBEX. Information regarding any available support may be obtained from the Owner(s) using the information provided in the appropriate READ.ME files or listed elsewhere on the media.

Should the manufacturer(s) or other Owner(s) cease to offer support or decline to honor any offer, SYBEX bears no responsibility. This notice concerning support for the Software is provided for your information only. SYBEX is not the agent or principal of the Owner(s), and SYBEX is in no way responsible for providing any support for the Software, nor is it liable or responsible for any support provided, or not provided, by the Owner(s).

Warranty

SYBEX warrants the enclosed media to be free of physical defects for a period of ninety (90) days after purchase. The Software is not available from SYBEX in any other form or media than that enclosed herein. If you discover a defect in the media during this warranty period, you may obtain a replacement of identical format at no charge by sending the defective media, postage prepaid, with proof of purchase to

SYBEX Inc.
Customer Service Department
1151 Marina Village Parkway
Alameda, CA 94501
(510) 523-8233
Fax: (510) 523-2373
e-mail: info@sybex.com

After the 90-day period, you can obtain replacement media of identical format by sending us the defective disk, proof of purchase, and a check or money order for $10, payable to SYBEX.

Disclaimer

SYBEX makes no warranty or representation, either expressed or implied, with respect to this media or its contents, its quality, performance, merchantability, or fitness for a particular purpose. In no event will SYBEX, its distributors, or dealers be liable to you or any other party for direct, indirect, special, incidental, consequential, or other damages arising out of the use of or inability to use the media or its contents even if advised of the possibility of such damage.

The exclusion of implied warranties is not permitted by some states. Therefore, the above exclusion may not apply to you. This warranty provides you with specific legal rights; there may be other rights that you may have that vary from state to state. The pricing of the book with the Software by SYBEX reflects the allocation of risk and limitations on liability contained in this agreement of Terms and Conditions.

Shareware Distribution

This Software media may contain various programs that are distributed as shareware. Copyright laws apply to both shareware and ordinary commercial software, and the copyright Owner(s) retains all rights. If you try a shareware program and continue using it, you are expected to register it. Individual programs differ on details of trial periods, registration, and payment. Please observe the requirements stated in appropriate files.

Copy Protection

None of the files on the disk is copy-protected. However, in all cases, reselling or redistributing these files without authorization is expressly forbidden except as specifically provided for by the Owner(s) therein.

Charles Perkins: To Mom and Dad
Matthew Strebe: To my wife

Acknowledgments

Charles Perkins: I would like to thank my family and friends for their support; James Chellis, EdgeTek, and Sybex for giving me the opportunity to write this book; Michael Moncur for pointing me in their direction; Kim Wimpsett, Neil Edde, and June Waldman for their patience; and John Schroeder for his perspicacity. Thanks especially to Christy Strebe for letting me steal so much of her husband's time.

Matthew Strebe: I thank my wife for her support and patience; James Chellis for his support and patience; everyone at Sybex (Kim, Neil, June, and the mysterious JFS) for their support and patience; my family, especially daan for being daan; Mike and Laura; Dylan and Joan; Steve; Mike and Katy; Chuck; Farrell; Dawni; and the refugees from LL.

Thanks also to the production team who worked so hard on this book: Nathan Johanson, production coordinator; Susan Glinert Stevens, desktop publisher; and Patrick Dintino, graphic illustrator.

Contents at a Glance

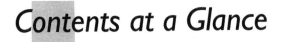

Table of Contents

Table of Exercises

Introduction

TODAY PERSONAL COMPUTERS ARE more powerful than even mainframes and supercomputers were a few years ago. Personal computer users often have gigabytes of hard disk space, megabytes of memory, and even hundreds of megahertz of processing power at their disposal. Personal computers are being used for much more than their original purposes of editing text and calculating spreadsheet values. The incredible computing capacity of today's computers is being used to combine audio, video, and textual information in multimedia software, to edit and present three-dimensional graphics and animation, and to communicate with other computers around the world via the Internet— to name just a few of the tasks of personal computers today.

Windows NT is the operating system that Microsoft developed to support today's computing requirements. The NT stands for New Technology. The new technology in Windows NT Workstation enables software writers to create sophisticated software and makes it easier for users to work with that software. Windows NT supports applications written for earlier Microsoft operating systems and is closely tied to Microsoft's premier operating system Windows NT Server, guaranteeing Windows NT Workstation's place in the future of personal computing.

Whether you are just getting started or are ready to move ahead in the computer industry, the knowledge and skills you have are your most valuable assets. Microsoft, recognizing this asset, has developed its Microsoft Certified Professional (MCP) program to give you credentials that verify your ability to work with Microsoft products effectively and professionally. The MCP credential designed for professionals who work with Microsoft networks is the Microsoft Certified Systems Engineer (MCSE) certification.

This book covers the Microsoft Windows NT Workstation operating system. Here you will find the information you need to acquire a solid foundation in the field of computer networks, to prepare for the Windows NT Workstation exam, and to take a big step toward MCSE certification.

Is This Book for You?

If you want to learn the basics of how Windows NT Workstation works, this book is for you. You'll find clear explanations of the fundamental concepts you need to grasp.

If you want to become certified as a Microsoft Certified Systems Engineer (MCSE), this book is also for you. The MCSE is *the* hot ticket in the field of professional computer networking. Microsoft is putting its weight behind the program, so now is the time to act. This book will start you off on the right foot.

What Does This Book Cover?

Think of this book as your guide to Windows NT Workstation. It begins by covering the most basic of Workstation concepts:

- What is it?

- How do you install it?

Next you will learn how to perform important tasks, such as

- Administering users and groups

- Configuring file systems and security

- Configuring local and network printing

- Networking Windows NT Workstation

You will also learn how to configure aspects of the operating system, tune your workstation's performance, work with applications, and troubleshoot your system.

How Do You Become an MCSE?

Attaining Microsoft Certified Systems Engineer (MCSE) status is a serious challenge. The exams cover a wide range of topics and require dedicated study and expertise. Many people who have achieved other computer industry credentials have had troubles with the MCSE. This challenge is, however, why the MCSE certificate is so valuable. If achieving MCSE status were easy, the market would be quickly flooded by MCSEs and the certification would quickly become meaningless. Microsoft, keenly aware of this fact, has taken steps to ensure that the certification means its holder is truly knowledgeable and skilled.

To become an MCSE, you must pass four core requirements and two electives. Most people select the following exam combination for the MCSE core requirements for the 4.0 track (the most current track):

CLIENT REQUIREMENT

70-73: Implementing and Supporting Windows NT Workstation 4.0

NETWORKING REQUIREMENT

70-58: Networking Essentials

WINDOWS NT SERVER 4.0 REQUIREMENT

70-67: Implementing and Supporting Windows NT Server 4.0

WINDOWS NT SERVER 4.0 IN THE ENTERPRISE REQUIREMENT

70-68: Implementing and Supporting Windows NT Server 4.0 in the Enterprise

For the electives, you have about 10 choices. The two most popular electives at present are

70-53: Internetworking Microsoft TCP/IP on Microsoft Windows NT 3.51 (4.0 will be available soon)
70-75: Implementing and Supporting Microsoft Exchange Server 4.0

For a complete description of all the MCSE options, see the Microsoft Roadmap to Education and Certification *on the CD that comes with this book.*

This book is a part of a series of Network Press MCSE Study Guides, published by Sybex, that covers four core requirements and two electives—the entire MCSE track.

Where Do You Take the Exams?

You may take the exams at any of more than 800 Authorized Prometric Testing Centers (APTCs) around the world. For the location of an APTC near you, call 800-755-EXAM (755-3926). Outside the United States and Canada, contact your local Sylvan Prometric Registration Center.

To register for a Microsoft Certified Professional exam:

1. Determine the number of the exam you want to take.

2. Register with the Sylvan Prometric Registration Center that is nearest to you. At this point you will be asked for advance payment for the exam—as of September 1996 the exams are $100 each. Exams must be taken within

one year of payment. You can schedule exams up to six weeks in advance or as late as one working day prior to the date of the exam. You can cancel or reschedule your exam if you contact Sylvan Prometric at least two working days prior to the exam. Same-day registration is available in some locations, subject to space availability. Where same-day registration is available, you must register a minimum of two hours before test time.

You will receive a registration and payment confirmation letter from Sylvan Prometric.

3. Call a nearby Authorized Prometric Testing Center (APTC) to schedule your exam.

When you schedule the exam, you'll receive instructions regarding appointment and cancellation procedures, ID requirements, and information about the testing center location.

What the Windows NT Workstation Exam Measures

The Windows NT Workstation exam covers concepts and skills required for the support of Windows NT Workstation computers. It emphasizes the following areas of Workstation support:

- Standards and terminology
- Planning
- Implementation
- Troubleshooting

This exam can be quite specific regarding Windows NT requirements and operational settings, and it can be particularly detailed about how administrative tasks are performed in the operating system. It also focuses on fundamental concepts relating to Windows NT Workstation's operation. Careful study of this book, along with hands-on experience with the operating system itself, will be especially helpful in preparing yourself for the exam.

Tips for Taking the Windows NT Workstation Exam

Here are some general tips for taking the exams successfully:

- Arrive early at the exam center so you can relax and take one last look at your study materials, particularly tables and lists of exam-related information.

- Read the questions carefully. Don't be tempted to jump to an early conclusion. Make sure you know *exactly* what the question is asking.

- Don't leave any unanswered questions. They count against you.

- Use a process of elimination to get rid of the obviously incorrect answers first on multiple-choice questions that you're not sure about. This method will improve your odds of selecting the correct answer if you need to make an educated guess.

- Save the hard questions for last because they will eat up the most time. You can move forward and back through the exam.

How to Use This Book

This book can provide a solid foundation for the serious effort of preparing for the Windows NT Workstation 4.0 exam. To best benefit from this book, you might want to use the following study method:

1. Study a chapter carefully, making sure you fully understand the information.

2. Complete all hands-on exercises in the chapter, referring to the chapter so that you understand each step you take.

3. Answer the exercise questions related to that chapter. (You will find the answers to these questions in Appendix A.)

4. Note which questions you did not understand and study the corresponding sections of the book again.

5. Study each chapter in the same manner.

6. Try the practice exams included on the CD that comes with this book. They will give you a good idea of what you can expect to see on the real thing.

If you prefer to use this book in conjunction with classroom or online training, you have many options. Both Microsoft-authorized training and independent training are widely available. Free network training referral services, such as Keeler Education at 800-800-1638 can help you locate available resources.

To learn all the material covered in this book, you will need to study regularly and with discipline. Try to set aside the same time every day to study and select a comfortable and quiet place in which to do it. If you work hard, you will be surprised at how quickly you learn this material. Good luck.

What's on the CD?

The CD contains several valuable tools to help you study for your MCSE exams:

- CBT System's *Windows NT 3.5x to 4.0: Upgrade* computer-based training. This program provides eight hours of interactive NT 4.0 training.

- Microsoft's *Roadmap to Education and Certification*, an online course catalog and exam preparation guide that provides an overview of the process of becoming an MCSE.

- An evaluation copy of Microsoft's *Personal Exam Prep*, which includes official Microsoft exam preparation software that can further test your knowledge of Windows NT Workstation.

- TechNet *Technical Information Network* demo, a vast database of information related to Microsoft products and technologies. It includes more than 100,000 pages of articles, technical notes, service packs, and Knowledge Bases.

- Transcender Corporation's *Certification Sampler* gives you a clear idea of the types of questions you'll see when you take your MCSE exams.

- Several programs required for the exercises in various chapters of the book.

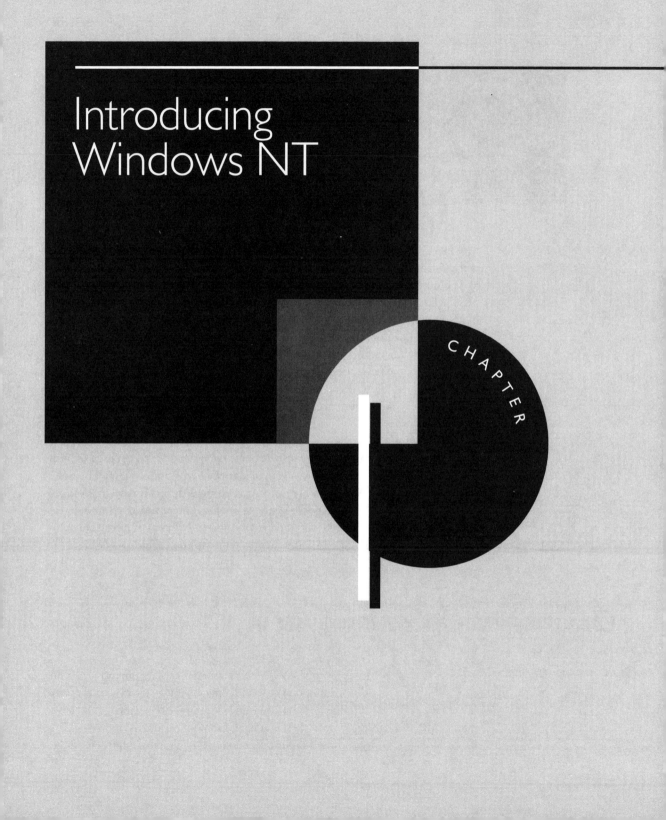

Introducing Windows NT

Windows NT IS THE FOUNDATION upon which Microsoft's networking strategy rests. Microsoft intends to provide a networking environment that is unified from bottom to top; from desktop clients to industrial-strength enterprise servers. Windows NT is the operating system that makes this strategy possible.

Windows NT's main competitor, Novell NetWare, provides powerful enterprise networking capabilities, but it is not useful as a desktop operating system. NT Server and NT Workstation are essentially the same software, with Server providing additional functionality and control for network environments.

Windows has established itself as a major contender to Novell NetWare's dominance in the network operating system market. Considering its more robust architecture, its flexibility, and its ability to support important fundamental improvements like multiprocessing, Windows NT may eclipse NetWare in the near future.

This book will take you on a guided tour of Windows NT Workstation and introduce the powerful features of the operating system. Our coverage of Windows NT Workstation starts with a general overview of Windows NT. Chapter 2 will help you install Windows NT, and succeeding chapters introduce components of Windows NT such as file systems, security, networking components, and printing. Then you'll see in detail how Windows NT runs applications, how the boot process works, and finally how to troubleshoot Windows NT.

Choosing an Operating System

Windows NT WORKSTATION is a very demanding operating system. It does not support the broad range of legacy hardware supported by Windows 95, and running Windows NT requires quite a bit more RAM and hard disk space than you need for Windows 95. Windows NT Workstation's security and multitasking scheduling puts more of a burden on the computer, causing noticeably slower performance for desktop applications compared to their performance on Windows 95.

Two primary considerations come into play when you select an operating system: what you have and what you want. What you have is the computer in which you will be installing an operating system. What you want is fulfillment of your computing requirements.

Operating System Hardware Requirements

Table 1.1 shows the official Microsoft minimum standards for its various operating systems.

Table 1.2 shows how an experienced network integrator would determine which operating system to run. The Microsoft minimum standards show the minimum requirements to load and run the operating system alone. Many users will actually want to use additional software. Use the criteria shown to determine which Microsoft operating system will be the best fit for your computer.

TABLE 1.1
Microsoft OS Minimum Requirements.

PLATFORM	PROCESSOR	RAM	HARD DISK
MS-DOS	8086	512KB	Not required
Windows 3.11 Enhanced Mode	386SX 16MHz	2MB	8(10)MB
Windows 95	386DX 20MHz	4(8)MB	40MB
Windows NT Workstation	486DX 33MHz	12(16)MB	120MB
Windows NT Server	486DX 33MHz	16MB	130MB

Values in parentheses indicate Microsoft recommended minimums.

Validating Your Hardware for Windows NT

Prior to Windows NT 4.0, the only way to find out about a hardware incompatibility problem was to attempt to install the operating system and fail. This involuntary method takes a bit of time, is very frustrating, and usually doesn't give you much information about what exactly is wrong.

TABLE 1.2 Selecting an Operating System.	**LESS POWERFUL**	**COMPUTER**	**MORE POWERFUL**
	Windows 3.11 for Workgroups	386, 16MB RAM, 400MB HD	Windows 95
	Windows 95	486/66, 32MB RAM, 500MB HD	Windows NT Workstation
	Windows 95	Pentium, 16MB RAM, 500MB HD	Windows NT Workstation
	Windows NT Workstation	Pentium Pro, 32MB RAM, 1GB HD	Windows NT Server
	Windows NT Workstation	RISC, 32MB RAM, 1GB HD	Windows NT Server

Microsoft has remedied this problem with the Windows NT Hardware Qualifier (NTHQ), a program that runs under DOS and inspects your computer for hardware incompatibilities without actually installing the operating system.

To use NTHQ, you must first create the NTHQ disk as shown in Exercise 1.1. You can run this program from any operating system that can run MS-DOS programs.

EXERCISE 1.1

Creating the Windows NT Hardware Qualifier (NTHQ) Disk

1. Boot MS-DOS or open an MS-DOS session in any operating system that supports running MS-DOS programs.

2. Insert the Windows NT Workstation CD-ROM.

3. Insert a formatted 1.44MB floppy disk into the A: drive.

4. Change drives to your CD-ROM.

5. Type **CD \SUPPORT\HQTOOL**.

6. Type **makedisk** and press Enter.

7. Remove the floppy disk and label it *NT Hardware Qualifier.*

After creating the NTHQ disk, you are ready to use it to validate your computer. Exercise 1.2 shows how to use the NTHQ disk.

EXERCISE 1.2

Using the Windows NT Hardware Qualifier (NTHQ) Disk

1. Boot the NTHQ floppy you created in Exercise 1.1.

2. Click Yes to continue at the query tool screen.

3. Click Yes for comprehensive detection. If this process locks up your computer, start over at step 1 and click No at this step.

4. Note the information detected about your computer.

5. Click the compatibility button.

6. Review each device listed as not compatible.

7. Ensure that you have third-party drivers for each device in this list or remove the device before attempting to install Windows NT.

Once you have installed Windows NT, you can attempt to re-install any devices you removed for incompatibility reasons.

Operating System Features

Determining if an operating system will run on your computer is only the first step. You must also determine whether the operating system fulfills your computing requirements.

Your requirements will be determined by

- Your hardware

- Your need for security

- The software you currently use

- The software used by others in your organization

- The software you want to use

- Your need for reliability and fault tolerance

- How responsive you want your computer to be

- The type of user interface you want to use

You are not likely to find an operating system that will meet all of your needs. Prioritize your requirements to find the best operating system for you. For instance, if you must have fault tolerance, but you'd like to support an old printer that Windows NT doesn't support, ask yourself how important that printer really is. If you can live without it (or upgrade it), you should use Windows NT.

You may find that your requirements cannot be fulfilled by the computer you currently own because it can't run the operating system you've decided will work best for you. Your best option in this case is to upgrade your computer. Use Table 1.3 to decide which operating system comes closest to fulfilling your requirements.

What Is Windows NT?

WINDOWS NT IS A 32-bit, preemptive, multitasking operating system that belongs to the Microsoft Windows family of operating system products.
It comes in two versions:

- **Windows NT Workstation:** Designed to work as member of a Windows NT Workstation workgroup, as a client of a Windows NT Server domain, as a Novell NetWare client, or on a stand-alone workstation. It is aimed toward users who need a reliable operating system with a high level of security.

- **Windows NT Server:** Essentially the same as Windows NT Workstation but with added features that enable it to work as a network operating system.

Windows NT Workstation comes with client software for NT Server and Novell NetWare.

Because these two products have so much in common, we'll look at their shared features first and then explore their differences.

Unlike previous versions of Windows, Windows NT really is a complete, true operating system in itself, not relying on DOS for lower-level functions. When a computer with Windows NT starts up, it starts immediately in Windows NT.

TABLE 1.3
Operating System Features.

REQUIRE-MENT	MS-DOS	WIN 3.11	OS/2 WARP	WIN 95	NT WS	NT SERVER
DOS software	√	√	√	√	1	1
Win16 software		√	√	√	√	√
Win32 software				√	√	√
Plug and Play				√		
Power management			√	√		
File level security			√		√	√
RAID						√
Preemptive			√	2	√	√
Multiprocessing					√	√
RISC CPU					√	√
Peer networking		√	√	√	√	√
Network server						√
Win16 drivers		√		√		
DOS drivers	√	√	3	√		
POSIX compliance					√	√
Peer Web services					√	
Internet host						√
Runs OS/2 1.3			√		√	√
Runs OS/2 2.0 PM			√			

1. Windows NT will not allow hardware access. DOS programs requiring such access will not run.
2. Windows 95 preemptive multitasking is not as fault tolerant as Windows NT.
3. OS/2 does not support all DOS mode drivers.

Windows NT Features

Windows NT is a secure, 32-bit computer operating system with a graphical interface. It is not a revision of any of the other Windows operating systems such as Windows 3.*x* or Windows for Workgroups 3.*x*, but rather an entirely new operating system.

Earlier versions of Windows NT used the graphical interface from Windows 3.*x* and Windows for Workgroups, but Windows NT 4.0 uses the Windows 95 graphical interface. Figure 1.1 shows the new face of Windows NT 4.0.

With Windows NT, Microsoft was able to go beyond the 16-bit limitations imposed by the MS-DOS operating system while maintaining support for MS-DOS applications (as well as Win16, Win32, OS/2, and POSIX environments). Windows NT Workstation supports existing files structures, in addition to the new file structure it introduces.

Windows NT has many features that we'll cover in detail in later chapters, but a few that are especially noteworthy are described in the following sections.

FIGURE 1.1
The latest graphical
interface on Windows NT.

Portability

Unlike most operating systems, Windows NT can run on a variety of platforms. This flexibility can be a great advantage when implementing a computer strategy for an organization because it can free you from being tied to a narrow selection of hardware platforms. Whereas DOS, for example, was written for the Intel 8086/8088 family of microprocessors, Windows NT was designed to support Intel 80386DX, 80486, and Pentium-based computers, as well as Reduced Instruction Set Computers (RISC)–based computers. Windows NT supports the following microprocessors:

- IBM PowerPC

- MIPS R4x00

- DEC Alpha AXP

- Intel 386 and descendants

Microsoft is able to port Windows NT easily to a variety of platforms because of the modular nature of Windows NT architecture. The hardware-specific components of NT architecture are stored apart from the rest of the operating system in a special module called the Hardware Abstraction Layer (HAL). This architecture enables NT developers to adapt Windows NT to various platforms simply by making changes to the HAL, rather than to an entire, monolithic operating system.

Multitasking Operations

From the perspective of the end user, *multitasking* means that different types of applications can run simultaneously. While the user is working on one application, another application can be running in the background.

An operating system achieves this effect by rapidly switching tasks, not—as it seems—by scheduling the microprocessor to work on more than one task at the same time. The microprocessor alternates so quickly from task to task that the user might think the machine is processing several different tasks at the same time. Windows NT actually supports two kinds of multitasking: preemptive and cooperative.

PREEMPTIVE MULTITASKING   Under previous versions of Windows, poorly written applications could seize control of a computer's processor and cause it to hang. Windows NT corrects this problem with *preemptive multitasking*. This type of multitasking allows the operating system to manage the processing of application *threads* in separate sessions without surrendering control of the processor.

COOPERATIVE MULTITASKING   Some multiple 16-bit Windows applications share the same processing session. In this case Windows NT relies on *cooperative multitasking* (rather than preemptive multitasking) under which the sharing of the session time is not managed by the operating system. Instead, each 16-bit Windows application must cooperate by releasing control of the processor so that the other applications can use it. Consequently, a poorly written application may be able to hang the other 16-bit applications running in the same 16-bit session, but it will not be able to affect the operation of Windows NT or other 32-bit processes. Windows NT is never hobbled by its ability to run cooperative multitasking applications.

Multithreading Operations

While running on a Pentium or RISC-based processor, Windows NT can actually execute multiple pieces of code—or *threads*—from a single application simultaneously. This capability is called *multithreading*. It helps to speed up applications and allows them to be executed more smoothly.

A thread is the most basic unit of code that can be scheduled for execution. A process is composed of one or more threads.

For example, under Windows 3.*x* you may have had the experience of running a multimedia application that was unable to produce smooth video while sound was playing. This situation could have been caused by Windows 3.*x* failing to process the application's video and audio threads in the correct distribution. If Windows 3.*x* had been able to multithread, as Windows NT does, it could have executed both the video and the audio threads smoothly.

File Systems

Windows NT supports a variety of file systems, including FAT, NTFS, and VFAT:

- **File Allocation Table (FAT):** The file system used with DOS

- **New Technology File System (NTFS):** The file system introduced by Windows NT

- **Virtual File Allocation Table (VFAT):** The file system introduced by Windows 95

Windows NT supports filenames of up to 256 characters, thus offering the "long filenames" feature that is a popular part of Windows 95.

Previous versions of Windows NT supported HPFS, but this feature was eliminated in the first release of NT 4.

Security

Microsoft designed Windows NT with security in mind. Windows NT's security features, such as a mandatory logon procedure, memory protection, auditing, and limited network access have been developed so that Windows NT can be used in accordance with the U.S. Department of Defense's Class C2 security specification.

Support for Many Clients

The following clients can serve as workstations on a Windows NT network:

- Windows 3.*x*

- Windows for Workgroups

- MS-DOS

- Windows 95

- Macintosh

- OS/2

- Windows NT Workstation

Because Windows NT Workstation is designed to work well with Windows NT Server, it is excellent as a client on a Windows NT network.

In addition, Windows NT has been designed to operate well on the same network as Novell NetWare and UNIX file, print, and application servers. Windows NT includes a suite of tools to provide seamless connectivity to NetWare servers.

MultiProcessor Support

Windows NT has the scalability to run on computers with multiple micro-processors, thereby enabling multiprocessing applications to run on more than one processor. This feature is referred to as *scalability* because the number of processors can be scaled to the demands of the task. When running on multiple processors, the Windows NT operating system manages the micro-processors as well as the memory, which they share.

The two main multiprocessing techniques are asymmetrical and symmetrical:

- **Asymmetrical multiprocessing (ASMP):** One processor is typically reserved for the operating system and the I/O devices, while the other processor(s) run application threads and other tasks. The problem with this approach is that it can be an inefficient way to use microprocessor resources, since one processor can end up being busier than another.

- **Symmetrical multiprocessing (SMP):** The available processors share all tasks, including operating system tasks, user processes, and application threads. This approach is the most efficient way to do multiprocessing, but designing an operating system to handle SMP is difficult. Fortunately, Windows NT was designed to support this type of multiprocessing.

To truly exploit the advantages of a multiprocessing operating system, an application must be specifically designed to execute multiple threads of code simultaneously.

Compatibility with Applications

Windows NT can run the following types of applications:

- DOS 16-bit applications

- Windows 3.*x* 16-bit (Win16) applications

- POSIX-compliant (POSIX is a UNIX implementation) applications

- OS/2 1.*x* character-based programs (and OS/2 1.*x* Presentation Manager applications if you obtain a special add-on package from Microsoft)

- New 32-bit (Win32) applications

Windows NT's compatibility with a variety of applications is critical to its success in the marketplace. For example, corporate MIS departments can switch to NT without needing to purchase new applications, which would mean large expenditures and massive retraining.

Storage Space

Windows NT supports a virtually limitless amount of memory and hard disk space. The specific numbers are as follows:

- **RAM:** Windows NT supports 4 gigabytes.

- **Hard disk space:** Windows NT supports 16 exabytes.

Networking Connectivity

Windows NT supports the following network protocols:

- TCP/IP

- DLC

- NetBEUI

- AppleTalk

- NWLink (Microsoft's 32-bit Windows NT IPX/SPX)

Because Windows NT was designed to be an operating system within an existing network, its developers provided support for the following network operating environments:

- AppleTalk networks

- Banyan Vines

- DEC Pathworks

- IBM LAN Server

- IBM SNA networks

- Microsoft LAN Manager

- Microsoft Windows 95 Peer Networking

- Microsoft Windows for Workgroups

- Novell NetWare

- TCP/IP networks

Windows NT Architecture

Before we head further into the services and features offered by Windows NT, and the differences between Windows NT Workstation and Windows NT Server, let's quickly detour into the guts of the Windows NT operating system. Figure 1.2 diagrams the Windows NT architecture.

A good understanding of the Windows NT architecture is crucial to understanding its inner workings.

Windows NT is based on a *modular* operating system. Rather than weaving all of the different components of the operating system into a complex, monolithic system, the designers of Windows NT decided to separate different operating system functions into independent components that work together to provide the complete functionality of a network operating system.

The Windows NT operating system uses objects. The word objects here is a general term that describes combinations of data and functions representing a service that can be shared by more than one process. These objects can be of different types, can be given different attributes, and can be protected by NT's security system.

Each component, while integrated with the rest of the operating system, is still distinct and has unique functionality. In fact, the modules are so distinct that they do not even share any code.

Dave Cutler headed the Windows NT design team. Cutler also designed the VMS operating system that runs on the DEC VAX system.

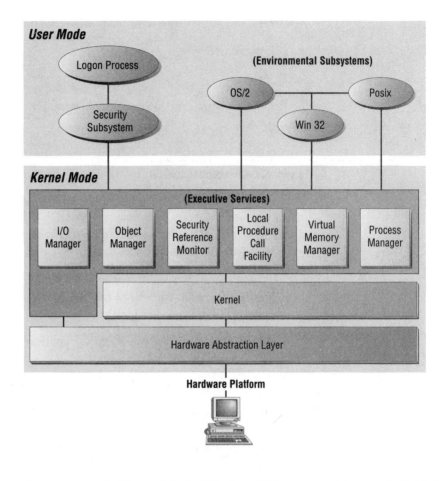

As you can see in Figure 1.2, the Windows NT system architecture is divided into two modes: User and Kernel. Let's begin by looking at the mode that is closest to us, the end users of NT.

The User Mode

The *User mode* is the operating system mode in which user applications and environmental subsystems are executed. It is a nonprivileged mode in which applications must call executive services in order to access memory and hardware. You'll learn more about executive services in just a few moments.

Several important subsystems run in User mode. Two of them are

- Environment

- Security

Let's take a quick look at these fundamental modules of the Windows NT architecture.

Environment Subsystems

As we mentioned earlier, Windows NT can run applications that are native to other operating systems. For example, Windows NT can run POSIX or OS/2 applications. Windows NT is able to do this because of the *environment subsystems* that reside in User mode.

The environment subsystems follow:

- **Win32** subsystem (the Windows NT 32-bit subsystem) supports Windows NT, DOS, and Windows applications.

- **POSIX** subsystem supports POSIX.1 applications, but these applications have limited functionality.

- **OS/2** subsystem provides limited support for OS/2.

Each of these subsystems contains an Application Programming Interface (API) that allows applications to run by emulating their native operating system. The Win32 subsystem, however, has a unique role in that it also controls the user interface.

The environmental subsystems are referred to as server objects, *while the applications are referred to as* client objects.

Security Subsystem

This subsystem handles the logon process. It works directly with the security reference monitor in the Kernel mode to verify the password. Here's how the security subsystem works: A user enters a password. The security subsystem then builds and sends an authentication package into the Kernel mode to the security reference monitor where it is checked against the security account database. If the password is correct, the security reference monitor builds and sends an access token back to the security subsystem.

One of the first things you may have noticed about Windows NT is that you log on by pressing Ctrl+Alt+Del. This key combination directly invokes the Windows NT logon routine, which resides in a secure area of Windows NT architecture that cannot be manipulated by would-be hackers.

Kernel Mode

The *Kernel mode* is also called the privileged processor mode. It is the inner core of the operating system. Unlike the User mode, this mode has execution priority over all User mode processes and cannot be swapped out to disk by the virtual memory manager (described later in this chapter).

User applications cannot access machine resources directly. To access system hardware and data, User mode applications make requests to the Kernel, then the Kernel executes the request and returns the resulting data. This method prevents a badly written program from destroying system resources or leaving the computer in an unstable state. Think of the Kernel as the teller in a bank. When you go into a bank to retrieve your money, the bank won't just let you walk into the vault. Instead, you must make a request to a teller, who enters the vault, retrieves your valuables, and returns them to you. The teller also makes a record of the transaction, which can be reviewed in a future audit. In this way the bank protects itself from both innocent and malicious loss and also keeps a record of all important accesses.

The Kernel mode is composed of three modules:

- The NT Executive
- The Kernel
- The HAL

These three modules are often called the *Executive services*. They are responsible for the fundamental functions of the operating system, including the processing of the microprocessor, as well as access to memory, hard disks, printers, and so on.

Executive

The NT Executive serves as the interface between the Kernel and the environmental subsystems in the User mode. It provides a set of services to support the native mode environments and contains six modules:

- **Object Manager:** Provides the rules for the retention, naming, and security of objects. It allocates objects, tracks their use, and removes them when they are no longer required.

- **Security reference monitor:** Is responsible for handling the logon process and the security protected subsystem (which is in User mode).

- **Process manager:** Creates and deletes processes and is also responsible for tracking process objects and thread objects.

- **Local procedure call facility:** Provides a client/server relationship between applications and the environmental subsystems.

- **Virtual memory manager:** Maps virtual addresses to physical pages in memory and makes sure that virtual memory is used efficiently.

- **I/O manager:** Handles all input and output for the operating system. When the I/O manager receives a request for an I/O service from an application, it determines which driver should be used and then sends a request to the driver.

Kernel

The nucleus of the entire operating system is the *Kernel*. The Kernel schedules all system activities (threads) for optimum performance. The Kernel queues data, channels it to the microprocessor, and the processed data directs it in the appropriate route. Windows NT has 32 thread-priority levels—the Kernel enforces and manages execution according to thread priority.

The Kernel is responsible for synchronizing multiple microprocessors.

Because the Kernel is responsible for the flow of activity in the microprocessor, it cannot be paged out to virtual memory (you'll learn more about virtual memory and paging later in the next section).

Hardware Abstraction Layer (HAL)

As mentioned earlier, one of the major features of Windows NT is its portability. The designers of Windows NT facilitated portability by creating the *Hardware Abstraction Layer* to hide the individual differences between different types of hardware platforms. The HAL effectively makes the hardware transparent to the rest of the operating system.

When NT is ported to a new platform, the HAL is rewritten, but most of the rest of the operating system is left untouched. Because the HAL is separate from the rest of the operating system, rewriting it is relatively easy.

Windows NT Memory Architecture

THE FOLLOWING FEATURES ARE the most important aspects of the Windows NT memory model:

- Virtual memory

- Demand paging

- 32-bit, flat, linear address space

Let's take a closer look at these features.

Virtual Memory and Demand Paging

If typical computers had hundreds of megabytes of RAM, virtual memory would probably not be an issue. But because most workstations have a limited amount of memory, virtual memory compensates for the shortfall.

Virtual memory refers to the practice of using the hard drive to fool the operating system and applications into behaving as if there is more RAM than actually exists. By using a local, physical disk as an extension of physical memory, Windows NT is able to create virtual memory. When actual RAM fills up, virtual memory is created on the hard drive.

When Windows NT runs out of physical memory, the virtual memory manager chooses sections of memory that have not been recently used and are of low priority and writes their contents to the virtual memory file, thus freeing that RAM for use by other processes. When that information is needed again, the same process occurs to make room for it in RAM and the original information is restored from the virtual memory disk file. This disk file is also known as the *swap file*.

All of this activity is hidden from the application, which sees both virtual and actual memory as the same. By centrally managing the memory addresses, Windows NT can keep memory used in one application separate and protected from interference by other applications. This arrangement provides greater stability for applications

Each application running under Windows NT is given a unique virtual address space composed of equal blocks called *pages*. *Demand paging* refers to the process of moving data into paging files and then paging it back into physical memory when the application needs it.

The down side of virtual memory is, of course, that it is much slower than physical memory; hard drives are far slower than RAM.

When you run Windows NT on a machine with insufficient RAM, the amount of paging to the hard drive will become very noticeable and the computer will run very slowly.

32-bit, Flat, Linear Addressing

Windows NT treats memory as one large contiguous block—there are no physical divisions and Windows NT can address up to 4GB at one time. This type of memory architecture is called a *flat* or *linear address space*, without the divisions of conventional, upper, expanded, and extended used in DOS and previous operating systems. Windows NT does use 2GB of this memory space for user mode applications, and it protects 2GB for kernal mode processes.

If you are familiar with the Windows for MS-DOS memory architecture, you will know that memory is broken into segments with a maximum length of 64K. This division presents major challenges to programmers who write large applications for Windows. The contiguous block of memory in Windows NT makes the programmer's job much easier.

Server and Workstation Differences

Windows NT Server is essentially Windows NT Workstation with enhanced features that allow it to function as a network operating system. Here's a brief look at the chief differences between the two products:

- Server allows unlimited inbound client sessions, while Workstation allows only 10.

- Server can support four processors (out of the box), while Workstation can support only two.

- Server allows up to 256 simultaneous sessions through Remote Access Service (RAS, which allows users to dial in across a modem), while Workstation allows only one.

- Server can import and export directory replication, but Workstation can only import it.

- Server offers services for Macintosh, logon validation, and disk fault tolerance. Workstation offers none of these.

For a detailed exploration of Windows NT Server, see the companion book MCSE: NT Server Study Guide, *also published by Sybex.*

Chapter Summary

We began our general overview of Windows NT by defining Windows NT as a 32-bit, preemptive, multitasking operating system. We examined its major features—platform portability, multitasking, multithreading, integral network connectivity, support for different client operating systems, multiprocessor support, and compatibility with legacy applications.

Next, we explored the modular design of Windows NT and its modes of operation:

- User mode, which includes

  - The environment subsystems

  - The security subsystem

- Kernel mode, which includes

  - The NT Executive

  - The Kernel

  - The HAL

After exploring the various modules of the architecture, we investigated the Windows NT memory system, which has the following characteristics:

- Virtual memory

- Demand paging

- 32-bit, flat, linear address space

In the last part of this chapter, we briefly compared Windows NT Server and Windows NT Workstation.

Exercise Questions

1. Windows NT Workstation is another name for Windows 95.

   A. True

   B. False

2. Windows NT 4.0 uses the same graphical user interface as Windows and Windows for Workgroups.

   A. True

   B. False

3. Windows NT Server can run the same software as Windows NT Workstation.

   A. True

   B. False

4. The _____ allows Windows NT to run on many different platforms with only minor changes.

5. Multiprocessing is

   A. Running more than one process at a time on one microprocessor

   B. Using more than one microprocessor in the same computer

6. Windows NT divides memory into_____.

   A. user and protected modes

   B. conventional and expanded modes

   C. conventional and extended modes

   D. Windows NT does not segment memory.

7. Windows NT is not available for which of the following computers:

   A. Intel 386–class machines

   B. Digital Alpha–based computers

    C. MIPS-based computers

    D. Power PC–based computers

    E. VAX minicomputers

8. Which of the following does Windows NT support?

    A. Asymmetrical multiprocessing

    B. Symmetrical multiprocessing

    C. Coherent multiprocessing

    D. Incoherent multiprocessing

9. Which of the following network protocols does Windows NT not support?

    A. TCP/IP

    B. NWLink (Microsoft's 32-bit Windows NT IPX/SPX)

    C. NetBEUI

    D. AppleTalk

    E. XNS

10. The core of the Windows NT operating system is called

    A. The Kernel

    B. The Executive

    C. Privileged mode

    D. Process Manager

Installing
Windows NT

WINDOWS NT 4.0 can be very easy to install if it's done right. In this chapter we will explain the process of planning and executing a successful NT installation. We will also show you how to upgrade to NT 4.0 from 3.*x*. Furthermore, for those occasions when you need to undo things, you'll see what it takes to uninstall Windows NT 4.0.

This chapter leads you through the installation process—from determining the hardware required for supporting Windows NT to installation via CD-ROM and via a network to the text and graphical portions of the installation process to the final reboot and finally to a functioning and installed Windows NT Workstation 4.0 operating system.

Before You Install Windows NT

BEFORE YOU LOAD WINDOWS NT on your computer, you need to be sure that it meets certain minimum hardware requirements. You must also know whether or not your hardware is on the Microsoft Hardware Compatibility List (HCL). Once you have the correct hardware, you must configure the hardware settings (IRQ and DMA numbers, etc.) to work correctly with Windows NT.

Hardware Requirements

In order for Windows NT 4.0 to work properly, your computer must meet the minimum requirements listed in Table 2.1.

The amount of memory on a machine greatly influences NT performance. You need to have at least 16MB of RAM on the computer. RISC computers require more memory than Intel-based computers, so you should install additional memory (half-again to twice as much) if your computer is RISC based.

	COMPONENT	INTEL	RISC
TABLE 2.1 Minimum Hardware Requirements for Windows NT 4.0.	Microprocessor	80486/33 or higher	MIPS, PowerPC, or Digital Alpha
	Disk storage	120MB	150MB
	Memory	12MB (16MB is recommended; 24 will reduce virtual memory usage and increase performance)	16MB (24MB is recommended; 32 will reduce virtual memory usage and increase performance)
	Display	VGA or higher resolution video display adapter	VGA or higher resolution video display adapter
	Required additional drive	CD-ROM or access to files from a networked CD-ROM	SCSI CD-ROM drive or access to files from a networked CD-ROM

Windows NT requires a more powerful microprocessor than Window 95 does to achieve an equal level of responsiveness to the computer user. Windows NT requires the extra processing power because its advanced capabilities provide a more robust, secure, and flexible environment than the Windows 95 environment provides.

The Hardware Compatibility List

The computer hardware market today gives you an almost unlimited array of computers and hardware devices (network adapters, video cards, etc.) to choose from. Windows NT supports most of the computers and hardware devices you can purchase today, as well as many hardware devices that are no longer manufactured but that you may still have around from earlier computers. However, Windows NT does not support every computer and every hardware device ever manufactured. Some hardware devices, while they may initially work with Windows NT, may conflict with other hardware devices or may cause Windows NT to become unstable.

The Windows NT Hardware Compatibility List contains computers certified by Microsoft to run Windows NT. Using a computer from the Hardware Compatibility List will reduce or eliminate incompatibility problems and will assist the Microsoft help line in resolving any difficulties you may have.

The Hardware Compatibility List (HCL) is part of the Windows NT documentation package that ships with Windows NT and lists hardware that Microsoft has tested and found to be compatible with Windows NT. (The list is also available in electronic form on Microsoft's Web site and on the NT CD-ROM.) The types of hardware covered include

- Storage devices including SCSI and RAID I/O subsystems

- Monitors, modems, network adapters, CD-ROMs, UPS systems, keyboards, and pointing devices

- CPUs

Many device drivers for Windows NT come with the Windows NT distribution CD-ROM. You are much more likely to find a device driver on the CD-ROM for your device if your device is on the Hardware Compatibility List.

If your hardware is not on the Hardware Compatibility List, you may be able to obtain drivers from the hardware manufacturer. If you buy new hardware that is not on Microsoft's list, make sure that the manufacturer includes a Windows NT device driver with the hardware.

Preparing the Hardware

Once you have purchased (or assembled) the hardware that will constitute your Windows NT computer, you will need to configure the components to run Windows NT. Windows NT will automatically detect many kinds of hardware during the installation process. The autodetect process detects the presence of hardware devices, but does not change hardware settings, such as the IRQ and DMA numbers and base memory addresses. Windows NT does not yet support Plug and Play. (Plug and Play is a hardware standard that automatically configures hardware settings such as IRQ and DMA numbers for hardware devices that are designed to the Plug-and-Play specification.) Microsoft has promised Plug-and-Play support with the future release of NT, code-named "Cairo."

Some computers will configure Plug-and-Play cards as a BIOS power-on function, and NT will be able to use the settings thus chosen; other computers let the operating system or the user (you) configure the Plug-and-Play cards. You should check the documentation for your computer and your cards to see how Plug and Play will affect your installation of Windows NT.

Until then, you'll need to make sure that the cards in your system do not conflict with each other for

- Interrupt Request lines (IRQs)

- Base I/O port addresses

- DMA channels

- Base memory addresses

If you are upgrading from a previous operating system, or if your computer comes completely assembled and configured from the manufacturer and everything is working well, you probably don't have a thing to worry about. If you do have some concerns, be sure to check the manufacturer's documentation that comes with the card(s) that you are concerned about.

Installing versus Upgrading

AFTER YOU HAVE PREPARED your hardware for Windows NT, you must decide whether you will upgrade an existing Windows operating system to Windows NT Workstation 4.0 or perform a fresh installation of the Windows NT operating system.

If your computer already has Windows 3.*x*, Windows for Workgroups, Windows 95, or an earlier version of Windows NT, you may wish to *upgrade* to Windows NT Workstation 4.0. The difference between installing and upgrading is that when you upgrade, many of the settings for the existing version of Windows are transferred into the new Windows NT Workstation 4.0 configuration.

You may wish to *upgrade* when

- You want to transfer desktop settings such as the wallpaper or sound settings.

- You want to transfer password files.

- You will not need to boot to the other version of Windows.

You may wish to *install* when

- You want to be able to boot the other version of Windows.

- You are installing to a large number of computers, and you want all of the computers to be the same.

The upgrade process does not transfer all settings from your current Windows operating system to your Windows NT Workstation because many of the current settings may not apply to Windows NT Workstation 4.0. What is transferred also varies from one original operating system to another. (Almost all of the Windows NT 3.51 settings, including security, user accounts, etc. are transferred when you upgrade. Much less information is transferred when you upgrade to NT 4.0 from Windows for Workgroups, for instance.)

The "upgrade" from Windows 95 to Windows NT version 4.0 is more like a new install, as NT will not carry forward any of the Windows 95 Registry settings or installed program information. Microsoft has pledged to resolve this problem with the next releases of Windows and NT.

Windows NT Workstation 4.0 does not support an upgrade path from Windows 95. Instead, you should install NT Workstation to a directory different from your Windows 95 directory. You should also allow Windows NT to install a dual boot configuration so that you can boot either Windows NT or Windows 95. This configuration is the default behavior of the installation program when you install Windows NT to its own directory.

When upgrading a DOS computer to Windows NT, very little operating system information is transferred to the new installation. However, having a DOS boot option can be very helpful when you need to configure hardware devices (some hardware devices require DOS setup programs that will not run under Windows NT) or troubleshoot computer problems. You should keep a DOS partition with DOS installed on it and install Windows NT to a separate directory. If you have a separate partition that you can devote to Windows NT, you should install Windows NT to that directory and convert that partition to NTFS. If you do not have a partition with DOS on it when you install Windows NT, you should try to install a DOS partition and the DOS operating system before you install Windows NT. By following this procedure, the NT boot manager will contain a menu option for booting DOS as well.

Booting Multiple Operating Systems

WINDOWS NT WILL COEXIST happily with other operating systems on your computer. Windows NT can be installed in its own NTFS volume (the best choice), or it can be installed alongside another operating system in a FAT volume. The Windows NT boot loader allows you to choose between the operating systems installed in your computer.

When you first install Windows NT, the Windows NT boot loader is installed in the boot partition of your computer. Initially, the boot loader's boot menu contains two entries for your Windows NT Workstation operating system, as well as one for DOS or Windows if you had either operating system installed on your computer before you installed Windows NT. Each successive installation of Windows NT adds to the boot loader menu, so you can, for example, install Windows NT Server and Windows NT Workstation along with Windows 95 on the same computer, each with its own boot menu option.

Chapter 16 explains how to configure the boot.ini file to support multiple operating systems and to remove entries for operating systems that are no longer on your computer.

Planning the Windows NT Installation

WINDOWS NT 4.0 HAS MANY LIVES. Computer support professionals and inexperienced computer users will be installing Windows NT 4.0 in many different computers in many different environments—in stand-alone home computers, in small LANs, and in large corporate networks. In some cases Windows NT will be installed and configured individually for each computer in a workgroup; in other cases an automated installation process will install identical copies of the operating system to all of the clients on a large network.

The Windows NT installation process is flexible. This flexibility is a result of the many different environments in which Windows NT will be installed. Because of this flexibility, however, you will need to make some decisions about how you will install Windows NT. Some of the decisions you will need to make or information you must have are as follows:

- How you will partition your computer's hard drive

- Whether you will use boot floppies during the installation

- Whether you will install from CD-ROM or from the network

- Whether your CD-ROM is supported by the Windows NT boot loader program

- Whether you will perform an unattended installation

- Which file systems you will install

- Windows NT system directory name

- Whether you will do a typical, portable, compact, or custom install

- Kind of mouse (Microsoft serial mouse, bus mouse, etc.)

- Type of keyboard and keyboard layout

- Computer network name

- Network adapter configuration

- Workgroup name or domain name

- Administrator password

Partitioning the Hard Drive

Before you proceed with the software installation of Windows NT, you may need to partition your computer's hard drive. Most hard drives come from the manufacturer configured with one large partition that encompasses all of the available hard disk space. Windows NT installations usually have at least two partitions—one from which a FAT file system boots and one for an NTFS file system to store Windows NT files. Partitioning the hard drive divides the space on the hard drive into parts—Windows NT can treat each partition as a different drive and format each with a different file system.

For running Windows NT on Intel-based computers, you should partition your computer's hard disk into at least two partitions—one DOS boot partition, formatted with the FAT file system, and one for Windows NT system files, user applications, and user files, formatted with the NTFS file system. (See the end of this section for a brief discussion of FAT and NTFS. You can learn more about FAT and NTFS in Chapter 5 "File Systems.")

If you install Windows NT on an Intel-based computer, you should make your boot partition 200MB, which will allow enough space for DOS and Windows 95 to be installed.

If you have more than one hard disk drive, you may wish to have only one partition on each drive. This option is best when you have one small hard disk drive (200MB or less) and one or more larger disk drives. You could then reserve one drive (the smaller drive) for the FAT boot partition and use the other drive(s) for Windows NT NTFS partition(s).

If you wish to install Windows NT to the same FAT partition that contains DOS or another version of Windows, you can leave your hard drive as one large partition. Windows NT will operate on a FAT partition, but it will not be able to take advantage of the advanced features that NTFS provides.

After you repartition your hard disk drive, you may need to reinstall DOS or Windows 95 to the FAT partition. You will have to do this reinstall only if partitioning your hard disk drive affected those partitions and you wish to be able to dual boot to DOS or Windows.

To partition a hard disk before you have installed Windows NT, you use the DOS FDISK program. Exercise 2.1 shows you how to partition a single-partition hard disk drive partition into two smaller partitions.

EXERCISE 2.1

Partitioning a Hard Disk Using the DOS FDISK Program

1. Boot your computer to the DOS command prompt.

2. Type **FDISK** and then press Enter.

3. Select choice 4, Display partition information, and then press Enter. You will be shown the partitions on the hard disk.

4. Press Esc to continue.

5. Select choice 3, Delete partition or logical DOS drive, and then press Enter.

6. Do one of the following depending on the partition you saw in step 3:

- If the partition you saw in step 3 was a primary DOS partition, select choice 1, Delete primary DOS partition, and press Enter.

- Otherwise, select the type of partition that you saw in step 3 and press Enter.

EXERCISE 2.1 (CONTINUED)

7. Type **1** when you are asked which partition to delete and then press Enter.

8. Type the volume label as it appears at the top of the screen when you are asked to do so. (If there is no volume label, just press Enter.)

9. Type **Y** to confirm the deletion and then press Enter.

10. Press Esc to continue.

11. Select option 1, Create DOS partition or logical DOS drive, and then press Enter.

12. Select option 1, Create primary DOS partition. You will be asked if you wish to use the maximum available space.

13. Type **N** and then press Enter.

14. Type **200** and then press Enter when you are asked to enter the partition size in megabytes.

If you have a hard disk drive that has more than 500MB, you should create a primary DOS partition of at least 200MB so that you can run DOS and Windows 95 comfortably in it. You can leave the remainder unpartitioned for the Windows NT install process to use.

15. Select option 2, Set active partition, and then press Enter.

16. Type **1** to select the partition you just created and then press Enter.

17. Press Esc to continue.

18. Press Esc to exit FDISK.

19. Reboot your computer. You may wish to reinstall DOS and Windows 95 to the new FAT partition you have just created.

WARNING

Partitioning your hard disk will destroy any data you have on your hard disk. Do not partition your hard disk if you have programs, data files, or an operating system installation that you wish to keep. Windows NT can share a partition with another operating system, so you do not have to create a partition for Windows NT. However, Windows NT will perform best if it has its own partition that it can format for its own use.

Floppy or Floppy-Less Install

The Windows NT Workstation software package contains three floppy disks in addition to the Windows NT installation CD-ROM. You do not need to have a previously installed operating system on your computer's hard disk drive if you install Windows NT using these floppy disks. The Winnt and the Winnt32 programs on the installation CD-ROM can re-create these floppy disks if they become damaged or lost.

You do not, however, have to use the floppy disks to install Windows NT. In order to perform a floppy-less install, you need to have a bootable partition that the Winnt or Winnt32 program can copy temporary files to and boot from. Although this method takes a little more space, it is an easier installation method than using the boot floppies because you do not have to keep track of several floppies and insert them at the correct time and in the right order. This method is also necessary if the setup disks do not directly support the CD-ROM drive, for example, non-IDE or SCSI drives.

Both methods of installation (floppy-less and floppy) perform the same function—they transfer the installation files from the CD-ROM (or network directory) to the hard disk drive on your computer.

The /B option of Winnt and Winnt32 tells the installation program to perform a floppy-less installation.

The /O and the /OX options of the Winnt and Winnt32 programs re-create the Windows NT installation boot floppies. The /O option creates boot floppies that you can use to install Windows NT from a CD-ROM that the Windows NT Setup program does not support. When you use boot floppies created with the /O option to install Windows NT, you must copy the Windows NT installation files to your computer's hard disk before turning control over to the Windows NT Setup program to finish the install. If you use the /OX option, the boot floppies do not copy the installation files to your hard disk first; instead, the Setup program reads the installation files from the CD-ROM. This installation process requires less disk space than the /O option but works only if the Windows NT Setup program supports your CD-ROM.

To re-create the floppy disks from your installation CD-ROM, perform the steps described in Exercise 2.2.

EXERCISE 2.2

Re-creating Windows NT Boot Floppies

1. Go to the command prompt. (In Windows NT and Windows 95, select Start ➤ Programs ➤ MS-DOS Prompt; in earlier versions of Windows, exit Windows.)

2. Change drives to the CD-ROM drive. (At the command prompt, type the letter of the drive. For instance, if your CD-ROM is drive F, type **F** and then press Enter.) Change to the I386 directory.

3. Do one of the following, depending on your current operating system:

- If you are at a Windows NT command prompt, type **Winnt32 /O** or **/OX** and then press Enter.

- If you are at a Windows 95, an earlier version of Windows, or a DOS command prompt, type **Winnt /O** or **/OX** and then press Enter.

4. Label a blank, formatted floppy disk as *Windows NT Workstation 4.0 Setup Disk 3* and place it in the disk drive. Press Enter. The program will transfer files to the floppy disk and then ask for the second disk.

5. Label another disk as *Windows NT Workstation 4.0 Setup Disk 2* and place it in the disk drive. Press Enter. The program will copy files to this second disk and then ask for the final disk.

6. Label a third disk as *Windows NT Workstation 4.0 Boot Disk*, insert it in the disk drive, and then press Enter.

7. Remove the boot disk from the drive after the program has finished transferring information to the boot disk.

Preparing for a Network Installation

If you will be installing Windows NT to many computers throughout a network, you may wish to put the Windows NT installation files on the file server and perform a network install at each of the client computers. If you have many identically configured computers, you can automate the process by using several of the installation program's software switches.

An additional advantage of installing from the network is that when you reconfigure your Windows NT workstation (by adding an adapter card such as a new modem or video card, for instance), the operating system will look to the network for the operating system files it needs instead of requiring you to insert the installation CD-ROM again.

However, if you are not attached to the network or if you prefer to use the simplest method of installing Windows NT or if you do not want to devote the file server hard drive space to Windows NT installation files, you can install Windows NT from a CD-ROM drive installed in your workstation.

You can perform a network install only if you already have an operating system installed on your computer (or on floppy disk) that can attach to the network file server and if you have a FAT file system on your hard disk drive with at least 120MB of free disk space. You map a drive to the shared network directory and use Winnt /B (from DOS) or Winnt32 /B (from Windows 95) to install from the network. This method does not require the Windows NT installation boot floppies.

Creating a Network Installation Share on the File Server

Before you can install the Windows NT Workstation 4.0 operating system to your workstation from the network, you must create a network share that contains the Windows NT installation files. If you have a large number of computers on your network, the best way to create the network share is to copy the installation files to a subdirectory on the file server's hard disk and then share that directory.

On the installation CD-ROM, the subdirectory with the name of that architecture contains the basic installation files for a particular computer architecture. The Intel files, for example, are in the i386 directory, and the PowerPC files are in the PPC directory. Other directories off the root directory of the CD-ROM contain additional files that are not a basic part of the operating system (e.g., new device driver software, demo programs).

If all the computers on your network use the same type of microprocessor (MIPS or Intel, for example), you may create shared network directories only for the installation files for those microprocessors. (In this case you would copy only the files in the MIPS or the i386 subdirectories, respectively.)

Exercise 2.3 shows you how to create a shared installation subdirectory on your Windows NT 4.0 file server.

EXERCISE 2.3

Creating a Network Share of the Windows NT Workstation 4.0 Installation Files

1. Log on as an administrator.

2. Place the Windows NT Workstation 4.0 installation CD into the CD-ROM drive.

3. Click on the *Browse This CD* button in the Windows NT CD-ROM window that will automatically start up when you insert the CD.

4. Open the My Computer icon on the desktop.

5. Open the drive icon that will contain the directory for the installation files.

6. Drag the subdirectory that contains the installation files from the CD-ROM window to the drive window. For example, to copy the Intel installation files to your C: drive, drag the `i386` directory to the (C:) window.

The files will be copied to the hard disk drive from the CD-ROM. This process may take a while. When the file copies are done, a new subdirectory will be present on the disk drive. It will be selected (highlighted).

7. Select File ➤ Sharing in the drive window. Select Shared As in the Directory Properties window.

8. Click the Permissions button at the bottom of the screen. Change the Type of Access for *Everyone* to *Read* in the Access Through Share Permissions window. Click OK.

9. Click the OK button at the bottom of the Directory Properties window.

10. Close the CD-ROM window, close the drive window, and close the My Computer window.

Unattended Install

Y OU CAN CONFIGURE THE Windows NT installation so that you do not have to respond to any prompts from the installation and Setup programs while NT is being installed. This way of installing Windows NT is called an unattended install. It takes a little more preparation to begin with, but if you have to install or upgrade a large number of machines, the unattended install option can save you a lot of time and effort.

In order to perform the unattended install, you must have unattended script files and answer files customized for your particular installation. These script and answer files must contain the information that you otherwise would type in to prompts and dialog boxes during the installation process. The unattended install is useful because if you have a large number of computers that are all configured mostly the same, you only have to type the information once into the unattended install files.

The UNATTEND.TXT file on the Windows NT Workstation 4.0 CD-ROM will allow you to install Windows NT in a simple configuration or to upgrade Windows NT versions 3.51 and earlier to Windows NT Workstation 4.0. (You have to customize the file for your particular installation.) This file is the simplest possible UNATTEND.TXT file. It can be simple because a basic installation requires very little information, and a Windows NT upgrade from an earlier version of Windows NT will use most of the earlier Windows NT operating system's configuration information.

If you wish to make unattended installation files for a more complex installation of Windows NT, you will need to use the Computer Profile Setup utility or the Setup Manager utility. (Refer to the Resource Kit documentation for instructions on how to use the Computer Profile Setup utility.) The Setup Manager is explained in the next section.

Using an Unattended Answer File

You can use the SETUPMGR.EXE program on the Windows NT installation CD-ROM to create unattended answer files. The Setup Manager program will allow you to specify, before you install the operating system, the answers to questions that you would otherwise have to enter during the installation process.

If you are using an Intel-based computer, you can find the Setup Manger program in the \Support\Deptools\I386 subdirectory of the Windows NT Workstation installation CD-ROM. Executing SETUPMGR.EXE enables you to configure the General Setup, Networking Setup, and Advanced Setup portions of the unattended installation text file. You access each portion (General, Networking, and Advanced) through its own button. Buttons for selecting a new unattended installation file, saving the file, and exiting the program are at the bottom of the window.

General

- **User Information tab:** Enter the user's name, the organization name, the name for the computer, and the product ID.

- **General tab:** Confirm the hardware settings, run a program during setup, and select the type of upgrade you are performing if you are upgrading rather than installing Windows NT.

- **Computer Role tab:** Determine which NT operating system you are installing (Workstation or Server) and the network architecture (Workgroup or Domain). If the operating system is Server, determine whether it will be a primary or backup domain controller. You will enter additional information here also, such as the domain or workgroup name and an (optional) computer account name.

- **Install Directory tab:** Tell the installation program to install to the default directory, ask the user for a directory, or install to a specified directory.

- **Display Settings tab:** Set the display configuration.

- **Time Zone tab:** List time zone settings for the computer's time clock.

- **License Mode tab:** Applies only to Server installations. From this tab, you can configure a Windows NT Server computer to have a certain number of per-seat or per-server network connection licenses.

Networking

- **General tab:** Specify that networking will be configured during the installation process or that you will configure networking from the Setup Manager program. If you select Unattended Network Installation (which requires you to configure networking from the Setup Manager), you can specify that the setup program will detect and install a network card using defaults or that the setup program will detect the card from a list you provide or that the setup program will install the network driver for the card you specify.

- **Adapters tab:** Select adapter cards to be installed or detected and specify their communications parameters.

- **Protocols tab:** Specify the protocols to be installed and set their parameters.

- **Services tab:** Specify the services to be installed and set their parameters.

- **Internet tab:** Set which of the Internet services will be installed and specify where the Internet services will store their information (for server computers only).

- **Modem tab:** Configure what type of modem is connected to your computer and set the modem configuration. (Use this tab only if the RAS service is installed and configured to use one or more ports.)

Advanced

The advanced options have a number of settings that you will not want to change unless you have a good understanding of the install process and a need to perform an unorthodox installation. One setting that you may wish to change, however, is the Convert to NTFS option in the File System tab. This option will convert the Windows NT installation partition to NTFS. Check this option if you wish to use advanced NTFS features.

Once you have selected the installation settings in the Setup Manager program, select Save from the Setup Manager main screen. Then you will select a directory and filename for the unattended installation file. If you have created a network share containing the Windows NT setup files, you should save the unattended installation file there.

Exercise 2.4 shows you how to create an unattended installation answer file. This exercise assumes that the answer file will be used to install a computer as part of a domain called DOMAIN and that the computer name is MY_WORKSTATION. The username is Isaac Newton, the organization name is Gravatic Technologies, and you have an NE2000 compatible ethernet driver and an Intel-compatible computer.

EXERCISE 2.4

Creating an Unattended Installation Answer File

1. Insert the Windows NT Workstation 4.0 installation CD-ROM into the CD-ROM drive.

2. Double-click the My Computer icon.

3. Open the CD-ROM icon in the My Computer window. Select *Browse This CD-ROM* from the autorun window.

4. Select Support ➤ Deptools ➤ I386.

5. Open the Setupmgr program.

6. Click the New button at the bottom of the screen.

7. Click the General Setup button.

8. Type the following in the User Information tab: **Isaac Newton** is the Username, **Gravatic Technologies** is the Organization, and **MY_WORKSTATION** is the Computer Name.

9. Click the Computer Role tab. In the *Select the role of the computer* field, select *Workstation* in *Domain*. Type **DOMAIN** into the Domain Name field.

10. Click the other tabs to observe the settings of each tab. You don't have to change them for a simple installation.

11. Click the OK button at the bottom of the screen.

12. Click the Networking Setup button.

13. Select Unattended Network Installation in the General tab. Then select Specify adapters to be installed.

14. Click the Adapters tab. Click the Add button. In the Adding Adapters window, select Novell NE2000 Adapter. Click OK.

15. Click the Parameters button. Enter **5** for the interrupt number and **320** for the I/O Base Address. Click OK.

16. Click the Protocols tab. Click on the Add button. Select NETBEUI in the Adding Protocols window. Click the OK button. You do not have to set the parameters for NETBEUI.

17. Click OK at the bottom of the Networking Options window.

18. Click Advanced Setup ➤ File System tab. Select the Convert to NTFS option. Click OK at the bottom of the Advanced Options window.

19. Click the Save button at the bottom of the Windows NT Setup Manager window. Type **C:\temp\test.txt** in the Name field. Click Save to save the unattended installation file as TEST.TXT in the temp directory of your C: drive.

20. Click the Exit button.

Using the Unattended Answer File with Winnt and Winnt32

The /U option in Winnt and Winnt32 allows you to specify an unattended answer file for a Windows NT installation. The /U option requires the /S option to also be selected, specifying the source directory for Windows NT installation files (including the unattended installation file). After the /U option you type the file-name of the unattended installation file.

Using a Text Editor to Create the Uniqueness Database File

If you have to install Windows NT workstation to a large number of similarly configured computers, you can use the unattended installation file. This file (which you create just once) contains the configuration information common to all of the computers on which you will install Windows NT. The unattended installation file works in conjunction with a uniqueness database file (UDF) that identifies differences between installations, such as the computer name and the username for that installation. You can then use the /UDF option of Winnt and Winnt32 to specify a UDF file that customizes the installation for a particular computer. The following UDF file customizes the installation for three computers.

Example UDF File

```
; UDF file to customize the installation for three
  computers
;
[UniqueIds]
u1 = UserData
```

```
u2 = UserData
u3 = UserData
[u1:UserData]
FullName = "Charles Perkins"
OrgName = "Charles Perkins Elucidation"
ComputerName = YOYO
[u2:UserData]
FullName = "Matthew Strebe"
OrgName = "Netropolis"
ComputerName = BOOMERANG
[u3:UserData]
FullName = "Henry J Tillman"
OrgName = "Tillman World Enterprises Inc."
ComputerName = POGO
```

UDF Organization

Each computer in the above example has a different username, organization name, and computer name. The installation program merges the settings of the unattended text file and the uniqueness database file at the graphics portion of the installation process. All other settings will be taken from an unattended installation answer file.

When you select the UDF option for Winnt or Winnt32, you can also specify the uniqueness ID for that installation. The example UDF above has three uniqueness IDs listed: u1, u2, and u3. When specifying u1 with the above UDF file, Winnt will cause the setup program to use the first set of example information.

The format of the UDF file is simple, and it is very similar to the format of the unattended installation answer file. The [u1:UserData] section heading, for example, specifies that the data following it will add to or replace, for the u1 installation, information found in the [UserData] section of the unattended installation file. The FullName setting of "Charles Perkins" will replace, for the u1 installation, the FullName information stored in the unattended installation file.

The UDF file is different from the unattended answer file in that it has a [UniqueIDs] section containing identifiers for unique installation, and the unique ID prefixes each section of the answer file that contains information just for the unique ID.

Creating and Using the UDF

You can create UDF files using a text editor such as Notepad. If you intend to use a UDF file to customize the installation process for several computers, you will need to provide unique settings for at least the computer name for each installation. Use the format outlined above to create UDF entries for each computer.

You use the UDF by specifying the UDF file and the uniqueness identifier for the installation on the Winnt or Winnt32 command line. The UDF file is used with the unattended answer file option (explained in the previous section "Using an Unattended Answer File"). You use the /UDF option to specify that setup will use a UDF file; here's the format:

```
/UDF:ID[,database_filename]
```

If you have created an unattended answer file unatl.txt using Setup Manger and you have created a UDF file udfl.txt, which contains a unique ID of idl, with your text editor and the installation files (including the answer file and the UDF file) reside on a network share mapped to the F: drive, you can type the following command from a DOS command prompt:

```
winnt /s:f:\ /u:unatl.txt /UDF:idl,udfl.txt
```

Using the Sysdiff Utility

If you further wish to customize the installation of Windows NT to one or more computers over a network, you can use the Sysdiff utility. Sysdiff records the difference between a normal Windows NT installation and an installation to which you have added files. Sysdiff can perform in any of the following modes:

- **Snap:** Sysdiff takes a snapshot of the state of the Windows NT operating system Registry and the state of the file system files and directories. The information it records is written to a snapshot file.

- **Diff:** Sysdiff records the differences between the state of a previous snapshot of a Windows NT installation and the state of the installation at the time sysdiff is run again. Sysdiff /Diff creates a difference file.

- **Apply:** Sysdiff applies the data in the difference file to a Windows NT installation.

- **Inf:** Sysdiff creates an inf file and installation data from the difference file. This data can be applied to a server-based share of the Windows NT installation files so that the differences captured with the Diff command are automatically applied to installations of Windows NT made from that server-based share.

- **Dump:** This command produces a file for you to review that details the contents of the difference file.

```
sysdiff /snap [/log:log_file] snapshot_file
sysdiff /diff [/log:log_file] snapshot_file
  difference_file
sysdiff /apply [/log:log_file ] difference_file
sysdiff /inf [/u] sysdiff_file oem_root
sysdiff /dump difference_file dump_file
```

The command line parameters are defined as follows:

- **snapshot_file** contains the state of the original installation.

- **difference_file** contains the differences between the original installation and your custom installation.

- **log_file** describes the operation of the sysdiff utility.

- **oem_root** is the directory containing the additional directories and files for your custom installation.

- **dump_file** describes the data in the difference file.

Exercise 2.5 illustrates the simplest way to use the sysdiff utility.

EXERCISE 2.5

Using the Sysdiff Utility to Customize an Installation

1. Install the Windows NT software to a typical computer.

2. Create a shapshot file with the sysdiff /snap option.

3. Install to a typical computer the software that you wish to be distributed to each installation.

4. Create a difference file with the /diff option.

5. Install Windows NT to each of the destination computers.

6. Run the sysdiff utility with the /apply option after each installation is complete.

The Sysdiff utility is a powerful tool that can automate the distribution of both operating system and application software to a large number of computers. However, you must be very familiar with the installation process and the operation of the Windows NT operating system and applications before you can use the sysdiff utility to its fullest extent.

Beginning the Install

Y OU ARE READY TO BEGIN the first part of the Windows NT Workstation 4.0 installation. This portion of the installation process (optionally) transfers all of the necessary installation files to your computer and then starts the Windows NT installation Setup program.

In order to install Windows NT from a CD-ROM or from the network, you must first have a DOS boot floppy, the Windows NT installation boot disks, or a DOS formatted hard disk boot partition. You must also have enough free disk space to perform a new Windows NT Workstation 4.0 install (120MB for Intel-based computers and 150MB for RISC-based computers).

Exercise 2.6 does not require you to have a CD-ROM that the Windows NT installation program supports. Exercises 2.7, 2.8, and 2.9 show you how to install Windows NT Workstation version 4.0 from the network using DOS, Windows 95, and Windows NT operating systems versions 3.51 and earlier. Exercise 2.10 shows you how to install Windows NT Workstation version 4.0 using the installation boot floppies and a supported CD-ROM.

EXERCISE 2.6

Beginning a Windows NT Workstation 4.0 Installation from CD-ROM (Intel-Based Computers; Floppy-Less Install)

1. If you are using DOS or a version of Windows earlier than Windows 95, boot your computer to the DOS prompt.

Or if you are using Windows 95, select Start ➤ Programs ➤ MS-DOS Prompt.

2. Change drive to the CD-ROM drive from the command prompt and then change directory to the i386 directory on the CD-ROM.

EXERCISE 2.6 (CONTINUED)

3. If you are running DOS and the version of DOS you are using is DOS 7 (you can type **VER** at the DOS prompt to find out), type the **LOCK** command. This step disables long filename support, which is necessary because long filename support interferes with the Windows NT installation program's access of the disk drive.

4. If you are running DOS or Windows 95, type **winnt /b** for a floppy-less install with a minimum of prompts from the installation program.
Or if you are running Windows NT, type **winnt32 /b** for a floppy-less install.

5. Respond to the prompt for the location of the installation files. (The current (i386) directory should be displayed.)

6. Press Enter to accept the displayed source directory.

The Installation program will begin to copy files to your hard disk drive.

EXERCISE 2.7

Beginning a Windows NT Workstation 4.0 Installation from the Network for DOS Computers (Floppy-Less Install)

1. Boot your computer to the DOS prompt. If network services are not started by a batch file, start network services now.

2. Map a drive letter to the network shared directory containing the installation files. If the files are stored in the i386 share of the boomerang server and if you have the drive letter G free, you may type the following: **net use g: \\boomerang\i386**.

3. Change drives to the drive you have just mapped. (Type the drive letter and then press Enter. The drive letter in this example is G.)

4. Type **winnt /b** to perform a floppy-less install.

5. Respond to the prompt for the location of the installation files. The current (i386) directory should be displayed. Press Enter to accept the displayed source directory.

6. The Installation program will begin to copy files to your hard disk drive.

EXERCISE 2.8

Beginning a Windows NT Workstation 4.0 Installation from the Network for Windows 95 Computers (Floppy-Less Install)

1. Open the Network Neighborhood icon on your desktop.

2. Find the file server in the list of computers in the Network Neighborhood window. If it is not listed directly, you may have to open the Entire Network icon and then the Microsoft Networks icon to find it.

3. Double-click on the icon for the file server. The network shares for that file server will appear. Select the share that contains the installation files. Select File ➤ Map Network Drive. Select a drive letter for the share and then press enter.

4. Select Start ➤ Run and then type **{drive:}winnt32 /b** in the Open: field. Press OK to perform a floppy-less install.

5. Respond to the prompt for the location of the installation files. The current (i386) directory should be displayed. Press Enter to accept the displayed source directory.

The Installation program will begin to copy files to your hard disk drive.

EXERCISE 2.9

Beginning a Windows NT Workstation 4.0 Installation from the Network for Windows NT Version 3.51 and Earlier Computers (Floppy-Less Install)

1. Open the Main icon on your desktop.

2. Start the MS/DOS icon.

3. Map a drive letter to the network shared directory containing the installation files. If the files are stored in the i386 share of the boomerang server and if you have the drive letter G free, you may type the following: **net use g: \\boomerang\i386**.

4. Change drives to the drive you have just mapped. (Type the drive letter and then press Enter. The drive letter in this example is G.)

5. Type **winnt32 /b** to perform a floppy-less install.

6. Respond to the prompt for the location of the installation files. The current (i386) directory should be displayed. Press Enter to accept the displayed source directory.

The Installation program will begin to copy files to your hard disk drive.

EXERCISE 2.10

Beginning a Windows NT Workstation 4.0 Installation from the Installation Boot Floppies

1. Place the Windows NT Workstation 4.0 installation boot disk into the computer's disk drive and place the Windows NT Workstation installation CD-ROM into the CD-ROM drive.

2. Turn on the computer. Replace the boot floppy with installation disk 2 when prompted.

To begin installing Windows NT from a CD-ROM to your (Intel-based) computer without using floppy disks, perform the steps outlined in Exercise 2.6.

From DOS, to begin installing Windows NT from a network share to your (Intel-based) computer without using floppy disks, perform the steps outlined in Exercise 2.7. This exercise assumes that you have network access to Microsoft networking shares using the Net Use command.

From Windows 95, to begin installing Windows NT from a network share to your (Intel-based) computer without using floppy disks, perform the steps outlined in Exercise 2.8.

From Windows NT version 3.51 and earlier, to begin installing Windows NT from a network share to your (Intel-based) computer without using floppy disks, perform the steps outlined in Exercise 2.9.

To begin installing Windows NT from floppy disks and from a supported CD-ROM regardless of the computer's operating system (or even if the computer does not have an operating system), perform the steps outlined in Exercise 2.10.

The Winnt and the Winnt32 programs perform the same function and take the same command line switches. The difference between them is that the Winnt32 program runs in the Windows 95 and Windows NT 32-bit environment.

The command line switches are as follows:

```
[winnt | winnt32] [/S[:]sourcepath] [/T[:]tempdrive]
    [/I[:]inffile] [/O[X]] [/X | [/F] [/C]] [/B]
    [/U[:scriptfile]] [/R[X]:directory]
```

- **/B** Installs without installation boot floppies.

- **/C** Skips free space check on installation boot floppies (not available in Winnt32).

- **/F** Copies files from the boot floppies without verifying the copies (not available in Winnt32).

- **/I** Specifies the filename (but not the path) of the setup information file. The default is `dosnet.inf`.

- **/O** Creates boot floppies only.

- **/OX** Creates boot floppies for CD-ROM or floppy-based installation.

- **/S** Specifies the source location of Windows NT setup files. Sourcepath must be fully qualified, that is, of the form `<driveletter>:\[<path>]` or `\\<servername>\<share>[\<path>]`. The default is the current directory.

- **/T** Specifies the drive to contain the temporary setup files.

- **/U** Specifies unattended operation and optional script file.

The Windows NT Setup Program

ONCE YOU HAVE PERFORMED one of the beginning installation exercises (Exercises 2.6 through 2.10), the Windows NT Setup program executes. The process from here is the same regardless of the method of installation (network, CD-ROM, floppy-less, or with the installation boot disks).

In this portion of the installation process, you must respond to a sequence of text screens that will examine your computer's hardware and allow you to select which partition you will use with Windows NT, which file system you will use on the NT partition, and which directory will contain the Windows NT files. Then the Setup program copies essential files (but not all of the files) to your hard disk.

Exercise 2.11 will lead you through the process of using the Windows NT Setup program. Each step will be explained in the text that follows.

EXERCISE 2.11

Using the Windows NT Setup Program

1. Press Enter at the initial setup screen.

2. Insert the third floppy disk if necessary. At the hardware identification screen press **S** if you need to specify additional adapters.

3. Press Enter to continue.

4. Select *The above list matches my computer* and then press Enter.

5. Select the partition you created for Windows NT in Exercise 2.1 and then press Enter.

6. Press **C** to convert the partition to NTFS.

7. Accept the default directory location of \WINNT.

8. Press the Escape key.

The Initial Setup Screen

The initial setup screen displays four options:

- To learn more about Windows NT Setup before continuing, press F1.

- To setup Windows NT now, press ENTER.

- To repair a damaged Windows NT version 4.00 installation, press R.

- To quit Setup without installing Windows NT, press F3.

Press Enter to continue (Exercise 2.11, step 1).

Hardware Identification

The Setup program automatically detects many types of hard disk and CD-ROM controllers, but it cannot detect every type of controller. This screen allows you to select additional adapter drivers and if necessary to provide additional adapter drivers on floppy disk. This step is necessary because the Setup program must be able to access a hard disk drive before it can install Windows NT, and you may have an unusual drive that NT does not automatically detect.

If you are installing from the installation boot floppies, you should insert the third floppy disk now. (Exercise 2.11, step 2.)

At this point you can press S to specify additional SCSI adapters, CD-ROM adapters, or special disk controllers. You can choose from the list of supported devices or specify a floppy disk from the manufacturer that contains a driver for the adapter if the device in your computer is not in the Setup program's list.

When you are done, or if you do not need to specify additional adapters, press Enter to continue. (Exercise 2.11, step 3.)

If NT is already installed on your computer, Setup skips to Exercise 2.11, step 7. Otherwise, the next screen shows the computer, display, keyboard, layout, and pointing device (mouse). You can select and change each item, or select *The above list matches my computer* to continue.

In most cases the list that the Setup program provides will be correct. Select *The above list matches my computer* and then press Enter. (Exercise 2.11, step 4.)

File Systems and Partitions

The next screen displays a list of existing partitions and unpartitioned space. You can install Windows NT on an existing partition or on the unpartitioned space. You can also create and delete partitions.

Select the partition you created for Windows NT in Exercise 2.1 and then press Enter. (Exercise 2.11, step 5.)

If the partition you chose is unformatted or is of type FAT, the Installation program gives you the choice of converting the file system to NTFS or of leaving the file system as FAT. You can make the partition NTFS even if it is the boot partition of the hard drive. However, if you do so, the partition will be unavailable to other operating systems. If you are following the recommended procedure and have created a second (large) partition for Windows NT, you should choose the option to convert the file system to NTFS.

The differences between FAT and NTFS and the best uses for each are covered in Chapter 5, "File Systems." At this point, if you have created a partition for use with NT, you should choose NTFS as the format for the partition.

You need to confirm that you wish to convert the partition to NTFS. Setup warns you that this step will make the partition unavailable to other operating systems, such as DOS, Windows, and OS/2.

Press C to convert the partition, which will actually occur just before the graphical portion of the installation process when you reboot to the actual NT operating system. (Exercise 2.11, step 6.)

Windows NT System Directory Location

If you already have an operating system installed on the partition, you must decide whether you are going to upgrade the current operating system or install a new operating system.

If you have another version of Windows installed on the computer, Windows NT will recognize it and ask if you want to install a new version of Windows or upgrade the current version. If you choose to install a new version and give the same file directory name as a version of Windows that is already installed, NT will warn you that this installation will destroy the existing version of Windows.

You will be prompted for the location for installation of Windows NT system files. The default location is \WINNT. You should keep this default unless you have a good reason to choose a different location. (One good reason is that you do not want to overwrite another version of Windows.)

Accept the default directory location of \WINNT. (Exercise 2.11, step 7.)

Hard Disk Examination and Exhaustive Secondary Examination

The final screen of the second (text-based) part of the installation process allows you to select whether the Setup program will perform a cursory hard disk examination or an exhaustive examination before your computer reboots and the graphical portion of the installation begins.

The simple examination may take a few seconds if you had a freshly formatted or unformatted drive before you began the installation process, or it may take several minutes if you have many files stored on your hard drive. The exhaustive examination will test every location on your hard drive in order to find any bad locations and may take several minutes.

Press Enter to perform the exhaustive secondary examination (don't press yet) or press Esc to skip the exhaustive examination.

Press Enter. (Exercise 2.11, step 8.)

Once the examination is complete, the Setup program continues, copying more files to your hard disk drive. When it is done copying files, your computer will reboot and then continue with the graphical portion of the installation.

As we explained in Chapter 1, Windows NT supports two file systems:

- **FAT** (file allocation tables): A file system that is compatible with DOS, OS/2, and Windows NT.

- **NTFS** (NT file system): The file system developed for Windows NT.

(File systems and partitions will be covered in detail in Chapter 5.)

Up through version 3.51, Windows NT supports HPFS, the file system developed and used by OS/2. Version 4.0 does not support HPFS. All HPFS partitions must now be converted.

When installing Windows NT, you have the opportunity to select a file system. Your system configuration as well as security requirements will help you determine which file system to select.

NTFS has several advantages over FAT. These include

- NTFS supports long filenames—up to 256 characters—with mixed-case letters. NTFS automatically generates the 11-character filenames that FAT supports, so the system also has access to a standard DOS name.

- NTFS has complete support for NT security.

- NTFS logs disk activity so that activities can be rolled back in the event of a system failure. In other words, the directory structure can be automatically rebuilt.

- NTFS supports POSIX files.

But NTFS also has a few disadvantages, including the following:

- DOS cannot see or work with NTFS partitions.

- On small disks (<200MB) NTFS is less efficient than FAT.

If you are running NT on an Intel machine, the only major reason *not* to use NTFS on the NT partition is if you also have DOS (or OS/2) installed and DOS (or OS/2) needs access to the partition.

RISC computers require a system partition of at least 2MB formatted with the FAT file system. You can, however, format other partitions using NTFS.

You can convert a FAT partition to NTFS without destroying any data, but you cannot convert an NTFS partition to FAT without destroying data on the hard drive. In order to convert from NTFS to FAT, you need to backup the data, perform the conversion, and then restore the data.

If DOS requires access to the file system, you should choose the FAT file system.

Keep in mind that although DOS cannot see or work with NTFS, DOS applications running under NT can.

Graphical Portion of the Installation

THE THIRD PORTION OF THE INSTALLATION process is mostly graphical, and your computer is running Windows NT while performing this part of the installation.

The first thing the computer will do after it reboots is to check the file systems on each of the hard disks. Windows NT requires each file system to be in a consistent state (i.e., the directory structure of the file system cannot contain any errors). At this time Windows NT will convert the file system to NTFS if you selected the Convert option earlier in the installation process. Windows NT will reboot after checking the file systems and converting a file system to NTFS. This portion of the install process is still text based, but the computer is now running NT instead of the Windows NT Setup program.

Windows NT displays a graphical interface and shows you a license agreement. You must accept the agreement and enter a key number if required. If you do not do so, you will not be able to continue with the installation process.

Once you have accepted the license agreement and entered the key, Windows NT proceeds with the installation. It first copies some more files, and then you help Windows NT gather information about your computer, install networking components, and finish the setup process by configuring miscellaneous information (e.g., the date and time zone) and then copying the rest of the files that the operating system needs.

Exercise 2.12 takes you through the graphical portion of the installation process.

EXERCISE 2.12

Proceeding with the Graphical Portion of the Windows NT Workstation 4.0 Installation Process

1. Select Typical at the Installation Options page and then click Next.

2. Enter your name in the Name field.

3. Enter the name of your organization in the organization field.

4. Press Next.

EXERCISE 2.12 (CONTINUED)

5. Enter a name in the Name field and then click Next.

6. Enter the Administrator account password twice and then click Next to continue.

7. Select Yes to create an emergency repair disk and then click Next to continue.

8. Select *Install most common* and then click Next to continue.

9. Click Next to continue past the first Configure Network screen.

10. Check the *Wired to the network* checkbox.

11. Make sure that the *Remote access to the network* checkbox is not checked.

12. Click Next.

13. Select *Search for Network Adapter* and click Next when the network adapter appears in the list.

14. Select the NetBEUI protocol and make sure that the other protocols are not selected. Click Next.

15. Click Next to install the components.

16. Respond to any requests for information. (You may need to inform the operating system of the IRQ and DMA numbers and the base memory address of your network adapter.) Click Next to continue.

17. Click Next to start the network.

18. Select Workgroup or Domain. Enter the workgroup or domain name.

19. Supply the account name and password for the Administrator account on the domain if you are joining a domain and if the administrator for the domain has not already created an account for your computer.

20. Click Next to continue.

21. Click Finish.

22. Select the correct time zone in the Time Zone tab of the Date/Time properties window. Click on the Close button.

EXERCISE 2.12 (CONTINUED)

23. Click OK when the Detected Display window shows you what kind of display adapter it has detected.

24. Click the Test button in the Display Properties window and click OK in the Testing mode window that tells you that it will display a test screen. Click Yes when the Testing mode window returns and asks if you saw the test screen properly.

25. Click OK in the Display Settings window and then click OK in the Display Properties window.

26. Insert a blank disk on which to create the emergency repair disk and click OK.

27. Remove any floppy disks from drives in the computer and click the Restart Computer button at the prompt.

Options

The first set of configuration options concerns how you will proceed with the installation process. The four options are

- Typical
- Portable
- Compact
- Custom

Typical installs the most frequently used software that comes with Windows NT in the most common configuration. Portable optimizes the configuration of Windows NT for a computer that will be used in several locations and may or may not be attached to a network. Compact minimizes the amount of disk space used by Windows NT. Custom allows you to select which NT software components to install on your workstation.

Choose Typical and then click Next. (Exercise 2.12, step 1.)

You will then be asked to provide the name and an organization that this copy of Windows NT is licensed to. You must provide this information to continue with the installation.

Enter your name in the Name field.

Enter the name of your organization in the organization field.

Click Next. (Exercise 2.12, steps 2 through 4.)

The Computer Name

The next screen asks you for the name for this computer. The name you enter here appears in workgroup and domain browse lists. (See Chapter 11 "Workgroups, Domains, and Network Browsing" for more information about workgroups, domains, and browsers.)

The computer name you select can be up to 15 characters long. You should make it simple and easy to type.

Enter a name in the Name field and then click Next. (Exercise 2.12, step 5.)

Next you need to enter an Administrator account password. Although you can install Windows NT without an Administrator account password (by leaving both fields blank), some Windows NT functions expect this password and will not operate correctly without it.

You should choose a password that is difficult to guess but that you will not forget. You should not write it down in a place that is easy for others to get to (such as on a yellow sticky note stuck to the computer's monitor), but if you are configuring this workstation for use in an organization, you should make sure that at least one other (trusted) individual in the organization has the password or can get the password in case you are not available to administer the computer. You could lock a sticky note in a safe.

Enter the Administrator account password twice and then click Next to continue. (Exercise 2.12, step 6.)

Emergency Repair Disk

The next screen asks you if you wish to create an emergency repair disk. The emergency repair disk can rescue your Windows NT installation from system corruption such as can happen when the power goes out unexpectedly or when a program or other operating system has disturbed the operating system's boot or system files.

Select Yes and then click Next to continue. (Exercise 2.12, step 7.)

Common Components

You will then be asked which components you wish to install. The choices are

- Install most common

- Show list from which to choose

Select Install most common and then click Next to continue. (Exercise 2.12, step 8.)

Network Adapter Configuration

Next you will need to configure your network adapter card. The first screen simply informs you that you will now be configuring your network. Click Next. (Exercise 2.12, step 9.)

The first choice you have is whether your computer will be participating in a network. Your choices are

- Do Not connect this computer to a network at this time

- This computer will participate on a network at this time

If you select the second option, the following checkboxes become available:

- Wired to the network

- Remote access to the network

Check the first box (Wired to the network) but not the second (Remote access). You will learn how to install and configure remote access services in Chapter 12, "Remote Access Service."

Click Next. (Exercise 2.12, steps 10 through 12.)

Next you will configure the network adapter for your Windows NT workstation. First, Windows NT must know what type of adapter is installed in the computer. You can instruct Windows NT to search for the adapter, or you can select the adapter from a list.

Select Search for network adapter. (Exercise 2.11, step 13.)

If Windows NT finds an adapter, it will display the adapter and you can click Next to continue. If it does not find the adapter, you must select it from a list or provide drivers for the adapter on a floppy disk.

Even if you do not have a network adapter installed in your computer, you can still install the networking portions of the operating system by selecting the MS Loopback Adapter from the list of adapters. The MS Loopback Adapter pretends to be an adapter but it does not really control a hardware device. It simply makes it appear as an adapter in the computer. You will not, of course, be able to connect to a network using the MS Loopback Adapter.

Protocols

The next screen displays checkboxes for the three default networking protocols for Windows NT networking. You may check or uncheck each one. A checked protocol will be installed and configured during the installation process; an unchecked protocol may be installed later. Chapters 8, 9, and 10 show you how to install and configure each of these protocols after Windows NT Workstation has already been installed. The default protocols to choose from are

- TCP/IP Protocol

- NWLink IPX/SPX Compatible Transport

- NetBEUI Protocol

You can select from the additional protocols list to add other protocols (such as AppleTalk) to the list of protocols to install at this time.

Select NetBEUI and make sure that the other protocols are not selected. NetBEUI is the simplest protocol and requires the least configuration during the installation process. Click Next. (Exercise 2.12, step 14.)

When the next screen appears, you should click Next to install the selected components. (Exercise 2.12, step 15.)

At this point you have to go through a configuration sequence for each of the networking components that you have just selected.

We have selected the simplest configurations, but you might have to enter IRQ and DMA numbers and the base memory address of your network adapter card. Each card is different, and some require more information than others. Enter the information that you gathered about your hardware settings when you configured your hardware in preparation for installing Windows NT. (Exercise 2.12, step 16.)

If you had selected TCP/IP or IPX/SPX at the protocol screen, you would now be required to enter TCP/IP and IPX/SPX information. We will show you how to configure these protocols in later chapters.

Click Next to start the network and continue with the configuration. (Exercise 2.12, step 17.)

Workgroups and Domains

After the network components of Windows NT have been started, you can select how your Windows NT workstation will participate on the network. You have two basic participation choices: Your workstation can be a part of a workgroup or part of a domain. Your choice will depend primarily on what type of network you will be connecting to. The differences, advantages, and disadvantages of workgroup versus domain are covered in Chapter 11.

If your network is workgroup based, choose Workgroup. If your network is domain based, choose Domain. Then in the workgroup or domain name field, enter the name of your workgroup or domain. The default workgroup name is WORKGROUP, and the default domain name is DOMAIN.

If you choose Domain, you can also create an account on the domain for this computer. A computer account is a little different from a user account. Each computer that is a part of a domain must have a computer account on that domain. You can create the account at this time by supplying an Administrator account name and password for the domain. Or the administrator of your network can create an account for you, using the Server Manager program on a Windows NT server computer. If you are not supplying the Administrator account name and password above, the administrator must do so before you proceed to the next step.

Click Next to continue. (Exercise 2.12, steps 18 through 20.)

Click Finish finish the networking installation. (Exercise 2.12, step 21.)

Miscellaneous Settings

After setting up the network, you will still need to configure some miscellaneous components of your Windows NT workstation. First you will need to configure the date, time, and time zone. The real-time clock on your computer will most likely have the correct date and time.

In the Time Zone tab of the Date/Time Properties window, select the correct time zone. Click Close. (Exercise 2.12, step 22.)

The next part of the installation allows you to configure your video adapter and monitor settings. The default configuration is standard VGA with 16 colors. You will learn how to configure display settings in Chapter 4, "Configuring Windows NT Workstation." Accept the default display settings.

The next screen shows you what kind of display adapter Windows NT has detected. Click OK. (Exercise 2.12, step 23.)

You must test the display before you go on, or Windows NT will present you with a warning box. The display settings you are testing are the current display settings, but you should test them anyway.

In the Display Properties window, click the Test button. Click OK in the Testing mode window and watch the test screen. Wait until the Testing mode window returns; if you saw the test screen properly, click Yes. (Exercise 2.12, step 24.)

Click OK to save the settings.

Click OK in the Display Properties window. (Exercise 2.12, step 24.)

Finishing the Installation

INALLY, WINDOWS NT WILL COPY a few accessories, applications, and DLLs to the Windows NT partition. It will set up the Start menu and shortcuts and then remove temporary installation files. If you have installed to an NTFS partition, it will also set security on system files.

Windows NT saves the configuration of the operating system and then creates the Emergency Repair Disk. (Exercise 2.12, step 26.) The last step is to remove any floppy disks and click the Restart Computer button. (Exercise 2.12, step 27.)

Your computer will then restart to an installed version of Windows NT Workstation version 4.0. Once you log on as an administrator, you can create a user account (the process is explained in Chapter 3) and configure your printers (see Chapter 13).

Removing Windows NT

I F YOU DECIDE TO GO BACK to a previous operating system, you simply install that operating system over Windows NT. Although Windows NT does not have a specific "de-install" routine, you will need to use a few tricks to "remove" it and reinstall the previous operating system. Follow these three steps:

1. Remove the NTFS volume if necessary.

2. Change the bootstrap routine.

3. Delete the Windows NT directory.

Removing an NTFS Volume

If you have used the NTFS file system for your Windows NT installation, you should remove the NTFS partition before installing another operating system. If you have data files on the NTFS partition that you want to keep, you will have to copy them onto another mass storage device or back them up to a tape that the operating system you are moving to can read. Copying these files to a FAT volume is an effective and fast way to make certain they will be available to your new operating system.

After moving or archiving any data you wish to keep, you are ready to delete the NTFS partition. Removing an NTFS volume can be difficult because some versions of the MS-DOS FDISK program cannot delete an NTFS volume. No version of the MS-DOS FDISK program can remove an NTFS logical drive in an extended MS-DOS partition.

Perhaps the easiest way to remove an NTFS partition is with the Windows NT setup program used to create them, as explained in Exercise 2.13.

Do not perform the following exercise unless you actually intend to remove an NTFS partition. This exercise can destroy information on your hard disk.

Removing the NTFS partition in which Windows NT is installed automatically removes the Windows NT files.

EXERCISE 2.13

Deleting an NTFS Partition

1. Insert the Windows NT Setup disk #1 and restart your computer.

2. Insert Setup disk #2 when prompted.

3. Press Enter at the *Welcome to Setup* screen.

4. Press Enter to automatically detect your mass storage devices or press **S** if you need to specify them manually.

5. Insert Setup disk #3 when prompted.

6. Press Enter when you have specified all necessary device drivers.

7. Press page down at the license page until you reach the end of the license agreement and then press F8.

8. Change your computer settings as necessary and press Enter.

9. Select the NTFS partition you wish to delete in the partition screen and press **D**.

10. Press **L** to confirm deletion. Note that the partition now shows up as free space in the partitions list.

11. Press F3 twice to exit NT Setup.

12. Press Enter to restart your computer.

Changing the Boot Operating System

Changing the boot operating system involves simply replacing the boot record of the primary hard disk with the boot loader for the operating system you will be using. Exercise 2.14 shows how to change the boot loader to MS-DOS in an existing FAT partition, and Exercise 2.15 to do so on a disk from which the NTFS partition has been removed.

This command replaces the bootstrap routing on the boot hard disk with the system files for MS-DOS. If you boot the MS-DOS Setup disk #1 to install MS-DOS, this step will be performed for you.

EXERCISE 2.14

Changing the Boot Loader to MS-DOS in an Existing FAT Partition

1. Boot an MS-DOS floppy disk containing the `sys` utility or MS-DOS Setup disk #1.

2. Exit to the command prompt, if necessary.

3. Type **SYS C:** at the A prompt.

4. Restart the computer.

Do not perform this exercise unless you intend to create an MS-DOS boot partition. The exact steps shown in this exercise will not apply if you have other existing partitions on your disk. Use caution when partitioning a disk that contains other partitions.

EXERCISE 2.15

Creating an MS-DOS Boot Partition

1. Boot an MS-DOS floppy disk containing the FDISK and format utilities or boot the MS-DOS Setup disk #1.

2. Exit to the command prompt, if necessary.

3. Type **FDISK** at the A prompt.

4. Select option 1, *Create MS-DOS primary partition.*

5. Answer **Y** when asked if you wish to use the entire space available and make the partition active.

6. Press Esc to exit FDISK and reboot the computer.

7. Exit to the command prompt if necessary after the computer reboots the system floppy.

8. Type **FORMAT C: /S** at the A prompt.

9. Remove the floppy disk and reboot the computer when the format finishes.

Other operating systems use other methods too numerous to cover. Usually, the operating system installation has an option to replace your current boot strap routine. If you are installing another operating system such as OS/2 or a version of UNIX, select the boot option that will replace the Windows NT boot loader.

Removing NT from a FAT Partition

If you have installed Windows NT in a FAT partition, removing it is simple. You need only delete the contents of two directories and a few boot files. Exercise 2.16 shows how to remove a Windows NT installation from a FAT volume in MS-DOS.

EXERCISE 2.16

Removing NT from a FAT Partition

1. Boot MS-DOS from a system disk containing the `deltree` utility.

2. Type **DELTREE WINNT** (or the name of your Windows NT directory) at the C prompt.

3. Type **CD PROGRA~1**.

4. Type **DELTREE WINDOW~1**.

5. Type **DEL NTLDR**.

6. Type **DEL NTDETECT.COM**.

7. Type **DEL BOOT.INI**.

8. Type **DEL PAGEFILE.SYS**.

9. Type **DEL BOOTSEC.DOS**.

Chapter Summary

NSTALLING WINDOWS NT WORKSTATION 4.0 requires careful planning. Although NT runs on almost any Intel-based computer and many RISC-based computers, Windows NT does not support every hardware adapter and computer configuration. For this reason, you should consult the Hardware Compatibility List before making any decisions about which hardware to use in your Windows NT workstation.

Before you install Windows NT, you must make sure that your computer is configured properly. One good indication that your computer will work correctly with Windows NT is that it works with another operating system such as Windows 95.

You should carefully plan your Windows NT installation. Before you begin, you should know the name for the computer, the name of the workgroup or domain it will reside on, the network adapter card settings, and so on.

Windows NT Workstation 4.0 can be installed in a variety of ways. You can install it with or without boot disks, over a network, or from a CD-ROM. If you do not use the installation boot disks to boot, you will use either the Winnt program (from within DOS or versions of Windows prior to Windows 95) or you will use the Winnt32 program (from within Windows 95 and Windows NT).

The installation process proceeds through several stages. The first stage loads the Setup program and (optionally) stores the setup files on your computer's hard disk. The text-based Setup program detects your computer's hardware and prepares the hard disk and file system for Windows NT installation. The third (graphical) stage installs the various Windows NT components and configures the Windows NT operating system. Finally, once Windows NT is installed, you can log on and create user accounts and configure printers and other devices.

Exercise Questions

1. Windows NT will run on any computer system.

   A. True

   B. False

2. A computer with an 80486 processor running at 33MHz with 120MB of disk space, a VGA video adapter, and 12MB of memory can run Windows NT Workstation 4.0.

   A. True

   B. False

3. A Sparc RISC-based computer running at 100MHz with 500MB of hard disk space and 64MB of memory will run Windows NT Workstation 4.0.

   A. True

   B. False

4. You must have a CD-ROM drive supported by the Windows NT installation program in order to install Windows NT from CD-ROM to your computer.

   A. True

   B. False

5. Windows NT requires more processing power than does Windows 95 to achieve the same level of responsiveness to the computer user.

   A. True

   B. False

6. Windows NT can automatically detect devices installed in your computer.

   A. True

   B. False

7. Windows NT Workstation 4.0 supports the Plug-and-Play standard.

   A. True

   B. False

8. Upgrading from some previous versions of Windows or Windows NT will transfer some of the configuration information of the operating system to the Windows NT installation.

    A. True

    B. False

9. If you install Windows NT Workstation on your computer, you will not be able to run other operating systems, such as Windows 95 or OS/2.

    A. True

    B. False

10. If Windows NT is run from a FAT partition, the advanced features of NTFS will not be available.

    A. True

    B. False

11. You must have three installation boot floppy disks in order to install Windows NT Workstation 4.0.

    A. True

    B. False

12. The graphical screens in the second portion of the installation process examine your computer's hardware; allow you to select the partition, file system, and directory for the installation; and copy essential files to your hard disk drive.

    A. True

    B. False

13. You can install Windows NT into unpartitioned hard disk space.

    A. True

    B. False

14. Windows NT can convert an existing FAT partition to NTFS.

    A. True

    B. False

15. If you select an installation directory that already contains a Windows or Windows NT operating system, you have the option of overwriting or upgrading the previously installed operating system.

A. True

B. False

16. The exhaustive hard disk examination examines only operating system files on the hard disk drive.

A. True

B. False

17. Your computer's name can be up to 31 characters long.

A. True

B. False

18. Windows NT will not function without an administrator password.

A. True

B. False

19. You cannot install the networking components if you do not have a network card in your computer.

A. True

B. False

20. AppleTalk is a default protocol for Windows NT Workstation 4.0.

A. True

B. False

21. AppleTalk is a protocol included with Windows NT Workstation 4.0.

A. True

B. False

22. HCL stands for _____ _____ _____.

23. For running Windows NT on Intel-based computers, you should partition your computer's hard disk space into at least _____ partitions.

24. You can use the DOS _____ program to partition your hard disk.

25. Under DOS and versions of Windows including Windows 95, you can use the _____ program to start the installation process.

26. Under Windows NT, you can use the _____ program to start the installation process.

27. The _____ option instructs the installation program that you wish to perform a floppy-less install.

28. The _____ and _____ options will re-create the Windows NT installation boot floppies.

29. In a _____ installation of Windows NT, the installation files reside in a shared directory on a file server.

30. The installation files for Intel-based computers reside in the _____ subdirectory of the CD-ROM.

31. Windows NT 4.0 supports two file systems: _____ and _____.

32. The _____ installation option allows you to select for yourself what software provided with Windows NT to install on your workstation.

33. The _____ installation option installs the most used software that comes with Windows NT in the most common configuration.

34. The _____ _____ adapter is a software driver that pretends to be a network adapter but does not really control a hardware device.

35. The default workgroup name is _____.

36. The default domain name is _____.

Users, Groups, and Policies

I N THE LAST CHAPTER you learned how to install Windows NT Workstation. In this chapter you will learn to build individual accounts so that different people can use the computer in different ways. You will start by learning how to construct user and group accounts and then begin exploring some fundamental NT security features.

Multiple-User Systems

M OST COMPUTERS IN A BUSINESS ENVIRONMENT are used by more than one person. Each person typically prefers different default settings and work styles and may also have files or programs that are private. One person—usually the primary user—may want to exercise some administrative control over the computer to maintain uniformity in the way files are stored or software is configured.

To accommodate the needs of different users, Windows NT Workstation implements user accounts and password security. Each person who needs to use a computer can have an account set up. User accounts perform many important functions:

- Allows computer access only to authorized users.

- Identifies the user's security permissions to determine whether access to files, folders, and programs on the computer is appropriate for that user.

- Identifies the user to a network if the computer is attached to one.

- Stores the user's individual passwords for shared resources such as dial-up accounts or NetWare file servers.

- Stores the user's personal preferences for many desktop features.

Customizing and maintaining numerous user accounts is difficult. An easier technique is to construct natural collections of users with similar requirements. In Windows NT these collections of users are called *groups*. Every user account that is a member of a group has all the permissions assigned to that group so that permissions do not have to be assigned to each user account. You can change permissions for any number of users by changing the permissions for their groups. In the following section, you'll learn to construct, manage, and assign user accounts to groups.

In many environments maintaining control over the use of a computer is important. Windows NT has numerous security features to help accomplish the level of control you need. You can limit when and how users are allowed to operate the computer, change the operations that a user or group is allowed to perform, and track many system activities. Chapters 6 and 7 cover all aspects of Windows NT security.

In the "Security Policies" section later in this chapter, you will learn how to implement account policies that control how passwords allow users to access the computer. You'll learn to set user rights that govern the operations a user can perform and how to use NT's Security log to keep a record of activities on the workstation. You'll learn to select the activities you want NT to track and how to view the Security log with the Event Viewer utility.

Users and User Accounts

USER ACCOUNTS MAINTAIN the privacy of information on a shared computer and help users work in ways that are comfortable to them by keeping track of their personal preferences. Windows NT uses the logon-authentication method to track computer usage. Each user has a specific username, which uniquely identifies him or her in the Windows NT user accounts database. In addition, each user is assigned a password when the account is created. Before Windows NT allows access to the computer, a user must enter a valid username and password in the dialog box that appears after pressing Ctrl+Alt+Del. When the user has finished working, he or she logs out, making the computer available for another user.

Network administrators should develop a consistent and coherent naming convention. A good naming convention has three characteristics:

1. It is easy to use and understand. If users don't understand the naming convention, they won't use it.

2. Anyone familiar with the naming convention should be able to construct an object name in a few moments. For a user, the name might include their full name and their function in the company. For a printer, the name might include the model number and configuration details, physical location in the building, and what kind of work the printer is intended for.

3. Given an object name, it should be obvious what the object corresponds to. If the object represents a printer, the name should correspond to the printer, for example, the Hewlett-Packard LaserJet III printer on the third floor. If the object is a user account, users should be able to determine that JASMITH corresponds to John A. Smith. Constructing a naming convention that produces meaningful names for objects is fairly easy; constructing a naming convention that translates easily in both directions is more difficult.

We recommend using the Internet e-mail name convention, which prefixes the last name with the first initial, for users. If that name is not unique, use the middle initial after the first initial.

The Default Accounts

Windows NT creates two accounts by default: the Administrator account and the Guest account.

The Administrator account is always present and should be protected with a strong password. This account manages the overall configuration of the computer and can be used to manage security policies, creating or changing users and groups, setting shared directories for networking, and for other hardware maintenance tasks. This account can be renamed, but it cannot be deleted.

The Guest account enables one-time users or users with low or no security access to use the computer in a limited fashion. The Guest account does not save user preferences or configuration changes, so any changes that a guest user makes are lost when that user logs off. The Guest account is installed with a blank password. If the password is left blank, remote users can connect to the computer using the Guest account. The Guest account can be renamed, but it cannot be deleted.

Creating User Accounts

You can add user accounts to your NT network in two ways: You can create new user accounts, or you can make copies of existing user accounts. In either case you may make changes in three areas:

- User account information

- Group membership information

- User account profile information

To add a new user account, you will be working with the New User dialog box, as shown in Figure 3.1.

Table 3.1 describes the properties of the user account that are accessible from the New User dialog box.

User accounts are administered with the User Manager administrative tool. Exercise 3.1 shows the process of creating new user accounts. (Subsequent exercises in this chapter assume that you have already opened the User Manager.)

You should record the Administrator account password, seal it in an envelope, and secure it in a safe or other secure location. Make sure at least one other trusted individual knows where the password is stored in case you get hit by a meteor.

FIGURE 3.1
The New User dialog box.

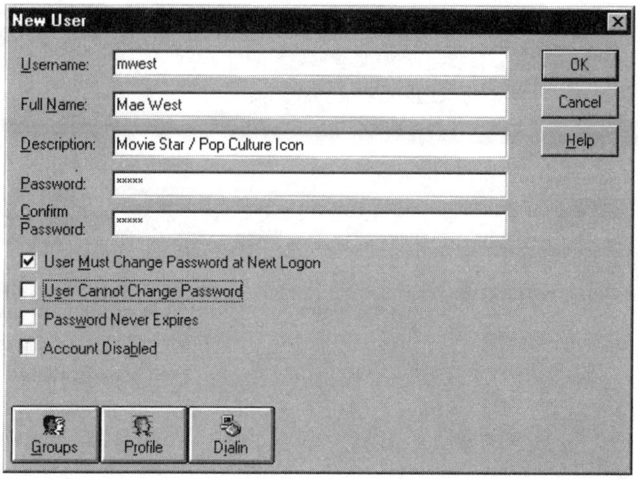

New User				
Username:	mwest			OK
Full Name:	Mae West			Cancel
Description:	Movie Star / Pop Culture Icon			Help
Password:	*****			
Confirm Password:	*****			

☑ User Must Change Password at Next Logon
☐ User Cannot Change Password
☐ Password Never Expires
☐ Account Disabled

Groups   Profile   Dialin

TABLE 3.1 User Account Properties.	**FIELD**	**VALUE**
	Username	A required text field of up to 20 characters. Uses both uppercase and lowercase letters except " / \ [ ] : ; | = , + * ? < > but is not case sensitive. This name must be unique among workstation users or among network domain members if attached to a network.
	Full Name	An optional text field typically used for the complete name of the user. For instance, a user whose full name is Mae West may have a username of mwest.
	Description	An optional text field used to more fully describe the user, his or her position in the firm, home office, etc. This field is limited to any 48 characters.
	Password	A required text field up to 14 characters; case sensitive. This field displays asterisks, rather than the characters typed, to keep your password secure.
	Confirm Password	A required text field used to confirm the password field. This method avoids typing errors, which result in unknown passwords. As with the Password field, the Confirm Password field also displays asterisks.
	User Must Change Password at Next Logon	A checkbox field used to force a password change at next logon. Note that Windows NT will not allow you to apply changes to a user account if this field and User Cannot Change Password field are both checked.
	User Cannot Change Password	A checkbox field that makes it impossible for users to change their own password. This feature is used for shared accounts (such as the Guest account) where a user changing the account password would make it impossible for other users of the account to log on. You would normally not check this account for typical users.
	Password Never Expires	A checkbox field that prevents a password from expiring according to the password policy. This setting is normally used for automated software services that must be logged on as a user. Note that setting *Password Never Expires* overrides *User Must Change Password at Next Logon*.

	FIELD	VALUE
TABLE 3.1 (cont.) User Account Properties.	Account Disabled	A checkbox field that when set prevents users from logging onto the network with this account. This field provides an easy way to place an account out of service temporarily.
	Account Locked Out	This option will be checked if the account is currently locked out due to failed logon attempts. You can clear it to restore access to the account, but it cannot be set.
	Groups button	Assigns Group membership.
	Profile button	Activates the user environment profile information.
	Dial-In button	Allows users to dial into this computer using Remote Access Service. See Chapter 12 for more information.

EXERCISE 3.1

Creating a New User Account

1. Log on to the network as an administrator.

2. Click the Start menu and select Programs ➤ Administrative Tools ➤ User Manager.

3. Select User ➤ New User.

4. Type **mwest** in the Username field.

5. Type **Mae West** in the Full Name field.

6. Type **Movie Star/Pop Culture Icon** in the Description field.

7. Type in any password you want in the Password field. A good password is at least eight characters long and includes at least one punctuation mark. Passwords are case sensitive.

8. Type exactly the same password in the confirm password field.

9. Leave the checkboxes as they are for now.

10. Click Add.

11. Do not record this password anywhere. If you forget it, use the Administrator account to assign a new password to this account.

Copying User Accounts

If you have to create accounts for a large number of users, for instance, in an academic environment where hundreds of students come and go every year, you can create a few basic user account templates and copy them as needed. A user account template is a user account that provides all the features new users will need and has its Account Disabled field enabled. When you need to add a user account, you can copy the template. When you copy a user account, Windows NT automatically copies some of the user account field values from the template and you provide the remaining information.

Windows NT copies these values from the template to the new user account:

- Description

- Group Account Memberships

- Profile Settings

- User Cannot Change Password

- Password Never Expires

Windows NT leaves the following fields blank in the new User account dialog box:

- Username

- Full Name

- User Must Change Password at Next Logon

- Account Disabled

The Username and Full Name fields are left blank for you to enter the new user information. The *User Must Change Password at Next Logon* checkbox is set by default. As a security precaution, leave this setting if you want to force new users to change from your assigned password when they first log on. Exercise 3.2 shows the process of copying a user account.

Notice that we assigned an initial password loosely based on the user's name, but mangled according to specific rules. This is a relatively secure initial password scheme to keep individuals outside your organization from easily guessing new user passwords. However, the only method that is entirely secure is to assign randomly generated passwords, which are passed to the user through some physical means. Your security needs may require more rigorous precautions to keep initial passwords from creating a hole in your security measures.

EXERCISE 3.2

Copying a User Account

1. Select the mwest user account in the User Manager.

2. Select User ➤ Copy or press F8.

3. Enter the following information into the Copy of mwest dialog box. Leave the checkbox fields in their default states.

4. Type **rvalentino** into the Username field.

5. Type **Rudolf Valentino** into the Full Name field.

6. Notice that the Description field is copied from the original New User dialog box. Although it remains correct in this example, you will usually change it.

7. Type **ruvaruva!** in the Password field.

8. Type **ruvaruva!** in the Confirm Password field.

9. Explore the User accounts profile and group settings to note that the assignments for mwest have been automatically assigned to rvalentino. To do this inspection, click the Profile and Group buttons and then click OK to return to the Copy of User2 dialog box.

10. Click OK to complete the creation of the rvalentino account.

Disabling and Deleting User Accounts

When access to the workstation is no longer appropriate for a user, that account should be disabled. Leaving unused active accounts in the user accounts database allows potential intruders to continue logon attempts after accounts they've already tried lock them out. Disabling an account prevents it from being used but retains the account information for future use.

This technique is useful for temporarily locking the accounts of employees who are absent or for temporarily denying access to an account that may have been compromised. Deleting an account removes all the user account information from the system. If a user account has been deleted and that user requires access again, you will have to set up a new account with all new permissions. Creating a new user account with the same name will not restore previous account information, as each user account is internally identified by a unique security identifier, not by username. See Chapter 7 "Windows NT Security" for more details on the security issue. Exercise 3.3 shows how to disable a user account.

EXERCISE 3.3

Disabling a User Account

1. Double-click user account rvalentino in the User Manager.

2. Check the Account Disabled field.

3. Click OK to complete the operation.

4. Log off and attempt to log on as rvalentino.

Follow the steps in Exercise 3.4 to reenable a disabled user account.

EXERCISE 3.4

Enabling a Disabled User Account

1. Double-click user account rvalentino in the User Manager.

2. Uncheck the Account Disabled field.

3. Click OK to complete the operation.

4. Log off and attempt to log on as rvalentino.

If a user will no longer be using the system, you should delete his or her account, rather than disable it. Deleting an account will destroy all user preferences and permissions, so be certain the user will never again require access before taking this step. Exercise 3.5 shows the process of deleting a user account.

Renaming User Accounts

You can rename any user account with the User Manager, including the Administrator and Guest default accounts. You may need to change a username if an account that is associated with a specific job is passed on to another individual or if your organization changes its network naming policy.

EXERCISE 3.5

Deleting a User Account

1. Log on to the network as an administrator. Go to the Start menu.

2. Select Programs ➤ Administrative Tools ➤ User Manager.

3. Click on user account rvalentino.

4. Select User ➤ Delete (or hit the Del key).

5. Click OK in the Warning dialog box.

6. Click Yes to confirm the deletion.

7. Log off and attempt to log on as rvalentino.

Changing the name does not change any other properties of the account. You may want to change the names of the Administrator and Guest accounts so an intruder familiar with Windows NT default user account names cannot gain access to your system simply by guessing a password. Figure 3.2 shows the Rename dialog box that allows you to change a user's name. Exercise 3.6 will walk you through the steps.

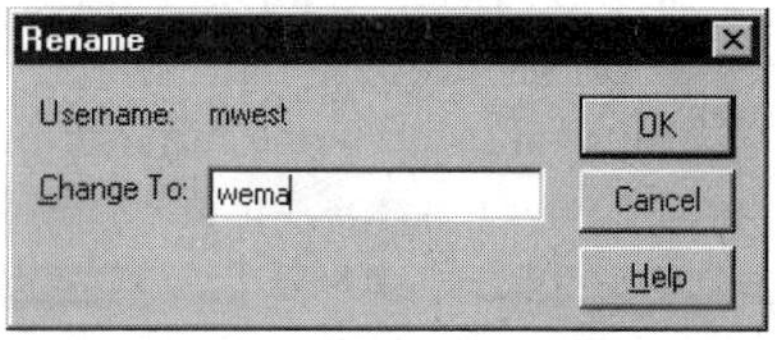

FIGURE 3.2
The Rename dialog box allows you to rename a user account.

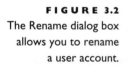

Editing User Environment Profiles

User environment profiles allow you to change some default behavior of Windows NT based on which user is logged on. For instance, they allow you to change the default file location based upon the current user or to map a drive letter to a user's home directory on a server if the person is logging on to a network.

User environment profiles also allow you to run a batch file or executable program that changes as each user logs on. This batch file can be used to set paths and environment variables, or for any other purpose that will change from user to user.

EXERCISE 3.6

Renaming a User Account

1. Log on to the network as an administrator and go to the Start menu.

2. Select Programs ➤ Administrative Tools ➤ User Manager.

3. Select mwest in the User Accounts list.

4. Select User ➤ Rename.

5. Type **wema** in the Change To box.

6. Click OK to complete the operation.

WARNING

You should not use user environment profiles simply to start a program when users log on unless the profile somehow depends upon the users name. The Startup folder provides a much easier method for running programs automatically.

Logon Scripts

Logon scripts help maintain a consistent set of network connections, and they provide a way to migrate users from older network operating systems that use logon scripts to Windows NT without changing the user's familiar environment. They are generally not used for individual workstations.

A logon script is usually implemented as a DOS batch file (with a BAT extension), but it can be an executable file under Windows NT 3.5 and later. Certain environment variables can be used to change settings from within a logon script:

- %PROCESSOR% changes to the CPU type of the machine.

- %HOMEDRIVE% changes to the system hard disk drive.

- %HOMEPATH% changes to the user's home path.

- %HOMESHARE% changes to the user's home share name.

- %OS% changes to the operating system being used.

- %USERDOMAIN% changes to the user's home network domain.

- %USERNAME% changes to the user's name.

If you are migrating from Novell NetWare, you can take advantage of Windows NT Server's ability to process NetWare login scripts without changing them to Windows NT logon scripts.

Home Directories

Home directories give users a place to store their own files. By changing the home directory through the user profile, each user can have a private location in which to store files. In general, you should set permissions on home directories so that only the user specified has access to the data in the directory.

Windows NT makes the home directory the default save location for programs that do not specify one in their Save dialog box. The home directory is also the default directory when launching an MS-DOS prompt. Figure 3.3 shows the user environment profile where you can change these settings. Follow the steps in Exercise 3.7 to change a user's environment.

Windows NT cannot create more than one level of directory structure automatically in the User Environment Profile dialog box. If we had entered the path above without having created the user directory first, Windows NT would have set the profile but warned us to create the directory manually. Creating the path for user directories prior to changing the profile information ensures you will not forget this step or misspell the username when you create the directory.

FIGURE 3.3
The User Environment Profile dialog box.

User Environment Profile
User: wema (Mae West)
User Profiles
User Profile Path: \\HENRY\Boot\Winnt\Profiles\wema
Logon Script Name:
Home Directory
⊙ Local Path:
○ Connect [▼] To

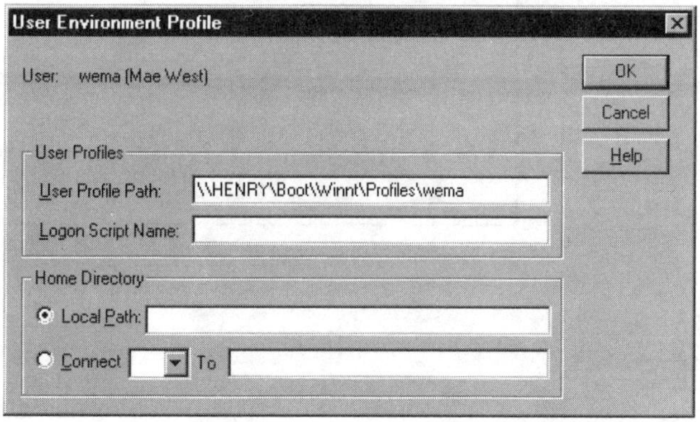

EXERCISE 3.7

Changing a User's Environment

1. Log on to the network as an administrator.

2. Open the My Computer icon.

3. Open the C: drive.

4. Click the right mouse button and select New ➤ Folder.

5. Name the folder "users" and go to the Start menu.

6. Select Programs ➤ Administrative Tools ➤ User Manager.

7. Double-click wema in the User Accounts list.

8. Click the Profile button.

9. Select the Local Path box.

10. Type **C:\users\%username%** in the text box.

11. Click OK to close the User Environment Profile dialog box.

12. Click the Profile button again. Notice that Windows NT has replaced the environment variable %username% with wema, the name of our user. (Using the %username% variable ensures that the name will be changed when you copy user templates.)

13. Click OK to close the User Environment Profile dialog box.

14. Click OK to close the User dialog box.

15. Click Close in the User Manager.

16. Open the users folder.

17. Notice that Windows NT has created a directory called wema.

Groups

 ETTING SPECIFIC PERMISSIONS for many users of a workstation can be an error-prone and time-consuming exercise. Most organizations do not have security requirements that change for every user. Setting permissions is more manageable with the security groups concept, where permissions are assigned to groups rather than to individual users. Users who are members of a group have all the permissions assigned to that group. Group memberships are especially important in large networks and are discussed in more detail in the companion book *MCSE: Networking Essentials Study Guide*.

Groups are useful in many situations. For instance, the finance department in your organization can have permissions set to access all the financial data stored on a computer. You would then create a group called Finance in the User Manager and make each individual in the finance department a member of this group. Every member of the Finance group will have access to all the financial data.

Groups also make changing permissions easier. Permissions assigned to a group affect every member of the group, so changes can be made across the entire group by changing permissions for the group. For instance, adding a new directory for the Finance group requires merely assigning the group permission to the directory to give each member access. This process is much easier than assigning permission to a number of individual accounts.

The two basic types of groups are local groups and global groups. *Local groups* affect only the workstation and are the primary focus of this chapter. *Global groups* affect the entire network and are stored on the primary domain controller.

One individual account can belong to many groups. This arrangement facilitates setting up groups for many purposes. For instance, you might define groups corresponding to the functional areas in your organization—administration, marketing, finance, manufacturing, etc. You might create another group for supervisors, another for network support staff, and another for new employees. This procedure enables you to set default permissions for all members of the Finance group. In addition, you can modify the permissions if an individual happens to be a member of more than one group, as we explained earlier in this chapter.

For example, a member of the Finance group may have permission to access accounting information and financial statements, but a member of the New Users may not have permission to access accounting information. By assigning membership in both groups, you would be allowing access to financial statements without permitting access to accounting information until the new user becomes a trusted employee and is removed from the New Users group.

Windows NT has a default group called Users that can be used to assign rights and permissions for every user on the network. When accounts are created, they are automatically assigned membership in the default Users group.

Changing permissions assigned to the default Users group will change permissions for everyone who has access to the computer.

Microsoft Exchange uses the Windows NT group information to define its groups. Therefore, all members of a security group defined now will also become message groups when you install Microsoft Exchange.

Planning Groups

Planning your groups correctly will make administering the users on your workstation easier. Experienced administrators seldom assign access rights to individual accounts. Instead, they create a group and then make individual accounts a part of that group. For instance, rather than giving individual users the access rights to back up the system, the administrator creates a Backup group with those rights and then adds users to that group. That way, when the backup process changes, only the group account must be changed to match the new process. Also, the administrator now has a convenient way to send messages to all of the individuals who can back up the network.

Windows NT Server uses global groups to maintain groups across all computers on a network. They are different from the local groups you can create using Windows NT Workstation. If you are planning Network groups, please refer to Mastering Windows NT Server 4, *also published by Sybex.*

Assigning users to groups allows you to keep track of who needs what resource. For example, word processing users might need access to the word processing package itself, its data files, and also a shared directory that contains your organization's common documents and templates. You can give all three rights to a group, called Word Processing, and then in one action give the rights to an individual account by adding the account to the group.

In Windows NT, you can give rights to everyone by assigning those access rights to the group Users.

When you are creating the network groups for your network, you should determine which network resources the users on your network will need to access.

Observe what different users have in common and create groups to give users that access. Ideally, you will assign rights to groups and grant rights to users by making them a part of the appropriate groups. You can base groups on the following criteria:

- Organization functional units (marketing, etc.)

- Network programs (word processing or graphics, etc.)

- Events (company party)

- Network resources (laser printer)

- Location (hanger 18)

- Individual function (backup operator, etc.)

When a user is a member of many groups, some of those groups may specifically allow access to a resource, while other group memberships deny it. A specific denial always overrides access to a resource.

User and group permissions are cumulative. However, if for any reason the user has a No Access permission for that resource, the user cannot access the resource. Another exception is if share permissions and NTFS user access permissions differ, then the most restrictive of the two are used.

Chapter 6 explains exactly how Windows NT determines security permissions for system objects like files and shares. Chapter 7 describes the technical details behind security and permissions. Exercise 3.8 shows you how to assign user accounts to groups.

The Built-in Groups

NT creates six groups at installation that are meant to provide convenient group features for a basic workstation. They may be all you need, but if you have many users you will probably modify these default groups and add your own. These built-in groups are

- Administrators

- Power Users

- Users

- Guests

EXERCISE 3.8

Assigning User Accounts to Groups

1. Log on to the network as an administrator and go to the Start menu.

2. Select Programs ➤ Administrative Tools ➤ User Manager.

3. Double-click on user wema in the username list.

4. Click the Group button in the User Properties box.

5. Review the Group Memberships dialog box.

6. Select Power Users in the Not Member Of box.

7. Click Add.

8. Click OK to close the Group Memberships dialog box.

9. Click OK to close the User Properties dialog box.

User wema is now a member of the Power Users group.

- Backup Operators

- Replicator

You can use a special group, named Everyone, to assign global permissions or rights to all local users. Table 3.2 shows the Windows NT built-in groups and the permissions assigned to them.

Administrators

Administrators have full rights and privileges over all files and other resources on the workstation. The default Administrator account and the Initial user account, if created automatically, have membership in the Administrators group. If the workstation is part of a network domain, then all domain administrators are members of the Administrators group automatically.

	GROUP	CAPABILITIES
TABLE 3.2 Groups Built into Microsoft Windows NT Workstation.	Administrators	Can fully administer the workstation
	Users	Have normal user rights and permissions
	Guests	Have guest user rights and permissions
	Power Users	Can share directories and printers
	Backup Operators	Can bypass security to back up and restore all files
	Replicator	Supports file replication in a network domain

Power Users

Power Users can add Program Manager groups, share directories, and modify the system clock. Furthermore, they can install, delete, share, and manage printers. Additionally, they can create users and groups. Finally, they can manage and delete any users and groups they created.

Even if you are the only user of your workstation, you should create an account that has Power User group membership and use it as your primary access to the computer. This designation will keep you from accidentally changing important system information, and if anyone ever acquired your Power User account password, that person could not lock you out because you would still have Administrator access.

Users

The Users group is designed for the vast majority of people who need to use the workstation, but are not system or network administrators. Members of the Users group can run applications, manage files on the workstation, and use local and network printers. They can create and manage their own local groups and may manage their own profile. All new User accounts you create will automatically have membership in the Users group.

Guests

The Guest group provides limited access to basic workstation resources. The Guest user account is a member of the Guest group. If you are attached to a network, any user on the network may log on to your workstation as a member of the Guest group.

Backup Operators

Backup Operators can use the Backup and Restore commands provided with NT to back up and restore all the files on the workstation. All users can use Backup and Restore to backup and restore files they have full access to. Members of the Backup Operators group are granted full rights for all files on the workstation, but only while using the Backup and Restore commands.

Replicator

The Replicator group is used to set up the Replicator service, which automatically updates files from one workstation to another. The Replicator service applies only to computers attached to a network.

Creating Groups

You create groups much like you create users. Select New Local Group from the User menu in the User Manager window. Then you can enter the Group Name, Description, and Members in the New Local Group dialog box (see Figure 3.4).

The Group Name field identifies the local group. The group name has the same restrictions as a Username. It must be unique and can contain any uppercase or lowercase letters, numbers, or symbols other than the following:

" / \ : ; | = + * ? < >

The Description field is where you type a description of the group.

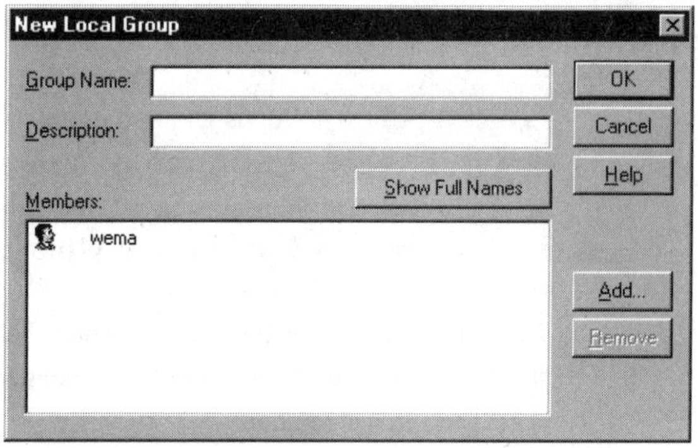

FIGURE 3.4
The New Local Group
dialog box allows you to
create a group and add
users to that group.

Security Policies

ECURITY POLICIES PROVIDE a way to implement systemwide security features that affect all aspects of the Windows NT security manager. Security policies control how your computer implements the various Windows NT security features. Permissions, on the other hand, merely grant or deny access to resources.

When implementing security policies, you should give users access to everything they need to perform their jobs and deny them access to everything else. This measure may sound extreme, but remember that users can accidentally—and easily—misconfigure computers, rendering them inoperable until a knowledgeable professional (usually you) repairs them.

Security policies are managed from the User Manager utility, and only an administrator can manage them.

NT provides three security policies to govern the activities of your workstation users:

- Account policy controls passwords.

- User rights policy determines which operations a user can perform on the workstation.

- Audit policy determines which user activities NT records in its log files.

Account Policy

Account policy governs the use of passwords for a user account. Because Windows NT assigns security at logon, any changes you make will be in effect only after current users have logged off. Table 3.3 lists the audit account policy features available in Windows NT Workstation.

The default Administrator account cannot be locked out. This ensures that no matter how strict your security policies are, the Administrator account can always log on to restore access to the workstation.

Account Policy is set through the Account Policy screen (Figure 3.5). Exercise 3.9 will show you how to change the default account policy settings assigned when you installed Windows NT Workstation.

TABLE 3.3 Account Policy Features.	ACCOUNT POLICY	OPERATION	RESTRICTIONS	DEFAULTS
	Maximum Password Age	Time until next password change is required.	1–999 days or never expires	Expires in 42 days
	Minimum Password Age	Time before users are allowed to change their password.	1–999 days or immediately	Allow Changes Immediately
	Minimum Password Length	Minimum length of a valid password or length for a blank password; default length is six characters.	1–14, or 0 when blank passwords are allowed	Permit Blank Password
	Password Uniqueness	Keep track of previous passwords and do not allow users to recycle passwords from the list of those recently used.	Maintain a list of the last 1–24 passwords this user has employed, or keep no list and allow recurring use of passwords	Do Not Keep Password History

TABLE 3.3 (cont.) Account Policy Features.	ACCOUNT POLICY	OPERATION	RESTRICTIONS	DEFAULTS
	No account locking and Account lockout	With No account locking engaged, account will not be locked out after attempts to log on with an incorrect password.	Choose one	No account locking
	Lockout after	Number of bad password logon attempts before account is locked out.	1–999	Blank
	Reset count after	Maximum number of minutes between two bad password logon attempts for those bad attempts to count toward the Account Lockout count.	1–99,999 minutes	Blank
	Lockout Duration	Minutes that a lockout is enforced. Forever will require an administrator to unlock the account.	1–99,999 minutes or Forever	Blank
	Users must log on in order to change password	When engaged, users must log on to their account before changing their password. If the password has expired, they cannot log on and cannot change their password, so they must get help from an administrator.	Checkbox	Clear

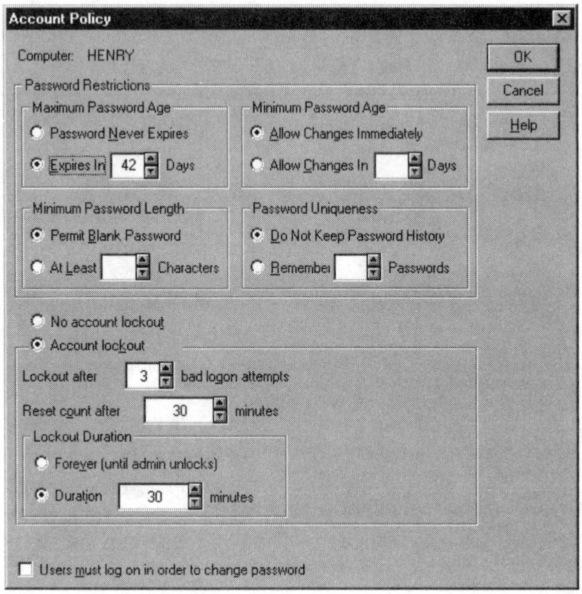

FIGURE 3.5
The Account Policy
screen allows you to view
and control passwords.

EXERCISE 3.9

Change Default Account Policy

1. Log on as an administrator and go to the Start menu.

2. Select Programs ➤ Administrative Tools ➤ User Manager.

3. Select Policies ➤ Account.

4. Set Maximum Password Age to 30 Days.

5. Set Minimum Password Length to 8 characters.

6. Set Minimum Password Age to Allow Changes Immediately.

7. Set Password Uniqueness to Remember 3 Passwords.

8. Set Account lockout to Lockout after 5 bad logon attempts.

9. Set Lockout Duration to 180 minutes.

10. Click OK.

User Rights Policy

User rights allow a user to perform certain restricted activities on the workstation. User rights apply to the entire computer, unlike permissions, which apply to specific resources on the computer such as directories and printers. User rights are managed from the Policies menu of User Manager.

Inappropriate changes to user rights policy can have undesired effects on the operation of your workstation. Do not change user rights unless you fully understand the effects of your changes.

NT provides ten user rights. Of these, only a few are of interest, and they are listed below. Although these rights may be assigned to both groups and users, a good administrative practice is to assign user policies only to groups and then to assign group membership to apply policy to individual users. Figure 3.6 shows the User Rights Policy dialog box.

Table 3.4 lists the user rights, what they do, and the groups that have these rights by default.

Exercise 3.10 will show you how to view specific user rights.

As an administrator, you will occasionally need to modify the default user rights structure by granting a user right to a group or removing a user right from a group that currently has that right.

Exercise 3.11 shows how to grant a right to a group and Exercise 3.12 shows how to revoke a right assigned to a group.

On the rare occasion when you wish to grant a user right to an individual user account instead of to a group, click the Show Users button in the Add Users and Groups dialog box. In its default operation, the Show Users and Groups dialog box only shows groups.

FIGURE 3.6
The User Rights Policy dialog box allows you to view and configure user rights.

User Rights Policy

Computer: HENRY

Right: Access this computer from network

Grant To:
Administrators
Everyone
Power Users

OK
Cancel
Help
Add...
Remove

☐ Show Advanced User Rights

		GROUPS THAT HAVE THESE RIGHTS BY DEFAULT
USER RIGHT	**FUNCTION**	
Access this computer from network	Allows users to connect to shared resources on this workstation	Administrators, Everyone, Power Users
Backup files and directories	Allows users to make backups of data on this machine	Administrators, Backup Operators
Change system time	Allows users to change the computer's internal real-time clock	Administrators, Power Users
Force shutdown from a remote system	Allows users to shut down the computer by issuing a command over the network	Administrators, Power Users
Load and unload device drivers	Allows users to change the drivers used to provide system services	Administrators
Log on locally	Allows users to use the workstation	Administrators, Backup Operators, Everyone, Guests, Power Users, Users
Manage and audit Security log	Allows users to change security policy	Administrators
Restore files and directories	Allows users to restore a previous backup	Administrators, Backup Operators
Shut down the system	Allows users to issue the shut down command; prohibits a user from simply shutting off the computer	Administrators, Backup Operators, Everyone, Power Users, Users
Take ownership of files or other objects	Allows users to assert authority over system objects	Administrators, Backup Operators, Everyone, Guests, Power Users, Users

TABLE 3.4
The Bill of Rights.

EXERCISE 3.10

View User Rights

1. Log on as an administrator and go to the Start menu.

2. Select Programs ➤ Administrative Tools ➤ User Manager.

3. Select Policies ➤ User Rights.

4. Select Load and unload device drivers from the Right drop-down list.

5. Note that this user right is granted only to administrators.

6. Select Log on locally from the Right drop-down list.

7. Note that this right is granted to all six of the default groups.

8. Click OK.

EXERCISE 3.11

Grant a User Right to a Group

1. Log on as an administrator and go to the Start menu.

2. Select Programs ➤ Administrative Tools ➤ User Manager.

3. Select Policies ➤ User Rights.

4. Select *Back up files and directories* from the Right drop-down list.

5. Note that this right is granted to Administrators and Backup Operators.

6. Click Add to grant the selected right to a user or group.

7. Select the Power Users group and click Add.

8. Click OK.

9. Note which groups now have the *Back up files and directories* right.

10. Click OK to return to User Manager.

EXERCISE 3.12

Remove a User Right from a Group

1. Log on as an administrator and go to the Start menu.

2. Select Programs ➤ Administrative Tools ➤ User Manager.

3. Select Policies ➤ User Rights.

4. Select *Back up files and directories* from the Right drop-down list.

5. Select the Power Users group from the Grant To: box.

6. Click Remove.

7. Note which groups now have the *Back up files and directories* right.

8. Click OK.

Advanced User Rights

Advanced user rights are generally associated with software development, not workstation administration. Use Exercise 3.13 to browse through the advanced user rights.

Audit Policy

NT can keep a record of many operating system activities. The actions you direct NT to track are recorded in a log file.

If you direct NT to log all possible activities, the auditing process overhead will slow down the system. The log file will grow so quickly that searching for interesting events will be very cumbersome.

You should enable auditing only for those activities that are specifically required by your organization's security policy. You direct NT to audit system activities using the Audit Policy dialog box (see Figure 3.7).

Security Policies **101**

EXERCISE 3.13

View Advanced User Rights

1. Log on as an administrator and go to the Start menu.

2. Select Programs ➤ Administrative Tools ➤ User Manager.

3. Select Policies ➤ User Rights.

4. Check *Show advanced user rights* at the bottom of the dialog box.

5. Select *Create a Pagefile* from the Right drop-down list.

6. Note this right is granted to the Administrators group.

7. Click OK.

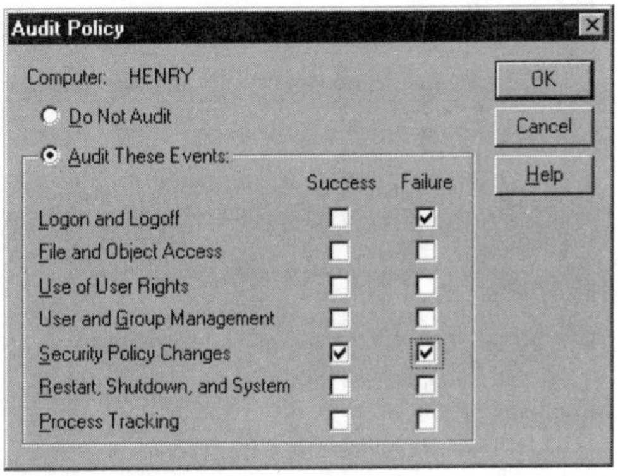

FIGURE 3.7
The Audit Policy
dialog box.

Auditing is organized by activity. For each activity you can audit only successful attempts, only unsuccessful attempts, or both. Table 3.5 lists the activities you can audit.

Exercise 3.14 shows how to enable auditing. Remember that auditing will slow down your computer. After you've completed this chapter, be sure to go back through this exercise and disable all the audit policies you enable.

TABLE 3.5 Activities You Can Audit with NT.	**ACTIVITY TO AUDIT**	**AUDIT SUCCESS OR FAILURE**	**EVENTS THAT ARE LOGGED**
	Logon and Logoff	Success	User logged on or off the workstation or some other system on the network
	Logon and Logoff	Failure	User attempted but failed to log on or off the workstation or some system on the network
	File and Object Access	Success	User accessed a directory, printer, file, or some other object set for auditing
	File and Object Access	Failure	User attempted but failed to access a directory, printer, file, or some other object set for auditing
	Use of User Rights	Success	User succeeded in the use of a user right other than logon and logoff
	Use of User Rights	Failure	User failed in an attempt to use a user right other than logon and logoff
	User and Group Management	Success	User created, modified, or deleted a user or group account or modified a password
	User and Group Management	Failure	User failed in an attempt to create, modify, or delete a user or group account or failed to modify a password
	Security Policy Changes	Success	User made changes in User Rights or Audit Policies
	Security Policy Changes	Failure	User attempted but failed to make changes in User Rights or Audit Policies
	Restart, Shutdown, and System	Success	User restarted or shutdown the system, or a system security event occurred
	Restart, Shutdown, and System	Failure	User failed to restart or shutdown the system

	ACTIVITY TO AUDIT	AUDIT SUCCESS OR FAILURE	EVENTS THAT ARE LOGGED
TABLE 3.5 (cont.) Activities You Can Audit with NT.	Process Tracking	Success	Provides detailed tracking information for a variety of user actions, including program activation, handle duplication, object access, and process exit
	Process Tracking	Failure	Provides detailed tracking information for a variety of user failed actions, including program activation, handle duplication, object access, and process exit

EXERCISE 3.14

Enable Auditing

1. Log on as an administrator and go to the Start menu.

2. Select Programs ➤ Administrative Tools ➤ User Manager.

3. Select Policies ➤ Audit.

4. Enable *Audit These Events*.

5. Make the following selections:

ACTIVITY	SETTING
Select Restart, Shutdown, and System	Success
Select User and Group Management	Success & Failure
Select Logon and Logoff	Success & Failure

6. Click OK.

7. Exit the User Manager.

8. Select Shut Down from the Startup menu.

9. Select *Restart the computer.* These activities will write a few events to the Security log.

10. Click Yes.

Network Policy

The network administrator can use the System Policy Manager to allow or disallow the modification of many Control Panel settings. This utility is not included with Windows NT Workstation, but you should be aware that if you are on a network, the domain administrator may have changed your settings policy. This topic is covered in Chapter 17, "Troubleshooting."

Working with the Security Log

After you have instituted an audit policy, each occurrence of an audited event is written to the Security log. The Security log may become very large quickly if your computer is very active and you have audited many activities. Finding specific events is difficult when the Security log is very large.

Windows NT provides some basic search and selection tools to help find events quickly. For example, the Event Viewer utility (see Figure 3.8) allows you to view the Security log and select the log items of interest. You can also use the Event Viewer to examine other logs that we discuss in later chapters.

Exercise 3.15 shows you how to view and clear the Security log.

You may want to go back to the User Manager program and clear the audit policies if you are not concerned about tracking these events. If you don't remember how to perform this step, see Exercise 3.14.

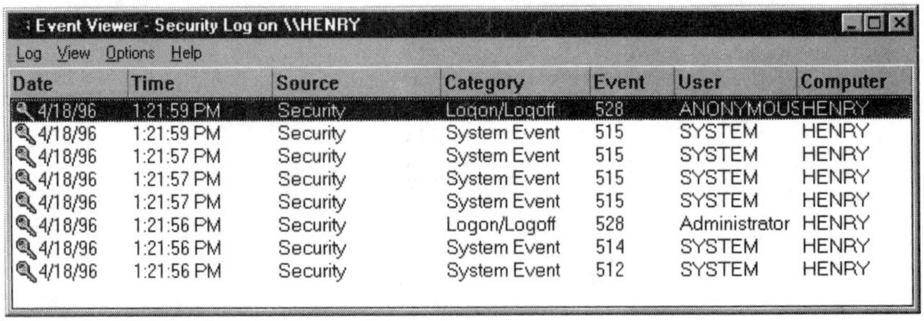
Event Viewer - Security Log on \\HENRY
Log View Options Help
Date Time Source Category Event User Computer
4/18/96 1:21:59 PM Security Logon/Logoff 528 ANONYMOUS HENRY
4/18/96 1:21:59 PM Security System Event 515 SYSTEM HENRY
4/18/96 1:21:57 PM Security System Event 515 SYSTEM HENRY
4/18/96 1:21:57 PM Security System Event 515 SYSTEM HENRY
4/18/96 1:21:57 PM Security System Event 515 SYSTEM HENRY
4/18/96 1:21:56 PM Security Logon/Logoff 528 Administrator HENRY
4/18/96 1:21:56 PM Security System Event 514 SYSTEM HENRY
4/18/96 1:21:56 PM Security System Event 512 SYSTEM HENRY

FIGURE 3.8 Windows NT Event Viewer showing security events.

EXERCISE 3.15

Viewing and Clearing the Security Log

1. Log on as an administrator and go to the Start menu.

2. Select Programs ➤ Administrative Tools ➤ Event Viewer.

3. Select Log ➤ Security.

4. Double-click on any event in the log.

5. Notice the information NT reports about the event.

6. Click Next to view events that occurred prior to this event; click Previous to view events that occurred after this event.

7. Close the Event Detail window.

8. Select Log ➤ Clear All Events.

9. When NT asks to save the log before clearing it, choose No; then click Yes in the Confirmation dialog box.

10. Close the Event Viewer.

Chapter Summary

EVERY USER OF A WORKSTATION must log on through a user account. Windows NT 4.0 installs two default user accounts: Administrator and Guest. (Windows NT 3.51 also has an optional initial user account.) User accounts maintain information such as individual permissions to use resources, group membership, passwords, and policy constraints.

Groups are a way of arranging users in logical sets, based on shared characteristics. Permissions and policy assigned by group apply to all members of that group. Windows NT Workstation can create only local groups, and local groups can contain only user accounts, not other groups. Six default groups are available at installation:

- Administrators
- Power Users
- Users
- Guests
- Replicator
- Backup Operators

Windows NT manages security policy with three distinct policy types:

- Account policy governs the operation and maintenance of passwords.
- User rights policy governs system activities by group membership or user account.
- Audit policy governs which activities are recorded in the Security log.

You can use the Event Viewer utility to review and search the Security log.

Exercise Questions

1. Windows NT 4 Workstation creates two default user accounts.

    A. True

    B. False

2. In NT 4 you can add new users in two ways.

    A. True

    B. False

3. The Administrator account cannot be renamed.

    A. True

    B. False

4. The Username, Full Name, and Description fields are left blank when copying user accounts.

    A. True

    B. False

5. Copying user accounts can save you time when you have many user accounts to create.

    A. True

    B. False

6. Since account permissions are based on the username, you will have to reassign permissions if you change an account username.

    A. True

    B. False

7. You should audit most system activities.

    A. True

    B. False

8. Deleting and disabling accounts are the same thing.

A. True

B. False

9. The default Administrator account can never be locked out.

A. True

B. False

10. Policies should usually be set by group, not by user.

A. True

B. False

11. Deleting an account removes information, but permissions can be restored by creating a new account with the same name.

A. True

B. False

12. A good administrative practice is to assign permissions to groups rather than to users.

A. True

B. False

13. Only administrators can create groups and assign permissions.

A. True

B. False

14. Only administrators can manage policies.

A. True

B. False

15. Windows NT does not ensure that permissions are the same across local groups with the same name on different workstations.

A. True

B. False

16. Policy changes are effective only after the current users log off.

  A. True

  B. False

17. The _____ account provides limited access to the computer for users with low or no security access.

18. The _____ account has the highest level of permissions of any user.

19. Windows NT provides _____ to make assigning permissions easier among a large number of users.

20. _____ policy controls passwords.

21. All user and group administration functions are performed through the _____ utility.

22. The _____ utility is used to view the Security log.

23. The _____ checkbox prevents users from using an account when checked.

24. A Windows NT Workstation installation contains _____ default groups.

25. When a user leaves your organization, you should _____ that account.

26. Which of the following is not a default group?

  A. Power Users

  B. Backup Operators

  C. Administrative Assistants

  D. Users

27. When copying user accounts, which of the following fields is not copied into the New Account dialog box?

  A. Profile Settings

  B. Description

  C. Group Memberships

  D. User Must Change Password at Next Logon

28. Account policy governs the use of what?

    A. User account permissions

    B. Passwords

    C. Accounting practices

    D. Security identification

29. Which of the following is not a user right?

    A. Change system time

    B. Load and unload device drivers

    C. Add/remove software

    D. Shutdown the system

    E. Access this computer from network

30. A user has been reassigned from sales to marketing. You should

    A. Change his user permissions

    B. Change her group assignment from sales to marketing

    C. Delete this account and then create a new one with new permissions

    D. Do nothing

31. You suspect someone may be attempting to gain unauthorized access to the system. To verify your suspicion, you should

    A. Lock out all accounts and then grant access to people who show photo identification

    B. Force all users to change their passwords at the next logon

    C. Audit failed logon attempts

    D. Audit use of shared resources

    E. Change the Administrator account password

Configuring Windows NT Workstation

I N CHAPTER 3 YOU CREATED accounts for users and groups. In this chapter you will find out how to use Windows NT tools to configure the workstation settings and to configure the Windows NT environment to match the preferences of individual users. This chapter introduces the Control Panel, which is your interface to most Windows NT settings, and the Registry, which keeps track of the Windows NT configuration data.

The Control Panel

Y OU CAN CONTROL ALMOST ANYTHING that has to do with the appearance or function of your workstation from the Control Panel. This section describes the functions that are represented by icons in the Control Panel and guides you through the use of the ones you will most likely need to use to configure your NT Workstation.

Many of the items shown in Figure 4.1 appear in the Control Panel of your NT Workstation. However, some icons (the one for Dial-Up Monitor, for instance) will not appear if the services they support have not been loaded. (Dial-Up Monitor appears only if the Remote Access Service has been installed.)

Other items in the Control Panel may not have much use, depending on how your computer is configured and what hardware has been installed. The PC Card item, for example, will not do much if your computer does not have PC Card slots, and the SCSI Adapters item is much less useful if you do not have a SCSI adapter.

Some computer settings can be set differently for each user (the desktop background, for instance, because each user can have a different pattern or picture in the background). Other computer settings are the same for everyone who uses the computer. The Network settings are an example of system settings that all users share.

FIGURE 4.1
The Control Panel
is where you will
configure most aspects
of your Windows NT
Workstation.

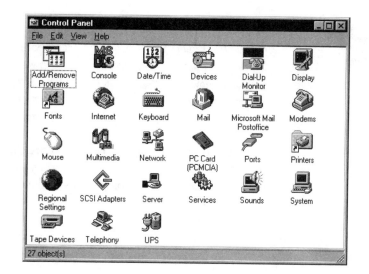

System Settings

SOME SETTINGS FOR HARDWARE and software remain the same for all users. You can use the icons in the Control Panel to help you manage these settings. Since these settings affect every user of the system, only members of the Administrators group can modify them. Some of the Control Panel icons that you can use to modify system settings are

- **Devices:** Allows you to start and stop hardware devices

- **Network:** Allows you to install and configure network components

- **Fonts:** Contains the system fonts available to programs on the workstation

- **Services:** Allows you to start and stop system services such as the Remote Access Server and simple TCP/IP services

- **Date/Time:** Allows you to set the time and date of the computer's clock

- **System:** Allows you to modify system settings such as the default startup parameters, system environment variables, and paging options

An item in the Control Panel may modify the system configuration or it may modify the user profile (settings that may be different for each user, explained in the next section) or it may modify both. For example, Display allows you not only to specify user profile settings such as window colors, but also to change the display driver, which is a part of the system configuration. Windows NT security ensures that only users with the appropriate security permissions can modify system configuration data.

Several of these items are topics for entire chapters in themselves (networking, for instance, is covered in Chapters 8 through 12). This section on system settings introduces the following components of the Control Panel: System, Date and Time, Ports, and UPS.

System

The System icon on the Control Panel holds many of the critical settings of your Windows NT Workstation. It controls six aspects of NT operation:

- General
- Performance
- Environment
- Startup/Shutdown
- Hardware profiles
- User profiles

Each component has a tab in the System Properties window. We will cover each tab in turn.

General

The General tab describes the operating system version, licensing information, and summary system data of your Windows NT Workstation. The summary information includes the type of computer and the amount of memory it has. This part of the System Properties window does not have any settings for you to modify.

Performance

The Performance tab allows you to adjust the application performance and virtual memory settings for your computer.

You can adjust the performance advantage the foreground application receives in relation to the other applications running in your computer. (The *foreground application* is the application that receives your keyboard strokes and mouse clicks.)

The Change button in the virtual memory section brings up the Virtual Memory window (see Figure 4.2) in which you can set initial and maximum sizes for the *paging file* for each of the drives in your computer. The process that

Paging

Windows NT uses a technique called *paging* to allow your computer to run more programs than its physical memory would normally allow. NT accomplishes this use of memory by dividing the memory in your computer into pages and by swapping pages of data belonging to inactive programs out to your disk in order to make room for program data that is being actively used. In this manner the operating system can actually use more memory than is physically present in your computer.

FIGURE 4.2
The Virtual Memory window shows how much virtual memory you have configured and which drives hold swap files.

```
Virtual Memory                                                  [X]

Drive [Volume Label]        Paging File Size (MB)      [  OK   ]
C:  [GBOF]                        43 - 93              [ Cancel ]
D:                                                     [  Help  ]



Paging File Size for Selected Drive
   Drive:              C: [GBOF]
   Space Available:    374 MB
   Initial Size (MB):    [43  ]
   Maximum Size (MB):    [93  ]         [  Set  ]

Total Paging File Size for All Drives
   Minimum Allowed:    2 MB
   Recommended:        43 MB
   Currently Allocated: 43 MB

Registry Size
   Current Registry Size:        3 MB
   Maximum Registry Size (MB):   [8  ]
```

performs this function is called the *virtual memory manager*. It is a key part of the Windows NT operating system.

The data is stored on the disk in a virtual memory page file called PAGE-FILE.SYS. You can have several paging files under Windows NT, one in each of the hard drives in your system. Windows NT combines the paging space from each of the files to get the maximum file space allocated for paging, and Windows NT operates fastest when the number of page files equals the number of hard drives.

When Setup calculates how big to make your initial page file, it chooses a size that is 11MB bigger than your physical memory size. So if you have 16MB of memory, then Setup will give you an initial page file size of 27MB. Microsoft suggests that the minimum commitment should be 22MB.

The minimum page file size you select is not necessarily the page file size that the system will use. When Windows NT reaches the capacity of its page file, it will expand the page file. Frequent page file expansions slow down the system.

The Virtual Memory window also shows you the current Registry size and allows you to set the maximum Registry size, as Figure 4.2 shows.

Environment

The Environment tab of the System Properties window shows you the system and user environment variables. You can modify current variables and add new variables from this window. We will encounter the Environment tab later in this chapter in the section called "User Profiles."

Startup/Shutdown

The Startup/Shutdown tab (see Figure 4.3) allows you to choose the default operating system for the boot loader and to specify how long the boot loader will wait before booting that default selection.

When you install Windows NT, you also install the Windows NT boot loader. The boot loader appears while your computer boots and allows you to choose between Windows NT and other operating systems you may have installed on your computer, such as DOS or Windows 95. The boot loader can also allow you to choose between several versions of Windows NT.

FIGURE 4.3
The Startup/Shutdown
section controls the
system default boot
behavior and how NT
handles a system error.

System Properties

| General | Performance | Environment |
| Startup/Shutdown | Hardware Profiles | User Profiles |

System Startup

Startup: "Windows NT Workstation Version 4.00"

Show list for 30 seconds

Recovery

When a STOP error occurs, do the following:

☐ Write an event to the system log

☐ Send an administrative alert

☐ Write debugging information to:

%SystemRoot%\MEMORY.DMP

☑ Overwrite any existing file

☐ Automatically reboot

OK   Cancel   Apply

*The Windows NT boot loader installs two Windows NT selections by default: Windows NT 4.0
and Windows NT 4.0 VGA mode. (It also installs a Windows 95 or DOS boot option.) The
VGA mode selection boots Windows NT in a safe video mode that will most likely operate
even if NT has the wrong video driver or video settings configured. VGA mode allows you
to fix any misconfigurations of the video system without necessarily having to reinstall the
whole operating system.*

This tab also allows you to select how Windows NT will behave in the event
of a system crash. You can require the system to perform one or all of the following actions: write an event to the event log, send an administrative alert,
write a copy of the contents of memory to the disk, and restart automatically.

Hardware Profiles

The Hardware Profiles tab of the System Properties window is where you can
set several hardware configurations for your Windows NT workstation. This

tab is useful for systems that change configuration often. For example, a laptop that is sometimes attached to a docking station—giving it a network interface, additional memory, and hard drive storage—might have two hardware profiles set up in this section. One profile would have these additional devices enabled; the other would not. When booting, Windows NT will either detect the correct hardware profile or request the user to select the hardware profile it should use. You can also set a timeout and a default hardware profile for when the user does not specify which profile to use.

In the Hardware Profiles tab of the System window, you can create additional profiles using the Copy button. Once you have created a profile, you can modify which devices and services to use with that profile from the Devices and Services icons in the Control Panel. Each device or service can be started or stopped for a particular hardware profile. This feature is useful for a computer that will be used in several different settings, such as with or without a network connection, or in or out of a docking port.

If you have several hardware profiles configured for your computer, and Windows NT is not able to detect at startup time which profile to use, you will be asked to select which profile to use at boot time. In the Hardware Profiles tab you can specify how long the startup program will wait before choosing the first profile on the list, or you can set it to wait Forever for the menu choice from the user.

User Profiles

From this section you can copy and delete user profiles. The user profiles (discussed in more detail later in this chapter) contain the user preferences for things like screen backgrounds and sound schemes. From this section you also can change the type of the profile from local to roaming and back. See Figure 4.4 for a typical User Profiles view.

Changing System Settings

In Exercise 4.1 you will change the boot delay and reduce the paging file size.

When you log on to the computer again, you may receive a warning message that the page file is improperly sized. This warning appears because you have reduced the page file below the amount of paging space that Windows needs to operate with the amount of physical memory you have in your computer. You should restore the page file to its original size.

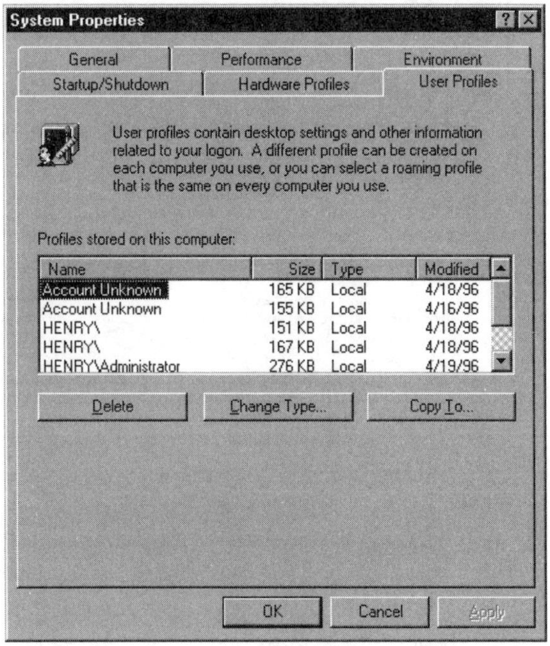

FIGURE 4.4
You can view and
delete user profiles
from the User Profiles
tab in the System
Properties window.

FIGURE 4.4
You can view and delete user profiles from the User Profiles tab in the System Properties window.

EXERCISE 4.1

Changing the Boot Delay and Reducing the Paging File Size

1. Click Start.

2. Click Settings ➤ Control Panel.

3. Double-click the System icon within the Control Panel.

4. Click the Startup/Shutdown tab within the System Properties window.

5. Change the Show list for value to 5 seconds.

6. Click the Performance tab in the System Properties window.

7. Click the Change button in the Virtual Memory section.

EXERCISE 4.1 (CONTINUED)

8. Click the drive that has numbers listed in the Paging File Size (MB) column within the Virtual Memory window. (This step selects that drive so that the changes you make in step 9 will affect that drive.)

9. Change the initial size to 2MB.

10. Click Set. Click OK. Click Close.

11. Click Yes.

Date and Time

The Date and Time Control Panel item has two tabs: Date and Time and Time Zone. The Date and Time tab displays a graphical representation of a calendar and a clock. These settings represent the system time that the computer uses to put time stamps on files and messages.

Windows NT can automatically adjust for the start and end of daylight savings time; it notifies you of the change the next time you log on and asks you to confirm that the new time is correct. You can configure the date and time not to automatically correct for daylight savings time. In that case you will have to set the new time yourself.

Ports

This Control Panel item allows you to specify the communications settings for the serial ports on your computer. From the Ports window you can view the configurations of installed ports, add ports, and delete ports. From the Settings window (reached by clicking the Settings button), you can set the baud rate, data bits, stop bits, and flow control. Advanced settings allow you to change the COM port number, base address, Interrupt Request number, and FIFO (serial buffer) setting.

Windows NT defaults to a conservative setting for the ports. You may wish to increase the baud rate for ports that have modems attached to them and turn on FIFO support if the port has a FIFO. (You will have to check the documentation for your computer or motherboard, or ask your vendor, to determine the capabilities of the ports on your computer.)

Services

The Services control panel allows you to stop and start services and to control when they are loaded by the system. Services may need to be stopped occasionally if they malfunction or if they are interfering with another resource. For instance, if RAS is configured to answer incoming calls, you will need to stop the RAS service before you can use the modem for dialing out.

The following startup options allow you to control how services start:

- **Automatic** means that the system starts automatically when you boot your computer.

- **Manual** means that other processes stop and start the service as necessary when they need its functionality.

- **Disabled** means that the service cannot be started.

Chapter 13, "Printing," includes an example of stopping and starting a service to clear a document jammed in the print spooler.

Telephony

WINDOWS NT 4.0 INCLUDES a common interface for application programs and services to use telephones and telephony devices such as modems and fax machines. This interface is called the Telephony Application Programming Interface, or the Telephony API. You can configure aspects of the Telephony API from the Telephony icon in the Control Panel.

The Telephony API maintains information common to any program that uses the telephone system, such as the location you are calling from, including the area code and how you access an outside line, and calling card information. It also allows you to specify multiple locations so that if you move your computer from place to place you can automatically switch between telephony setups.

The Telephony Drivers tab in the Telephony window contains the drivers for devices that use the phone system. You can select and modify the configuration of the drivers from this tab. You can also add and remove drivers from this tab.

Exercise 4.2 adds a new location to the telephony settings for your Workstation.

EXERCISE 4.2

Adding a New Location to the Telephony Settings

1. Open the Control Panel (Start ➤ Settings ➤ Control Panel).

2. Click the Telephony icon.

3. Click the New button in the Properties window.

4. Click OK in the window that informs you that a new location has been created.

5. Replace the highlighted text in the *I am dialing from:* field with **San Diego**.

6. Type **801** in *The area code is:* field.

7. Type **9** in the *To access an outside line first dial:* field.

8. Click OK at the bottom of the Dialing Properties window.

UPS

The UPS item in the Control Panel (see Figure 4.5) lets you configure how Windows NT will respond in the event of a power failure. UPS stands for "uninterruptible power supply," and a UPS is an external device that attaches to your computer and provides power from batteries when regular power fails.

FIGURE 4.5
The UPS window allows you to configure how your computer will respond to a power failure.

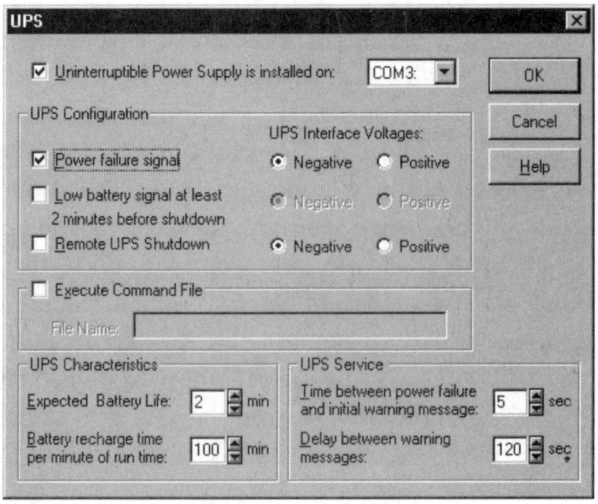

The UPS may provide power for several minutes or for several hours before signaling to the computer that its battery is low and the computer must shut down.

The UPS communicates with Windows NT through a standard RS-232 cable. The UPS does not send text messages to the computer—instead, it assigns special meanings to several of the control lines of the RS-232 cable. The control lines are as follows:

- **Power failure:** The UPS signals with the clear to send (CTS) line when regular power fails.

- **Low battery:** The UPS signals a low-battery condition with the data carrier detect (DCD) line.

- **Remote UPS shutdown:** The computer requests the UPS to shut down by signaling with the data terminal ready (DTR) line.

Not every UPS supports each of the above signals. You must check the documentation of your UPS device to determine which signals it does support. You also need to know if each signal is negative or positive. When you configure the UPS via the UPS icon in the Control Panel, you also need to know which serial port the UPS is connected to.

Windows NT settings that you can configure to handle a power failure include

- **Execute Command File:** You can select a command file (CMD, BAT, COM, or EXE) for Windows to execute 30 seconds before it shuts down.

- **UPS Characteristics:** The expected battery life and battery recharge time settings will guide NT's behavior in shutting down the system if the UPS does not support a low-battery signal.

- **UPS Service:** The time to initial warning message is the delay before the system warns you of a power failure. This delay prevents momentary power fluctuations from disrupting the network. Only a prolonged power failure will cause a system shutdown. The delay between warning messages allows you to set the frequency of warning messages that the system sends to users when power fails.

When power fails, the following events occur in a Windows NT system:

- The Server service pauses.

- The Event Viewer logs a Power Out event.

- The administrator receives a Power Out alert.

If power is restored before the initial warning message is sent, the following events occur:

- The Server service continues.

- The Event Viewer logs a Power Back event.

- The administrator receives a Power Back alert.

If power was not restored, the following occurs:

- Users who are connected to your workstation receive a Power Out message. The system sends the message periodically until power is restored or the system shuts down.

- The system raises a Power Out alert and then raises it periodically until power is restored or the system shuts down.

If power is restored before automatic shutdown, the following events occur:

- The system sends a Power Back message to the local user and all users who are connected to the workstation.

- The Event Viewer logs a Power Back event.

- The administrator receives a Power Back alert.

If a low-battery signal is received or the expected battery life setting has been reached, the following events occur:

- The Server service stops.

- The system sends a Power Shutdown Final message to the local user and all users connected to the workstation.

- The system writes a UPS Shutdown entry to the error log.

- The system sends the Power Shutdown alert. Windows NT shuts down.

Configuring Hardware

ALTHOUGH INSTALLATION AND CONFIGURATION details for specific devices vary, the general procedures used to install, configure, and remove hardware in a running Windows NT environment are always the same. You should follow these general procedures for any type of hardware.

Installing Hardware

The general procedure for installing a hardware device is described below. Use this procedure when installing any hardware device in a working Windows NT computer.

1. Determine which hardware settings you will use.

2. Verify that these resources are free in the running Windows NT Workstation environment.

3. Configure and install the device. If necessary, boot MS-DOS and run the software configuration utility provided with the device.

4. Boot Windows NT and add the NT driver.

5. Reboot the computer to make the device available.

If you have problems after installing a hardware device, such as your computer failing to boot, remove the device and look for hardware conflicts. Computers with Plug-and-Play BIOS options may re-assign interrupts when you add a new hardware component, potentially confusing services and drivers that rely upon interrupt number assignments. Disable Plug-and-Play BIOS settings if possible and manually assign interrupts to PCI slots.

Only experienced computer technicians should perform hardware component installation, configuration, and removal. You should not perform these exercises unless you actually need to install or remove a hardware component.

Removing Hardware

Removing hardware from a computer is somewhat simpler than installing hardware because there's no potential for new conflicts to arise. Remove any software drivers and services that rely on the presence of the hardware *before* removing the device.

1. Uninstall the device driver.

2. Power down the computer.

3. Remove the device.

4. Restart the computer.

If removing a device causes a malfunction not related to losing the service of that device, you should make sure that your Plug-and-Play BIOS settings haven't caused a reassignment of interrupts. If you suspect this is the case, use the following procedure to correct the problem.

1. Install the device again. It is not necessary to reconfigure the operating system.

2. Power up the computer.

3. Go to the BIOS settings page and record the values that the Plug-and-Play BIOS assigns for the current configuration.

4. Disable the Plug-and-Play BIOS.

5. Set all the BIOS settings manually—except for the device you will remove—to the values assigned by the Plug-and-Play BIOS.

6. Power down the computer.

7. Remove the device.

8. Restart and check the operation of your computer.

The following sections include exercises for installing and removing specific hardware components.

Network Adapters

More services depend upon the proper installation of network adapters than any other single hardware device. However, unlike many devices, Network adapters are not critical for the operation of stand-alone computers, so they are easy to work with and troubleshoot.

Most adapter configurations are performed during the installation process. Each network adapter uses a unique installation script to configure that particular device. Since this script changes for each device, you will have to use the manual that comes with your network adapter to configure it for use in your network.

Installing a network adapter is easy, especially if the driver is included on the Windows NT installation disk. Exercise 4.3 shows how to install a network adapter.

EXERCISE 4.3

Installing a Network Adapter

1. Turn off your computer. Make any physical jumper or switch settings necessary on the adapter card to configure it for your computer.

2. Install the network interface card.

3. Boot MS-DOS and run the configuration utility if your card is software configured. Record the IRQ, DMA, and port settings in case they are required by the Windows NT driver for the device.

4. Reboot your computer.

5. Right-click Network Neighborhood on the desktop.

6. Select the Adapters tab.

7. Click Add.

8. Select the driver for your card from the list or click Have Disk.

9. Enter the path to the Windows NT Workstation CD-ROM or the floppy disk containing the driver for your device.

10. Click Close.

11. Add any information necessary to the dialog boxes raised by your installed transport protocols.

12. Restart your computer.

Removing a network adapter is even easier. You need only remove the adapter driver in the networking control panel and physically remove the device. Exercise 4.4 shows you how to remove a network adapter.

EXERCISE 4.4

Removing a Network Adapter

1. Right-click Network Neighborhood on the desktop.

2. Select the Adapters tab.

3. Select the adapter driver you want to remove.

4. Click Remove.

5. Click Close.

6. Answer No when asked if you want to restart your computer.

7. Shut down and power off your computer.

8. Remove the network adapter.

SCSI Adapters

Installing a SCSI adapter properly can be the most difficult portion of a Windows NT installation. The dependence of the entire operating system upon a booting SCSI disk complicate the myriad of problems that can occur with a SCSI installation.

You can minimize these problems by following these rules of thumb:

- Use SCSI controllers listed on the Windows NT hardware compatibility list.

- Search the Microsoft Windows NT Knowledge base at www.microsoft .com, search key "SCSI", to identify any compatibility issues associated with the SCSI controllers you are considering for use with Windows NT.

- Be certain you've properly terminated the SCSI bus before attempting to install Windows NT. Validate your SCSI configuration before installing Windows NT using the SCSI Tool included with Windows NT or an MS-DOS boot disk and MS-DOS SCSI utilities. The correct method for terminating a SCSI bus is covered in Chapter 17, "Troubleshooting."

- Use the NTHQ to identify and resolve SCSI adapter issues before attempting to install Windows NT.

- Disable the Plug-and-Play BIOS of your computer and manually assign interrupts to PCI slots. Check your adapter documentation to see if its SCSI BIOS requires a certain BIOS to boot.

- Enable the SCSI BIOS to boot the hard disk attached to SCSI ID 0, and install Windows NT in the first primary partition of that disk.

Using IDE to Boot a SCSI System

If boot performance is not an issue, consider disabling the SCSI adapter BIOS and installing the operating system on a small IDE hard disk. This method has a number of benefits:

- Windows NT uses a single IDE driver embedded in the operating system, making it much more compatible than most SCSI adapters.

- An IDE bus has fewer points of failure.

- You can use the entire capacity of multiple SCSI disks for stripe or volume sets—that is, you don't need a separate boot/system partition.

- You can boot your operating system in the event of a SCSI controller failure

- Most motherboards have two IDE controllers built in, which provides a small measure of redundancy.

Booting SCSI

The Windows NT installation program cannot identify the SCSI ID number of the booting SCSI disk. If you have set your adapter BIOS to boot a disk other than SCSI ID 0, the computer will not boot properly when you restart it because the ARC path to the boot disk in the BOOT.INI file will be incorrectly set to

SCSI ID 0. You can boot another operating system such as MS-DOS to edit the BOOT.INI file according to the procedures shown in Chapter 16, "Booting Windows NT."

If you are using a SCSI adapter supported by the SCSI tool (Adaptec and Buslogic cards are the only brands currently supported), you can use this tool to make certain that you have no device conflicts and that all devices are available on the bus. Otherwise, create an MS-DOS boot disk with the ASPI drivers provided by the card manufacturer and the test software that comes with the SCSI adapter to make certain everything is working correctly prior to installing Windows NT. Exercise 4.5 shows you how to create the SCSI tool disk.

EXERCISE 4.5

Creating the SCSI Tool Disk

1. Boot MS-DOS or open an MS-DOS session in any operating system that supports running MS-DOS programs.

2. Insert the Windows NT Workstation CD-ROM.

3. Insert a formatted 1.44MB floppy disk into the A: drive.

4. Change drives to your CD-ROM.

5. Type **CD \SUPPORT\SCSITOOL**.

6. Type **makedisk** and press Enter.

7. Remove the floppy disk and label it SCSI Tool.

Exercise 4.6 shows how to use the SCSI tool to validate your SCSI configuration.

Exercise 4.7 shows the process for adding a SCSI adapter that will not be used as the boot adapter to a running Windows NT installation.

Exercise 4.8 shows the process for removing a SCSI adapter from a running Windows NT installation. Note that if you remove a SCSI adapter supporting a disk containing either your boot or system partitions, you must use the procedure shown in Exercise 4.9 to replace it with another SCSI adapter.

Exercise 4.9 shows the procedure for exchanging SCSI controllers in a running Windows NT environment.

EXERCISE 4.6

Using the SCSI Tool to Diagnose SCSI Problems

1. Insert the SCSI tool disk and reboot your computer.

2. Select your adapter manufacturer or All at the SCSI Interrogator menu.

3. View your adapter settings in the SCSI Interrogator window.

4. Click SCSI Devices.

5. Use the scroll bar to view all the SCSI devices attached to your adapter. Make sure that all the devices attached to your system show up correctly before installing Windows NT.

6. Remove the SCSI tool disk and reboot your computer.

EXERCISE 4.7

Installing a SCSI Adapter

1. Set your SCSI adapter to the IRQ and port address you wish to use if the adapter uses jumpers or manual switches. Install or remove termination resisters if necessary.

2. Power off your computer and install the SCSI controller; attach all SCSI cables.

3. Power up the computer. If your adapter is software configured, boot the MS-DOS configuration program and make any necessary changes to the default settings. Reboot your computer.

4. Change the SCSI adapter BIOS settings during the boot process if necessary for the configuration you want. If you do not intend to boot a SCSI device, disable the SCSI BIOS.

5. Boot Windows NT.

6. Open the Control Panel by selecting Start ➤ Settings ➤ Control Panel.

7. Click SCSI Adapters.

8. Click the Driver tab.

EXERCISE 4.7 (CONTINUED)

9. Click Add.

10. Select your SCSI adapter from the list or click Have Disk if you are using an adapter not included on the basic set.

11. Enter the path to the Windows NT Workstation 4.0 installation CD-ROM or the floppy disk containing the SCSI driver in the Driver path window.

12. Click Yes to restart your computer after the driver copies.

EXERCISE 4.8

Removing a SCSI Adapter

1. Open the Control Panel by selecting Start ➤ Settings ➤ Control Panel.

2. Click SCSI Adapters.

3. Click the Driver tab.

4. Select the driver for the adapter you will be removing.

5. Click Remove.

6. Click Yes to confirm.

7. Click Close to complete the removal.

8. Shut down and power off your computer.

9. Remove the adapter.

Tape Drives

Adding tape drives to Windows NT is easy for most tape devices—simply run the Tape devices control panel and click the Detect button. Windows NT will load each tape driver it knows about and scan for the presence of a supported device. If found, it will automatically install the driver.

EXERCISE 4.9

Exchanging SCSI Controllers in a Windows NT Environment

1. Open the Control Panel by selecting Start ➤ Settings ➤ Control Panel.

2. Click SCSI Adapters.

3. Click the Driver tab.

4. Select the driver for the adapter you will be removing.

5. Click Remove.

6. Click Yes to confirm.

7. Click Add.

8. Select your SCSI adapter from the list or click Have Disk if you are using an adapter not included on the basic set.

9. Enter the path to the Windows NT Workstation 4.0 installation CD-ROM or the floppy disk containing the SCSI driver in the Driver path window.

10. Click No if asked to restart your computer after the driver copies.

11. Shutdown and power off your computer.

12. Remove the adapter you are replacing.

13. Set the SCSI adapter you are installing to the IRQ and port address you wish to use if the adapter uses jumpers or manual switches. Install or remove termination resisters if necessary.

14. Install the new SCSI controller and attach all SCSI cables.

15. Power up the computer. If your new SCSI adapter is software configured, boot the MS-DOS configuration program and make any changes to the default settings necessary. Reboot your computer.

16. Change the SCSI adapter BIOS settings if necessary for the configuration you want during the boot process.

17. Boot Windows NT. If you have a boot problem, try setting the new SCSI adapter to the same settings as the adapter you removed. Follow the troubleshooting procedures outlined in Chapter 17, "Troubleshooting." If all else fails, install your old adapter again and attempt to isolate the problem. Use the SCSI tool and the Windows NT Diagnostic program to help isolate the problem with your new controller.

For tape devices that Windows NT can't automatically detect, the procedure is only slightly more complicated. The procedure for adding a tape device and driver to Windows NT is shown in Exercise 4.10.

EXERCISE 4.10

Adding a Tape Device and Driver to Windows NT

1. Power down the computer.

2. Make any physical jumper or switch settings necessary on the tape drive for your computer. Set the SCSI ID for SCSI tape devices; use the Master/Slave setting for IDE tape devices.

3. Install the tape device.

4. Boot the computer.

5. Select Start ➤ Settings ➤ Control Panel to launch the Control Panel.

6. Select the Drivers tab.

7. Click Add.

8. Select the driver for your device from the list or click Have Disk.

9. Enter the path to your Windows NT Workstation CD-ROM or the floppy disk containing the driver for your device and click OK.

10. Answer Yes when asked to restart your computer.

Removing a tape device and driver is just as easy. This procedure is shown in Exercise 4.11.

UPS

Because Windows NT was primarily designed as a network operating system, it includes strong built-in support for uninterruptible power supplies (UPS). Most UPS devices interface through a serial port.

You do not have to install a UPS driver to use the device. The driver is necessary only if you want the computer to shut itself down in the event of a power

EXERCISE 4.11

Removing a Tape Driver and Device

1. Select Start ➤ Settings ➤ Control Panel to launch the Control Panel.

2. Select the Drivers tab.

3. Click Remove.

4. Click Yes to confirm.

5. Click OK.

6. Shut down your computer.

7. Remove the tape device.

failure. In fact, many simpler UPS devices do not have an interface to alert the computer to an impending power failure—they rely upon the human operator to shut the computer down. This method does not work for computers such as servers that operate unattended.

One snag complicates UPS use: The NTDETECT procedure probes serial ports for the presence of a mouse during the initial stages of a Windows NT boot. Some UPS devices interpret the signal sent by NTDETECT as the signal to shut down. If your computer shuts down suddenly during the boot process, follow Exercise 4.12 to correct the problem.

Installing UPS support is easy, but you will need to have the hardware manual for your UPS at hand to enter the correct settings for your device. Exercise 4.13 shows how to configure the UPS control panel to shut down your computer in the event of a power failure.

To remove UPS support, simply uncheck the *Uninterruptible Power Supply is installed on* setting in the UPS control panel.

CD-ROMs

Windows NT automatically supports many CD-ROMs. Simply attach the CD-ROM device to the IDE or SCSI bus, and the CD-ROM drive will be ready for use when you boot your computer.

EXERCISE 4.12

Disabling NTDETECT Serial Mouse Automatic Detection

1. Unplug your UPS device serial cable from your computer.

2. Boot Windows NT.

3. Double-click My Computer.

4. Double-click the drive that contains your system partition. Usually, this is the C: drive.

5. Right-click the BOOT.INI file. If you cannot see a BOOT.INI file, select View ➤ Options. From the View tab, select Show all files and click OK. Now right-click the BOOT.INI file.

6. Select Properties.

7. Clear the Read Only check.

8. Click Close.

9. Select Start ➤ Programs ➤ Accessories ➤ Notepad to launch the notepad utility.

10. Select File ➤ Open.

11. Select All Files in the Files of Type drop-down list box.

12. Select the drive containing the system partition in the Look In drop-down list box.

13. Select the BOOT.INI file.

14. Append **/NOSERIALMICE=COMX** to the end of each line containing the word multi(0) or scsi(0). Replace the final X with the COM port number to which your UPS will be attached. Leave the COMX off if you don't know to which COM port your UPS is attached.

15. Close Notepad.

16. Answer Yes to save changes.

17. Power down your computer, reattach the UPS serial cable, and reboot.

EXERCISE 4.13

Adding Support for an Uninterruptible Power Supply

1. Select Start ➤ Settings ➤ Control Panel to open the system Control Panel.

2. Double-click UPS.

3. Set the *Uninterruptible Power Supply is installed on* checkbox.

4. Select the COM port to which your UPS cable is attached in the *Uninterruptible Power Supply is installed on* drop-down list box.

5. Use your UPS manual to select the appropriate settings in the UPS Configuration control group.

6. Enter the command line if you want to execute a program prior to shutdown, such as a communication program to notify your pager of the power loss. The program must be able to operate without user input of any sort, or your computer will not shut down.

7. Click OK.

However, some CD-ROM drives require special drivers—usually proprietary bus CD-ROM drives that have special interface cards, for example, many early Sony and Mitsumi drives that came out before the ATAPI (IDE) standard for CD-ROM devices was adopted.

To install support for these devices, follow the procedures outlined in Exercise 4.14. These devices are installed through the SCSI adapter control panel as if they were SCSI adapters. You may have to modify this procedure for some proprietary CD-ROM drives or for drives not included on the Windows NT CD-ROM.

EXERCISE 4.14

Installing a CD-ROM Drive

1. Power off your computer.

2. Set your CD-ROM adapter card to the IRQ and port address you wish to use if the adapter uses jumpers or manual switches. Install or remove termination resisters if necessary.

EXERCISE 4.14 (CONTINUED)

3. Install the CD-ROM adapter card and attach the CD-ROM cables.

4. Power up the computer. If your CD-ROM adapter is software configured, boot the MS-DOS configuration program and make any changes to the default settings necessary. Reboot your computer.

5. Boot Windows NT.

6. Open the Control Panel by selecting Start ➤ Settings ➤ Control Panel.

7. Click SCSI Adapters.

8. Click the Driver tab.

9. Click Add.

10. Select your CD-ROM adapter from the list or click Have Disk if you are using an adapter not included on the basic set.

11. Enter the path to the Windows NT Workstation 4.0 installation CD-ROM or the floppy disk containing the CD-ROM driver in the Driver path window.

12. Click Yes to restart your computer after the driver copies.

Use the procedure outlined in Exercise 4.15 to remove a CD-ROM driver from a Windows NT computer.

Display Drivers

The initial display driver is installed when Windows NT is installed, and a display driver must be present for Windows NT to operate. You can change display drivers through the Display Type button on the Settings tab of the Display control panel.

Because Windows NT must have a display driver in order to operate correctly, you should remove your old driver and install the new one prior to shutting down your computer and swapping display cards. You should also set your display resolution to VGA to ensure that you will be able to see the screen when you reboot. This procedure is shown in Exercise 4.16.

EXERCISE 4.15

Removing a CD-ROM Driver

1. Open the Control Panel by selecting Start ➤ Settings ➤ Control Panel.

2. Click SCSI Adapters.

3. Click the Driver tab.

4. Select the driver for the CD-ROM adapter you will be removing.

5. Click Remove.

6. Click Yes to confirm.

7. Click Close to complete the removal.

8. Shut down and power off your computer.

9. Remove the adapter and CD-ROM device.

EXERCISE 4.16

Changing Video Adapters

1. Right-click the desktop.

2. Select Settings.

3. Select the Settings tab of the Display control panel.

4. Slide the Desktop Area slider down to the lowest setting.

5. Set the color palette to 256 Colors.

6. Set the refresh rate to 60Hz.

7. Click Test.

8. Click Apply.

9. Click Display Type.

EXERCISE 4.16 (CONTINUED)

1. Right-click the desktop.

2. Select Settings.

3. Select the Settings tab of the Display control panel.

4. Slide the Desktop Area slider down to the lowest setting.

5. Set the color palette to 256 Colors.

6. Set the refresh rate to 60Hz.

7. Click Test.

8. Click Apply.

9. Click Display Type.

10. Click Change.

11. Select the video adapter installed in your system or click Have Disk.

12. Enter the path to the Windows NT Workstation CD-ROM or the floppy containing the display driver.

13. Shutdown and power off your computer.

14. Remove your old display adapter and insert the new one.

15. Reboot your computer. If you cannot see anything when the GUI portion of the boot process occurs, reboot your computer and select the VGA boot option.

Keyboard Drivers

You can change keyboard drivers through the General tab of the Keyboard control panel, which is where you specify regional and language settings for your keyboard. Exercise 4.17 shows the procedure for changing your keyboard driver.

EXERCISE 4.17

Changing the Keyboard Driver

1. Open the Control Panel by selecting Start ➤ Settings ➤ Control Panel.

2. Double-click Keyboards.

3. Select the General tab.

4. Click Change.

5. Select the device you want to change or click Have Disk.

6. Enter the path to the Windows NT Workstation CD-ROM or the floppy disk containing your keyboard driver files if requested.

7. Click Close.

8. Click Yes to restart your computer.

Mouse Drivers

You change mouse drivers through the General tab of the Mouse control panel, which is used to change the behavior of your mouse. Exercise 4.18 shows the procedure for changing a mouse driver.

Installing Applications

MOST WINDOWS NT PROGRAMS are added through their own setup programs. Normally, you will launch these setup programs by selecting the run option in the start menu and entering the path to the installation program.

Windows NT also provides a control panel for installing and removing applications. For the install/uninstall control panel to work with an application, the

---

EXERCISE 4.18

Changing the Mouse Driver

1. Open the Control Panel by selecting Start ➤ Settings ➤ Control Panel.

2. Double-click Mouse.

3. Select the General tab.

4. Click Change.

5. Select the device you want to change or click Have Disk.

6. Enter the path to the Windows NT Workstation CD-ROM or the floppy disk containing your keyboard driver files if requested.

7. Click close.

8. Click Yes to restart your computer.

---

application must register with the control panel. For this reason, only a few applications installed on your computer can actually be used with this control panel.

Exercise 4.19 shows how to install a program through the add/remove program control panel.

EXERCISE 4.19

Using the Add/Remove Program Control Panel to Install Software

1. Select Start ➤ Settings ➤ Control Panel.

2. Double click the Add/Remove Program control panel.

3. Insert the installation floppy disk or CD-ROM.

4. Click Install.

5. Click Finish to run the install program.

Exercise 4.20 shows how to install a program through the add/remove program control panel.

EXERCISE 4.20

Using the Add/Remove Program Control Panel to Remove Software

1. Select Start ➤ Settings ➤ Control Panel.

2. Double click the Add/Remove Program control panel.

3. Select the program to remove in the programs list box.

4. Click Add/Remove.

5. Answer Yes when asked if you would like to remove the program and all of it's components.

6. Click OK when the Uninstaller completes removing the program.

7. Click Close.

User-Specific Settings

N THE PREVIOUS SECTION of this chapter, we explained how to view and change many system settings from icons in the Control Panel. This section will show you how to change the environment of each individual user to match that user's preferences. You can change the following items in the Control Panel on a per-user basis:

- Display

- Keyboard

- Mouse

- Regional Settings

- Sounds

The items in this list are primarily concerned with user preferences; other Control Panel items can also modify settings on a per-user basis. Any Control Panel item can change system settings as well as user preferences.

User Profiles

User preferences are stored in a user profile. A user profile is created for a user from the default user profile the first time the user logs on. Any personal changes that the user makes are saved in the user profile so that the next time the user logs on the changes will be in effect. For example, one user may prefer the Flying Windows screen saver, while another user may prefer not to have a screen saver.

The user profile also stores other environmental settings. For example, the user profile stores recently edited documents so that when you select Documents from the Start button, you see a list of the documents that you have opened most recently. The user profile also stores your preferences for browsing files and directories in the Explorer. You can modify your Start menu, for example, adding programs or changing the menu's location and appearance, and these settings too are stored in your user profile. The two types of profiles are

- Local profiles
- Roaming profiles

Local Profiles

When a new user logs on for the first time, Windows NT creates a profile for that user from the default profile and stores it in the Profiles subdirectory of the Windows NT directory. The user profile is actually a directory with several files and subdirectories within it. Windows NT programs (many in the Control Panel) access the data stored in the user profile, and Windows NT uses the profile data stored in these directories to configure your working environment for you.

The name of your user profile directory is the same as the username that you type to log on.

Each local profile is specific to the computer on which it is stored. If you have accounts on two different Windows NT workstations, each with a local profile, a change you make to your preferences on one computer will not be transferred to the other computer.

Roaming Profiles

Roaming profiles are normally stored on a Windows NT server. By storing one profile on the server, instead of storing a local profile on each of the Windows NT workstations that you use, changes to your environment will be in effect for all of the workstations you use, rather than on just the one on which you made the change.

When you specify a roaming profile in the user settings for your user account, the profile is downloaded from the server every time you log on. Changes you make to the server are then sent back to the server so that they will still be in effect the next time you log on and download the profile.

You create a roaming profile by specifying a path to the profile that includes a server name. `\\Yoyo\Profiles\June` is a valid roaming profile path if that directory on the Yoyo server has a profile for June.

Profile Location

User profiles are usually found in the Profiles subdirectory of the Windows NT directory. Each profile is itself a directory containing several files and subdirectories. The profile directory name is the same as that user's logon name. For instance, if user Bob works on Windows NT Workstation Yoyo with the Windows NT directory of `C:\Winnt`, the name of Bob's profile directory will be `C:\Winnt\Profiles\Bob`.

You can set the profile directory to another location through the Profiles section of the User Manager program.

Display

The Display Properties window shown in Figure 4.6 (reachable by opening the Display icon in the Control Panel) has five sections, represented by tabs at the top of the window.

- **Background** allows you to set the pattern or image that will appear in the background of your computer screen.

- **Screen Saver** allows you to select the screen saver you wish to appear when your computer has been inactive for a period of time.

- **Appearances** configures the colors and sizes of Windows NT screen elements such as borders, windows, icons, menus, and the desktop. You can also create and manipulate schemes, which contain predefined or user-defined settings for the screen elements.

- **Plus!** allows you to select the icons for certain desktop icons and to change certain behaviors of the Windows NT desktop, such as the size of icons, whether windows should appear as solid or as outline shapes when you move them, and whether icons should be shown in all possible colors.

- **Settings** is where you configure the hardware settings of the display. You can set the resolution, the number of colors of the display, and the refresh rate. This tab is also where you configure the device driver that Windows NT will use to talk to the video card in your computer. These settings apply to every user, and therefore are not a part of the user profile. The user may view the settings, but if the user does not have the right access permissions, Windows NT will not allow the user to change the settings.

To select a screen saver (Flying Objects) for the current user, perform the steps outlined in Exercise 4.21.

EXERCISE 4.21

Selecting a Screen Saver

1. Click the Start menu.

2. Click Settings ➤ Control Panel.

3. Double-click the Display icon within the Control Panel. (Or right-click on the desktop and choose Properties.)

4. Click the Screen Saver tab of the Display Properties window.

5. Select Flying Objects (OpenGL) from the Screen Saver drop-down list in the middle of the Display Properties window.

6. Click OK.

Keyboard

The Keyboard Properties window is where you configure the keyboard speed and layout. The Speed tab allows you to set the cursor repeat delay, rate, and blink rate. The Input Locales tab provides multiple key mappings so that you can remap the keyboard for other languages or preferred key placements. The General tab is a system configuration tab, and you will most likely leave the setting on the default PC/AT Enhanced Keyboard setting, but if you have an unusual keyboard attached to your computer, here is where you will configure it.

Mouse

The Mouse Properties window is where you configure the buttons, pointers, and motion of the mouse. Each aspect has a tab. You can use the General tab to select the type of mouse attached to your computer.

- **Buttons** allows you to set the handedness of the mouse for each user, switching the functions of the left and right buttons on the mouse. Here you also set how fast you have to click the mouse button in order for it to be recognized as a double-click.

■ **Pointers** lets you customize the appearance of the mouse pointer (see Figure 4.7). Many activities of the system can be represented by a different mouse icon, and you can select which icon will represent which activity. For instance, you can select a watch icon to replace the standard hourglass icon to indicate that the system is busy, and you can change the default pointer into a pointing hand. You can also select and modify pointer schemes, such as the Windows Animated scheme, which replaces the default static icons with colorful animated ones.

■ **Motion** customizes how fast the mouse pointer sweeps across the screen when you move the mouse. You can also select the Snap to Default option, which will make the mouse cursor go to the default button on a window when it appears. For instance, if you have Snap to Default enabled, and you select Save As from the File menu of your application, your mouse will move automatically to the Save button, which is the default button for that window.

You can select the Dinosaur pointer scheme shown in Figure 4.7 by following the steps in Exercise 4.22.

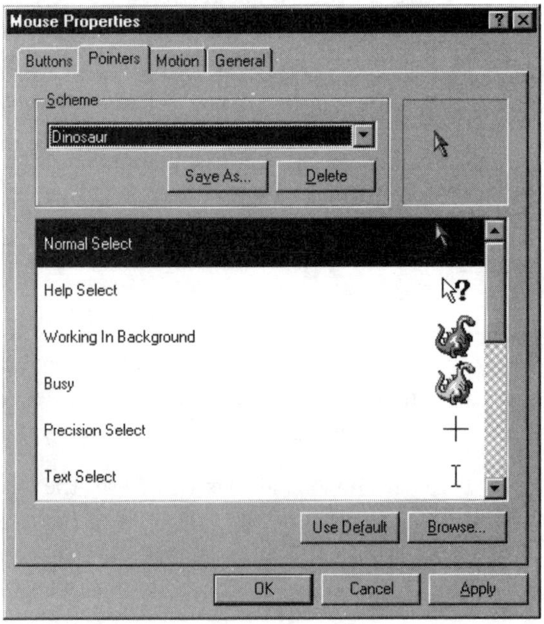

FIGURE 4.7
You can choose from many mouse pointer schemes.

EXERCISE 4.22

Selecting a New Pointer Scheme

1. Click Start.

2. Select Settings ➤ Control Panel.

3. Double-click the Mouse icon within the Control Panel.

4. Click the Pointers tab in the Mouse Properties window.

5. Select the Dinosaur scheme in the Scheme drop-down box.

6. Click OK.

Regional Settings

The Regional Settings window allows you to set the language, time zone, number currency and time representations, and input locales for the current user.

Sounds

The Sounds Properties window (see Figure 4.8) allows you to associate sounds with system events, such as a window opening or the system shutting down. You can associate individual sounds with individual events, or you can select a sound scheme that associates sounds with events for you.

You can change the sound associated with a system event by performing the steps in Exercise 4.23.

Environment Variables

The system maintains certain environment variables for Windows NT to use, but each user can also have environment variables set up for their own user account. You can use the System icon on the Control Panel to view and modify your environment variables even if you do not have permission to modify the system environment variables. The Environment tab in the System Properties window (see Figure 4.9) has two lists: one for system variables and the other for user variables. You can click on a variable to view it—and to change it if you

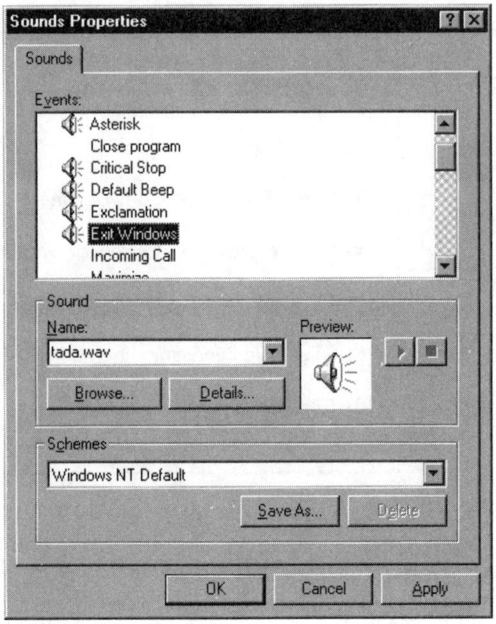

FIGURE 4.8
You can associate
sounds with system
events under
Windows NT.

EXERCISE 4.23

Changing the Sound Associated with a System Event

1. Click Start.

2. Select Settings ➤ Control Panel.

3. Double-click the Sounds icon within the Control Panel.

4. Click Close program in the Events section.

5. Select TADA.WAV in the Name drop-down box in the Sound section.

6. Click OK.

have permission. You can enter a new variable name and variable value in the fields below the lists. Click Set to add it to the environment variables. To add the environment variable Job_Function to the environment of the current user, follow the steps outlined in Exercise 4.24.

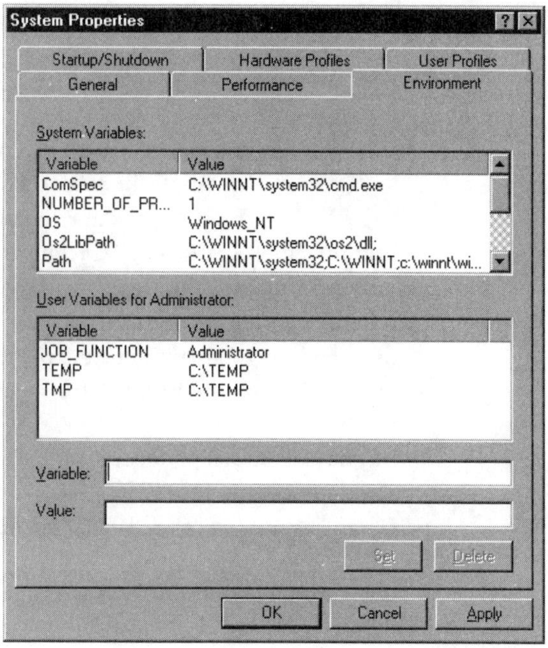

FIGURE 4.9
You can modify
system and user
environment variables
from the Environment
tab in the System
Properties window.

FIGURE 4.9
You can modify
system and user
environment variables
from the Environment
tab in the System
Properties window.

EXERCISE 4.24

Adding an Environment Variable

1. Click Start.

2. Select Settings ➤ Control Panel.

3. Double-click the System icon within the Control Panel.

4. Click the Environment tab in the System Properties window.

5. Type **Job_Function** in the Variable field in the System Properties window.

6. Type **Administrator** in the Value field in the System Properties window.

7. Click the Set button.

8. Click OK.

The Registry

W E RECOMMEND THAT YOU configure Windows NT settings through the Control Panel. However, you can also directly modify the data managed by the Control Panel items by using a program called REGEDIT.EXE. This program, also called the Registry Editor, directly manipulates the Registry, which is where Windows NT stores all of its important configuration information. This part of the chapter introduces the Registry and the Registry Editor, explains the structure of the Registry, and shows you how to search the Registry for specific items.

The Registry is a very important part of the Windows NT operating system. You should be familiar with its structure and operation in order to use your Windows NT computer to its maximum potential and to do well on the Microsoft exams.

You can think of the Registry as a database that contains Windows NT configuration information. Some things that Windows NT stores in the Registry are

- Hardware configuration data

- System software configuration data

- User security data

- Current user data

- Application configuration data

The Registry does for Windows NT what system and configuration files do for other operating systems. You may be familiar with AUTOEXEC.BAT and CONFIG.SYS for MS-DOS and SYSTEM.INI and WIN.INI for Windows. The Windows NT Registry contains all of the information that these other configuration files hold for their respective operating systems and more. Windows NT maintains versions of these files for compatibility with programs written for older versions of Windows.

The parts of Windows NT also can communicate via the Registry. NTDETECT, the Windows NT Kernel (NTOSKRNL), device drivers, Control Panel items, as well as other configuration tools, setup programs, and application programs all can view and set information in the Registry.

- When Windows NT starts up, a program called NTDETECT.COM executes. The purpose of NTDETECT is to detect hardware configuration changes in your computer. If you change the amount of memory, add an adapter card, or upgrade the processor, NTDETECT informs the rest of Windows NT by updating the Registry to reflect the changes.

Current versions of Windows NT do not automatically configure Plug-and-Play devices the way that Windows 95 does. However, devices you purchase should include drivers for Windows NT and have documentation instructing you how to install the devices in your Windows NT computer.

- The Windows NT Kernel (NTOSKRNL.EXE) extracts the hardware configuration from the Registry when it loads and uses that information to determine which device drivers to load and in what order to load them. The Kernel also places information about itself, such as its version number, in the Registry.

- The device drivers exchange information with the Registry, retrieving configuration information such as IRQ number and memory address and storing information such as what resources they are using and their current status.

- Control Panel items and other configuration tools, such as the User Manager and Windows NT Diagnostics, which are both found in the Administrative Tools section of the Start menu, permit you to modify the Registry in a safe manner. The various Control Panel items enable you to use a graphical interface to access settings that are stored in the Registry. This interface allows you to perform system configuration tasks much more easily than if you had to use the Registry Editor. The Control Panel items also list the valid values for system settings by listing possible values for you to select, rather than requiring you to know the correct values for various settings. The Registry Editor is harder to use than the icons.

- Setup programs will enter new information into the Registry for the application program or system device that the Setup program installs.

- Application software can read and store application-specific information in the Registry and also read system information and adapt the application's behavior to match the configuration of your system.

You should be aware that there are two versions of the Registry Editor shipped with version 4.0 of the Windows NT Workstation operating system. One, REGEDIT.EXE, is the registry editor that is also used with Windows 95. It presents a unified tree of keys, with the My Computer at the top. The other, REGEDT32 .EXE, shows each of the top level keys in a separate window. REGEDT32.EXE also is safer to use because it allows you to save or abandon a session of changes to the registry. In addition, REGEDIT32.EXE has additional security features concerning permissions, auditing, and ownership.

Before you explore the Registry, you will need to create a Start menu selection for the Registry Editor, REGEDIT.EXE (see Exercise 4.25).

EXERCISE 4.25

Creating a Start Menu Selection for the Registry Editor

1. Click Start.

2. Select Find ➤ Files or Folders.

3. Type **REGEDIT.EXE** in the Named part of the Find: All Files window.

4. Click the drop-down button in the Look In drop-down list.

5. Select Local Hard Drives.

6. Click the Find Now button. REGEDIT.EXE will appear in the window when Windows NT finds the file.

7. Drag the REGEDIT.EXE entry to your start button and then let go.

8. Close the Find window.

The REGEDIT.EXE program will appear in your Start menu. You should now be able to run REGEDIT.EXE by clicking the Start button and then selecting the REGEDIT.EXE menu item.

Use REGEDIT.EXE with caution. You can damage your operating system by entering inappropriate values or removing important Registry information. Therefore, we do not recommend modifying the Registry entries directly if you can use another more conventional way to change your system settings, such as through the Control Panel or through the User Manager.

Components of the Registry

The Registry stores a great deal of essential information. Figure 4.10 shows the Registry Editor and the top level of the Registry. The structure of the Registry is hierarchical, much like the file system on your computer's hard drive. Keys and subkeys correspond to directories and subdirectories. Values are much like files in that they have names and types and hold the data in the registry.

FIGURE 4.10
The Registry holds important Windows NT system configuration data.

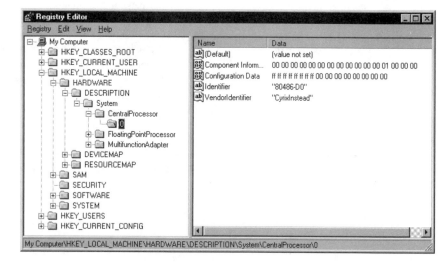

At the top of the Registry, which corresponds to the root of a file system, are five subtrees. The subtrees are like top level directories. Keys and subkeys within each subtree hold information about your Windows NT computer. Refer to Table 4.1 for an explanation of the Registry elements.

The values in the Registry can have one of three value types: DWORD, string, and binary. Refer to Table 4.2 for an explanation of the Registry value types.

Registry Structure

Every Windows NT 4 Workstation Registry has these five subtrees, and each subtree contains information for a different part of the Windows NT system.

- **HKEY_CLASSES_ROOT** contains information for use with OLE and file associations. This subtree helps maintain compatibility with the Windows 3.1 registration database.

TABLE 4.1 Registry Terms.	**ITEM**	**EXPLANATION**
	Values	Values contain the information that is stored in the Registry. Each value has three parts: a name, a data type, and a configuration parameter that contains the actual information.
	Keys and subkeys	Keys and subkeys are containers for subkeys and values.
	Subtree	The subtree (sometimes called subtree key or a predefined key handle) is a top level key. A Windows NT workstation Registry has five subtrees.
	Hive	A hive is a set of keys, subkeys, and values from the Registry that is stored in its own file in the location \<winnnt_root>\ SYSTEM32\CONFIG. A hive has its own transaction log to ensure that the data is valid.

TABLE 4.2 Registry Value Types.	**VALUE DATA TYPES**	**STRUCTURE AND CONTENTS**
	DWORD	1–8 hexadecimal digits; contains a single value
	String	A string data type of variable length
	Binary	A string of hex digits; each pair of digits forms a byte value

- HKEY_CURRENT_USER contains information about the current user. Each user's profile information (described earlier in this chapter) is stored in a separate hive in the Profiles subdirectory of the Windows NT directory. When a user logs on, the profile for that user is attached to the Registry under the subtree HKEY_CURRENT_USER. This information also can be found in the HKEY_USERS subtree under the user's Security ID (SID), which is defined in more detail in Chapter 7.

- HKEY_LOCAL_MACHINE contains the hardware and software configuration that does not change between user logons. Information in this subtree is used to boot the system, configure devices, load device drivers, and start system services.

- **HKEY_USERS** contains two subkeys: DEFAULT, which contains the system default settings that are used during the logon process (when the user presses Ctrl+Alt+Del), and a key with the SID of the current user (mentioned above).

- **HKEY_CURRENT_CONFIG** contains additional configuration information about the current configuration of the system.

HKEY_LOCAL_MACHINE

HKEY_LOCAL_MACHINE contains a great deal of information and contains the most critical system data.

Five keys are located directly below HKEY_LOCAL_MACHINE in the Registry:

- HARDWARE

- SAM

- SECURITY

- SOFTWARE

- SYSTEM

HARDWARE is generated automatically every time the computer boots and is not associated with a hive file and log. The other four keys do have hives stored in the \<winnt_root>\SYSTEM32\CONFIG directory. For instance, the hive for SAM is called SAM and the log is SAM.LOG.

HARDWARE HARDWARE contains hardware information that is provided when the system boots. System programs and user applications can view information in this key to determine the computer's hardware configuration and to see the type and state of devices attached to the computer.

SAM The SAM, or the Security Account Manager, holds local user and group account information. Applications that view information in the SAM key must do so through the appropriate Application Programming Interface (API), and the user running the application must have sufficient permissions to access the information. This information can also be found under the SECURITY key in the key SAM.

The SAM also holds the domain user accounts database if the computer is running Windows NT Server instead of Windows NT Workstation.

SECURITY SECURITY contains all security information for the local computer. Applications must use the correct API to make changes to the SECURITY information, and the user performing the task must have the privileges required.

SOFTWARE This key holds information about software that is independent of user profiles. The manufacturers and version numbers of software are stored here, as well as file associations and OLE information.

SYSTEM SYSTEM contains information about the devices and services on the system. As devices are installed and modified, they store their configuration information here. The SYSTEM hive is stored in the SYSTEM and SYSTEM.ALT files in the Config directory.

Searching the Registry

The information stored in the Registry is exhaustive, and very few individuals know where everything is in it. Select Edit ➤ Find in the Registry Editor to search for keys, values (names), and data. You can find exact matches for the text you type or find all occurrences of the text you type. Once you find a match, you can press F3 to continue your search or click Find Next in the Search window.

All searches start from the currently highlighted key. They will not branch back. If you wish to search the entire Registry, you must first select the My Computer key at the top of the Registry.

You can find occurrences of the word *Administrator* in the Registry by performing the steps in Exercise 4.26.

Microsoft Windows NT Diagnostics (WINMSD)

The Windows NT Diagnostics utility will show you the most useful and most often viewed Registry values in a graphical and logically arranged format. To find Windows NT Diagnostics from the Start menu, select Programs ➤ Administrative Tools. Figure 4.11 shows an overview of Windows NT Diagnostics functions.

EXERCISE 4.26

Finding Occurrences of a Word in the Registry

1. Start the Registry Editor.

2. Highlight My Computer.

3. Select Edit ➤ Find from the Registry Editor (or hit Ctrl+F).

4. Type **Administrator** in the Find What field.

5. Click the Find Next button.

6. Press F3 to find additional occurrences of *Administrator* in the Registry.

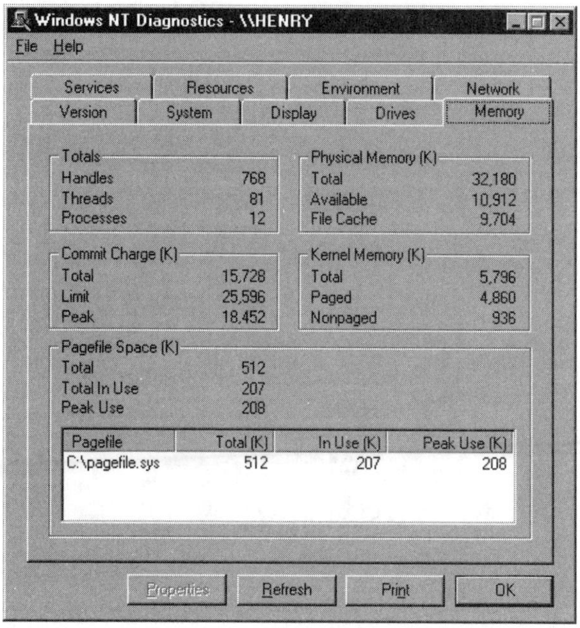

FIGURE 4.11
Windows NT Diagnostics displays many of the important settings stored in the Registry.

Chapter Summary

THE CONTROL PANEL ALLOWS YOU to control most system configuration options. You can change Control Panel settings on per-user or a per-system basis, but you must have appropriate permissions in order to change system settings. System settings are settings that affect every user on the system. Device drivers and network protocols are system settings. Per-user settings are settings that change with the user's preferences. Background colors, sound schemes, keyboard mappings, and mouse icons are per-user settings.

Per-user settings are stored in user profiles. User profiles can be local to a certain computer or can be roaming. User profiles are usually stored in the Profiles subdirectory of the Windows NT directory.

All of the critical information maintained by the Windows NT operating system is stored in the Registry. You can use the Registry Editor to view and change information in the Registry.

The five subtrees within the Registry are as follows:

- HKEY_CLASSES_ROOT

- HKEY_CURRENT_USER

- HKEY_LOCAL_MACHINE

- HKEY_USERS

- HKEY_CURRENT_CONFIG

The five subkeys within HKEY_LOCAL_MACHINE are as follows:

- HARDWARE

- SAM

- SECURITY

- SOFTWARE

- SYSTEM

Exercise Questions

1. All Windows NT Workstation computers have the same icons visible in the Control Panel.

   A. True

   B. False

2. The Network settings are an example of system settings that all users share.

   A. True

   B. False

3. You can use icons in the Control Panel to modify system settings or to modify user profile settings, but not to modify both.

   A. True

   B. False

4. Windows NT can use only one page file at a time.

   A. True

   B. False

5. A user profile is created for a user from the default user profile the first time the user logs on.

   A. True

   B. False

6. Screen saver settings are stored in the user's profile.

   A. True

   B. False

7. Paging file settings are stored in the user's profile.

   A. True

   B. False

8. You can add programs to the Start menu that will appear only when you log on under your username.

   A. True

   B. False

9. The system maintains certain environment variables for Windows NT to use, but users can also set up some environment variables to customize their own user accounts.

   A. True

   B. False

10. The Registry stores device configuration data only. Security information and user settings are stored in `INI` files.

    A. True

    B. False

11. You can easily render your Windows NT system unusable by making inappropriate changes to the Windows NT Registry.

    A. True

    B. False

12. Six keys are located directly below `HKEY_LOCAL_MACHINE` in the Registry.

    A. True

    B. False

13. The HARDWARE key is generated automatically every time the computer boots. The HARDWARE key does not have a hive.

    A. True

    B. False

14. The SYSTEM key is generated automatically every time the computer boots. The SYSTEM key does not have a hive.

    A. True

    B. False

15. Anything that has to do with the appearance or function of your workstation will most likely be controlled from the _____ _____.

16. Settings that affect every user of the system can only be modified by members of the _____ group.

17. Windows NT uses a technique called _____ to allow your computer to run more programs and larger programs than the physical memory in your computer would allow.

18. The process that performs the paging function is called the _____ _____ Manager.

19. The paging data, when it is stored on the disk, is stored in a virtual memory page file called _____ . SYS.

20. When Setup calculates how big to make your initial page file, it chooses a size that is _____ MB bigger than you physical memory size.

21. The _____ loader appears while your computer boots and allows you to choose between Windows NT and other operating systems you may have installed on your computer.

22. The _____ _____ section of the System Properties window is where you can set several hardware configurations for your Windows NT workstation.

23. UPS stands for _____ _____ _____ .

24. The UPS communicates with Windows NT through a standard _____ cable.

25. User preferences are stored in a _____ _____ .

26. _____ profiles are normally stored on a Windows NT server.

27. The recommended method of configuring Windows NT settings is through the _____ _____ .

28. You can directly modify the data in the Registry that the Control Panel items change by using a program called _____ .EXE.

29. The _____ is where Windows NT stores all of its important configuration information.

30. In order to organize the information in the Registry, it is structured in a _____ manner, much like the file system on your computer's hard drive.

31. A _____ is a set of keys, subkeys, and values from the Registry that is stored in its own file in the location \<winnnt_root>\SYSTEM32\CONFIG.

32. The values in the Registry can have one of three value types: _____ , _____ , and _____ .

33. Fill in the Control Panel item that performs the described function:

A. _____ allows you to start and stop hardware devices.

B. _____ allows you to install and configure network components.

C. _____ contains the system fonts available to programs on the workstation.

D. _____ allows you to start and stop system services such as the Remote Access Server and simple TCP/IP services.

E. _____ allows you to set the time and date of the computer's clock.

F. _____ allows you to modify system settings such as the default startup parameters, system environment variables, and paging options.

34. From where can you delete user profiles?

A. The Services Control Panel

B. The Server Control Panel

C. The User Manager program

D. The System Control Panel

35. Match the UPS condition to the control line:

A. Power failure   **1.** DCD

B. Low battery   **2.** DTR

C. Remote UPS shutdown   **3.** CTS

36. Match the Registry subtree with the information stored in it:

A. HKEY_CURRENT_USER   **1.** Contains information for use with OLE and file associations

B. HKEY_CLASSES_ROOT   **2.** Contains information about the user currently logged in

C. HKEY_LOCAL_MACHINE   **3.** Contains the hardware and software configuration that does not change between user logons

D. HKEY_CURRENT_CONFIG   **4.** Contains the subkey DEFAULT and the subkey corresponding to the SID of the current user

E. HKEY_USERS   **5.** Contains additional information about the current configuration of the system

File Systems

WHEN YOU INSTALLED the Windows NT Workstation operating system (the topic of Chapter 2), you chose a partition and a file system in which to install it. This chapter will show you how to work with partitions and file systems under Windows NT Workstation.

First, you will learn how Windows NT organizes hard disk storage space into partitions, volumes, directories, and files. Next, you'll learn about the two hard disk file systems supported by Windows NT: File Allocation Table (FAT) and the Windows NT File System (NTFS). Finally, you'll learn how to use the Disk Administrator to configure and manage the volumes in your computer.

Windows NT supported read and write access to OS/2 High Performance File System (HPFS) partitions through version 3.51. This support has been removed in Windows NT version 4.0.

The exercises in this chapter can wreck the data on your computer if you're not careful. If you do not already know what a partition is, or if you know that you have only one partition on your hard disk, you'll want to study this chapter without performing the exercises.

You will need a partition (or free space) other than the partition that contains your important data that is larger than 50MB in order to complete the exercises in this chapter.

File Storage

THE MEMORY IN YOUR COMPUTER is volatile, which means that it goes away when the power is turned off. Computers also have nonvolatile storage in which to place operating system data, application data, and files. Hard disks and floppy disks (and to an increasing extent, CD-ROMs) are the most popular forms of nonvolatile (or persistent) storage in personal computers.

Hard disks must store a great deal in today's computers. If you want to organize and store thousands of operating system files, application programs and data, and user files, the file system on the hard drive helps you find what you need and manage the file space.

The two file systems for hard disks that Windows NT supports (FAT and NTFS) are described in the following sections, but first we will cover topics in common to all file systems: files, directories, volumes, and partitions.

A file system is a method of organizing files. In Windows NT this method is implemented as an operating system module that controls the storage and retrieval of data to the disk.

Files and Directories

Everything you store in a computer goes into a file. A file is simply a named sequence of data stored somewhere. A file contains information, just the way a piece of paper can contain text, pictures, tabular accounting data, or blueprints. Imagine the piece of paper can be cut to any size to represent any amount of information.

Just as the print device determines what goes on paper, the program that generates a file interprets its contents. A graphics program may store pictures in a file, and a word processor may store documents in a file. Windows NT doesn't care about the contents of the file; it is merely concerned with storing them and keeping track of them.

Directories are sometimes called *folders*—they contain files just the way a file folder does. If you carry the analogy two steps further, the file drawer that holds the folders can be considered a volume. And then the cabinet itself can be considered a hard disk.

Windows NT also stores application software and its modular software components as files. Although these files contain executable code, Windows NT stores them the same way it stores data files, such as spreadsheets or word processing documents.

Structure of a Hard Disk

Hard disks, like file cabinets, are not simply vast places to put data. They have a very defined structure that allows the various file systems to coexist peacefully on the same disk. You will encounter these structural components—partitions and volumes—again when you learn how to use the Disk Administrator (later in this chapter).

Partitions

The basic subdivisions of a hard disk are its partitions. Each partition contains one volume maintained by any file system. Note that a partition may be created and maintained by any operating system, not just by Windows NT. Some operating systems, including Windows NT, support creating volumes that span several partitions. These multiple partition volumes have a single drive letter assigned to them. We cover multiple partition volumes later in this chapter.

Partitions allow a hard disk to appear as many hard disks. This arrangement allows you to divide your hard disk according to function or to support foreign file systems on the same physical hard disk. (*Foreign file systems* are file systems that are not recognized by Windows NT, such as UNIX or OS/2 file systems.)

Changing the partitions of a disk requires destroying all the data in the partitions being changed. Consequently, you should take the time to partition your hard disk correctly the first time.

Unless you have a reason to do otherwise, create one partition as large as your disk will support.

The initial portion of the Windows NT installer program runs under MS-DOS, which does not support partitions with more than 1,024 cylinders. During the installation process, you may get a warning that your disk has more than 1,024 cylinders. If so, you should enable sector translation (SCSI disks) or large block allocation (IDE disks) in the BIOS of your disk controller to allow Windows NT access to the entire disk without partitioning it. If your controller does not support sector translation, you will have to create multiple partitions with fewer than 1,024 cylinders.

MASTER BOOT RECORD The master boot record is the first portion of data on a hard disk. It is reserved for the BIOS bootstrap routine, which contains low-level code that redirects the loading of the operating system to the partition marked as active. This method of redirecting the bootstrap routine to a partition allows up to four bootable operating systems to exist on the same disk.

THE PARTITION TABLE The partition table is the index of partitions used by the bootstrap routine to identify distinct portions of the disk. File systems can create volumes only within partitions. If your hard disk doesn't have any partitions, you cannot create any volumes. Partition entries in the partition table contain a simple starting position on the disk and the length (and therefore size) of the partition.

Volumes

A volume is the structure imposed upon a partition to allow the indexing of files. A volume contains the table of contents of the disk called the *root directory*. The volume also maintains allocation tables that show what space in the volume is occupied, thus ensuring that no file overwrites another by being stored in the same location. File systems operate with volume information to determine where to store files and how to retrieve them.

Some file systems, such as NTFS, can create logical volumes that extend across more than one partition. Volume sets and stripe sets are examples of multiple partition volumes. Volume and stripe sets are covered in detail later in this chapter.

DRIVE LETTERS Drive letters are assigned to volumes to help identify them when referring to the exact location of a file. MS-DOS assigned drive letters as it found devices when booting, starting with C: for hard disks. Windows NT allows the administrator to assign drive letters as necessary. This arrangement allows you to migrate drives from DOS to Windows NT while retaining the original drive letters, even if a new disk is installed.

For example, if you install a new hard disk as your primary hard disk and make your old hard disk (with all your software on it) your second hard disk, MS-DOS will automatically assign drive letter D: to your old disk. This process wreaks havoc with all your programs that rely on exact path locations to their files. With Windows NT you can simply assign C: to your old drive and D: to the new one to keep your applications happy.

FAT

THE FILE ALLOCATION TABLE (FAT) file system was introduced with MS-DOS in 1981. Because of its age, almost all computer operating systems, including Windows NT, Windows 95, MacOS, and most UNIX operating systems, support the FAT system in some way. Its universality makes the

FAT appropriate for use on volumes that will be used by more than one operating system.

The FAT file system keeps track of files in a partition using a file allocation table (hence the FAT acronym) stored on the first few clusters of the partition. Each cluster on the disk has an entry in the FAT that indicates whether the cluster is in use. A root directory that contains file and directory entries that point to the remaining files on the disk is stored on the disk immediately after the FAT.

In the FAT file system, a directory is a list of file entries consisting of a filename limited to 8 characters, a period, and a three-letter extension. File entries also contain a date and time stamp, and some attribute bits that show the status of the file, such as read only and hidden. If the attribute bit "directory" is set, the file is interpreted as another directory containing its own list of file entries.

Because the root directory contains pointers to other directories and those directories can contain pointers to other directories, the FAT file system is referred to as a linked-list file system.

The FAT file system is a simple file system that does not prevent files from becoming corrupted in abnormal shutdowns such as power failures. Over time, FAT volumes can become increasingly corrupt. MS-DOS (version 5 and newer), Windows 95, and Windows NT all come with a utility to scan for and correct discrepancies in the FAT file system. However, it cannot detect or correct all discrepancies, and it does not run unless you specifically invoke it.

The FAT file system was also designed to be used with DOS, which is a single-user operating system. The FAT file system therefore does not record security information such as the owner or access permissions of a file or directory.

The simple structure of the FAT file system does give it some advantages over more complex file systems such as NTFS—primarily for volumes smaller than 200MB. The FAT file system requires less overhead for small volumes (data structures used to keep track of information in the system) than does NTFS and is the most widely supported file system type. Therefore, if several operating systems must share a volume, the FAT file system is a good choice.

FAT versus VFAT

Two versions of the FAT file system are available: the original version, used in versions of DOS and Windows (up to version 6.22 of MS-DOS and version 3.11 of Windows), and VFAT, which is used in MS-DOS version 7 (the never officially released version of DOS that runs within Windows 95), Windows 95, and Windows NT versions 3.51 and 4.0.

The main difference between the versions has to do with filenames. VFAT is an extension to FAT that allows newer programs and operating systems to use long filenames, while still allowing older programs to use the shorter filenames that they expect.

FAT Filename Conventions

The FAT filename conventions are as follows:

- The name must start with either a letter or a number; it can contain any character except the following:

  " / \ [ ] : ; | = , ^ * ?

- The name cannot contain any spaces.

- The name cannot have more than eight characters before an optional extension that starts with a period.

- The extension cannot have more than three characters.

- Only one period is allowed.

- The following names are reserved: CON, AUX, COM1, COM2, COM3, COM4, LPT1, LPT2, LPT3, PRN, NUL.

- Names are not case sensitive and do not preserve case.

VFAT Filename Conventions

VFAT relaxes some of the restrictions of the FAT naming conventions:

- The name can be up to 255 characters.

- The name can contain multiple spaces and multiple periods, but the text after the last period is still considered the extension.

- Names are not case sensitive, but they do preserve case.

POSIX-compliant applications and utilities are case sensitive under Windows NT.

Filename Conversions from VFAT to FAT

To maintain backward compatibility with the FAT file system, VFAT actually creates a normal FAT file system directory entry equal to the first few characters of the filename plus special characters to ensure that the name is unique in the directory. VFAT ignores these mangled filenames and instead shows the full, long filename information to programs that understand long filenames.

Long filename information is also stored in the FAT file system directories. VFAT sets four DOS attribute bits (volume, read only, system, and hidden), which are an undefined combination in the FAT file system and thus ignored completely. This arrangement effectively hides the long filename information from the FAT file system while preserving it for the VFAT file system in a compatible manner.

Using FAT file system utilities like CHKDISK or SCANDISK to repair VFAT volumes will probably cause the loss of long filename information. Use only Windows 95 or Windows NT 3.51 or later disk utilities to repair VFAT volumes.

When VFAT creates a FAT file system directory entry, it uses the first six characters from the long filename, then the tilde (~) character, then a digit serially assigned to ensure uniqueness, and the extension if any. For example:

```
C:\Do you like long filenames?\This is another file.txt
```

would become

```
C:\DOYOUL~1\THISIS~1.TXT
```

This mangled filename is called the FAT alias. Programs designed for Windows 95 and NT replace these aliases with long filenames, but you can use the FAT alias to specify a folder or file if you want to. This shortcut can be handy when you would otherwise have to type a very long filename.

The FAT file system root directory has a hard-coded limit of 512 entries. Since a single long filename could take up to 21 of these entries, you should use long filenames with moderation in the root directory.

When a VFAT filename is stored on the disk, one directory entry is used for the FAT alias and one additional entry is used for each 13 characters of filename length. Consequently, a long filename could potentially use 21 directory entries. See Exercise 5.1 for an example of how to view the FAT alias of a VFAT long filename.

EXERCISE 5.1

Creating a VFAT Filename and Viewing Its FAT Alias

1. Select Programs ➤ Accessories ➤ Notepad in the Start menu.

2. Type anything into the body of the Notepad document.

3. Select File ➤ Save As.

4. Select the Root Directory in the directory hierarchy browser.

5. Click the New Folder icon.

6. Type **Delete This Directory** as the name of new folder.

7. Double-click the new folder.

8. Select the Filename input box.

9. Type **This is a long filename.txt** in the Filename input box.

10. Click the Save button.

11. Close the Notepad by clicking the Close button.

12. Select Programs ➤ Command Prompt in the Start menu.

13. Type **cd \delete this directory** at the command prompt.

14. Type **dir /x** at the command prompt.

15. Notice the long filename and the FAT alias.

16. Close the command prompt by clicking the Close button.

FAT File System Considerations

Despite the FAT file system's security and corruptibility drawbacks, you might decide to use the FAT file system on your computer for many reasons. If you use more than one operating system, such as Windows, OS/2, or DOS, and you want to access files in both systems, you will need to have a FAT file system partition.

Many Plug-and-Play configuration utilities for network adapters, modems, video adapters, and other hardware devices will not run under Windows NT, which does not allow hardware-level access to User mode programs. These programs will have to reside in a FAT partition in order to be accessed from MS-DOS. If these conditions apply to your system, keep an MS-DOS boot partition large enough to contain hardware configuration utilities and foreign operating system file storage.

The Windows NT installation program requires a FAT partition for the initial portion of the installation, and Windows NT running on microprocessors other than the Intel 386 family can boot Windows NT only in a FAT partition.

Here is a summary of the advantages of the FAT system:

- FAT supports files and partitions as large as 4GB.

- FAT is accessible by many operating systems, including MS-DOS, Windows NT, Windows 95, OS/2, MacOS, and many variants of the UNIX family of operating systems. FAT is a nearly universal file system.

- FAT has the least file system overhead of any modern file system, which makes it suitable for small partitions (less than 50MB).

- FAT is the only PC-compatible file system that is used on floppy disks.

- Many removable hard disks are too small to take advantage of NTFS.

NTFS

THE NEW TECHNOLOGY FILE SYSTEM (NTFS) is the preferred file system for use with Windows NT, was created for Windows NT, and represents the culmination of file system development at Microsoft. NTFS implements many protective features to ensure the reliable storage and retrieval of data.

NTFS is supported only by Windows NT. If you need to share files with another operating system on the same computer, you will need to choose a file system that is compatible with both operating systems.

The following characteristics make NTFS the file system of choice for Windows NT computers:

- Fault tolerance

- Security

- File and partition sizes

- File compression

- POSIX support

- Performance

NTFS Features

NTFS has numerous features that make it more appropriate than the FAT file system for Windows NT. If you are only using Windows NT on your computer, you should seriously consider using NTFS as your primary file system. You may want to retain a FAT partition for the reasons explained in the FAT file system section, but it does not need to be your primary file system. The many virtues of NTFS are extolled next.

Fault Tolerance

NTFS logs all changes to the file system, which means that every file or directory update can be redone or undone to correct discrepancies arising from system failures or power losses. This process prevents the inconsistencies that occur in the FAT file system, which eventually lead to data loss if left uncorrected.

NTFS also uses a method called *hot fixing* that repairs hard disk failures on the fly without returning an error message to the calling application. After NTFS writes to a hard disk, it rereads the newly written data to verify its integrity. If the data is corrupt, NTFS flags that portion of the hard disk as bad and then rewrites the data to another location on the hard disk.

Security

Windows NT objects maintain the permissions and auditing features implemented by the Windows NT security model. Files created or copied into a directory inherit the security permissions of the directory. Files moved into a directory retain their original permissions and attributes.

NTFS supports security on files and directories, but does not support data encryption. You will need to use third-party data encryption utilities if your security environment requires encryption.

File and Partition Sizes

NTFS can store files up to 16 exabytes in length. An exabyte is 2^{64}, or 4GB x 4GB. Windows NT extends considerably the maximum file and partition sizes when compared to those of FAT and HPFS.

The recommended minimum partition size for NTFS is 50MB. If you have a partition smaller than this, you should consider using the FAT file system because of the overhead required for NTFS.

Windows NT provides no method to undelete a deleted file under NTFS. Note that when you drag a file to the recycle bin, it is not deleted. Dragging files to the recycle bin merely copies them to a hidden area on the disk. Files are not actually deleted until the size of your recycle bin exceeds the threshold programmed for automatic deletion or until you specifically empty the bin. To retrieve files from the recycle bin, simply double-click the bin and drag the files out as if you were copying files between folders.

File Compression

In addition to greatly increased file and partition sizes, NTFS provides real-time file compression. File compression removes redundancy from files, thereby decreasing their physical size.

NTFS compresses files on a file-by-file basis, which means that if anything goes physically wrong with a portion of data on the disk, the defect affects only one file. This situation is different from compression schemes for MS-DOS, which can lose an entire volume of data if a small portion of the disk goes bad.

Because NTFS is far more fault tolerant than earlier operating systems and because it implements compression on a file-by-file basis, you need not be cautious about file compression. Compressing directories that contain infrequently used information or programs is a good practice.

NTFS compression is a native part of the file system, so it is supported throughout Windows NT. This feature is unlike FAT file system compression schemes, which use a number of clever techniques to emulate the FAT file system file under what amounts to an entirely different compressed file system.

NTFS can compress or decompress an individual file or all of the files in any directory. A compressed attribute bit is set when a file or the content of a directory are compressed. This bit tells the system whether or not to decompress the file when it is read.

Because compression requires a small amount of overhead, compressing files that contain little or no redundancy could possibly make them larger. Although NTFS will leave the compression bit set, it will not actually compress files that would not benefit from compression.

NTFS favors speed over size when compressing and decompressing files. The average compression ratio for Windows NT is about two to one, which means you should be able to store about twice as much data on a disk if you enable file compression. The file compression ratio depends on the amount of redundancy in a file and varies greatly.

When compressed files are moved or copied, the compression bit is maintained in the same manner as all permission information. When files are copied, the compression bit is set to that of the target directory. When files are moved within the same partition, the compression bit remains the same regardless of the target directory's compression setting. A move across partitions actually copies a new file and deletes the old. Therefore, when files are moved across partition boundaries, the compression bit is inherited from the target directory.

POSIX Support

Windows NT supports POSIX standard network naming conventions such as case sensitivity, last-access-time stamping, and hard links.

Under POSIX applications README.TXT, Readme.TXT, and readme.txt are three different files. You will not be able to test this feature with Windows NT applications such as the Explorer, because they treat filenames as case insensitive.

Although Windows NT and NTFS support case-sensitive filenames, Windows NT applications including the Explorer, File Manager, and DOS command prompts treat filenames as case insensitive. Using Windows NT utilities to manage files created by POSIX applications can result in ambiguities that can cause data loss.

Hard links are two directory entries that point to the same file on the disk. These are fundamentally different from shortcuts, which are actually small files containing information that Windows NT uses to locate the original file.

To fully support POSIX, NTFS filenames can include any characters except the following: ? " / \ < > * | :

Performance

To decrease fragmentation, Windows NT always attempts to save files in contiguous blocks. Windows NT implements a B-tree directory structure similar to that used by the OS/2 high performance file system rather than the linked list directory structure used by the FAT file system. The B-tree speeds file searches considerably and reduces the possibility of a missing link resulting in data loss.

Converting to NTFS

Most computers come with MS-DOS, Windows 95, or OS/2 factory installed, but few currently ship with Windows NT Workstation installed. Most users will want to convert their existing FAT or OS/2 file systems to NFTS after they've become comfortable with Windows NT Workstation as their primary operating system.

Converting a file system to NTFS is a one-way process. You cannot convert a file system back to the FAT file system or OS/2 if you change your mind.

Converting File Systems to NTFS

Windows NT includes a conversion utility called, appropriately, CONVERT.EXE, which can convert FAT and OS/2 HPFS volumes into NTFS volumes without erasing them or deleting any files. The conversion utility uses command line syntax. You can launch it either from an MS-DOS box or from the Run option in the Start menu.

Because NTFS has more overhead than FAT and HPFS, you may not have enough free room on a partition to perform the conversion, especially on partitions smaller than 50MB. The conversion utility will alert you to this problem without changing the contents of your partition.

The correct way to run the conversion utility is shown in Exercise 5.2.

EXERCISE 5.2

Converting FAT or HPFS Volumes to NTFS

1. Select Programs ➤ Command Prompt from the Start menu.

2. Type **CONVERT D: /FS:NTFS** at the command prompt and press Return.

Notice the progression of the conversion utility.

The convert utility does not retain OS/2 security attribute information. If you need to retain security attributes of an HPFS386 volume used by LAN Manager or OS/2 Warp Server, get the ACLCONV.EXE utility from Microsoft and read the associated readme file.

Other File Systems Supported by NT

WINDOWS NT CAN SUPPORT many different file systems. Also included in the basic Windows NT installation are the CD-ROM file system and the Named Pipes file system. Other file systems from third-party vendors can be added to access foreign file systems such as the network file system implemented by many UNIX computers and for access to legacy data stored on old computers and media.

Compact Disk File System (CDFS)

Compact Disk File System (CDFS) supports read-only operations on ISO9660 formatted CD-ROMs. Since the file system is read only, the only file management operations that you can perform are open, read, and copy.

Networks as File Systems

Many network redirectors and programming interfaces are implemented as file systems to abstract the boundary between local and network file storage. When you map a drive to a network path, Windows NT is redirecting file requests to make the network appear as a large local disk. This implementation allows programs to use network files easily and across any type of network supported by Windows NT.

For instance, Client Services for NetWare, named pipes, mailslots, Workstation, and Server are all implemented as file systems by Windows NT. Therefore, Windows NT Explorer can browse network resources in the same manner as it browses a local disk. (See Chapter 8 for more information on networks.)

Working with the Disk Administrator

THIS SECTION WILL SHOW YOU how to use the Windows NT Disk Administrator to create partitions and volume sets; how to format volumes; and how to create, extend, delete, stripe, and make active volume sets.

To reach the Disk Administrator from the Start menu, select Programs ➤ Administrative Tools. The Disk Administrator shows you a graphical view of the hard disks and partitions that exist in your Windows NT workstation. The graphical display shows the drives, their capacities, the volumes with their volume names, volume characteristics (stripe set, mirror set, volume set), file system types, volume size, and drive letters. See Figure 5.1 for a view of the main Disk Administrator window.

The Disk Administrator program performs all of the functions of the older programs FDISK and Microsoft LAN Manager Fault Tolerance character-based applications and more.

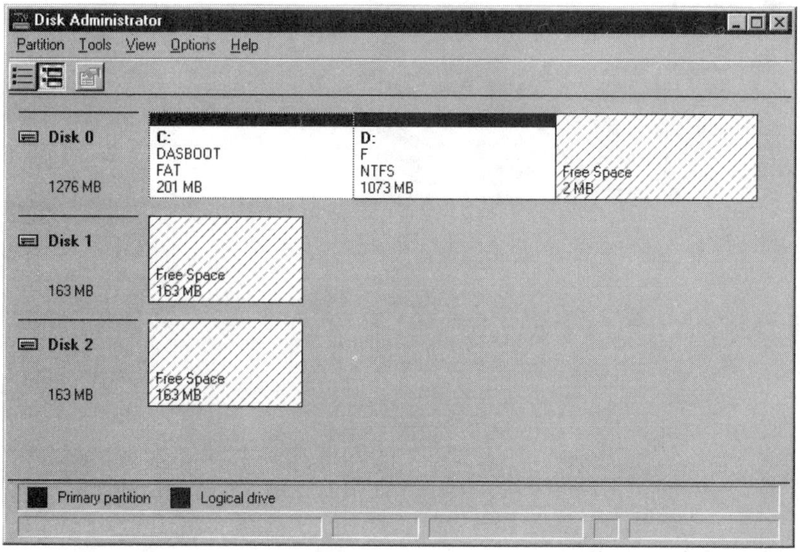

FIGURE 5.1
You use the
Disk Administrator to
manage volumes and
partitions on a
Windows NT
workstation.

Creating and Deleting Partitions

A disk must be partitioned before it is formatted with a file system. Some hard disks come prepartitioned and preformatted (usually with the FAT file system), but some do not. You may need to partition a new hard drive before installing it.

A disk with no partitions set up on it is completely given over to free space. You can create a partition on a hard disk only when free space is available on that hard disk and the partition will be taken from that free space. Deleting a partition returns the space occupied by that partition to the free space for that drive. If you have two DOS partitions on a drive, for example, and you wish to make one large NTFS partition, you will first have to delete the two DOS partitions so that you can create the NTFS partition. Figure 5.2 shows the Create Primary Partition window.

You may create a partition as large as the available free space or any size (in megabytes) smaller. Any area not used by the new partition will remain as free space, which you can use to make more partitions. Exercise 5.3 steps through the process of creating a partition.

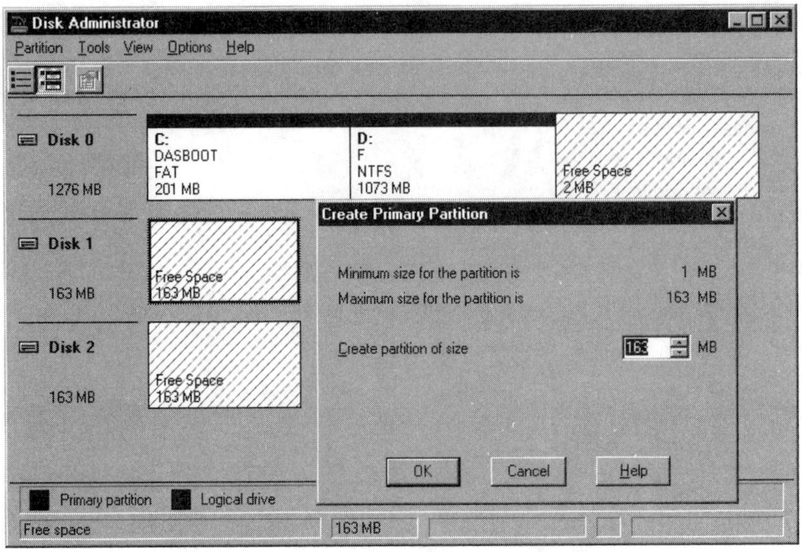

FIGURE 5.2
The Create Primary
Partition window is where
you select the size of the
new partition.

EXERCISE 5.3

Creating a Partition

1. Select Programs from the Start menu; then select Administrative Tools ➤ Disk Administrator.

2. Select the free space on the drive that will contain the new partition.

3. Select Partition ➤ Create.

4. Click OK when you are prompted for the size of the partition to accept the default amount of free space left on the drive.

5. Select Partition ➤ Commit Changes Now.

6. Select Yes in the confirmation window.

7. Click OK in the window that announces that Disk Administrator has performed the operation successfully.

Deleting a partition will destroy any information stored in a file system on that partition, so be very careful when you delete partitions.

The Disk Administrator will warn you when you are attempting to delete a partition that has a file system installed on it. Exercise 5.4 shows you how to delete a partition.

Do not perform Exercise 5.4 on any partition except the one created in Exercise 5.3, or you will lose data.

EXERCISE 5.4

Deleting a Partition

1. Select Programs from the Start menu; then select Administrative Tools ➤ Disk Administrator.

2. Select the partition you wish to delete.

3. Select Partition ➤ Delete. The Disk Administrator announces that all data on the partition will be lost and asks if you wish to proceed.

4. Select Yes.

5. Select Partition ➤ Commit Changes Now.

6. Select Yes in the confirmation window.

7. Click OK when you see the announcement that Disk Administrator has performed the operation successfully.

Windows NT assigns a drive letter to each partition as you create it. Windows NT may rearrange the drive letters when it does so, and the change may confuse programs or users who expect files to be on certain drives.

You do not have to leave the partitions with the drive letters that the Disk Administrator has assigned. You can use the Disk Administrator to assign drive letters to partitions (see Figure 5.3). As you install and remove hard drives in

FIGURE 5.3
You can assign specific
drive letters from the
Disk Administrator.

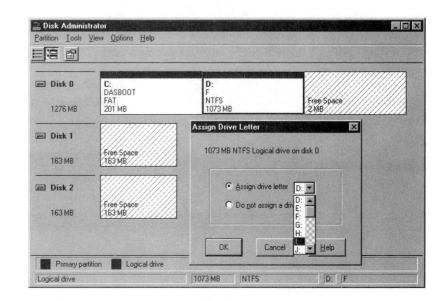

your computer, you should make sure that the drive letters for partitions that hold programs remain the same; otherwise, some programs may fail to work.

Primary and Extended Partitions

When you create a partition it can be either a primary or an extended partition. The Create menu item in the Partition menu creates a primary partition in the free space of the hard drive. To create an Extended partition, use the Create Extended menu selection instead.

The maximum number of primary partitions on a hard disk is four. This restriction is an artifact of how early IBM PC compatible computers organized information on hard disks. Early DOS computers using the FAT file system could not handle a disk partition greater than 32MB, but hard disks grew to sizes much larger than 128MB, so it was soon clear that four partitions would not be enough.

To overcome the four-partition limitation, you may designate any one (but only one) of the four partitions as an *extended* partition. Within the extended partition, you can create many logical drives.

MS-DOS 5.0 and earlier versions of DOS could see only one primary partition. These versions of DOS do not see any other primary partitions even if they have been formatted with a DOS file system. Versions of DOS earlier than 3.3 will not be able to use a partition larger than 32MB.

Active Partitions

The partition that your computer boots when it is turned on is the active partition. You mark a partition active by selecting Partition ➤ Mark Active (in the Disk Administrator utility). Only one primary partition may be marked active at a time.

In IBM-compatible computers, only a primary partition can be a system partition, and the Windows NT boot loader must reside in the primary partition that has been set as the System partition. However, Windows NT can reside in any sufficiently large portion on any of the hard disk. This partition, which contains Windows NT itself, is called the boot partition. The Windows NT boot partition will load the Windows NT operating system from wherever it has been installed.

In order for the Windows NT boot loader to run, the active partition must contain the Windows NT startup files, which include NTLDR, BOOT.INI, and NTDETECT.COM. In Windows NT terminology, the partition that contains the startup files is called the *system partition*. The partition with the Windows NT operating system files (the partition that has the System32\ directory) is called the *boot partition*. The boot partition can be the same as the system partition, or it can be in another volume or on another hard disk drive.

Committing Changes

When creating and deleting partitions with the Disk Administrator utility, the changes you make are not committed (saved) to the hard disk until you either exit the program and confirm the changes or select Commit Changes Now from the Partition menu. Unlike some other operating systems, in windows NT an administrator can delete, reconfigure, format, and use a partition without rebooting the computer.

Volumes and Volume Sets

A volume is one or more partitions treated as a single unit and given a single drive letter. When between 1 and 32 partitions are combined into one volume, the result is called a *volume set*. That volume set can be treated as a single partition for the purposes of formatting and file system use by the operating system. The partitions combined into a volume set do not have to be the same size or on the same drive or same type of drive (SCSI, ESDI, or IDE) to be combined into one larger partition. For instance, a 340MB partition on one drive can be combined with a 500MB partition on another drive to make a single 840MB partition. The E: drive in Figure 5.4 is a volume set.

When data is stored to a volume set, the data is stored to the partitions, one partition at a time. When one partition is full, the next partition will be used.

The system and boot partitions cannot be a part of a volume or stripe set.

You might wish to create a volume set if you have several small partitions on a hard disk or if you have several smaller hard disks that you want to treat as one large hard disk.

Volume sets do not provide fault tolerance to your file storage because they do not implement fault or error-recovery information beyond what is already provided by the file system. In fact, if a fault occurs within any one partition in a volume set, the whole volume set may be unusable. Exercise 5.5 shows you how to create a volume set.

FIGURE 5.4

The E: drive in the Disk Administrator window is an example of a volume set.

Disk Administrator				
Partition Tools View Options Help				

Disk 0 1276 MB	C: DASBOOT FAT 201 MB	D: F NTFS 1073 MB	Free Space 2 MB
Disk 1 163 MB	E: VOL NTFS 50 MI	Free Space 113 MB	
Disk 2 163 MB	E: VOL_TEST NTFS 163 MB		

■ Primary partition	■ Logical drive	□ Volume set		
Volume set #1		213 MB	NTFS	E: VOL_TEST

EXERCISE 5.5

Creating a Volume Set

1. Select Programs from the Start menu; then select Administrative Tools ➤ Disk Administrator.

2. Select the free space from which you will make the first part of the volume set.

3. Hold down the control key and select the free space on the drive that will contain the extension to the volume set. (Repeat this step for as many additional partitions as will be part of the volume set.)

4. Select Create Volume Set from the Partition menu. You will be prompted for the size of the volume set. The default is the current size plus the amount of free space left on the drive.

5. Click OK.

6. Select Partition ➤ Commit Changes Now.

7. Select Yes in the Confirmation window.

8. Click OK in the window that announces that Disk Administrator has performed the operation successfully.

You may be informed that you have to reboot your computer in order for the changes to take effect.

Extending Volume Sets

If you have formatted a volume set with NTFS, you can extend a volume set. You may wish to do so if the file system on the volume set is full or almost full.

You can only create and extend volume sets. You cannot shrink a volume set—instead you must delete the volume set, returning the space occupied by the volume set to free space (discarding all information that was stored in the volume set). You can then create a new volume or volume set that is smaller than the original. Follow the steps outlined in Exercise 5.6 to extend a volume set.

EXERCISE 5.6

Extending a Volume Set

1. Select Programs from the Start menu; then select Administrative Tools ➤ Disk Administrator.

2. Select the volume set that you want to extend.

3. Hold down the Control key and select the free space on the drive that will contain the extension to the volume set. (Repeat this step for as many additional partitions as will be part of the volume set.)

4. Select Extend Volume Set from the Partition menu. You will be prompted for the new size of the volume set. The default is the current size plus the amount of free space left on the drive.

5. Click OK.

6. Select Partition ➤ Commit Changes Now.

7. Select Yes in the confirmation window.

8. Click OK in the window that announces that Disk Administrator has performed the operation successfully.

You may be informed that you will have to reboot your computer in order for the changes to take effect.

Creating Stripe Sets

A stripe set is like a volume set except that the partitions that are a part of a stripe set must be on different drives and should be about the same size. The space from each drive is combined into one large volume as it is in a volume set, but in a stripe set the data is stored evenly across all of the partitions of the stripe set instead of being stored to one partition at a time. Figure 5.5 shows a stripe set of two drives.

Because of the way data is stored to a stripe set, stripe sets can transfer data much faster than volume sets—or even faster than single partitions. The reason is that a stripe set with multiple disk drive controllers (or a sophisticated disk drive controller that can communicate with several drives at a time) can transfer more information than a single drive controller connected to a single drive can transfer.

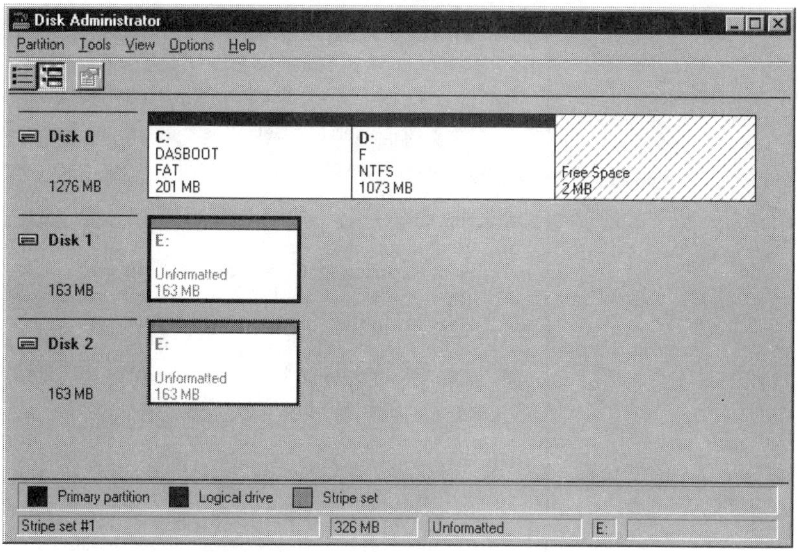

FIGURE 5.5

The E: drive is a stripe set
that has not yet been
formatted with NTFS.

FIGURE 5.5
The E: drive is a stripe set that has not yet been formatted with NTFS.

In a stripe set the data is stored evenly across all of the disks, one row at a time, in 64K blocks. This process allows the operating system to divide the commands among the drives and issue concurrent commands to each drive; the drives can then perform the operations simultaneously. This arrangement can enhance read and write performance in the file system, especially if several hard drive controllers are present or if the hard drive controller is sophisticated enough to issue multiple commands to multiple drives.

Exercise 5.7 explains how to create a stripe set.

EXERCISE 5.7

Creating a Stripe Set

1. Select Programs from the Start menu; then select Administrative Tools ➤ Disk Administrator.

2. Select the free space on the first drive that will be a part of the stripe set.

3. Hold down the Control key and select the free space on the drive that will contain the next partition of the stripe set. (Repeat this step for as many additional partitions as will be part of the stripe set.)

EXERCISE 5.7 (CONTINUED)

4. Select Create Stripe Set from the Partition menu. You will be prompted for the size of the stripe set. The default is the smallest free space among the drives multiplied by the number of drives selected.

5. Click OK.

6. Select Partition ➤ Commit Changes Now.

7. Select Yes in the confirmation window.

8. Click OK in the window that announces that Disk Administrator has performed the operation successfully.

You may be informed that you will have to reboot your computer in order for the changes to take effect.

Drive Letters

Windows NT assigns drive letters in the same order as MS-DOS; however, unlike MS-DOS, you can change the order of assignments any way you want. This is called static drive letter assignment.

The MS-DOS drive letter assignment order follows these rules:

- Hard disk drive letter assignments start with C:.

- Hard disk drive letter assignment always proceeds in physical drive number order.

- The primary partitions of each drive are assigned drive letters.

- The logical drives of each drive are assigned drive letters.

- The remaining partitions of each drive are assigned drive letters.

Exercise 5.8 shows the static assignment of drive letters. Keep in mind that you can only assign "free" drive letters, or in other words, drive letters that are not already in use. If you want to free up a drive letter that is currently in use for assignment to another drive, simply assign that drive another drive letter and commit your changes. This will free up the letter you wish to assign.

EXERCISE 5.8

Assigning a Drive Letter

1. Select Programs from the Start menu; then select Administrative Tools ➤ Disk Administrator.

2. Select the volume to receive an assigned drive letter.

3. Select Assign Drive Letter from the Tools menu.

4. Select the drive letter for the volume from the list in the Assign Drive Letter window. Click OK.

5. Select Partition ➤ Commit Changes Now.

6. Select Yes in the confirmation window.

7. Click OK in the window that announces that Disk Administrator has performed the operation successfully.

You may be informed that you will have to reboot your computer in order for the changes to take effect.

Formatting a Volume

Once you have created a partition, whether it is a single partition, volume set, or stripe set, you must format the partition to make it usable by Windows NT. (The file systems supported on hard disks—FAT and NTFS—were described in detail earlier in this chapter.)

To format a partition, you must first select the partition to be formatted. (Click once on the partition in the Disk Administrator window.) The partition must have already been created; you cannot format the free space on a hard disk. You can then select Format from the Tools menu and choose a file system for that volume (see Figure 5.6). Select Change Format if the partition already has a file system.

Exercise 5.9 explains how to format a drive.

FIGURE 5.6
Choosing a file system
for a volume.

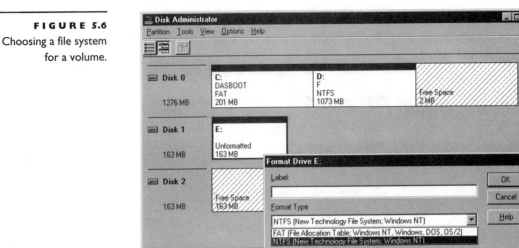

Formatting a Volume

1. Select Programs from the Start menu; then select Administrative Tools ➤ Disk Administrator.

2. Select the volume to format.

3. Select Format from the Tools menu.

4. Enter a label for the drive.

5. Select the file system type for the volume; your choices are FAT and NTFS.

6. Click OK. You will be warned that formatting the drive will destroy any data saved on the drive.

7. Click Yes.

8. Click OK when the format is complete.

Formatting a volume will destroy any data stored on that volume.

Recovering Disk Configuration Information

When you install Windows NT, you are asked if you wish to create an emergency repair disk on which to store the disk configuration information, among other things. After you make any changes to the configuration of your hard drives, the Disk Administrator allows you to save the configuration to the emergency disk.

You should save the configuration information to a floppy disk, because an emergency that would require you to recover the disk configuration information would most likely prevent you from accessing information on the hard disk drives.

You can use the RDISK.EXE in the SYSTEM32 subdirectory and the emergency repair disk to restore the hard disk configuration to the state it was in the last time you saved the configuration.

Chapter 17, "Troubleshooting," explains how to use the RDISK.EXE utility.

Chapter Summary

HARD DISK DRIVES PROVIDE your Windows NT workstation with persistent storage. The hard drives must be partitioned into volumes in order to be used. The active partition on the boot drive is the partition that will be booted by the operating system.

Windows NT supports two file systems for hard disk drives: the FAT file system and NTFS. The FAT is the same file system that DOS uses. NTFS is the native file system for Windows NT, and NTFS is the only file system that provides all of the security, reliability, and performance features that Windows NT supports.

The Disk Administrator is the tool that you use in Windows NT to manage your hard disk drives. You can use the Disk Administrator to partition the drives, create volume sets and stripe sets, format the volumes, assign drive letters, and set active partitions.

Exercise Questions

1. Files on a hard disk that contain programs are stored differently than normal data files because the program files contain instructions for the computer to execute.

    A. True

    B. False

2. Directories can contain either subdirectories or files.

    A. True

    B. False

3. The DOS FAT file system was introduced with the CPM operating system.

    A. True

    B. False

4. The DOS FAT file system is the most widely supported file system type.

    A. True

    B. False

5. The DOS FAT file system does not record security information such as the owner or file-sharing access permissions of a file or directory.

    A. True

    B. False

6. The DOS FAT file system has more overhead for small volumes than NFTS does.

    A. True

    B. False

7. The primary difference between the DOS FAT file system and VFAT has to do with file-sharing access permissions.

    A. True

    B. False

8. Under VFAT names are not case sensitive, but they do preserve case.

   A. True

   B. False

9. You must be careful not to create a new partition in the same space as an existing partition.

   A. True

   B. False

10. Windows NT assigns a drive letter to each partition as you create it.

   A. True

   B. False

11. Windows NT must reside in a primary partition.

   A. True

   B. False

12. The Windows NT boot loader must reside in the primary partition that has been set to be the boot partition.

   A. True

   B. False

13. The partitions combined into a volume set must be the same size and on the same drive.

   A. True

   B. False

14. The system and boot partitions cannot be a part of a volume set.

   A. True

   B. False

15. Volume sets provide fault tolerance to your file storage.

   A. True

   B. False

16. Because of the way data is stored to a stripe set, stripe sets can retrieve files much faster than volume sets can.

   A. True

   B. False

17. The system and boot partitions cannot be a part of a stripe set.

   A. True

   B. False

18. Windows NT always assigns the letter C to the active system partition unless you have selected another letter for the drive.

   A. True

   B. False

19. Formatting a volume will cause any data stored on that volume to be lost.

   A. True

   B. False

20. NTFS favors size over speed when compressing and decompressing files.

   A. True

   B. False

21. The memory in your computer is _____, which means that it goes away when the power is turned off.

22. Hard disks and floppy disks (and increasingly, CD-ROMs) are the most popular form of nonvolatile (or _____) storage in personal computers.

23. The two file systems for hard disks that Windows NT supports are _____ and _____.

24. Hard disks are subdivided into _____.

25. The _____ _____ _____ is the first portion of data on a hard disk and is reserved for the BIOS bootstrap routine.

26. Windows NT supports converting _____ to NFTS for the purpose of easing the migration of a computer from OS/2 to Windows NT.

27. Filenames under NFTS are limited to _____ characters.

28. _____ is the preferred file system for use with Windows NT.

29. A disk with no partitions set up on it is completely given over to _____ _____.

30. There can be only _____ primary partitions on a hard disk.

31. The partition that your computer boots when it is turned on is the _____ partition.

32. In Windows NT terminology, the partition that contains the startup files is called the _____ partition.

33. A _____ is one or more partitions treated as a single unit and given a single drive letter.

34. In a stripe set, the data is stored evenly across all of the disks, one row at a time in _____ K blocks.

35. Once you have created a partition, whether it be a single partition, volume set, or stripe set, you must _____ the partition to make it usable by Windows NT.

36. The recommended minimum partition size for NTFS is _____ MB.

37. File _____ removes redundancy from files, thereby decreasing their physical size.

File and Directory
Security

I N THE PRECEDING CHAPTERS you learned how to install Windows NT Workstation, configure the system, create user and group accounts, and prepare the hard disks and file systems.

In this chapter you will see how the user accounts, file systems, and Windows NT services interact to provide a secure and reliable environment. You will find out how to work with shared directories and how to use the security features of the Windows NT file system. You will learn about the principles of access permissions and ownership and how to audit files and directories. Finally, you will find out how to back up and restore data on your NT Workstation computer.

Planning for Security

W INDOWS NT PROVIDES a number of security options for you to protect the resources you share on your computer, but it's up to you to determine how to secure those resources. By default, Windows NT is very permissive with secured resources. Windows NT assumes that if you share a resource, you intend to provide full access to everyone. If this is not the case, you will have to modify your security settings for the shared resource.

We will cover securing the resources you share from your computer. Security for network sharing is covered in more detail in the companion book, *MCSE: NT Server Study Guide,* also published by Sybex.

How Much Security Is Enough?

Before you begin securing shared resources, you need to determine exactly what your security requirement is. If your organization has a security policy, you should read that document before implementing security on your computer.

Remember that the purpose of security is to prevent loss (including unauthorized disclosure) of any type. Before implementing security, ask yourself how likely different sorts of loss are. Remember that a good back-up policy will prevent most data loss, so you should really only be concerned with unauthorized disclosure in your security policy.

The following section will present a series of questions you should ask yourself before creating a security policy. The rest of this chapter will show you how to implement sharing and security.

What Are You Trying to Prevent?

You should understand what losses you are trying to prevent before implementing security. The following problems can occur on computer networks, so you should consider them when you create a security policy.

ACCESSORY TO COPYRIGHT VIOLATION The owners of computers that are used for public data receptacles are liable for the content on them. For instance, if you are running a BBS with your computer and one of your clients stores pirated software on it, you may be liable for copyright violation. This specific circumstance does not apply to most users, but similar problems may.

ACCIDENTAL LOSS Users may accidentally delete or change important data files or programs that they should have read access to. Preventing this is easy, but it does require specific action on your part because the default share permission is full control for everyone.

UNAUTHORIZED DISCLOSURE Trade secrets, privacy act information, and financial data are important information resources to protect, but they must also be shared among users on a network. For most shares containing this sort of data, you should deny access for everyone, and then allow access only for the specific groups that require it to perform their jobs.

MALICIOUS DESTRUCTION OF DATA This can occur when a computer isn't properly secured on the Internet or when someone gains physical access to your computer or network with the intent to destroy information. Assess the likelihood of this sort of access to your computer when formulating a security plan.

How Important Is Your Data?

This may seem obvious, but if your data doesn't have much value or is naturally secure, there isn't much reason to secure it.

For instance, directories that contain non-work-related software such as games or programs that can easily be re-installed if something goes wrong are not big security risks.

On the other hand, trade secrets or private employee information must be secured to prevent its accidental disclosure.

What Is the Risk of Intrusion?

If your computer is part of a physically secure network and you trust everyone who logs in, you don't have much risk of intrusion.

If, however, your computer is not secure from untrusted individuals or has sensitive information on it, you should take steps to prevent that information from being shared or restrict access to certain groups.

What Is the Probability of Accidental Loss?

Sometimes people with access to your files accidentally delete or change them without understanding the consequences. If your shared resources are accessible to inexperienced computer users, you may accidentally lose data.

Creating a Security Plan

If you have a rigorous security requirement, create a plan listing all the shared resources on your computer and the groups that will require access to them. When complete, use the exercises shown in the remainder of this chapter to implement security according to your plan.

Sharing Files and Directories

N A NETWORK ENVIRONMENT you will often need to share information that resides on your Windows NT workstation. You implement information sharing by creating *shared directories*. This section will show you how to start and stop sharing of directories. It will also identify the *default shares* that Windows NT provides as well as show you how to attach to a shared directory and detach from the shared directory.

In Windows NT Workstation 4.0, you can identify a directory that is being shared by the icon for shared directories. The shared directory icon has a hand underneath it to represent that the directory is being shared with other computers on the network.

In order for your computer to share directories, several network components must be in place:

- The Server service must be started on your computer. If you have installed the networking components of Windows NT, this service should start automatically when Windows NT starts.

- The user creating the network share of the directory must have access permissions to create the share. The default groups that are allowed to create shares are Administrators, Power Users, and Server Operators. A user who belongs to one or more of these groups can create a new directory share.

- The user attempting to view the share must have at least list permissions for that directory if it is on an NTFS partition.

Access and list permissions will be explained in the "NTFS Security" section of this chapter.

In order for you to perform the exercises in this chapter exactly as they are written, you will need to create a directory called `Dir_1` and two user accounts (see Exercise 6.1).

You will use the Bob and June accounts and the `Dir_1` directory as you perform the exercises in this chapter.

Sharing the Directory

You can share any directory on your NT workstation, regardless of the file system (DOS FAT or NTFS) or media type (hard disk, CD-ROM, or floppy disk).

NT Workstation allows you to set the sharing of the files and directories from several places, including from NT Explorer and from My Computer on the desktop. When you can see an icon of the directory you wish to share, you can usually right-click the icon to access the share properties of the directory.

To share a directory, follow the steps outlined in Exercise 6.2.

EXERCISE 6.1

Creating a Directory and Two User Accounts

1. Open My Computer on the Windows NT desktop.

2. Open the C: drive.

3. Select New Folder from the File menu.

4. Name the folder **Dir_1**.

5. Close the C: window.

6. Close the My Computer window.

7. Start the User Manager program.

8. Select the New User option from the User menu.

9. Type **Bob** in the Username field.

10. Enter a password in the Password and Confirm Password fields.

11. Click OK.

12. Add **June** as a user by repeating steps 9 through 11.

13. Close the User Manager window.

EXERCISE 6.2

Sharing a Directory for the First Time from the Desktop

1. Open My Computer on the Windows NT desktop.

2. Open the C: drive.

3. Select the Dir_1 directory by clicking the Dir_1 icon.

4. Select the Sharing menu option from the File menu in the My Computer window (see Figure 6.1).

5. Enable sharing by clicking on Shared As. See Figure 6.2 for an example of sharing a directory.

6. Select OK. Note that the icon for Dir_1 changes to a folder with a hand below it.

FIGURE 6.1
The Sharing option is in the File menu of the My Computer window.

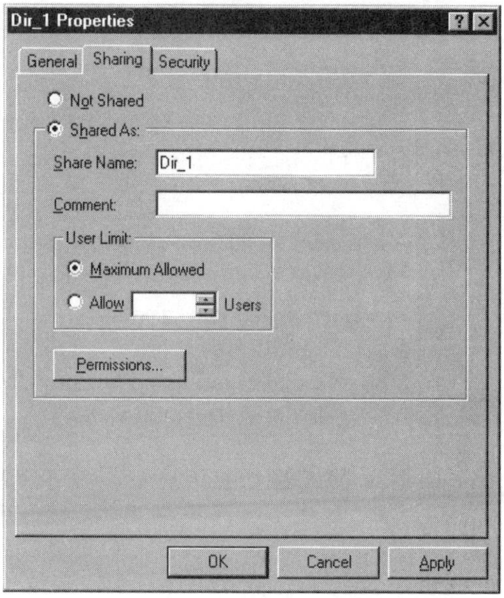

FIGURE 6.2
Enter the Share Name of a shared directory in the Properties window of that directory.

The share name of a shared directory does not have to be the same as the directory name. You may use a shorter name (limited to eight characters with an optional period and a three-character extension) for the directory if you expect MS-DOS–based clients to use the directory.

You can set the following controls in the Sharing tab of the Properties window of the directory (see Figure 6.2):

- **Not Shared** disables the sharing of a directory.

- **Shared As** enables sharing on the directory and uses the following fields (Share Name, Comment, User Limit, New Share, and Permissions) to configure the share.

- **Share Name** holds the name that will announce this share to browsing computers. If more than one name appears for this share, you can select which share you are viewing by selecting the share name in this field.

If the directory being shared has a long share name, it will not be accessible from some MS-DOS workstations. Windows NT will warn you of this situation when you create the share.

- **Comment** holds a description of the share that will be visible to browsing computers.

- **User Limit** allows you to set the share to accept the maximum allowed number of connections or to set it to allow fewer users.

The maximum number of users who can access a shared directory simultaneously is 10. You can set the number to a larger number in the Properties window, NT will still accept a maximum of 10 connections.

- **New Share** allows you to make a new share (with a new share name) for this directory.

- **Permissions** opens a Permissions window for this share. Permissions will be discussed later in this chapter.

Default Shares

Every time Windows NT Workstation boots, it creates default shares for each of the computer's hard drive volumes. These shares are used by both the NT Workstation operating system and the Windows NT server for administrative purposes and are not visible to computers browsing the network.

You can view the administrative shares by opening the Server icon in the Control Panel and then clicking the Shares button. A Shared Resources window will appear (see Figure 6.3). The default shares have a $ at the end of the name. The $ hides the shares from browsing requests. You can connect to these administrative shares only by specifying them by name (e.g., //Yoyo/C$ for the share on the server Yoyo corresponding to its C: drive), using the correct administrator name and password.

Admin$ is a special administrative share that always points to the Windows NT directory, and it is used for remote administration of a Windows NT computer. Other special shares created by NT include IPC$, for Inter-Process Communication between NT systems (such as for domain security authentication), and PRINT$, for sharing of printer information.

You cannot change the access control list (ACL) of an administrative share that was created automatically by the system. You can stop the sharing of an administrative share temporarily the same way you would stop the sharing of any other resource (described later in this chapter in the section "Stop Sharing"), but the default administrative share will be started again automatically the next time you reboot.

You can create your own hidden shares by appending a $ to the share name. A share so hidden will be just like any other share you create except that it will not show up in browser lists.

FIGURE 6.3
Share names ending with $ (visible in the Shared Resources window) do not appear on browse lists on other computers.

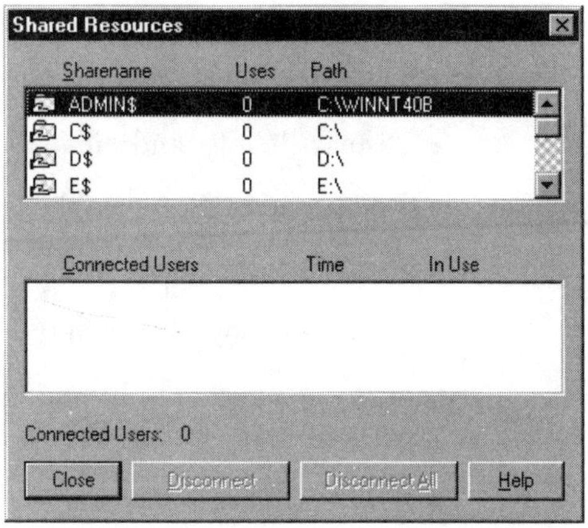

Shared Directory Permissions

Directories shared over a network are protected by permissions. Shared directory permissions are not the same as the NTFS permissions that will be present if the shared directory is on an NTFS partition. Shared directory permissions are in addition to NTFS permissions, and when the permissions differ for a user, the more restrictive permission prevails. Shared directory permissions, unlike NTFS permissions, do not depend on the partition type and are the same for DOS and NTFS partitions.

Shared directory permissions apply only to users accessing the share over the network. They do not apply to local users. When a share is created, the special global group Everyone is granted Full Control by default.

The four permissions for shared directories are

- No Access

- Read

- Change

- Full Control

These four access permissions levels are defined in more detail for NTFS partitions in the "NTFS Security" section in this chapter.

NO ACCESS This level of access allows a user to connect to the resource, but the user cannot access the directory or list the contents.

READ An individual with Read access can

- Display the files and subdirectories contained by the shared directory

- Run program files from the shared directory

- Access subdirectories of the shared directory

- Read and copy files from the shared directory

CHANGE In addition to having read capabilities, a user with Change permissions can

- Create subdirectories and files

- Delete files and subdirectories

- Read and write to files in the directory

- Change file attributes

FULL CONTROL In addition to having read and change capabilities, a user with Full Control of a share can

- Change file permissions
- Take ownership of files on an NTFS volume

Assigning Shared Directory Permissions

To assign permissions for Bob and June to the directory we created earlier in the chapter (Dir_1) and to remove the permissions of everyone else, perform the steps outlined in Exercise 6.3.

EXERCISE 6.3

Assigning Directory Permissions

1. Open the My Computer icon on your desktop.

2. Open the C: icon in the My Computer window.

3. Select the Dir_1 icon by clicking it once.

4. Select File ➤ Sharing.

5. Click the Permissions button in the Dir_1 Properties window.

6. Select Everyone ➤ Full Control permission in the window and click the Remove button to remove the default share permission that allows everyone access to the share.

7. Click the Add button.

8. Click the Show Users button in the Add Users and Groups window.

9. Find and select Bob and June. (Hold the control key to select more than one user.) Click the Add button. Bob and June should appear in the Add Names: space below the list of users and groups.

10. Click OK.

Note that Bob and June are assigned Read access by default when they are added. Changing the Type of access before clicking OK will affect each selected user.

11. Click OK in the Access through Share Permissions window and again in the Dir_1 Properties window.

Accessing the Shared Directory

To access shared resources external to your NT workstation computer, you can browse network shares with the Explorer or the Network Neighborhood icon on the desktop.

Mapping a Drive Letter to a Shared Directory

You can make a permanent connection by mapping a drive letter to the shared directory. Select the icon for the shared directory (clicking once on the icon) and then select File ➤ Map Network Drive in the window that contains the shared directory icon. A Map Network Drive window will appear. You can select

- The drive letter that the network drive will use

- Whether to reconnect to the shared network directory the next time you log on

- The username under which the connection will be made

After clicking OK, you may be asked for a password to go with the username.

Disconnecting a Drive Letter from a Shared Directory

You can disconnect from a shared directory in the following manner: Open the My Computer icon and select the drive letter to disconnect by clicking on it once. In the File menu of the My Computer window select Disconnect.

Exercise 6.4 shows how to connect to a network drive and how to connect using a different username than you are using in your current session.

Connecting from the Command Line

In addition to mapping drive letters to network resources through the Explorer, you can use the universal naming convention (UNC) path to access a locally shared resource.

UNC paths are constructed by taking the name of the server, followed by the share name, followed by the directory tree, and finally the file in which you are interested, as in the following example:

```
\\yoyo\matt\windows\tools\ping.exe
```

EXERCISE 6.4

Connecting to a Shared Resource

1. Double-click on Network Neighborhood.

2. Double-click on another computer on your network with a shared directory. You can select your own computer if you'd like.

3. Right-click on a share name.

4. Select Map Network Drive.

5. In the Drive list box, select the drive letter you would like to use.

6. Note the UNC name listed in the Path.

7. Enter the username to use for the remote computer connection. If you are logged in as administrator, use your regular username or vice versa.

8. Check the reconnect at logon checkbox if you would like this network mapping to persist through reboots.

9. The contents of the network drive will open in a new window.

In this example, `yoyo` is the name of the server, `matt` is the share name, `windows\tools\` is the directory path, and `PING.EXE` is the file we are specifying.

UNC names are useful for two purposes: when you must include a share name in a script or environment setting, and when accessing shared resources without assigning a drive letter. Exercise 6.5 shows how to use a UNC name to get a directory listing.

This is exercise exploits the hidden administrative share that is created for each drive on a computer with sharing turned on. You can use this feature to access files on other computers without sharing or mapping drives.

If you are participating on a TCP/IP intra/internet, you can also use the fully qualified domain name with utilities that understand Internet names. Fully qualified domain names are the same thing as Internet names, such as:

    www.microsoft.com

EXERCISE 6.5

Using Uniform Naming Convention Names

1. Log in as an administrator.

2. Select Start ➤ Programs ➤ Command Prompt

3. Type \\ followed by the name of your computer, followed by **\C$** and press Enter.

4. Note that you get a directory listing of your C: drive.

This name is looked up in a domain name server (DNS) and resolved to the TCP/IP address of the specified computer. You can use fully qualified domain names in Internet tools such as the Internet Explorer and Ping. You will use fully qualified domain names in many of the Internet-related exercises throughout the remainder of this book.

Stop Sharing

You can stop sharing a directory with other people on the network by selecting the Not Shared option in that directory's Properties window.

To stop sharing the directory Dir_1, follow the steps in Exercise 6.6.

EXERCISE 6.6

Stop Sharing a Directory

1. Open the My Computer icon on your desktop.

2. Open the C: icon in the My Computer window.

3. Select the Dir_1 icon.

4. Select File ➤ Sharing.

5. Select Not Shared in the Dir_1 Properties window.

6. Click OK.

NTFS Security

WHEN YOU USE THE NTFS under Windows NT, you have many security options that you do not have with a DOS FAT file system. This section explains how to set access permissions for files and directories in an NTFS partition.

NTFS Security Advantages

NTFS has several features that you can use to provide a more secure environment for network and local users. Some of the security features that NTFS provides in relation to files and directories are

- **Permissions**: NTFS keeps track of which users and groups can access certain files and directories, and it provides different levels of access for different users.

- **Auditing**: Windows NT can record NTFS security-related events to a log file for later review using the Event Viewer. The system administrator can set what will be audited and to what degree of detail.

- **Transaction logging**: NTFS is a log-based file system, which means that it records changes to files and directories as they happen and also records how to undo or redo the changes in case of a system failure. A log-based file system is much more robust than a FAT file system like DOS.

- **Ownership**: NTFS also tracks the ownership of files. A user who creates a file or directory is automatically the owner of it and has full rights to it. An administrator, or other individual with equivalent permissions, can take over ownership of a file or directory.

Using NTFS Permissions

In NTFS each file and each directory has permissions associated with it for users and groups. These permissions are in addition to the directory sharing permissions discussed in the previous section, and the most restrictive set of permissions prevails whenever a discrepancy exists. For instance, if a directory is shared with Full Access, but the user accessing that directory has only Read access under NTFS, then that user will only be able to read in that directory.

Viewing Permissions

You can view the permissions that a file or directory has by selecting File ➤ Properties and then selecting that file's icon, or by right-clicking the file's icon and selecting the Properties item in the pop-up menu. When the file's Properties window appears, select the Security tab and then click Permissions. The Directory (or File) Permissions window will appear, showing the users and groups that have access to the directory (or file). See Figure 6.4 for an example of a File Permissions window.

The Permissions window for a directory allows you to specify additional permissions for subdirectories and files stored in the directory. Figure 6.5 shows a Directory Permissions window.

A user who is not explicitly listed in the File Permissions or Directory Permissions window may still have access to the file or directory because the user may belong to a group that is listed in the window. In fact, you should never assign individual users access to files or directories. Instead, you should create a group to be given access permissions and then assign users to that group. This way you can change access rights for whole groups of users without having to modify each individual user account.

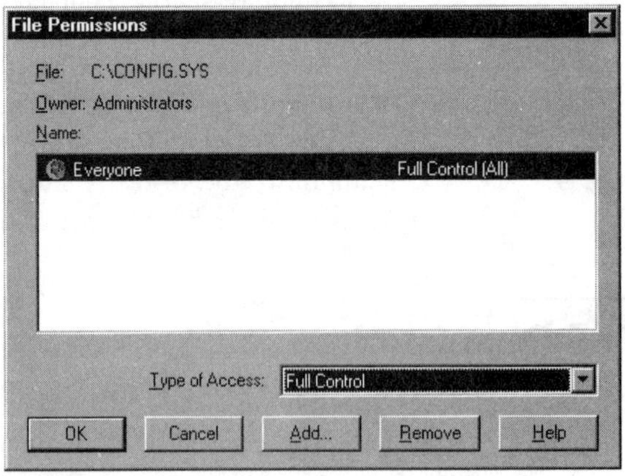

FIGURE 6.4
The File Permissions window shows the users and groups that have access to the file.

FIGURE 6.5
The Directory
Permissions window
shows the users and
groups that have access
to the directory.

Directory Permissions

Directory: C:\Dir_1

Owner: Administrators

☐ Replace Permissions on Subdirectories

☑ Replace Permissions on Existing Files

Name:

Administrators	Full Control (All) (All)
Bob	Read (RX) (RX)
CREATOR OWNER	Full Control (All) (All)
Everyone	Change (RWXD) (RWXD)
Server Operators	Change (RWXD) (RWXD)
SYSTEM	Full Control (All) (All)

Type of Access: Full Control

OK   Cancel   Add...   Remove   Help

Windows NT directories inherit access permissions in a different manner than network operating systems such as NetWare. The permissions in NetWare (called trustee *rights) for a parent directory apply to each child directory unless modified. If a trustee is changed on the parent directory, it also affects access rights to the subordinate directories. With NT each directory inherits a copy of the access control list of its parent when it is created, but the access control list of the new directory is independent of the access control list of the parent. If a change is made to the parent access control list, the change must be explicitly applied to all subdirectories (which is not the default action).*

NTFS defines access permissions that can perform a combination of operations under Windows NT, as shown in Tables 6.1 and 6.2. In Table 6.1 the X indicates that for that permission the operation can be performed, and the ? indicates that the availability of the operation for that file or directory depends on the special access settings of that particular directory.

Each of the access permissions performs a set of operations on the file or directory except for Special Access, which can allow or disallow any combination of tasks.

The File Permissions and Directory Permissions windows are similar, but not exactly the same. The permissions for users and groups listed in the Directory Permissions window (refer to Figure 6.5) have two sets of parentheses after the description—for example, Full Control (All) (All). The first of the two parentheses describes the special permissions for that directory and its subdirectories.

PERMISSION	R	X	W	D	P	O
No Access						
List (Directory only)	X	X				
Read	X	X				
Add (Directory only)		X	X			
Add & Read (Directory only)	X	X	X			
Change	X	X	X	X		
Full Control	X	X	X	X	X	X
Special Access	?	?	?	?	?	?

OPERATION	DESCRIPTION
R	Read or display data, attributes, owner, and permissions
X	Run or execute the file or files in the directory
W	Write to the file or directory or change the attributes
D	Delete the file or directory
P	Change permissions
O	Take ownership

Figure 6.6 shows you the permissions you can assign to users and groups for the directory. The Special Directory Access window controls the special permissions for the directory (see Figure 6.7).

The second set of parentheses describes the special permissions to be set on the current files in the directory and on any new files. The Special File Access window (see Figure 6.8) controls this setting.

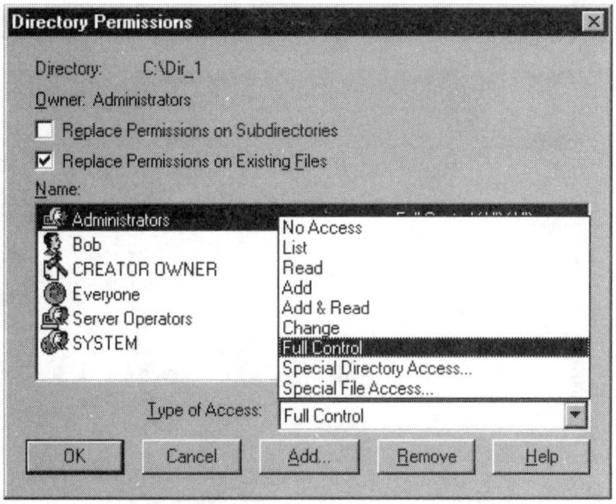

FIGURE 6.6
FIGURE 6.6
The Directory
Permissions window
shows the permissions
that users and groups
have for this directory.

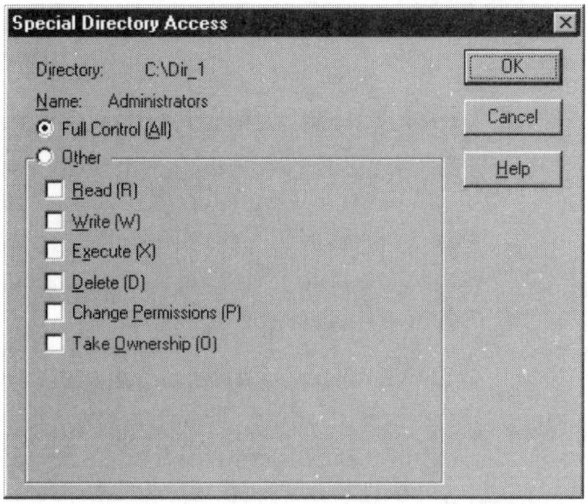

FIGURE 6.7
The Special Directory
Access window contains
special permissions
for directories.

Changing Permissions

In order to change permissions on a file or directory, you must meet one of the following three conditions:

- You have Full Control access to the file or directory.

- You have the Change Permission permission.

- You are the owner of the file or directory.

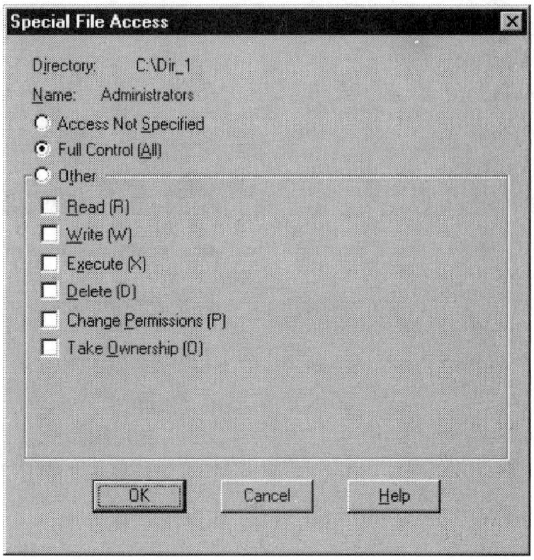

FIGURE 6.8
The Special File Access
window contains special
permissions for files.

FIGURE 6.8
The Special File Access
window contains special
permissions for files.

CHANGING PERMISSIONS GRAPHICALLY You set permissions for directories and files graphically from the Directory (or File) Permissions window.

The following exercise assumes that the C: drive on your Windows NT computer is an NTFS partition. Perform the steps outlined in Exercise 6.7 to remove the permission for Everyone to access the directory and to add the permission for June to access the directory.

CHANGING PERMISSIONS WITH CACLS CACLS.EXE is a command line utility that allows you to edit the access control list of files and directories. (We explain access control lists in detail in the next chapter.) You can use CACLS to change the permissions of files and directories on NTFS partitions.

CACLS has the following parameters:

```
CACLS filename [/T] [/E] [/C] [/G user:perm] [/R user
        […]] [/P user:perm […]] [/D user […]]
```

The parameters are described in Table 6.3.

The following exercise assumes that the C: drive on your Windows NT computer is an NTFS partition. To give Bob read access to the Dir_1 directory, perform the steps in Exercise 6.8.

You can set permissions on files using CACLS.EXE in exactly the same way you set permissions on directories.

EXERCISE 6.7

Changing Access Permissions for a Directory

1. Open the My Computer icon on your desktop.

2. Open the C: icon (or the icon for the NTFS partition in your computer) in the My Computer window.

3. Select the `Dir_1` icon by clicking it once.

4. Select File ➤ Properties.

5. Select the Security tab.

6. Click the Permissions button.

7. Select the Everyone group in the Directory Permissions window and then click Remove.

8. Click Add.

9. Click the Show Users button. Select June. The type of access defaults to Read for June.

10. Click Add and then click OK.

11. Click OK in the Directory Permissions window and then click OK in the Properties window.

EXERCISE 6.8

Using CACLS to Change Access Permissions

1. Select Start ➤ Programs ➤ Command Prompt.

2. Type **C:** and then press Enter.

3. Change directories to the root of the C: drive: Type **cd ** and then press Enter.

4. Give Bob read access to the `Dir_1` directory by typing **CACLS Dir_1 /e /p Bob:r** and then pressing Enter.

5. Review the access permissions to `Dir_1` by typing **CACLS Dir_1** and then pressing Enter.

	PARAMETER NAME	DESCRIPTION
TABLE 6.3 CACLS parameter table.	Filename	Display access control lists
	/T	Change the access control lists of specified files in the current directory and all subdirectories
	/E	Edit the access control list instead of replacing it
	/C	Continue changing the access control lists, ignoring errors
	/G	Grant specified user access rights (C Change, R Read, F Full Control)
	/R	Revoke specified user access rights (must use together with /E)
	/P	Replace specified user access rights (N None, C Change, R Read, F Full Control)
	/D	Deny specified user access

Default Permissions

The default permissions setting for a newly formatted NTFS partition is Full Control to the Everyone group. This setting makes an NTFS volume appear much like a FAT volume because any user can make any modification to any file. You may wish to restrict access to the NTFS permission by removing the Everyone group and assigning access permissions to a group with a more restricted set of users. You should, of course, make sure that the Administrators group has Full Control of the partition.

Copying and Moving Files and Directories with Permissions

When you copy a file (or a directory) from one directory on an NTFS partition to another directory, it inherits the permissions and owner of the receiving directory.

Moving a file or directory from one directory to another does not change it's permissions and owner.

The difference between copying and moving files is that when you copy a file, the original file still resides in its original location. You are essentially creating a new file in the new location that contains the same data as the old file. The new file (the copy) will have the receiving directory's default permissions for new files.

When a directory is copied, it receives the directory and default new-file permissions of its new parent directory. As new files are created within this new directory, they receive the new-file permissions of this directory.

When Windows NT moves a file or directory, it merely changes pointers in the directory structure on the NTFS partition instead of copying it. Even though the file or directory disappears from the old location and appears in the new location, it does not physically move on the hard disk. The permissions and ownership of the file or directory remain the same. This technique applies only to moving directories within the same NTFS volume.

When some programs perform a move command, they actually copy the file or directory to the new location and then delete it from the old location. In this case the moved object obtains new permissions from the receiving directory, just as it would in a regular copy operation. This process is sometimes called the container effect.

Permissions for Users and Groups

Windows NT determines whether or not a user can access a resource by combining all of the access permissions of the user and of the groups to which the user belongs.

If any one of the permissions is No Access for that resource, then access to that resource is denied. If the requested access is not specifically permitted by one of the user's permissions, then the user cannot perform that action.

For example, suppose that Bob is a member of the both Marketing group and the Management group. Marketing is allowed Change access to the Sales directory. Management is allowed Read access to the Sales directory as well as Full Control to the Projections directory. Management is given Full Access to the Party_Plans directory, but Bob has No Access to the Party_Plans directory. Table 6.4 shows the combined access permissions that result for Bob from this combination of permissions.

			MANAGE-	
	BOB	**MARKETING**	**MENT**	**RESULT**
Sales		Change	Read	Change
Projections			Full Access	Full Access
Party_Plans	No_Access		Full Access	No Access

TABLE 6.4
Combined Access
Permissions.

When a user or program requests permissions to access a resource, either all of the permissions requested are granted or none of them are. For example, if a user requests Read and Write access to a directory but the user has only Read access, no access will be granted. The user must request access only to the things for which he or she has permission.

Ownership

By default, the creator of a file or directory has ownership of that file or directory. On an NTFS partition, Windows NT keeps track of the owners of files and directories; the owner has full control of the file or directory and can change any of its permissions.

The Owner dialog box (see Figure 6.9) shows the current owner of the file or directory and allows you to take ownership of it if you have the permissions to do so. An administrator always has the permission to take ownership of a file or directory, even when the owner has restricted those rights.

No user can give ownership of a file or directory to another user. You can only become the owner by taking ownership. For users other than the administrator, however, the owner must allow the user the permission to take ownership of the file or directory.

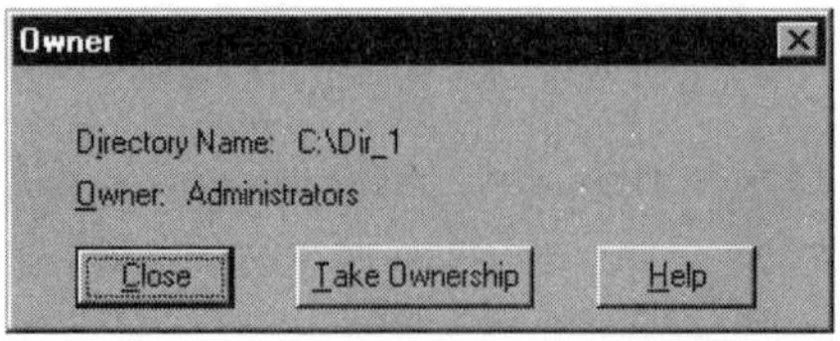

FIGURE 6.9
The Owner dialog box
allows you to take
ownership of a file or
directory if you have
permission.

Owner	✕
Directory Name: C:\Dir_1	
Owner: Administrators	
Close Take Ownership Help	

Auditing

NTFS supports the auditing of files and directories, which allows you to track the successful or unsuccessful attempts to access selected resources on your computer. The Directory Auditing and File Auditing windows allow you to specify which access attempts will be written to the Security log of the Event Viewer (see Figure 6.10).

Auditing must be enabled via the User Manager in order for auditing to be performed. Follow the steps in Exercise 6.9 to enable file and directory auditing.

To monitor every successful or unsuccessful attempt to take ownership of the Dir_1 directory by Everyone, perform the steps in Exercise 6.10 (which assumes that your C: drive is an NTFS partition).

FIGURE 6.10
The Directory Auditing window shows which accesses will be reported to the Security log.

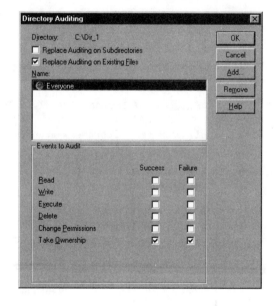

NT Backup

THE FIRST SECTION OF THIS CHAPTER showed you how to protect your data when you share it over the network. You were then introduced to the more sophisticated security measures that NTFS provides. This section will show you how to protect your data from accidental deletion and from physical failure of the computer equipment.

EXERCISE 6.9

Enabling File and Directory Auditing

1. Click Start and then select Programs ➤ Administrative Tools (common) ➤ User Manager.

2. Select Policies ➤ Audit.

3. Select Audit These Events.

4. Check the File and Object Access checkbox for Success. Also check the File and Object Access checkbox for Failure. This setting enables you to audit both successful and failed attempts to access objects.

5. Click OK.

EXERCISE 6.10

Auditing Attempts to Take Ownership

1. Open the My Computer icon on your desktop.

2. Open the C: icon in the My Computer window.

3. Select the Dir_1 icon.

4. Select File ➤ Properties.

5. Click the Security tab in the Dir_1 Properties window.

6. Click Auditing in the Dir_1 Properties window.

7. Click Add in the Directory Auditing window.

8. Select Everyone from the Names list in the Add Users and Groups window and click on the Add button.

9. Click OK.

10. Check the Success and Failure checkboxes for Take Ownership events.

11. Click OK and then close the Dir_1 Properties window.

Your final resort for protection from data loss is the backup process. Windows NT provides a backup utility that can help you make backup copies of your NT Workstation's data so that even the total destruction of your computer will not necessarily destroy all of your data.

A secure backup policy can reduce, but not eliminate, the risk of losing data. The data you have on backup tape will only be as recent as the last time you initiated the backup process.

You can use the Windows NT backup utility to back up files on FAT or NTFS partitions. Each of these file systems has an archive bit in the directory entries that can be asserted to indicate that the utility should back up the file.

Backup Sets, Family Sets, and the Catalog

A backup set is the group of files, directories, and drives stored together on a backup tape. When the volume of data to be stored on backup tape is greater than the capacity of a single tape, the backup sets can span multiple tapes; the set of tapes that contains the backup sets is called a *family set*. The backup sets on the tape are described in a catalog that is also stored on the tape. The catalog for a family set is stored on the last tape of the set.

Backup Permissions

You can use the backup tool to back up only the drives that you have permission to access. If you do not have rights to a file or directory, you may still be able to back it up if you are a member of the Backup Operators group. This membership allows you to bypass the normal file permissions while backing up and restoring files and directories.

Backup Methods

You can use the Windows NT backup utility to back up files and directories in one of five ways:

- **Normal** backs up and marks the files as having been backed up.

- **Copy** backs up and does not mark the files as having been backed up.

- **Incremental Backup** backs up the files if they have changed since the last backup. Marks those files as having been backed up.

- **Daily Copy** backs up the files that have changed that day. Does not mark those files as having been backed up.

- **Differential Copy** backs up the files if they have changed since the last backup. Does not mark those files as having been backed up.

The type of backup you perform depends on the circumstance of the backup. You should do a normal or copy backup often, because these options are the only ones that will copy every file, regardless of whether it has been backed up previously or not. In order to retrieve all of the backed up information from backup tapes, you will need to restore the data on the most recent normal or copy backup and all subsequent incremental, daily copy, or differential backups. Incremental, daily copy, and differential backups, however, take less time and require less storage space. The best backup policy is to interleave each normal backup (performed at night or on the weekend) with several incremental or daily copy backups.

Backup Options

The backup you perform can have one of five tape options:

- **Append** appends the new backup set after the last backup set on the tape.

- **Replace** replaces any backup sets on the tape with a new backup set.

- **Restrict Access to Owner or Administrator** allows only the administrator or the owner of the tape or members of the backup operators group to retrieve data from the tape.

- **Verify after Backup** confirms that the files were backed up accurately by comparing the data on the tape with the files on disk.

- **Backup Registry** also backs up the Windows NT Registry, which holds important system data.

You can also configure which backup operations the backup utility will write to a log file. The log file can report the following details:

- **Summary Only** logs only summary information, such as when a tape was loaded, a backup was started, or a file failed to open for backup.

- **Copy Full Detail** logs all details of the backup operation, including the names of the files and directories backed up to tape.

- **Don't Log** requests that no log be kept of the backup actions.

Restore Options

When you need to restore data from backup tape, you have the option of restoring the data to its original location or to another location on the same computer or on another computer. You can restore the data to another type of file system as well. Files backed up from an NTFS partition, for instance, can be restored to a FAT partition, and vice versa.

However, file permissions and other NTFS specific information may be lost if you restore a file from an NTFS partition to a FAT volume.

The Windows NT backup utility offers the following options for restoring files:

- **Verify after Restore** verifies that the data on disk after a tape restore is the same as the data on the tape and logs any exceptions.

- **Restore File Permissions** restores access control list information along with the file. If this option is not selected, then the restored file will receive default permissions from the directory to which it is restored.

- **Restore Local Registry** restores the Windows NT Registry, which holds important system data. You will have to restart the computer after restoring the Registry in order to have the changes take effect.

Scheduled Tape Backups

You cannot schedule a tape backup to happen at a certain time through the graphical interface of the Windows NT backup utility, but you can use the command line interface of Windows NT with the AT command to automate tape backups. All of the tape backup utility functions are available from the command line and you can write batch files that call the backup utility.

You can use automated tape backup to perform backup operations at times when the data on the network is relatively static and the backup won't interfere with the work of network. Many networks back up their data between midnight and 2 A.M. every night.

You can also use third-party tape backup utilities if you need more sophisticated backup automation features than those available in the Windows NT backup utility.

Chapter Summary

ANY WINDOWS NT USER who has Administrator or Power User permissions can create shared directories that are visible over the network when the Server service is running. The user must have at least List permissions to the directory to be shared.

You can assign permissions to shared directories that supplement the regular permissions of the directory.

You can share directories on any file system that NT supports, for example, FAT or NTFS.

NT Workstation creates several default administrative shares, as well as inter-process and printing shares, that are not normally visible to network users. These shares correspond to the root of each hard drive and the Windows NT directory, and their names end with a $. (The $ hides the shares from other users on the network.) You can also create shares that end with a $.

NTFS supports more security options than the FAT file system does. With NTFS you can set security on individual files and directories, as well as perform auditing on accesses and track ownership of files and directories.

The User and Group permissions combine to provide a flexible architecture for implementing security on an NTFS partition. A No Access permission always takes precedence over any other access permission, and the administrator always has access to an NTFS file or directory, regardless of permissions, and can always take ownership.

Moved files retain their ownership and permissions, whereas files that are copied obtain new permissions that depend on the directory to which they are copied and the user doing the copying.

The NT backup utility gives you an additional level of protection against data loss and interacts with the other permissions and ownership settings of an NTFS permission. You can backup any file system that NT recognizes (FAT or NTFS) and restore any partition, although permission and ownership information may be lost if the partition does not support the NTFS features.

Exercise Questions

1. Anyone can create a shared directory.

   A. True

   B. False

2. The user attempting to view the shared directory must have at least List permissions for that directory if it is on an NTFS partition.

   A. True

   B. False

3. You can only share directories that are on NTFS partitions.

   A. True

   B. False

4. The share name must be the same as the directory name.

   A. True

   B. False

5. You can use the `CACLS.EXE` program to change the access control list of an administrative share that was created automatically by the system.

   A. True

   B. False

6. When shared directory permissions and NTFS permissions differ, the shared directory permissions take precedence.

   A. True

   B. False

7. Shared directory permissions do not depend on the partition type and are the same for DOS FAT and NTFS partitions.

   A. True

   B. False

8. A user with No Access to a shared directory cannot connect to a shared directory.

   A. True

   B. False

9. A user with Read access to a directory can execute files in that directory.

   A. True

   B. False

10. A user with change access can delete files in a directory.

    A. True

    B. False

11. NTFS gives you many security options that you do not have with a DOS FAT file system.

    A. True

    B. False

12. An Administrator always has the permission to take ownership of a file or directory.

    A. True

    B. False

13. You can give ownership of a file or directory to another user only if you have the Owner Transfer permission.

    A. True

    B. False

14. You can use the Windows NT backup utility to back up files on DOS FAT or NTFS partitions.

    A. True

    B. False

15. You must restore to the same type of partition (DOS FAT or NTFS) from which you backed up the data.

    A. True

    B. False

16. Using the backup tool, you can back up only drives that you have permission to access.

   A. True

   B. False

17. Incremental, daily copy, and differential backups take more time and require more storage space than do normal and copy backups.

   A. True

   B. False

18. When you restore data from backup tape, you must restore the data to its original location.

   A. True

   B. False

19. You cannot schedule a tape backup to happen at a certain time through the graphical interface of the Windows NT backup utility.

   A. True

   B. False

20. All of the tape backup utility functions are available from the command line.

   A. True

   B. False

21. In a network environment, you will often need to share information that resides on your Windows NT Workstation. You do this by creating _____ directories.

22. The default groups that permit creating shares are _____, _____ _____, and _____ _____.

23. Windows NT Workstation has a limit of _____ simultaneous users accessing a shared directory.

24. _____ is a special administrative share that always points to the Windows NT directory.

25. You can make a permanent connection by mapping a _____ letter to the shared directory.

26. _____ . EXE is a command line utility that allows you to edit the access control lists of files and directories.

27. ACL stands for _____ _____ _____.

28. By default, the creator of a file or directory has _____ of that file or directory.

29. NTFS supports the _____ of files and directories, which allows you to track the successful or unsuccessful attempts to access selected resources on your computer.

30. With auditing you can specify which access attempts will be written to the _____ log of the Event Viewer.

31. Auditing must be enabled via the _____ Manager in order for auditing to be performed.

32. Each file system supports an _____ bit that can be asserted to indicate that the utility should back up the file.

33. A _____ _____ is the group of files, directories, and drives stored together on a backup tape.

34. The set of tapes that contain backup sets spanning multiple tapes is called a _____ _____.

35. The _____ for a family set is stored on the last tape of the set.

36. If you do not have rights to a file or directory, you may still be able to back them up if you belong to the _____ _____ group.

37. The default shares have the following at the end of the share name:

A. Default Administrative Share

B. (hidden)

C. $

D. Nothing

38. Which of the following is not a permission for shared directories?

A. No Access

B. Read

C. Full Control

D. Change Ownership

39. Match the NTFS feature with its description:

A. Auditing	**1.** Keeps track of which users and groups can access certain files and directories.
B. Permissions	**2.** Records security-related events to a log file.
C. Ownership	**3.** Records changes to files and directories as they happen and also records how to undo or redo the changes in case of a system failure.
D. Transaction logging	**4.** Tracks the individual who has full rights to a file or directory regardless of permissions.

40. Which of the following access permissions apply only to directories?

A. No Access

B. List

C. Read

D. Add

E. Add & Read

F. Change

G. Full Control

H. Special Access

41. Match the backup method with its description:

A. Normal	**1.** Backs up the files if they have changed since the last backup. Does not mark those files as having been marked up.
B. Copy	**2.** Backs up the files that have changed that day. Does not mark those files as having been backed up.
C. Incremental	**3.** Backs up the files if they have changed since the last backup. Marks those files as having been backed up.
D. Daily copy	**4.** Backs up and does not mark the files as having been backed up.
E. Differential copy	**5.** Backs up and marks the files as having been backed up.

Creating
Windows NT
Security Structures

SECURITY IS A PERVASIVE CONCERN, and not only in the realm of computers. The ignition lock on your car, the dead bolt on your door, the personal identification number on your automatic teller machine card, and the police officers who patrol your neighborhood are all examples of security measures in your everyday life. These measures attempt to prevent others from gaining access to you and your possessions without your permission. Although none of these measures makes intrusion impossible, they work because they make access difficult.

Accounting enhances security. For example, keeping a building secure is easier if you know who has entered and when. A full record of all financial transactions in a business helps keep its assets secure from misappropriation and mismanagement by ensuring that all of the money is accounted for. If a financial or physical malfeasance occurs, the records can help identify the culprit.

Security is more than control of a system to prevent theft. It is control to prevent loss of any nature. Accidental loss, especially in information systems, is quite common. Users sometimes delete files to make space without really knowing the contents or importance of the files they deleted. Computers can crash, sometimes losing data in the process. Files can be overwritten with a different document of the same name.

The security measures implemented in Windows NT are designed to prevent both accidental and intentional loss. Windows NT requires a logon, so that no access to information is given without accountability.

Windows NT also implements resource-level security whereby individual information resources are secured by type and access to the resource is controlled by lists of trusted users called *access control lists* (ACLs). These measures are quite effective in preventing loss, and they form an important part of the total networking process.

NT Security Model

W INDOWS NT ALLOWS ACCESS to resources based upon user identity or group membership, rather than requiring a password for each resource requested. This model is both less intrusive to the user and more deeply embedded in the system than requiring passwords for each access to a resource that requires security. In fact, Windows NT can control access to every type of Windows NT resource, not simply those chosen when the operating system was created.

Windows NT security is based around trusted access that is confirmed by passwords during the logon process. Once the user has logged on, Windows NT compares the user's identity to access permissions stored in objects to determine whether the user has the authority to access the object as requested.

Logon Authentication

The Ctrl+Alt+Del logon dialog box is the gatekeeper of a Windows NT computer and is presented when no user is logged on to a Windows NT workstation or server. This dialog box appears when the computer is booted and when a user has logged out but left the machine running.

Specific security features of the mandatory logon include

- **Mandatory logon:** Logon is mandatory for gaining access to the computer. Although you can provide a username and password automatically through the Registry, the logon process still occurs.

- **Restricted User mode:** You cannot run User mode programs until a valid logon occurs. This requirement prevents the use of "Trojan horse" programs that simulate the look and feel of the logon dialog box to steal user account names and passwords.

- **Physical logon:** Use of Ctrl+Alt+Del generates a hardware interrupt that signals the computer that the username and password are coming from a keyboard physically attached to the computer, not from some other source. Intercepting this key sequence is difficult for other programs, and it also prevents users from inadvertently rebooting Windows NT.

- **User preferences:** The logon procedure identifies you to Windows NT so it can use your user preference settings. Windows NT uses the user account information to specify preferences for desktops, network connections, and other user-specific options. Each user can have his or her own preferences restored when they log on.

The logon process creates an access token that identifies the user and his or her various security clearances to the system. We discuss access tokens in detail later in this chapter.

Windows NT Objects

Access is controlled to individual resources on the computer called *objects* not to the computer as a whole. Objects consist of data and the services that manipulate that data.

The data contained in an object are called *attributes*. Attributes describe such information as the filename, the data contained in a file, access permissions, and any other properties of the object.

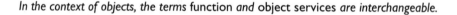

In the context of objects, the terms function *and* object services *are interchangeable.*

The actions that an object performs are called *services*. Some examples of object services are Open, Edit, Delete, or Close.

Permission is granted by object and service. For instance, a file contains information to which a user may have access (in other words, the user has Open access), but that user may not have access to the Save service of that object.

Windows NT represents all resources as objects, and all objects have an access control list, so you can set access permissions for any NT resource based upon a user's account or group membership. A typical object is shown in Figure 7.1.

In addition to attributes and services, objects also have types. Some examples of types include

- Directories

- Symbolic links

- Printers

- Processes

- Network shares

- Ports

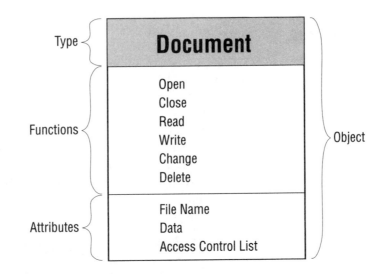

FIGURE 7.1
A document is a
Windows NT object.

- Devices

- Windows

- Files

- Threads

Every object also has an access control list that Windows NT uses to determine whether or not a certain user has the authority to access that object.

Access Control

ACCESS CONTROL IN WINDOWS NT is managed through a set of access tokens that are assigned when a user logs on. The tokens are compared to access lists containing access control entries. This process is somewhat like having the combination to a lock. When you log on, Windows NT assigns you a combination based upon the permissions assigned to you by the workstation administrator. Every time you access a resource, Windows NT compares your combination (an access token) against the list of valid combinations (the access control list) for that object. If your token matches an entry, access is granted. Otherwise, access to the resource is denied.

Access Tokens

When a user logs on, Windows NT assigns an access token that remains valid until the user logs off. This token is simply a representation of the user's account that Windows NT compares against entries in an object's access control list to determine if the user is permitted to perform the requested service.

After entering your user ID and password, Windows NT creates an access token that represents your username and the groups to which you belong. This token identifies you to all system objects during your session on the computer.

Access tokens are objects just like any other Windows NT object, so they contain attributes and services that describe them to the system and provide their services. Important attributes in the access token include

- **Security ID** representing the logged-on user

- **Group IDs** representing the logged on user's group memberships

- **Permissions** allowed for the user

Security ID

Windows NT creates unique security identifiers for each user and group in the user accounts database. Because these security IDs are unique, if an account or group is deleted, any new account or group created will not have the same permissions as its similarly named predecessor.

Group ID

Group IDs are like Security IDs in that they allow certain permissions. Unlike Security IDs, however, they do not represent a certain user. Rather, Group ID objects contain permissions assigned to groups of users based upon some common criteria, such as department or work function. When a user becomes a member of a group, the Group ID for that group is attached to the user's access token.

When the administrator grants or denies access to an object based on a group, that group's Group ID is added to the object's access control list along with the specific permission. Since the access token for a user contains the user's Security ID and all of the user's Group IDs, the access control list and the access token will contain a matching ID, telling Windows NT which permissions to allow. See the next section for more detailed coverage of access control lists and access control entries.

More than one ID match may occur if a user is a member of more than one group with permissions to the object. Windows NT always allows the lowest level of access specifically assigned when more than one matching permission exists.

Permissions

Permissions are the specific access control entries contained in an object's access control list. An access control entry contains either a security ID or a Group ID and the right to which that ID is assigned, such as Read access, Write access, or Full access. Access control entries are covered in the next section.

Attaching Access Tokens to Processes

When you turn on your Windows NT workstation, the Win32 subsystem starts the WinLogon process (a process is software that is currently running), which generates the logon dialog box. When a username and password are entered into the dialog box, the WinLogon process passes that information to the security accounts manager.

The security accounts manager queries the security accounts database to check if the username represents a valid user. If it does and the password for that user is correct, the security accounts manager generates an access token representing the user and the user's group memberships and passes it back to the WinLogon process.

Other authentication packages may be implemented as Dynamic Link Libraries so that third-party vendors may integrate their own custom security measures, such as those relating to a foreign network operating system, into Windows NT.

The WinLogon process then tells the Win32 subsystem to create a new process (usually the Explorer) for the user with the security token attached to the process.

All processes have access tokens, even those started by the system or by automatic software.

When a process attempts to access an object, the process's access token is checked against the object's access control list. If the access control list allows the specific access requested, the new process is started and the access token from the calling process is attached to it for the duration of its execution.

Since no process can be started without an access token and since all processes receive the access token of the process that initiated them, you cannot bypass the security subsystem by starting a process that has a higher security clearance than the process that called it.

Access Control Lists

Each object has an access control list attribute that describes which user or group accounts have what type of access to the object. A user must have an entry in the access control list that allows access to an object's service, or Windows NT will not allow that user to perform that service upon that object.

For instance, if a user attempts to open a file, the user must have Open access to that file or be a member of a group that has Open access to that file. Otherwise, NT will not allow the user to open the file. NT does not display a dialog box or warning to indicate that access is denied; rather, nothing happens when the user double-clicks the object.

The access control list for an object contains the user and group accounts that have access and permissions to the object. Instead of containing user or group names, the access control list maintains entries containing security identifiers (discussed in the following section).

When a user requests access to an object, Windows NT checks the security identifier against the permissions allowed by the access control list to determine whether the user is allowed to complete the request.

Access Control Entries

Each access control entry in an object's access control list describes a specific permission for a specific service for a user or a group (see Figure 7.2).

An access control entry is added to the access control list for each user or group that is specifically granted or denied access to an object. If an object does not have an access control entry for a specific user or group, the default access for the object service is granted.

Checking Permissions

When you request access to an object (when you invoke a service of an object), Windows NT compares the security identifiers in the access token of the calling process to each entry in the access control list to see if the access is explicitly

FIGURE 7.2
Access control entries in
an access control list.

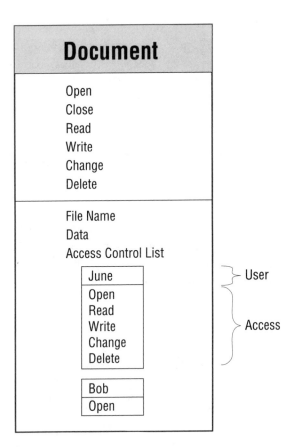

denied to you or to any group to which you belong. It then checks to see if the requested access is specifically permitted. It repeats these steps until a deny is encountered or until it has collected all the necessary permissions to grant the requested access. If permission for each requested access is not specifically granted by the access control list, access is denied.

Windows NT optimizes access control by performing all security access checking when the object is first opened. All allowable requested accesses are copied into the object's process table when the object is opened. Any subsequent accesses to the object will succeed if the access appears in the process table and will fail if it does not.

Owing to this optimization, Windows NT has very little computer overhead for security once an object is started. However, any change to a user's or group's permissions will not take effect for any process currently running until that process is shut down and restarted.

Also note that only those permissions requested when the object is opened are copied to the object's process table. Consequently, a file opened only for Read/Write access, for example, cannot be deleted until it is closed and then reopened with a delete request.

Customizing the Logon Process

YOU MAY NEED TO CHANGE the default behavior of the WinLogon process to meet your security requirements. Your security installation may require a warning to potential intruders, or you may wish to load a shell other than the Explorer when a user logs on. All Windows logon options are controlled by editing the WinLogon Registry Key in the following hierarchy:

```
\HKEY_LOCAL_MACHINE\SOFTWARE\Microsoft\
Windows NT\CurrentVersion\Winlogon
```

We will refer to this registry key as the WinLogon Registry Key from now on. Launching the Registry Editor and opening the WinLogon Registry Key is shown in Exercise 7.1. This method is one of many ways to launch a program in Windows NT, but for the Registry Editor it is perhaps the easiest. For the remaining exercises in this section, we will presume you already have the Registry Editor running and open to the WinLogon Registry Key prior to the first step. Note that you do not have to specifically save the changes you make in the Registry Editor as in previous versions of Windows NT. Closing the Registry Editor automatically saves any changes you made.

In the following sections, we will show you how to modify entries in the WinLogon Registry Key to change the default behavior of Windows NT to match your security requirements. We will be discussing the following options:

- Disabling the default username

- Adding a logon security warning

- Changing the default shell

- Enabling or disabling the WinLogon Shutdown button

- Enabling automated logon

EXERCISE 7.1

Opening the WinLogon Registry Key

1. Click the Start button.

2. Select Run.

3. Type **regedit** in the Open input box.

4. Click OK.

5. Double-click the HKEY_LOCAL_MACHINE key (or single-click the + to the left of the folder icon for the key).

6. Double-click the SOFTWARE key in the above hierarchy.

7. Double-click the Microsoft key in the above hierarchy.

8. Double-click the Windows NT key in the above hierarchy.

9. Double-click the Current Version key in the above hierarchy.

10. Click the WinLogon key in the above hierarchy.

Although the WinLogon Registry can control other facets of the WinLogon process, these functions are the functions promulgated by Microsoft. The Registry Editor is open and displaying the WinLogon Registry Key in Figure 7.3.

You should refrain from changing other entries in the Registry as they may cause your workstation to behave unpredictably.

Disabling the Default Username

The WinLogon process defaults to showing the username of the person who logged on last. This information would be valuable to an intruder who would then need only to guess the password to gain access. Exercise 7.2 explains how to disable the default username.

To restore the default behavior of the WinLogon process, select the DontDisplayLastUserName value and press the delete key, or change the value to 0.

FIGURE 7.3
The WinLogon
Registry Key.

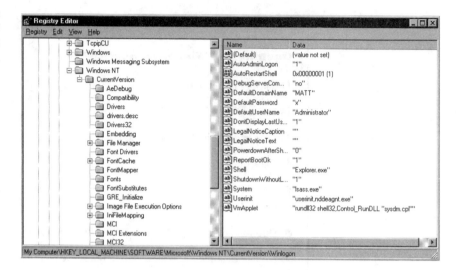

FIGURE 7.3
The WinLogon
Registry Key.

EXERCISE 7.2

Disabling the Default Username

1. Select the Edit menu in the Registry Editor with the WinLogon key open.

2. Move to the New option.

3. Select String value from the pop-up menu.

4. Type **DontDisplayLastUserName** in the Name field of the entry and press Enter.

5. Double-click the name you just added.

6. Type **1** in the entry field of the Edit String dialog box.

7. Click OK.

8. Close the Registry Editor.

9. Log out and log on again to check the results. Note that the username field in the logon dialog box is now blank.

Adding a Logon Security Warning

Many security installations (especially government facilities) require a warning of penalties for unauthorized use of a system to be displayed during or immediately prior to the logon process.

Setting the Values LegalNoticeCaption and LegalNoticeText of the WinLogon Registry Key to any value will cause Windows NT to display a warning dialog box containing the text of LegalNoticeText and the caption set by LegalNoticeCaption as a dialog box with an OK button after you press Ctrl+Alt+Del, but before the username and password dialog box is displayed. The only way to avoid this display is to remove these entries from the Registry. Exercise 7.3 shows how to change the WinLogon security warning.

To eliminate the warning box, double-click each value and clear the contents of their respective Edit String dialog boxes.

EXERCISE 7.3

Changing the WinLogon Security Notice

1. Follow the steps at the beginning of this section to open the WinLogon Registry Key.

2. Double-click the value named LegalNoticeCaption.

3. Type **Unauthorized Access Warning!** in the Entry field of the Edit String dialog box.

4. Click OK.

5. Double-click the value named LegalNoticeText.

6. Type **Unauthorized access to this system constitutes a felony punishable by a maximum fine of $10,000 dollars and six years in prison.** in the entry field of the Edit String dialog box.

7. Click OK.

8. Close the Registry Editor.

9. Log out and log on again to check the results. Note that a warning box titled Unauthorized Access Warning! with the LegalNoticeText now appears, and the user must respond.

Changing the Default Shell

To change the application launched by the WinLogon process from the Explorer to a custom application, you can edit the shell value of the WinLogon entry. Simply change the value *Shell* from EXPLORER.EXE to the name of the application you would like to launch at startup.

You might need to change the default shell if you have security procedures or emergency restoration procedures that are written to the Program Manager interface provided in Windows NT prior to version 4.0. Setting the default shell to the Program Manager will allow you time to change your procedures without waiting to implement Windows NT 4.0. You may also have users who prefer the simpler paradigm of the Program Manager to the Explorer interface.

You will not have access to normal Explorer services like My Computer, the Start menu, or the Task Bar if you change the shell value. If you do not want to deny access to the Explorer, put a shortcut to the application you want to start in the Startup folder.

You can always start other processes (allowed by your access privileges) by pressing Ctrl+Alt+Del, selecting Task Manager, and using the File ➤ New Task option.

If you prefer the Program Manager paradigm to the desktop objects paradigm, simply set the shell entry of the WinLogon key to PROGMAN.EXE. Windows NT will then launch the familiar Program Manager interface rather than Explorer. Exercise 7.4 shows you how to change the default shell.

WinLogon Shutdown

Windows NT 4.0 has a Shutdown button on the WinLogon dialog box that is enabled by default in Windows NT Workstation 4.0 and disabled by default in Windows NT Server 4.0. You can change the state of this button to enabled or disabled by default, regardless of which version of the operating system you are running, by changing the following value in the WinLogon Registry Key:

```
ShutdownWithoutLogon
```

Changing this value to **1** enables the button, and **0** disables the button.

EXERCISE 7.4

Changing the Default Shell

1. Follow the steps at the beginning of this section to open the WinLogon Registry Key.

2. Double-click the value named Shell.

3. Type **progman.exe** in the entry field of the Edit String dialog box.

4. Click OK.

5. Close the Registry Editor.

6. Log out and log on again to check the results. Note that the familiar Program Manager shell comes up after logging on. Windows NT does not create Program Manager groups or icons by default, so you will have to create them yourself.

To restore Explorer as the default shell:

1. Select the File menu in the Program Manager.

2. Select Run.

3. Type **regedit** in the Run Program dialog box.

4. Click OK.

5. Follow the procedures at the beginning of this chapter to select the WinLogon Registry Key.

6. Double-click the shell value.

7. Type **explorer.exe** in the Edit String dialog box.

8. Click OK.

9. Close the Registry Editor.

10. Select the File Menu in the Program Manager.

11. Select the Logoff option.

12. Click OK.

Enabling the Shutdown button on a Windows NT Server will allow anyone with physical access to the computer to shut it down without supplying a password. Also note that Windows NT does not require a password to turn off the computer.

Some computers have BIOS options that allow the computer to be physically turned off automatically at the end of the shutdown process. These computers will have an additional button: Shutdown and Power Off.

Notebook computers that have advanced power management and a Power Save mode called sleep will have an additional shutdown option, Sleep, that suspends processing and powers off all hardware except RAM. The computer can be awakened instantly and will resume processing at the point it was put to sleep without requiring a reboot. Exercise 7.5 walks you through the steps for enabling the WinLogon Shutdown button.

EXERCISE 7.5

Enabling the WinLogon Shutdown Button

1. Follow the steps at the beginning of this section to open the WinLogon Registry Key.

2. Double-click the value named ShutdownWithoutLogon.

3. Type **0** in the entry field of the Edit String dialog box.

4. Click OK.

5. Close the Registry Editor.

6. Log out and log on again to check the results. Note that the Shutdown button on the logon dialog box is disabled and grayed-out.

7. To re-enable the button, repeat this exercise and type **1** in step 3.

Automated Logon

For some users, security is not a concern. Either their computers are physically secure and accessible only to trusted individuals or the information stored on the computer or stored on the network does not have to be secured from unauthorized access. You can make the mandatory logon process more convenient for these users.

Although bypassing the Windows NT logon process is not possible, you can automate it by supplying a username and password through the Registry. Windows will then bypass the WinLogon dialog box and proceed directly to the shell application specified in the WinLogon Registry Key.

Automating the Windows NT logon process will allow anyone to access your computer without accountability. Use this feature with extreme caution and only in situations where absolute physical security exists or security precaution is not necessary.

You should never automatically bypass the Administrator account because this account has complete access to the computer. This account can modify the Registry Key to change the administrative password, thereby denying access to authorized users. Setting up a workstation to bypass the logon process restricts the workstation to that user account. This method restricts that workstation from modifying sensitive information such as the administrative password.

To enable the logon dialog box for a single session—to allow a user other than the default user to log on or to correct your password in the Registry—hold down the Shift key while logging off or rebooting.

The process for enabling automatic logon is shown in Exercise 7.6.

EXERCISE 7.6

Enabling Automatic Logon

1. Follow the steps at the beginning of this section to open the WinLogon Registry Key.

2. Double-click the value named DefaultDomainName.

3. Type the name of your domain in the entry field of the Edit String dialog box. If you are not sure what your default domain name is, log out and check the value shown in the Domain field of the Logon dialog box.

4. Click OK.

5. Double-click the value named DefaultUserName.

6. Type your username in the entry field of the Edit String dialog box.

7. Click OK.

EXERCISE 7.6 (CONTINUED)

8. Select the Edit menu.

9. Select New.

10. Select the String Value option in the pop-up menu.

11. Type **DefaultPassword** as the name of the value.

12. Double-click the DefaultPassword value.

13. Type your password into the Edit String dialog box.

14. Click OK.

15. Select the Edit menu.

16. Select New.

17. Select the String Value option in the pop-up menu.

18. Type **AutoAdminLogon** as the name of the value.

19. Double-click the AutoAdminLogon value.

20. Type 1 into the Edit String dialog box.

21. Click OK.

22. Close the Registry Editor.

23. Log out and log on again to check the results. Note that the logon security warning, if enabled, will still display before automatic logon occurs, but that the user specified is logged on without the system stopping to ask for the username or password.

To disable automatic logon, set **AutoAdminLogon** to **0**, or delete the value. You should also delete or clear the **DefaultPassword** value at the same time.

Automatic Account Lockout

WINDOWS NT PROVIDES a security feature to automatically lock user accounts after a number of invalid logon attempts. This feature can thwart intrusion by anyone attempting to guess passwords.

By far the easiest way to gain unauthorized access to a computer is by guessing a valid user's password. Windows NT default behavior allows an unlimited number of attempts at correctly typing (or remembering) your password. While this is convenient for authorized uses, it allows unauthorized users an unlimited number of attempts at guessing passwords. Most users can enter their passwords correctly and quickly by habit after only a few attempts and will rarely mistype it more than once.

If someone is really attempting to gain access to your computer, the intruder will attempt all valid usernames he or she knows. An unauthorized user who knows anything about Windows NT default accounts will most certainly attempt to gain access to your computer through the Administrator and Guest accounts. Therefore, you should consider renaming these accounts to prevent their possible compromise. The account lockout feature has two important settings:

- Number of attempts before lockout occurs

- Duration of lockout

Setting the number of attempts before lockout occurs allows you to control how many chances a user has to get his or her password right. Many security procedures specify this number as either three or five. Allowing more than five logon attempts enables intruders to penetrate your security measures more easily and does not make valid user logons easier.

The account lockout duration can be set to Forever to force a user to alert administration that his or her account has been locked out. Such notification can be important in security installations that are required to track intrusion attempts.

The Administrator account is not subject to the user lockout mechanism. A short delay will ensue after a number of bad attempts, but that delay is not the same as the lockout delay.

You can change the intruder lockout settings in the User Manager utility, shown in Figure 7.4 by modifying the system Account Policy, which affects all

FIGURE 7.4

The User Manager's
Account Policy dialog box.

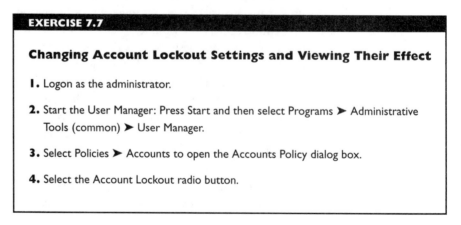

accounts for the system. An individual locked out account can be re-enabled by clearing the *Account Locked Out* checkbox for the account in the User Manager.

Exercise 7.7 changes the lockout settings in Windows NT.

EXERCISE 7.7

Changing Account Lockout Settings and Viewing Their Effect

1. Logon as the administrator.

2. Start the User Manager: Press Start and then select Programs ➤ Administrative Tools (common) ➤ User Manager.

3. Select Policies ➤ Accounts to open the Accounts Policy dialog box.

4. Select the Account Lockout radio button.

EXERCISE 7.7 (CONTINUED)

5. Set the Account Lockout parameters according to these policies:

- Lock out after 3 bad attempts.

- Reset count after 30 minutes.

- Lockout duration 60 minutes.

6. Close the dialog box by clicking OK, close the User Manager, and then log off.

7. Attempt to log on as a user other than administrator but use an incorrect password the first three times.

8. Notice the dialog box that appears on your fourth attempt. It specifies that the account logon cannot be completed because the account is locked.

9. Log on as administrator and start the User Manager.

10. Double-click the username used in step 7.

11. Clear the Account Locked Out checkbox.

Chapter Summary

WINDOWS NT PROVIDES significant security features to prevent both intentional and accidental loss and to encourage a more organized and coherent file system structure.

Windows NT provides a mandatory logon process that determines the identity of system users and provides an inherited mechanism for checking the user's security clearance each time a Windows NT resource is used. Windows NT represents all resources as objects.

When a user logs on, the system generates an access token object to represent the user to all objects subsequently accessed. The access token contains security identifiers specific to the user's identity, permissions, and group memberships. The access token also contains all relevant permissions that apply to groups to which the user belongs.

Windows NT security works by checking the user's identity or group membership against each object's access control list. This control list, containing access control entries, specifically allows or denies access to each service the object provides.

Each time a new object is opened, the access token created at logon for the user is attached to the new process by the calling process. This method ensures a constant chain of authentication through each service call and guarantees that a user can never launch a process that will sidestep Windows NT security.

Windows NT optimizes the security checking process by copying all requested allowed object services to the started process. Subsequent requests that are allowed will automatically go through and requests that are not allowed will generate an error because the process cannot respond to them.

The Windows NT logon process can be customized to meet the rigorous security requirements of some organizations by modifying values in the Windows NT Registry.

A security warning screen can be added prior to accepting the username and password. The default behavior of the username input box can be changed to show nothing. The Shutdown button on the logon screen can be enabled or disabled as necessary.

In addition, the default shell can be changed to a custom application or to mimic older versions of Windows NT. Finally, the logon process can be obviated by providing a default password in the Windows NT Registry.

Account Lockout can be enabled with the User Manager for security installations that require it. Accounts can be locked after any number of attempts and for any duration. Account Lockout does not apply to the Administrator account. A member of the Administrators group can clear any locked accounts through the User Manager.

Exercise Questions

1. Security is control of a system to prevent what? (Choose the best selection.)

   A. Intrusion

   B. Theft

   C. Loss of any nature

2. The _____ process implements the security user interface when the computer is booted.

3. If you delete a user account and then add it again, the permissions will remain the same because the name has not changed.

   A. True

   B. False

4. Permissions changed while a user is logged on do not take effect until the user has logged out and back on again.

   A. True

   B. False

5. Windows NT allows access to objects by default.

   A. True

   B. False

6. The Windows NT logon process can be eliminated by adding default user information and an AutoAdminLogon value to the Windows NT Registry.

   A. True

   B. False

7. The Windows NT logon process is useful for more than just security.

   A. True

   B. False

8. All Windows NT resources are represented as objects in the system.

   A. True

   B. False

9. All Windows NT objects have access control lists to implement security.

   A. True

   B. False

10. The _____ _____ is created by the Security Access Manager process and identifies the current user to all subsequent processes.

11. Objects are composed of _____ that contain data and of _____ that are functions that operate on that data.

12. An access token is a Windows NT object.

    A. True

    B. False

13. Your access token is attached to each object you open after you log on.

    A. True

    B. False

14. You should never change the default behavior of the WinLogon process.

    A. True

    B. False

15. The account lockout policy applies to all accounts.

    A. True

    B. False

Network
Environment

CHAPTER

8

INDOWS NT WAS DESIGNED for networking, so it comes with all the components necessary to perform everyday network functions, including file and print sharing, without adding software.

Windows NT can operate either as a client or as a server and can participate in a peer-to-peer network. In addition, Windows NT includes all necessary components for access to the global Internet. Internet connectivity is covered in detail in Chapter 9.

The component-based architecture of Windows NT allows the operating system to respond quickly to new developments and standards. For instance, adding the Internet access components to Windows NT 4.0 took very little effort because no code had to be changed in the operating system to allow for the added functionality. Component-based architecture means that a functioning operating system can serve as the foundation for new functionality. This type of design allows an operating system to take advantage of evolutionary changes in the state of the networking art without being replaced.

We start this chapter by covering the broad topic of network components and network component models. Then we introduce the specific Windows NT components that provide the various networking services by component category. Finally, we explain how to change the default network settings.

Network Component Models

INDOWS NT IS NOT a monolithic operating system. Rather, Windows NT provides a foundation for interfacing different software components that interoperate to provide the functionality of a computer workstation or a network server.

Component-based environments allow for future expansion and for the inclusion of components not written by the original software developer. These factors extend the life of a network operating system and ensure that it will remain compatible with future systems.

Component-based systems are also referred to as modular systems. *The term* module *in this case is synonymous with the term* component.

These components are organized into a model that describes how the various components operate. The model shows the minimum set of components required to implement a network and identifies the components that you can replace or upgrade. The Windows NT network model is discussed in detail in the next section.

How Software Components and Interfaces Work

Software components work together to provide a complete networking environment. Each component encapsulates some network function completely, providing an interface through which it imports and exports data to and from other components.

Components can be inserted and removed without affecting the functionality of other components unless they are bound to the other components. (Binding is discussed later in this chapter.) New components can also be introduced to existing networks to provide some additional utility.

Components communicate through interfaces known as boundary layers. *Boundary layers* translate data from a format that the sending component understands to a format that the receiving component understands.

The Open Systems Interconnect Model

The International Standards Organization developed the Open Systems Interconnect (OSI) model to provide a basis upon which different manufacturers could create interoperable network software components.

The OSI model describes seven standard layers to which all network software components in a modular operating system, such as Windows NT, should conform. The seven OSI layers are

- Application
- Presentation

- Session

- Transport

- Network

- Data Link

- Physical

Each layer provides a service to the layer directly above it by using the services of the layer below it. For instance, TCP, a Transport layer service, guarantees a reliable connection to the layer above it using the unreliable service of IP, a Network layer service. TCP does its work by making as many requests as necessary to IP for data until it gets what it needs to provide a consistent set of data to the layer above it. This system works in much the same way as a concierge guarantees that you'll have a pleasant stay at a hotel by taking care of many disagreeable details for you. This process is shown in Figure 8.1.

FIGURE 8.1
How network
components interact.

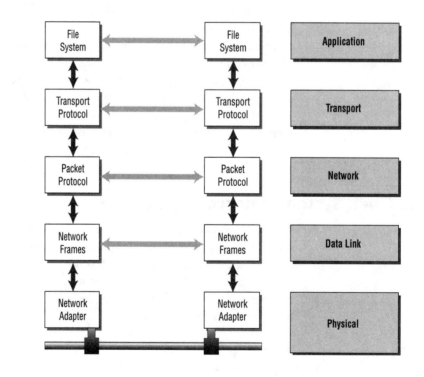

The OSI model represents an abstract ideal that is not always applicable to real-world considerations. For instance, many software components encompass more than one layer of the stack. The OSI model also encompasses some functionality that is not the responsibility of software at all. The physical and Data Link layers are implemented with electronic equipment and cables. The Data Link layer encompasses the functionality of the network adapter driver software, which is provided by the network adapter manufacturer, not the operating system manufacturer.

User applications are not prohibited from bypassing higher level modules and writing directly to lower level layers if they know how to interface with the lower level components. The upper layers abstract the differences between interchangeable software modules at lower levels, but user applications are not required to use this abstraction. For example, an application can interact directly with the TCP/IP layer even though NetBIOS is bound above it. The application will break if TCP/IP is replaced by IPX, however. An application that interacts with NetBIOS does not have to worry about which Transport layer is installed.

Taking this concept to the extreme, a network could be implemented by interfacing directly to the network adapter from the redirector, but the entire network would have to be implemented with exactly the same model network adapter and could never be upgraded to newer technology.

As you can see, the modular structure of NT allows layers to be independent of one another, which increases the life span of the operating system and supports cross-vendor compatibility.

In the following sections, we present each of the seven layers to help you understand the intent of modular, component-based networking. Notice that each layer depends upon the services provided by the layer above to implement its functionality.

Physical Layer

The Physical layer is simply responsible for sending bits (bits are the binary 1s and 0s of digital communication that you learned about in Chapter 2) from one computer to another. The Physical layer is not concerned with the meaning of the bits; it deals only with the physical connection to the network and with transmitting and receiving signals.

This level defines physical and electrical details, such as what will represent a 1 or a 0, how many pins a network connector will have, how data will be synchronized, and when the network adapter may or may not transmit the data.

Data Link Layer

The Data Link layer allows data to flow over a single link from one device to another. It accepts packets from the Network layer, packages the information into data units called *frames,* and sends it to the Physical layer for transmission. The Data Link layer adds control information, such as frame type, routing, and segmentation information, to the data being sent.

This layer provides for the error-free transfer of frames from one computer to another. A cyclic redundancy check (CRC) added to the data frame can detect damaged frames, and the Data Link layer in the receiving computer can request that the information be present. The Data Link layer can also detect when frames are lost and request that those frames be sent again.

Network Layer

The Network layer routes data between networks. The Network layer makes routing decisions and forwards packets for devices that are farther away than a single link. (A link connects two network devices and is implemented by the Data Link layer. Two devices connected by a link communicate directly with each other and not through a third device.) Larger networks may have *intermediate systems* between any two *end systems,* and the Network layer makes it possible for the Transport layer and layers above it to send packets without being concerned about whether the end system is immediately adjacent or is instead several hops away.

Transport Layer

The Transport layer ensures that packets are delivered error free, in sequence, and with no losses or duplications. The Transport layer breaks large messages from the Session layer (which we'll look at next) into packets to be sent to the destination computer and reassembles packets into messages to be presented to the Session layer. The Transport layer typically sends an acknowledgment to the originator for messages received.

Session Layer

The Session layer allows applications on separate computers to share a connection called a *session.* This layer provides services such as name lookup and security to allow two programs to find each other and establish the communications link. This layer also controls the dialog between two processes, determining who can transmit and who can receive at what point during the communication.

Presentation Layer

The Presentation layer translates data between the formats the network requires and the formats the computer expects. The Presentation layer does protocol conversion, data translation, compression and encryption, and character set conversion; it also interprets graphics commands.

Redirectors operate at this level. The redirectors are what make the files on a file server visible to the client computer. Redirectors also make remote printers act as though they were attached to the local computer.

Application Layer

The Application layer is the topmost layer of the OSI model. It provides services that directly support user applications, such as database access, e-mail, and file transfers. It also allows applications to communicate with applications on other computers as though they were on the same computer. When a programmer writes an application program that uses network services, the application program will access this layer.

Windows NT Network Model

MICROSOFT HAS DONE an admirable job of mapping its software components and boundary layers to layers in the OSI stack (see Figure 8.2). (Also included in the figure are physical disk I/O subsystems to show how the network redirector can make network connections look like local storage.) Note that many of the software components appear to cover more than one layer; in fact, they perform services in more than one layer, essentially embodying the function of the layers and interfaces in one package. In the sections that follow, we will introduce each component in Windows NT according to the layer in which it operate.

FIGURE 8.2
Windows NT and
the OSI model.

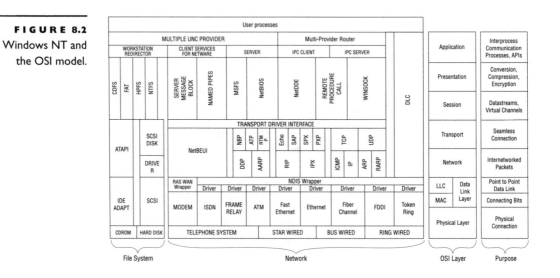

		OSI Layer		Purpose
File System	Network			

Do not confuse the Application layer of the OSI stack with software applications. The Application layer provides services to user applications, which run in the user space above the OSI stack.

Major NT Component Types

Windows NT components work together through interfaces called *boundary layers*. Each component implements a major network service. Each boundary layer provides a way for components to communicate but provides no other service. In some cases boundary layers are implemented as software switches that select the appropriate component to perform a service. In other cases boundary layers are not really software at all—they are simply rules by which programmers must write components in order for them to work under Windows NT. Components provide a certain service; boundary layers connect components. This relationship is shown in Figure 8.3.

Windows NT divides the network software component layers slightly differently than the OSI model does, so we will now change to using Microsoft terminology for these component layers. You should be familiar with the

FIGURE 8.3
Microsoft component
architecture.

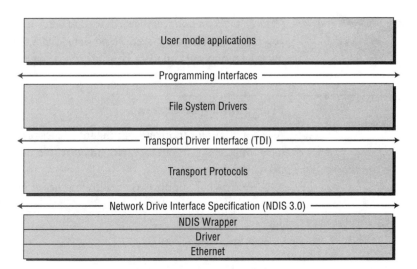

purposes of the different OSI layers and be able to match them up with their Windows NT counterparts when you finish reading this section.

Boundary layers facilitate the development of adapter drivers and network components such as protocols and file systems because the interfaces to the boundary layers are very well defined. Boundary layers help realize the goals of the OSI model.

The Windows NT components and boundary layers are

- Programming interfaces (boundary layer)

- File system drivers (component)

- Transport Driver Interface (boundary layer)

- Transport protocol (component)

- Network Driver Interface Specification (boundary layer)

- Adapter driver (component)

The boundary layers and components alternate in the above list because each boundary layer provides the interface between the components above and below it. The first boundary layer, programming interfaces, provides the boundary between the user's application and the network itself.

Although the term boundary layer *is used to describe the interface between components, notice that each boundary layer component includes the word interface in its name. The terms* interface *and* boundary layer *are synonymous.*

Programming Interfaces

As a boundary layer, programming interfaces provide an established method for user applications to interact with any one of a number of file system drivers and network services.

Windows NT supports the following programming interfaces:

- NetBIOS

- Windows Sockets

- Remote Procedure Calls

- Network Dynamic Data Exchange

These services call upon file system drivers as well as transport protocols to perform their functions.

Programming interfaces are the boundary between the Application layer and user applications in the OSI model.

File System Drivers

File system drivers are networking components that are treated the same as Windows NT local storage file systems. Windows NT provides file systems for many of its Application and Session layer components so applications do not have to treat local and networked storage differently. By making Application and Session layer components look like file systems to user applications, you can use applications written to work on your local computer across the network. Local storage file systems are covered in detail in Chapter 5.

These components include the Workstation and Server services, named pipes, and mailslots. All of these components call upon transport protocols to perform their services.

File system drivers are also called redirectors *because they redirect I/O to go over the network instead of to a local disk.*

Transport Driver Interface

The *Transport Driver Interface* (TDI) is a boundary layer that makes all the transport protocols look the same to higher level services such as file systems and redirectors. TDI is not software—rather, it is a specification to which all Windows NT transport protocols are written. For instance, NWLink, which implements Novell's IPX protocol, looks exactly like TCP/IP for Windows NT to upper layer file systems and redirectors.

In the OSI model, the TDI is an interface between the Transport layer and the Session layer.

Transport Protocols

Shared media networks are not always available to a computer: transmission errors occur, packets are dropped in routers, collisions happen. Transport protocols convert the unreliable inconsistent packet bursts delivered by network adapter drivers into smooth data transmission streams (albeit with nondeterministic delay characteristics) that can be used for file transmission.

Transport protocols perform such services as packet ordering, guaranteed delivery, connection maintenance, and data routing between networks.

The TDI allows you to run several protocols at once under Windows NT. Think of this service as being multilingual. If a server speaks TCP/IP, IPX, and NetBEUI, it can make reliable connections to clients running any one of those protocols.

Transport protocols make up the Network and Transport layers of the OSI model. They can be subdivided even further; for instance, TCP is the Transport layer and IP is the Network layer in the TCP/IP protocol.

Network Driver Interface

In Windows NT the Network Driver Interface is implemented by the Network Driver Interface Standard (NDIS 4.0).

NDIS is a small code wrapper that controls the interface between NDIS-compliant drivers and transport protocols. NDIS 4.0 allows multiple adapter drivers to be bound to an unlimited number of transport protocols.

Adapter Drivers

Adapter drivers are software components designed by adapter manufacturers to provide an interface between proprietary hardware and standard software. Adapter drivers know exactly how to make the specific adapter for which it was written perform a certain function, such as transmitting a packet.

The IEEE 802 model, which was developed in concert with the OSI model, further subdivides the Data Link layer into the logical link control (LLC) layer and the media access control (MAC) layer. The LLC layer is the network adapter driver. The MAC layer contains the network adapter and other devices that transmit a specific protocol such as Ethernet or Token Ring. Each model of adapter requires an adapter driver written specifically for it. To operate with Windows NT, these drivers must be NDIS 3 compliant, which means they must know how to respond to requests from NDIS.

Adapter drivers operate at the media access layer of the IEEE 802 model, whereas the adapter itself interfaces the media access layer with the Physical layer.

Default Components

A standard Windows NT installation includes a number of default components that satisfy the requirements of most users.

By default, Windows NT installs a complete set of network components to allow the majority of network users to begin using their network as soon as they perform the initial installation. This section describes the default components and how they interact. You will also learn how to install, remove, and configure each component in this chapter.

Also included with Windows NT, but not installed by default, are standard components that provide additional functionality, such as interoperation with NetWare file servers, and support networking via dial-up telephone lines. These components are covered in detail in their own chapters later in the book.

The following components are installed by default in Windows NT:

- NetBIOS interface

- TCP/IP protocol

- Workstation

- Server

- Computer browser (see Chapter 13 for details)

- Driver for your network interface adapter

- RPC configuration

Network Protocols

NETWORK TRANSPORT PROTOCOLS PROVIDE the core functionality required for computers to communicate on a network. Network transport protocols providing complete seamless communication channels between computers.

Think of a transport protocol as a registered mail service. You simply pass an envelope (data) to the post office, and it makes sure your mail gets to the addressee. In the same manner, a transport protocol ensures that the data you give it gets to its intended destination by verifying receipt of the data with the destination. It performs error checking and correction without requiring the intervention of higher levels.

Windows NT comes with three network transports, each intended for networks of different sizes with different requirements. They are

- NetBEUI

- NWLink (IPX/SPX compatible)

- TCP/IP

Each network transport has its own strengths and weaknesses. In general, NetBEUI is intended for small, single-server networks. NWLink is intended for medium-size networks (in a single facility perhaps) or for networks that require access to Novell NetWare file servers. TCP/IP is a complex transport sufficient for globe-spanning networks like the Internet. We cover the network transports in detail in the following sections.

NetBEUI

NetBEUI stands for NetBIOS Extended User Interface (NetBIOS stands for Network Basic Input Output System). NetBEUI implements the NetBIOS Frame (NBF) transport protocol, which was developed by IBM in the mid-1980s to support LAN workgroups under OS/2 and LAN Manager.

When IBM developed NetBEUI, it did not target networked PCs for enterprisewide connectivity. Rather, NetBEUI was developed for workgroups of 2 to 200 computers. NetBEUI cannot be routed between networks, so it is constrained to small LANs consisting of Microsoft and IBM clients and servers.

The version of NetBEUI shipped with all versions of Windows NT is the Microsoft update of IBM's NetBEUI protocol that shipped with LAN Manager.

Features of NetBEUI

NetBEUI can be thought of as the small, fast sports car of transport protocols. You can't rely on it for long trips (routing), but it's faster than any other TDI-compliant transport protocol for small networks that do not need to take advantage of routing to other networks. Here are some of the major features of NetBEUI:

- Very fast on small networks

- More than 254 sessions allowed (a limitation of earlier versions)

- Better performance over slow serial links than previous versions

- Easy to implement

- Self-tuning

- Good error protection

- Small memory overhead

Disadvantages of NetBEUI

NetBEUI is not suitable for long trips because it can't be routed. Because NetBEUI is not widely used outside the realm of Microsoft operating systems, very little software is available to help you analyze its problems. Here are a few of its disadvantages:

- No routing between networks

- Few tools (such as protocol analyzers) exist for NetBEUI

- Very little cross-platform support

NWLink

NWLink is Microsoft's implementation of the Novell IPX/SPX protocol stack used in Novell NetWare. IPX is an outgrowth of the XNS protocol stack developed by Xerox in the late 1970s.

NWLink is IPX for Windows NT. IPX is the protocol, and NWLink is the networking component that provides the protocol.

IPX is included with Microsoft Windows NT primarily to support an interconnection to Novell NetWare servers. Microsoft clients and servers can be added to existing network installations slowly over time, easing the migration between platforms and obviating the need for an abrupt change from one networking standard to another.

NWLink does not by itself allow file and print sharing to and from NetWare clients or servers. Those functions are performed by the Client Services for NetWare (CSNW) redirector that also comes with Windows NT.

NWLink also includes enhancements to Novell's version of the NetBIOS programming interface. NWLink will allow Windows NT to act as either the client or server in Novell IPX/NetBIOS client/server applications.

Features of NWLink

Think of NWLink as the sedan of network protocols. NWLink provides a reasonable middle ground between the simple, unroutable NetBEUI transport protocol and the complex, routable TCP/IP protocol. Like NetBEUI, IPX has many self-tuning characteristics. In addition, IPX

- Is easy to set up

- Supports routing between networks

- Is faster than the current Windows NT implementation of TCP/IP

- Connects easily to installed NetWare servers and clients

Disadvantages of NWLink

On the other hand, truly large networks (networks that connect many organizations) may find it difficult to work over IPX, as IPX does not have a central addressing scheme to ensure that two networks don't use the same address numbers (in contrast to TCP/IP, which has this service). IPX does not support the wide range of network management tools available for TCP/IP. In addition, IPX

- Lacked a centralized network numbering agency until recently, which stymies interconnection between independent organizations

- Is slower than NetBEUI over slow serial connections

- Doesn't support standard network management protocols

TCP/IP

TCP/IP is the Transmission Control Protocol and the Internet Protocol, as well as a suite of related protocols developed by the Department of Defense's Advanced Projects Research Agency (ARPA, later DARPA) under its network interconnection project started in 1969. TCP/IP is by far the most widely used protocol for interconnecting computers and is the protocol of the global Internet. ARPA originally created TCP/IP to connect military networks but provided the protocol standards to government agencies and universities free of charge.

Universities quickly adopted the protocol to interconnect their networks. A large number of academicians collaborated to create higher level protocols for everything from news groups, mail transfer, file transfer, printing, remote booting, and even document browsing.

TCP/IP became the standard for interoperating UNIX computers, especially in military and university environments. With the development of the Hypertext Transfer Protocol (HTTP) for sharing Hypertext Markup Language (HTML) documents freely on the large global network, the World Wide Web (WWW) was born and Internet use exploded into the private sector. TCP/IP rode this wave of expansion to eclipse IPX as the commercial protocol of choice among all network operating systems.

To support NetBIOS over TCP/IP, Microsoft has included NetBT (NetBIOS over TCP/IP) in accordance with Internet Protocol Request for Comments (RFC) 1001 and 1002.

TCP/IP protocol definitions are called **Requests for Comments (RFCs)**, *which are freely available on the World Wide Web. Protocol definitions tell software developers how to write their software in order to work with Internet standards properly. You can use RFCs to study the inner workings of all Internet protocols.*

Features of TCP/IP

If you have a network that spans more than one metropolitan area, you will probably need to use TCP/IP. TCP/IP is the truck of transport protocols. It's not fast or easy to use, but it is routable over wide, complex networks and it provides more error correction than any other protocol. Every modern computer and operating system supports TCP/IP. In addition, it provides

- Broad connectivity among all types of computers and servers

- Direct access to the global Internet

- Strong support for routing

- Simple Network Management Protocol (SNMP) support

- Support for Dynamic Host Configuration Protocol (DHCP) to dynamically assign client IP addresses

- Support for the Windows Internet Name Service (WINS) to allow name browsing among Microsoft clients and servers

- Support for most other Internet protocols such as Post Office Protocol, Hypertext Transfer Protocol, and any other acronym ending in *P*

Finally, centralized TCP/IP domain name and network number assignment allows internetworking between organizations.

Disadvantages of TCP/IP

Like a truck, TCP/IP has some down sides. It is the slowest of all the protocols included with Windows NT. It is also relatively difficult to administer correctly, although new tools like DHCP make this job a little easier. Here are some other disadvantages of TCP/IP:

- Centralized TCP/IP domain assignment requires registration effort and cost.
- Global expansion of the Internet has seriously limited the availability of unique domain numbers.
- Set up is fairly difficult.
- It requires relatively high overhead to support seamless connectivity and routing.
- TCP/IP is slower than IPX and NetBEUI.

Data Link Control

Unlike the other transport protocols provided with Windows NT, data link control (DLC) does not support higher level protocols at all. It is included primarily to support access to IBM mainframes through emulation software and to support printing to HP printers directly connected to the network.

However, you probably will not need this protocol in the majority of installations, as TCP/IP can also now be used for both functions.

 DLC does not support NetBIOS and cannot be used by the Windows NT redirector.

Features of DLC

DLC is the bicycle of transport protocols. It isn't going to get you very far, but it has specific uses. Microsoft included DLC because it was easy to add, and it allows some specific network installations to migrate to Windows NT very quickly. If you are supporting access to IBM mainframes and you don't want to install the TCP/IP protocol stack on the mainframe, you can use DLC. DLC has the following advantages:

- It supports direct connection to IBM mainframes.
- It supports direct network printing to HP printers.

Disadvantages of DLC

DLC is very limited, and its functionality has been completely supplanted by TCP/IP in most cases. Generally, you should use TCP/IP whenever possible. All IBM mainframes and HP printers now support TCP/IP. Here are some disadvantages of DLC:

- DLC does not support higher level protocols used to transfer files.

- DLC does not support routing.

- DLC provides only a primitive network transport that is not suitable for higher level services.

Interprocess Communications

NTERPROCESS COMMUNICATIONS (IPC) PROVIDES a common language for client computers to make requests for data (not necessarily files) from a server and for the server to respond to those requests.

Client/server applications are software applications that distribute the processing load across two machines: an interface application running on the client used to enter and view information and a server component used to respond to requests for information from the client.

Client/server applications are designed to put the processing burden on powerful, expensive machines called servers. Client computers can then be much simpler, as they need only to process data entry displays and forms.

Two examples of client/server applications are database servers, which respond to requests for sets of database records from clients, and Web browsers, which make requests to HTTP servers for data that they then display. IPC mechanisms are the protocols used to generate and respond to requests for data between the client and the server. They also have two components, of course—the IPC client and the IPC server. Note that these terms are generic and do not describe a specific part of the Windows NT operating system.

IPC mechanisms in Windows NT are broken down into two categories: file systems and programming interfaces. File systems perform the client/server file-sharing process. Programming interfaces handle conversations between clients and servers in a manner not based on files and consequently different for each programming interface.

File Systems

Windows NT comes with two file system IPC mechanisms: named pipes and mailslots. IPC mechanisms implemented as file systems route through the Windows NT redirector, so programs that implement client/server applications using these mechanisms can use simple file I/O commands, rather than complicated network IPC mechanisms.

Named Pipes File System

Named pipes provides connection-oriented message passing between clients and servers. The term *connection oriented* means that the receiver acknowledges receipt of the message much the same way that registered mail informs you that your letter got to its intended recipient. Because named pipes provides a reliable connection, it can run over unreliable transports like UDP/IP (discussed in Chapter 9) without failure.

The Windows NT version of named pipes includes a security feature called *impersonation*. When a client requests a service from a server, the named pipes mechanism on the server impersonates the client's security identifier to ensure that the client has the required permissions before returning data.

Mailslots File System

Mailslots is similar to named pipes, except that it is connectionless, which means it does not support acknowledgment of receipt from the receiver. Windows NT implements second-class mailslots most commonly used for communications that are not critical (that is, no user data is lost if they don't connect), such as registering computer, domain, and user names on the network, the computer browser service, and sending broadcast messages to computers or users.

Programming Interfaces

Programming interfaces implement specific IPC mechanisms appropriate for different types of client/ server applications. The client side of a client/server application must use the same programming interface as the server side in order to communicate. The authors of a client/server application will choose the programming interface that best suits their specific application.

NetBIOS

NetBIOS has been the standard PC client/server IPC mechanism since it was introduced by IBM in the early 1980s. Because of its age, NetBIOS is somewhat primitive compared to more flexible interfaces like named pipes and remote procedure call, both of which operate on a wider range of operating systems than NetBIOS does.

NetBIOS handles many of the basic functions of a Windows NT network, such as browsing network resources. For this reason, NetBIOS is required for a Microsoft Windows network to operate (although it may not be required if you are using non-MS Windows networking).

NetBIOS can communicate over any TDI-compliant transport, including the following:

- NetBEUI (NBF)

- NetBIOS over NWLink (NWNBLink)

- NetBIOS over TCP/IP (NetBT)

Windows Sockets

Windows Sockets provide a standard Windows interface to transports such as TCP/IP and IPX. Windows Sockets were developed in part to ease the migration of UNIX applications written to the Berkeley Sockets specification and in part to standardize a protocol across platforms.

Windows Sockets are typically used by programs descended from or originally developed on UNIX computers, such as Internet Web browsers and e-mail clients.

Remote Procedure Calls

Remote procedure calls (RPC) implements an IPC mechanism for starting programs on foreign computers, feeding them input, and accepting their output. This process allows computer networks to spread the processing load among a number of computers.

RPC allows the client and server portion of the application to exist on the same machine by using the local procedure calls (LPC) mechanism. Since this technique is transparent to the application, you can distribute the processing load among computers any way you please.

RPC has four major components:

1. The **remote procedure stub** packages the RPC request to be sent to the server.

2. The **RPC runtime** passes data and parameters between the local and remote computers.

3. The **application stub** accepts RPC requests from the RPC runtime, formats the RPC request for the executing computer, and makes the appropriate call to the remote procedure.

4. The **remote procedure** is the actual procedure called over the network.

Network Dynamic Data Exchange

NetDDE opens data exchange pipes between two applications across the network in the same way that Microsoft's DDE protocol opens data exchange pipes between applications on the same machine to facilitate data sharing and object linking and embedding. NetDDE is an extension of DDE to allow it to operate over a network.

By default, NetDDE services are installed by Windows NT, but they are not started (usable).

If you need to run NetDDE applications, you can start the NetDDE service using the Services control panel.

Redirectors

THE TWO MOST IMPORTANT FUNCTIONS that LANs implement are file sharing and print sharing. Local area networking was invented primarily to support these two functions.

Windows NT supports file sharing and print sharing through two Application layer components: Workstation and Server. Both are implemented as file system drivers that operate at the same level as the FAT and NTFS file system drivers.

The Workstation and Server components, as well as the Multiple Universal Naming Convention Provider (MUP) and the Multi-Provider Router (MPR) are called *redirectors*. They take a request for service from the client computer and *redirect* it to the appropriate network service provider. Redirectors are the top level networking components because they interface directly with user applications.

Workstation Service

The Workstation service allows computers to access resources on a network. The Workstation process facilitates functions such as logging in, connecting to shared directories and printers, and the different interprocess communications mechanisms.

The Workstation service consists of two components:

- The **User mode interface,** which determines which file system User mode requests refer to

- The **redirector,** which translates file and print requests and passes them on to lower level components

The Workstation service includes the redirector file system, which accesses shared directories on network computers. However, this file system may not be chosen to service the request if the request is on a local hard disk handled by the FAT or NTFS file system drivers.

In order for the Workstation service to operate, at least one TDI-compliant transport protocol and at least one Multiple Universal Naming Convention Provider must be running. MUPs are discussed in the next section.

The Windows NT redirector allows connection to Windows NT, LAN Manager, LAN Server, and other MS-Net servers. The redirector communicates with protocols via the TDI interface.

Server Service

The Windows NT Server service manages the creation and security of shared resources, such as directories and printers. The Server service also allows the computer to act as a server in a client/ server network to any number of clients (as limited by the license manager). In this capacity, the server processes the connection requests made by clients. A server may deny a connection request if the user does not have a user account in the domain or if a logon attempt fails.

The Server service is similar to the Workstation service in that it is implemented as a file system driver and uses other file system drivers to satisfy I/O requests. Server is also broken down into two components: SERVER . EXE, which manages connection requests from clients, and SRV.SYS, which is a file system that interacts with the network and with other file system drivers to satisfy requests for service.

Multiple Universal Naming Convention Provider

Windows NT can have more than one active redirector such as the NetWare redirector (CSNW), which manages connections to NetWare servers, and Workstation, which manages connections to Microsoft Windows Network shares. As with all other boundary layers in Windows NT, a common interface must exist to allow Windows NT to treat each redirector equally.

In Windows NT the single, unified interface to all network resources is called the *Multiple Universal Naming Convention Provider* (MUP). The MUP provides a link between applications that make Universal Naming Convention (UNC) requests and the different redirectors in the system. MUP frees applications from having to know anything about the number or type of redirectors installed by determining which redirector should handle a request based upon the UNC's share name.

How MUP Works

When the I/O manager receives a request containing a UNC name, it passes the request to MUP. MUP maintains a list of shares accessed in the last 15 minutes. If MUP knows about the share name, it passes the request to that redirector. If MUP does not know about the share name (meaning it has not been accessed within the last 15 minutes), MUP sends the request to each registered redirector and asks if it can handle the request. MUP selects the redirector with the highest registered priority response that claims it can establish a connection to the UNC name. This connection is then cached until no activity has transpired for 15 minutes.

UNC Names

UNC names consist of two backslashes followed by the server name, the shared resource name, the directory path, and the requested file name, all separated by backslashes, as follows:

```
\\computer\share\directory\path\filename.text
```

For example, the `readme` file located in the Word directory in the public storage directory of the server named tinman might be

```
\\tinman\public\Word\readme.txt
```

Multi-Provider Router

Not all programs use UNC requests, however. For those that use the Win32 API, the Multi-Provider Router (MPR) determines which redirector should handle the request. This routing service allows programs written to Microsoft specifications to operate as if they were written to UNC specifications. If the G: drive has previously been mapped to the server dorothy, a Win32 request might look like this:

```
G:\COMMON\TEMPLATES\WORD.DOT
```

MPR knows which redirector handles the G: drive, so it routes the request to that redirector.

MPR receives Win32 Network API calls (WNet) and passes them to the redirectors registered with it through DLLs. Every redirector installed to work with MPR must have a DLL exposing a common interface to MPR. The network vendor that provided the redirector also provides the DLLs. For example, CNSW is implemented as a DLL that exposes the correct interface to MPR, thus providing an interface as seamless as the native Windows NT redirectors.

Changing Network Settings

CHANGING NETWORK SETTINGS in Windows NT is very easy to do compared to the way most other network operating systems change their settings. You will need to have administrator privileges in order to change network settings. Components are installed and removed through the Network Settings control panel shown in Figure 8.4.

As with most settings in Windows NT 4.0, you can get to the Network control panel via a bewildering number of routes. Exercise 8.1 explains how to open the Network control panel, and the remaining exercises in this chapter assume that the Network control panel is open.

FIGURE 8.4
The Network
control panel.

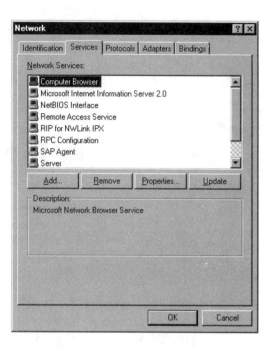

FIGURE 8.4
The Network
control panel.

EXERCISE 8.1

Opening the Network Control Panel

1. Right-click the Network Neighborhood icon on the desktop and select Properties.

-OR-

1. Click Start ➤ Settings ➤ Control Panels.

2. Double-click the Network control panel.

-OR-

1. Double-click the My Computer icon on the desktop.

2. Double-click the control panel application.

3. Double-click the Network Control Panel.

Installing and Removing Components

If the default setting does not meet your connectivity requirements, you will need to install other components. The following exercises walk you through process of installing and removing various components. Figure 8.5 shows the Select Network Service dialog box of the of the Network control panel Services tab.

Exercise 8.2 shows the process of removing a component. Be careful—removing the component shown will disable network access until you reinstall it in Exercise 8.3. You must have your Windows NT 4.0 Workstation CD available to perform these exercises.

Installing a Transport Protocol

Exercise 8.4 shows you how to install a transport protocol. Many networks will require IPX to communicate with NetWare servers, so we will use that situation as an example.

Configuring Individual Components

After a workstation is installed on the network, you may need to change configurations to attach the computer to a new or changed domain or to reconfigure a

---

EXERCISE 8.2

Removing a Service

1. Open the Network Settings control panel.

2. Click on the Services tab.

3. Select RPC Configuration.

4. Click the Remove button.

5. Click the Yes button in the confirmation dialog box.

6. Click the Close button to complete the operation.

7. Click Yes to restart your computer.

EXERCISE 8.3

Reinstalling a Removed Component

1. Open the Network Settings control panel.

2. Click on the Services tab.

3. Click on the Add button.

4. Select RPC Configuration from the Network Services option list and click OK.

5. Enter the path to your CD-ROM install files and click OK. Normally this path is `D:\I386`.

6. Click Close to complete the operation.

7. Click Yes to restart your computer.

---

service or protocol to reflect new network policy. For instance, if you start running out of IP addresses, you may may reconfigure computers to use DHCP once all your servers have been migrated to DHCP. Changing the domain or workgroup is shown in Exercise 8.5.

EXERCISE 8.4

Installing a Transport Protocol

1. Open the Network Settings control panel.

2. Click the Protocols tab.

3. Click the Add button.

4. Select *NWLink IPX/SPX compatible transport* from the Protocols option list and click OK.

5. Enter the path to your CD-ROM install files and click OK. Normally this path is `D:\I386`.

6. If you have RAS installed, Windows NT will ask you if you want to support it using this protocol. Click Cancel to leave it unsupported. Typical networks will need RAS bound to TCP/IP only for connections to the Internet or an enterprisewide WAN.

7. Click Close to complete the operation.

8. Click Yes to restart your computer.

EXERCISE 8.5

Changing the Domain or Workgroup

1. Open the Network Settings control panel.

2. The Identification tab should already be in front. If not, click the Identification tab.

3. Click the Change button. Record the current workgroup or domain settings on a piece of paper so you can restore them later in this exercise.

4. Select the Workgroup radio button.

5. Type a workgroup name that is different from your current workgroup or domain (if any).

6. Click OK to accept the change.

7. Click OK to acknowledge the welcome message. Close the Network Settings control panel.

8. Click Yes to acknowledge that you will have to restart the computer for the change to take effect.

9. Restart the computer to affect the computer name change.

10. Double-click the Network Neighborhood icon.

11. Double-click the Entire Network Hierarchy text line.

12. Double-click the Microsoft Windows Network Hierarchy text line.

13. Click the name of your new workgroup. Notice that your old workgroup name may also appear (depending on which computer is the master browser for your workgroup and discussed in Chapter 11).

14. Notice that only your computer exists in this new workgroup.

15. Open the Network Settings dialog box.

16. Click the Change button in the Identification tab.

17. Enter the previous settings you recorded on a piece of paper.

18. Click OK to accept the change.

19. Click OK to acknowledge the welcome message. Close the Network Settings dialog box.

20. Click Yes to acknowledge that you will have to restart the computer.

21. Restart the computer to restore your settings.

Binding Options

Binding is the process of linking Windows NT software components together to control how they communicate. You can bind a component to one or more components above or below it. The services provided by a component can be shared by all components bound to it. The Bindings tab of the Network Settings control panel is shown in Figure 8.6.

By default, the TCP/IP stack is bound to both the Server and Workstation services. If you install additional protocols, they are also bound by default.

FIGURE 8.6
Bindings in the Network
Settings control panel.

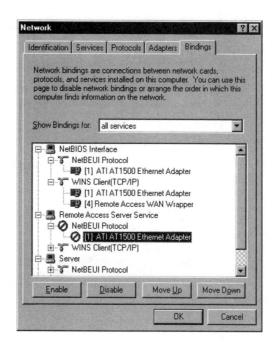

FIGURE 8.6
Bindings in the Network
Settings control panel.

By default, Windows NT enables as many bindings between components as possible.

Default Bindings

You can increase the performance of the system and decrease the possibility for error if you disable any protocol bindings that you will not use. For instance, If you will never remotely access a computer using the IPX protocol, you should disable the binding between the Remote Access WAN Wrapper (which shows up as an adapter in the bindings list) and the NWLink transport. Exercise 8.6 will walk you through the process of changing the default bindings. To perform this exercise, you must have the NWLink transport installed.

EXERCISE 8.6

Changing Default Bindings

1. Open the Network Settings control panel.

2. Select the Bindings tab.

3. Select all protocols in the *Show Bindings for* drop-down box.

4. Double-click the NWLink SPX protocol.

5. Click the *NWLink IPX/SPX Compatible Transport* binding that appears below the NWLink SPX protocol.

6. Click the Disable button.

7. Notice that both the binding and the protocol have become disabled. If you disable all bindings below a protocol, the protocol becomes disabled.

8. Click OK to accept the new bindings. You have now disabled the binding between SPX and NWLink.

9. Click Yes to restart your computer to affect the change.

10. Perform this exercise again to re-enable the binding after you've seen the effect of this change.

Binding Priorities

You may also want to change the priority of different bindings. Windows NT negotiates connections in protocol order. If two machines are running NetBEUI and TCP/IP, Windows NT will negotiate with whichever protocol is ranked higher in the services binding list. If both computers are running NetBEUI and NetBEUI is ranked higher than TCP/IP in the workstation or server bindings and both computers are on the same LAN, then the two computers will negotiate a faster connection, since NetBEUI is faster than TCP/IP. Exercise 8.7 will show you how to change the priority of transport protocols.

EXERCISE 8.7

Changing the Priority of Transport Protocols

1. Open the Network Settings dialog box.

2. Select the Bindings tab.

3. Select all services in the *Show Bindings for* drop-down box.

4. Double-click the Workstation service.

5. Select the NWLink NetBIOS protocol.

6. Click the Move Up button until this protocol is at the top of the list to make it the first choice when Windows NT establishes a connection.

7. Click OK to accept the new protocol order.

8. Click Yes to restart your computer to affect the change.

Chapter Summary

WINDOWS NT IS A MODULAR network operating system that adheres to the principles promulgated by the ISO with its OSI model for network operating systems.

Windows NT components such as file systems, transports, and adapter drivers can be interchanged freely as long as they conform to the specifications of the boundary layers that interconnect them.

Interprocess communications build upon the data transmission foundation provided by transports in order to provide direct communication between servers and clients. Distributed processing is achieved through the IPC mechanism.

Programming interfaces enable applications on one machine to communicate with applications running on another machine. Various programming interfaces are built into Windows NT to support a wide range of current and legacy applications.

File and print sharing between Windows NT computers is achieved through the Workstation and Server services. These services provide redirection between local resources and resources located on remote computers and servers. The Multiple Universal Naming Convention Provider is a mechanism for switching user requests among numerous installed redirectors, and the MPR provides a switch for Win32 API calls made by user applications.

Windows NT installs a basic set of default components that will allow most users to get up and running with very little effort. These include NetBIOS, TCP/IP, Workstation, Server, Computer Browser, an adapter driver, and the RPC Name Service Provider.

All installed network components are configured through the Network control panel. This control panel is divided into five areas: Identification, Services, Protocols, Adapters, and Bindings. Through these major sections, each Windows NT component can be configured for the unique network requirements of the host computer. Components are bound by default to all available services, but you can change binding settings to optimize system performance.

Exercise Questions

1. The NDIS boundary layer allows any number of adapters to be bound to any number of transport protocols.

    A. True

    B. False

2. Microsoft added networking support after Windows NT was already finished.

    A. True

    B. False

3. Programming interfaces are the boundary between the Application layer and user applications.

    A. True

    B. False

4. All Windows NT adapter drivers are written by Microsoft and included on the Windows NT CD-ROM.

    A. True

    B. False

5. IPC mechanisms are the protocols used to support client/server applications.

    A. True

    B. False

6. IPC components are required only if you intend to support client/server applications.

    A. True

    B. False

7. More than one redirector can be active in Windows NT.

    A. True

    B. False

8. NWLink provides all necessary functions for Windows NT computers to share files and printers with NetWare servers.

    A. True

    B. False

9. The Mailslots file system is not required if you do not install Microsoft Exchange.

    A. True

    B. False

10. The Multi-Provider Router determines which redirector should handle Win32 API calls.

    A. True

    B. False

11. The TDI is a required software component.

    A. True

    B. False

12. NetBIOS can communicate over any TDI-compliant transport.

    A. True

    B. False

13. Windows NT installs the NetDDE services by default.

    A. True

    B. False

14. Windows NT automatically determines the best bindings between components, which should not be changed.

    A. True

    B. False

15. Local area networking was developed primarily to support file sharing and print sharing.

    A. True

    B. False

16. Once a software component is installed in Windows NT, it must be removed before it can be reconfigured.

   A. True

   B. False

17. NWLink can be used only to attach to NetWare file servers.

   A. True

   B. False

18. Windows NT components match the OSI model exactly.

   A. True

   B. False

19. The _____ layer provides a reliable connection between computers.

20. The _____ allows Windows NT to run several transport protocols at once.

21. The Windows NT version of _____ includes a security feature called impersonation.

22. Remote procedure calls allow both the client and the server portion of a client/server program to reside on the same machine through the _____ mechanism.

23. The _____ service includes the Windows networking redirector.

24. In Windows NT the unified interface to all network resources is called

   A. The redirector

   B. The Workstation service

   C. The I/O Manager

   D. The Multiple Universal Naming Convention Provider.

25. Which type of component is named pipes?

   A. Programming interface

   B. File system

   C. Transport protocol

   D. Transport driver interface

26. Which of the following is not installed by default in Windows NT?

A. TCP/IP

B. NetBIOS

C. NWLink

D. Workstation

27. Which networking component is required to print to a shared printer?

A. Workstation

B. Server

C. TCP/IP

D. DLC

28. Which of the following is not an IPC mechanism in Windows NT?

A. NetBIOS

B. NetDDE

C. Windows Sockets

D. TDI

29. Which of the following transports cannot be routed?

A. TCP/IP

B. NWLink

C. NetBEUI

30. Which of the following is not a feature of TCP/IP?

A. Can be routed across wide area networks

B. Broad support across hardware and software systems

C. Faster than NetBEUI

D. Support for Internet protocols like SNMP

TCP/IP

EVERY TYPE OF NETWORK OPERATING SYSTEM has a native network protocol. You have already been introduced to NetBIOS and NetBEUI, which (together) make up Microsoft's native network protocol. The native protocol of NetWare is IPX/SPX. Transmission Control Protocol/Internet Protocol (TCP/IP) also has a native environment: UNIX workstations.

TCP/IP, however, has grown beyond its native realm of high-performance engineering workstations. The Internet grew out of a large academic and military internetwork that primarily used the UNIX operating system, and by extension TCP/IP, to route data between the local networks. Now TCP/IP is the most commonly used network protocol to transport data between dissimilar networks, and it is the network protocol of today's worldwide Internet.

In this chapter we first show you the structure of TCP/IP and how TCP/IP works. Then we explain how to install and configure TCP/IP and describe several important TCP/IP and Internet programs.

TCP/IP Architecture

CP/IP STANDS FOR Transmission Control Protocol and Internet Protocol, which are two significant parts of what is now also known as the Internet protocol suite. This section gives you some background information on how TCP/IP was developed, describes its major components, and explains how those components work together in Windows NT.

TCP/IP and Requests for Comments

TCP/IP is an outgrowth of a project that started in 1969 to link computer networks for the United States Department of Defense. (Refer to Chapter 8 for an overview of network protocols and more details on TCP/IP's origin.)

The feature that makes TCP/IP different from many other networking protocols is that it was designed to link networks together instead of just linking computers into a network. The design of TCP/IP allows each individual network to be managed separately, so different organizations that do not wish to give complete network access to each other (for instance a military research department and an academic computer science department) can still exchange information.

The first TCP/IP specifications were circulated as Requests for Comments (RFCs). The original developers and the Internet Engineering Task Force (the current open-membership standards body for TCP/IP and the Internet) maintained the tradition of producing RFCs that describe any new Internet standards or revisions to older standards. All of the RFCs for TCP/IP protocols are available for download on the Internet.

TCP/IP and the OSI Layers

TCP and IP operate at the Transport and Network layers of the OSI model. Above the Transport layer in the TCP/IP model is the Application layer, which corresponds to the Session, Presentation, and Application layers in the OSI model. Below the Network layer in the TCP/IP model is the Network Interface layer, which talks to the hardware. In the OSI model, these two layers are called the Data Link layer and the Physical layer. Refer to Chapter 8, "Networking Environment," for a description of the OSI model and the layers within it.

The Network Interface Layer

The Network Interface layer handles hardware-dependent functions and presents a standardized interface to the Internet layer of TCP/IP. You can have several different network interfaces in your Windows NT computer, each of which can carry the TCP/IP data traffic over a different type of physical network.

For instance, you may have an Ethernet card connecting your computer to an Ethernet network and a Token Ring card connecting your computer to a Token Ring network. In addition, you might have a serial connection through a modem to your Internet Service Provider (ISP). Each of these network interfaces uses different physical and data link protocols, but they all appear the same to the Internet layer of TCP/IP.

Under Windows NT the interface that the network interface layer presents to TCP/IP is Network Device Interface Standard 3 (NDIS 3). TCP/IP can use any device or software component that presents the NDIS interface to Windows NT as a Network Interface layer.

NDIS is not a TCP/IP standard; rather, it is a Microsoft-sponsored open standard for network device drivers. Any device driver that presents an NDIS interface can be used with any transport protocol that Windows NT supports. TCP/IP does not necessarily use NDIS under other operating systems.

The Internet Layer

The Internet layer is responsible for moving information from the source to the destination through a network. The source and destination computers may not be on the same LAN; in fact, the source and destination computers may be in different computers on different continents, and the data being transferred may have to go through many intermediate computers and networks to reach its destination.

- **Internet Protocol** is the core of the TCP/IP protocol suite. This protocol provides a connectionless *best-effort data delivery service* for data sent within and between networks. Therefore, data that is sent is not guaranteed to arrive at the destination and data packets are not guaranteed to arrive in the same order in which they were sent.

- **Internet Control Message Protocol** uses IP to control the flow of data over networks and to report error and congestion conditions on the network links.

- **Address Resolution Protocol (ARP)** is used in a local area network to determine a destination computer's physical hardware address when the source computer has the destination computer's Internet address. (We discuss hardware addresses and Internet addresses later in this chapter.)

- **Reverse Address Resolution Protocol (RARP)** is a mechanism whereby a computer that does not yet have an Internet address can obtain one. RARP is not used in the TCP/IP protocol stack implemented by Microsoft—DHCP is used instead.

- **Dynamic Host Configuration Protocol (DHCP)** is a newer protocol for obtaining an IP address as well as other TCP/IP information on an IP network. DHCP is more flexible than RARP and automates many tasks that must be done manually with RARP.

The Transport Layer

The Transport layer provides end-to-end data delivery services for the TCP/IP Application layer above it (which under Windows NT includes Session, Presentation, and Application layer services such as the network redirector, the Server and Workstation services, named pipes, the Windows Sockets interface, and NetBIOS.

Refer to Figure 8.1 for a view of the TCP/IP stack within the Windows NT architecture.

TCP/IP provides two types of Transport layer services. The nature of the network communication that the upper layer services need determines which service they use. The two Transport layer protocols provided by TCP/IP are

- **User Datagram Protocol (UDP)** adds very little to the underlying IP transmission service. Datagrams are small, fixed-sized packages of data sent over a network. Like IP, UDP neither guarantees that the data (transmitted as *datagrams*) arrives in order nor that the datagrams arrive at their intended destination. UDP is useful in applications when you are sending many small units of data, speed is more important than guaranteed delivery, and the application will make sure that data is received.

- **Transmission Control Protocol (TCP)** is a connection-oriented Transport layer protocol that ensures that the data arrives and arrives in the correct order. TCP sets up a connection between the sender and the receiver and uses the services of IP to send and receive data. TCP reorders information that is received out of order, and TCP will request that information that was not received be sent again.

Under Windows NT, as was mentioned in Chapter 8, a network transport protocol must conform to the TDI interface. Both UDP and TCP in the Microsoft implementation of TCP/IP communicate with the application layer through the TDI interface. The TDI interface, however, is a Windows NT standard, not a TCP/IP or Internet standard.

The Application Layer

The Application layer in a typical TCP/IP implementation contains the following network applications (some of which are also included in Windows NT Workstation):

- **Ping** is a utility that tests connectivity between computers on the Internet. It uses Internet Control Message Protocol echo request and echo reply packets to time how long it takes for information to get to the other computer and back.

- **Telnet** is a utility that gives you a character mode interactive session with another computer.

- **Rlogin** is like telnet in that it gives you a command line interface to another computer, but it also does more for UNIX computers to make the connection transparent to UNIX programs. Rlogin is not included in the Windows NT TCP/IP package.

- **Rsh** allows you to type commands on your local system that will be executed on the remote system. The results are returned to you on the local system. Rsh is not included in the Windows NT TCP/IP package.

- **File Transfer Protocol (FTP)** is a utility that transfers files to and from remote computers over TCP/IP. The remote computer must have an FTP server. Windows NT provides both an FTP utility and an FTP server.

- **Trivial File Transfer Protocol** is a file transfer protocol usually used to download operating system code for UNIX-networked client machines. Windows NT TCP/IP does not include TFTP.

- **Simple Mail Transfer Protocol (SMTP)** is used to send and receive Internet mail. Windows NT does not include an SMTP mail client, but many mail packages do.

- **Domain Name Service (DNS)** translates human-friendly Internet addresses such as `electriciti.com` to numerical Internet addresses such as `198.5.212.8`, which the computer needs to find the receiving computer. Windows NT workstations use the DNS protocol to look up names stored on DNS servers elsewhere on the network, such as on a Windows NT server.

- **Simple Network Management Protocol (SNMP)** has become the most widely used protocol for monitoring network devices such as hubs, routers, workstations, and computers. Windows NT supports SNMP.

The Windows NT Application level contains several operating system and network services that are not strictly part of the TCP/IP protocol suite but that can use the TCP/IP protocols in a Windows NT network:

- **Windows Internet Name Service (WINS)** performs for a Windows local area network the same service that DNS performs for a large TCP/IP internetwork and the Internet. WINS, however, is more automatic and easily configured. Windows NT Server 4.0 integrates the WINS and DNS services.

- **Server** responds to redirected file requests from other computers on the network.

- **Workstation, or Network Redirector,** forwards file and print requests to the server over the network. Workstation provides a file system interface to application programs.

- **Programming APIs** provide an interface to network services other than a file system interface. Windows Sockets is one such API—it provides an interface to TCP/IP that application programs can use to implement non–file system services such as e-mail, World Wide Web browsers, audio transmission, and remote terminals.

TCP/IP Configuration

W HEN YOU SET UP TCP/IP networking on your NT workstation, you will need certain information about your TCP/IP network:

- The IP address of your computer

- The subnet mask for your network

- The default gateway

- The domain name server

- Dynamic Host Configuration Protocol information

- Windows Internet Name Service information

Figure 9.1 shows the Microsoft TCP/IP Properties window, which contains these configuration settings.

This section will explain the TCP/IP networking settings and walk you through the process of installing TCP/IP on your workstation.

IP Address

The IP address uniquely identifies your computer on a TCP/IP network. It consists of four numbers separated by dots, and each number must be between 0 and 255. For instance, 128.110.121.42 is a valid IP address.

The first one to three numbers (depending on the subnet mask, described below) identify the network that your computer is on. The remaining number(s) identify your computer on that network. The address as a whole should uniquely identify your computer among all computers worldwide.

Microsoft TCP/IP Properties

IP Address | DNS | WINS Address | Routing

An IP address can be automatically assigned to this network card by a DHCP server. If your network does not have a DHCP server, ask your network administrator for an address, and then type it in the space below.

Adapter:
[1] Novell NE2000 Adapter

○ Obtain an IP address from a DHCP server
● Specify an IP address

IP Address: 128 .110 .121 .42
Subnet Mask: 255 .255 .0   .0
Default Gateway: .   .   .

Advanced...

OK   Cancel   Apply

If the first three numbers identify your network address (indicated by the subnet mask), then your computer is a part of a class C network. A class C network can contain up to 255 computers and is the most common Internet network size. If the first two numbers identify your network address, then you are on a class B network, which can have up to about 65,000 computers. (There are far fewer class B networks than there are class C networks.) Class B networks are usually very large corporate and university networks. If only the first number identifies your network and the remaining three identify the computers on the network, then you are on a class A network. Class A networks are reserved for other wide area internetworks with millions of computers that are linked to the Internet.

If your network is connected to other networks, then you will have received your network ID and perhaps your whole IP address from an outside source such as Internet Network Information Center (InterNIC) or from an Internet provider, which received the numbers from InterNIC.

IP addresses ending in 0 and 255 are special addresses in TCP/IP.

This address can be configured automatically if DHCP has been installed on your network, or you can enter the information manually.

Subnet Mask

The subnet mask, which usually looks like this—255.255.0.0—marks which part of the IP address is the network ID and which part is your station ID. A value of 255 means that the number is a part of the network ID. A value of 0 identifies your station ID. For instance, a subnet mask of 255.255.255.0 with an IP address of 198.5.212.40 means that your network is 198.5.212 and you are station 40 on that network.

TCP/IP uses subnet masks because some networks need a large number of station addresses and other networks need few. The subnet scheme provides for a large number of small networks and a small number of large networks.

Sometimes you will see a value other than 0 or 255 in the subnet mask. This additional value divides networks into even smaller subnets. For example, a subnet mask of 255.255.255.128 would give you a network with fewer than 127 available addresses for client stations. The topic of dividing subnets is beyond the scope of this book, but you should recognize when a network is being so divided.

The subnet mask is used to identify a message destination that is beyond your local network. When a destination network ID (identified from your subnet mask) is not the same as your network ID, then the message is sent to a gateway (see below), which will forward the message to the destination computer. This setting can be configured automatically if you have DHCP on your network, or you can configure the subnet mask manually.

Default Gateway

When the destination computer is not on the same network as your computer, the message must be forwarded from your network to the destination network. A special device or computer called a *gateway* handles the task of forwarding. When your computer recognizes that the destination computer is not on your local network (by combining the subnet mask with the destination IP address), your computer sends the message to the gateway instead.

For this reason the gateway must have an address that is on your local network. For instance, you could have a gateway on your network (198.5.212) at address 9. The default gateway IP address would be 198.5.212.9, and any address that did not have 198.5.212 as the first three numbers would not work.

If you do not have a valid gateway IP address, your computer, using TCP/IP, will be limited to communicating with computers on your local network only. This setting can be configured automatically if you have DHCP on your network, or you can configure the subnet mask manually.

Domain Name Server

Computers are very good at keeping track of numbers, but humans are better at dealing with names that mean something. Therefore, the designers of the Internet provided a means of converting human-friendly names into computer-friendly numbers. The Internet domain name service performs this function, and to use it you need the IP address (numbers) of the closest domain name server (DNS).

When you see an Internet address, such as `sybex.com`, `oeadm.org`, *or* `whitehouse.gov`, *you are seeing an address that the DNS must transform into numbers so that your computer can reach that destination computer.*

The DNS address will be a string of four numbers separated by dots like any other IP address, and it does not necessarily have to be on your local network. This setting can be configured automatically if you have DHCP on your network, or you can configure the DNS address manually. See Figure 9.2 for a view of the DNS tab of the Microsoft TCP/IP Properties window.

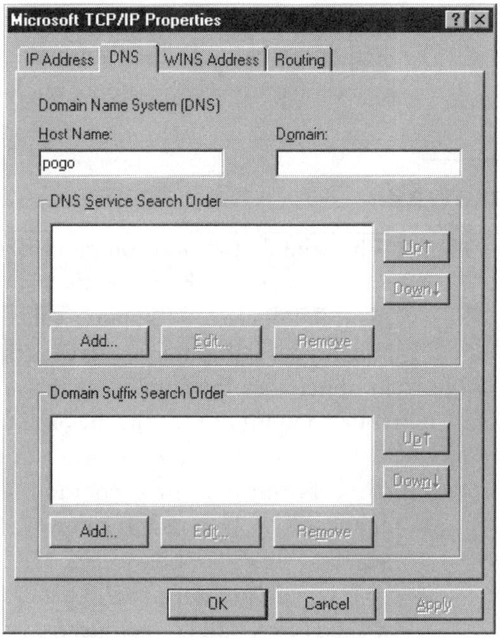

FIGURE 9.2
You can manually enter the location of domain name servers for your network.

Microsoft TCP/IP Properties

| IP Address | DNS | WINS Address | Routing |

Domain Name System (DNS)

Host Name: pogo   Domain:

DNS Service Search Order

Up↑
Down↓

Add...   Edit...   Remove

Domain Suffix Search Order

Up↑
Down↓

Add...   Edit...   Remove

OK   Cancel   Apply

Dynamic Host Configuration Protocol

You can configure your Windows NT workstation to be automatically configured by a DHCP server elsewhere on your LAN (most likely by your Windows NT server). This service is covered in detail in the companion book, *MCSE: NT Server Study Guide*.

Windows Internet Name Service

WINS is a protocol Microsoft developed to make managing Internet numeric addresses easier in a LAN. WINS performs the function of mapping Microsoft networking names to the numeric representation (e.g., 111.222.333.444) of the Internet number. WINS keeps track of Microsoft-style computer names in your LAN. On the other hand, DNS looks up addresses that use the hierarchical Internet naming scheme (e.g., www.whitehouse.gov). You can configure NT Workstation to use WINS, DNS, or both to translate computer names into Internet addresses. The WINS server will run on a Windows NT server somewhere in your network. See Figure 9.3 for a view of WINS configuration.

Installing and Configuring TCP/IP

The TCP/IP protocol is one of the protocol options available when you install Windows NT Workstation. If you already installed this protocol, you won't have to perform the steps outlined in Exercise 9.1. However, if you need to reconfigure TCP/IP, then you will need to perform the steps in Exercise 9.1.

Windows NT and the Internet

THE MOST COMPELLING REASON to configure your workstation to use the TCP/IP protocol suite is to connect you to the Internet. You can use the Internet to send e-mail messages to other computer users around the world, retrieve files from remote computers using FTP, use the World Wide

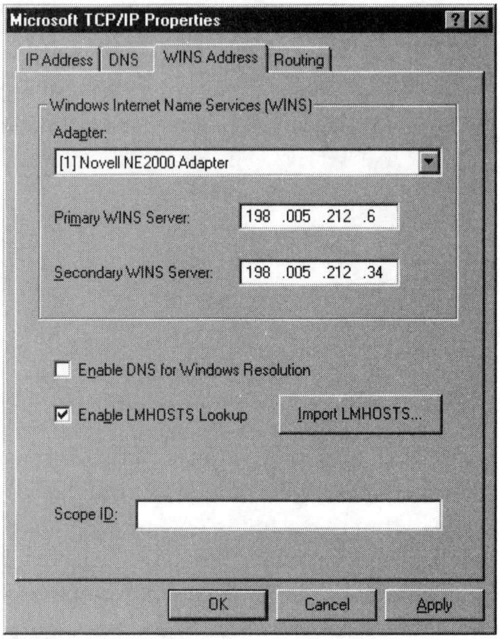

FIGURE 9.3
WINS translates
Microsoft-style network
names to numerical
Internet addresses
for you.

Web to search for specific information or browse Internet sites of interest to
you personally or professionally, and participate in the Internet News discussion forums on almost any topic imaginable. You or your company can use the
Internet to publish all kinds of information, such as your products and services,
prices, support resources, and literature; you can even use the Internet to distribute software and text data.

This section will show you the two ways you can connect to the Internet—by
using a direct Internet connection or by connecting via the Remote Access
Service of Windows NT. Then we will introduce several of the many Internet
tools that you can use to access information over the Internet.

Direct Internet Connection

A direct Internet network connection provides a constant connection between
your workstation or local area network and the Internet—you do not have to
start a service or make a connection to access an Internet resource. In addition

EXERCISE 9.1

Installing and Configuring TCP/IP

1. Select Settings ➤ Control Panel from Start.

2. Double-click the Network icon.

3. Click the Protocols tab in the Networks window.

4. Do one of the following:

- If you did not install TCP/IP when you installed the operating system, click Add.

- If you already installed TCP/IP, select the TCP/IP protocol from the list of protocols, click Properties, and then go to step 7.

5. Select TCP/IP Protocol from the list of protocols. You may be asked to insert the original installation CD-ROM.

6. Select Close in the Network window.

7. If your local area network has a DHCP server, select *Obtain an IP address from a DHCP Server.* Otherwise, enter the IP address for your computer in the IP address field. Specify the subnet mask and default gateway as well.

8. If you have a DNS server in your LAN or if you have a constant connection to the Internet, click the DNS tab and then enter the DNS address. *Or* if you have a WINS server in your network, click the WINS Address tab and then enter the WINS addresses. Click OK to close the TCP/IP Properties dialog box. You will receive a warning if you haven't specified a primary WINS address.

9. Click Close.

10. Restart your computer in order for the changes to take effect. Click Yes to restart your computer.

to making access to the Internet very convenient, this form of connection has a number of significant advantages over a dial-up connection:

- You can receive your Internet e-mail immediately rather than checking your mailbox at intervals throughout the day.

- Many computers on your LAN can share one Internet connection, rather than requiring each computer to dial and connect to an ISP individually.

- A direct Internet connection is usually a much faster connection than a dial-up modem connection.

- You can run Internet server programs such as World Wide Web servers and FTP servers, making selected information on your local network available to people worldwide.

- People in your organization can work remotely, accessing all of the services your network provides (files, printers, etc.) over the Internet as if they were directly connected to your network.

You can make the direct connection either with a device called an Internet router, which transfers TCP/IP information between the Internet service feed (usually a dedicated high-speed telephone line or an ISDN line) and your network, or with a computer on your network that performs the same service. In either case, a *gateway* (the computer or dedicated device) transfers TCP/IP data between the ISP and your local area network.

When you connect your network to the Internet via a gateway, your network becomes a subnetwork of the Internet. The computers on your LAN that are configured with TCP/IP become nodes on the part of the Internet that you manage.

Temporary Connection via Remote Access Service

If you do not have a direct Internet connection, you can connect your individual workstation to the Internet using the RAS software of Windows NT. RAS allows you to make networking connections using modems attached to your computer.

The individual connection you make to an ISP connects only your computer to the Internet because the ISP temporarily assigns one TCP/IP address to your workstation. Other computers on your network cannot share the connection because they would need a number in order to send and receive data over the Internet.

When you connect your workstation to the Internet via an individual Internet connection, your workstation becomes a node on the ISP's subnetwork. The ISP manages the network.

You will learn more about RAS and how to make RAS connections in Chapter 12.

Internet Tools

The appeal of TCP/IP does not lie in its technical sophistication, although it is a very sophisticated protocol suite, but rather in the unique tools that have been developed for use on a TCP/IP network.

One of the oldest and still one of the most useful Internet tools is Internet mail. Hundreds of thousands of messages are exchanged daily within and between companies worldwide via Internet mail. The most visible Internet tool today is the World Wide Web, which presents information textually and graphically and turns the Internet into an information resource and marketing tool unlike any other. Internet news gives individuals with common interests (from cooking to large system database administration) a new way to exchange information on almost any subject.

Once you have an Internet connection, whether it is a dedicated connection or a dial-up connection using RAS, you can use any of the following Internet tools.

The exercises that follow assume that you have a TCP/IP connection to the Internet from your workstation. If you do not have a direct Internet connection, you may need to refer to Chapter 12, "Remote Access Service," in order to establish a connection to an Internet Service Provider.

Internet Mail

You can use Internet mail to send e-mail messages to other individuals anywhere in the world. If you have a dedicated Internet connection and your LAN e-mail package is set up to route e-mail to the Internet, you do not have to do anything special to send Internet mail. In fact, you may not even need to have TCP/IP installed on your workstation if some other computer does the e-mail conversion.

If you are using Microsoft Exchange as your e-mail package, you can either use Microsoft Exchange Server to route your e-mail to the Internet, or if you checked the Internet option when you installed Exchange, you can send mail directly to the Internet from your workstation. Many Internet e-mail packages are available for Windows NT. Here are some of the popular e-mail features:

- Address books

- Inboxes and outboxes

- Mail boxes for specific correspondence

- Delayed message sending and offline mail reading

- Multiple e-mail account checking

- Automatic mail forwarding and mail checking

- Mail filters and automated mail processing

- File attachment and flexible mail formats

See Figure 9.4 for an example of a package that can send Internet mail. In Exercise 9.2 you will send an e-mail message over the Internet using Microsoft Exchange.

If Microsoft Exchange is not configured, you may have to configure it. Configuring Microsoft Exchange is beyond the scope of this book. Ask your network administrator to configure it, consult the Microsoft documentation, or consult the Network Press book MCSE: Exchange Study Guide.

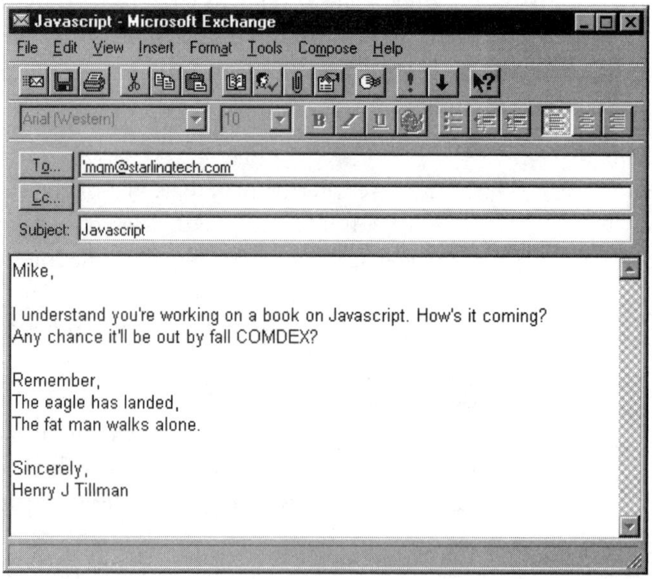

FIGURE 9.4
Microsoft Exchange can send e-mail over the Internet.

☒ **Javascript - Microsoft Exchange**

File Edit View Insert Format Tools Compose Help

To... 'mgm@starlingtech.com'
Cc...
Subject: Javascript

Mike,

I understand you're working on a book on Javascript. How's it coming?
Any chance it'll be out by fall COMDEX?

Remember,
The eagle has landed,
The fat man walks alone.

Sincerely,
Henry J Tillman

EXERCISE 9.2

Sending an Internet E-mail Message Using Microsoft Exchange

1. Start Microsoft Exchange (double-click on the Inbox icon on the desktop).

2. Select New Message from the Compose menu.

3. Enter the address **MCSEWSSG40@aol.com** in the To: box.

4. Enter **Exercise 9.2** in the Subject: box.

5. Enter the following message in the text area of the window: **Exercise 9.2 completed. I will be a Microsoft Certified Systems Engineer soon.**

6. Select Send from the File menu.

7. If you are working offline (check your configuration and refer to step 1 above), then in the Inbox-Microsoft Exchange window, select Tools ➤ Deliver Now Using ➤ Internet Mail option.

8. Select File ➤ Exit and log off.

World Wide Web

The World Wide Web has given businesses the most compelling reason since e-mail to connect to the Internet. Before the World Wide Web, the widely used Internet programs were character based. The World Wide Web allows graphical as well as textual information to be displayed, and new innovations in World Wide Web technology provide for continuous sound and video transmission and dynamic displays based on executable code.

You can use the World Wide Web to search for product information, download changes to software and firmware, keep abreast of information published in electronic newsletters, research any subject from auto mechanics to zoology, and much more.

You can also publish your own information on the World Wide Web. If you have a constant connection to the Internet, the information can be stored on your workstation or on your LAN server. If you have a dial-up connection, your ISP usually will provide space on its server for your Web information.

Several Web browsers are in wide use today. Netscape is a very popular and feature-filled Web browser. Microsoft includes a Web browser with Windows NT called the Windows Internet Explorer (see Figure 9.5). Web browsers may support some or all of these features:

- Bookmarks for favorite Web sites

- Multiple browsing windows

- Frames or multiple views within a window

- Multiple outstanding requests to Web servers

- User settings for colors and other aspects of screen appearance

- Web interface to FTP and Gopher Internet sites

- Secure data transmission

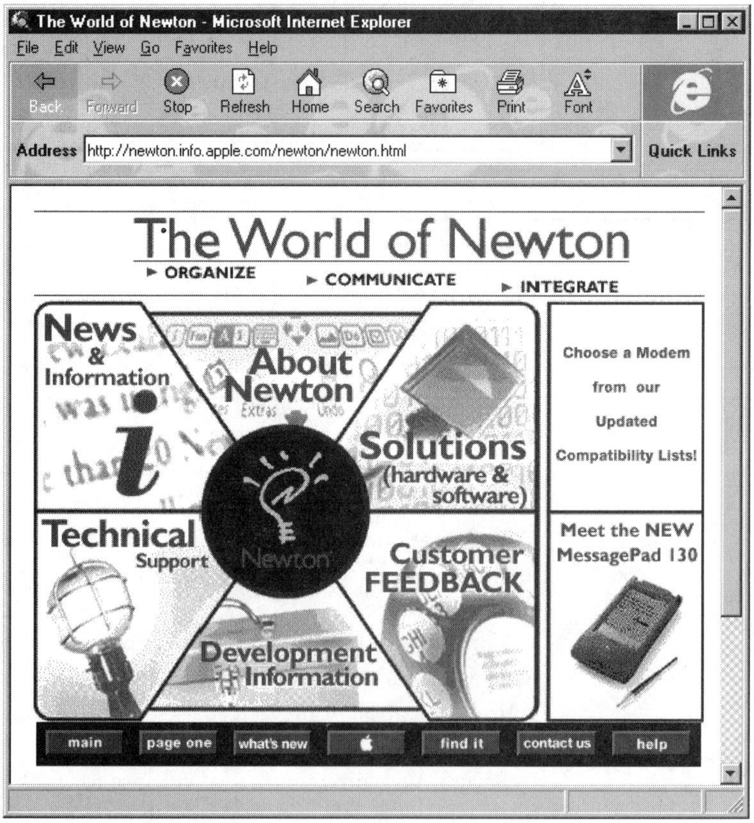

FIGURE 9.5
Internet Explorer is
your graphical interface
to the Internet.

- User-configurable helper applications for new data types

- Support for Java and other scripting languages

In Exercise 9.3 you will access and search the World Wide Web over the Internet using Microsoft's Internet Explorer.

EXERCISE 9.3

Access the World Wide Web Using Internet Explorer and Search for Windows NT Information

1. Start Internet Explorer (double-click on the Internet Explorer icon on the desktop).

If your Internet Explorer is in its default configuration, you will be viewing the Microsoft Network web site http://www.msn.com.

2. Replace http://www.msn.com in the Address field, with http://www .sybex.com and then press Enter.

Internet Explorer displays the Sybex Web page.

3. Select Add To Favorites from the Favorites menu. In the Add To Favorites window, press the Add button.

The Sybex Web page will appear in the Favorites menu.

4. Replace http://www.sybex.com in the Address field with http://www .yahoo.com and then press Enter.

This address takes you to the Yahoo home page where you will see a list of categories.

5. Click once on the underlined Computers and Internet category to go to the Computers and Internet subcategory.

6. Select *Search only* in the Computers and Internet search option.

7. Type **"Windows NT"** (including quote marks) in the text box before the Search button and then click the Search button.

Yahoo displays a list of Web pages that refer to Windows NT.

8. Select the Sybex entry from the Favorites menu. You will be returned to the Sybex home page.

9. Close Internet Explorer by selecting Exit from the File menu.

FTP

FTP is a protocol for transferring files over the Internet, and many FTP utilities are available for Windows NT. Microsoft ships an FTP utility with the Windows NT operating system; it is installed when you install the operating system.

The FTP utility that ships with Windows NT is a command line utility; you type commands from within the utility to perform the file transfer operations. You can set up an icon that will start the FTP utility, or you can invoke it from the Windows NT command line.

Many graphical FTP utilities translate the actions you perform on graphical objects (e.g., selecting a file from a file list on a remote computer and then clicking Get) into the textual commands that the FTP protocol expects (e.g., get "filename"). See Figure 9.6 for an example of FTP in action.

In Exercise 9.4 you will download a file from an Internet FTP site using the Microsoft provided FTP tool.

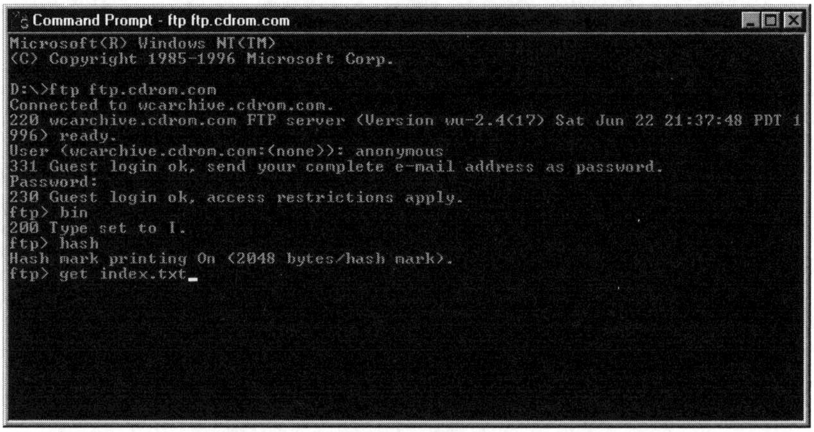

FIGURE 9.6
FTP is a tool to retrieve files over the Internet.

Telnet

Telnet is a utility that gives you a text terminal interface to another computer over a TCP/IP network. Telnet is usually used to connect to a remote UNIX computer.

If your ISP provides you with a UNIX shell account, telnet is most likely how you will access that shell account. If you have a dial-up connection, your mail will probably be delivered to this account. Although accessing this e-mail account is easier if you use a TCP/IP e-mail package as described above, you can use telnet

EXERCISE 9.4

Using the Microsoft FTP Tool

1. Select Run from the Start menu.

2. Type **FTP** in the Open entry and then click OK.

3. Type **open ftp.sybex.com** in the FTP window.

4. Type **anonymous** at the User prompt and then press Enter.

5. Type your e-mail address at the Password prompt.

6. Type **ls** when you see the *Guest logon ok* message and the ftp > prompt. Then press Enter to view the current ftp directory.

7. Change the ftp directory to the pub directory. (Type **cd /pub** and then press Enter.)

8. View the contents of this directory. (Type **ls** and press Enter again.)

9. Type **bin** and then press Enter to configure FTP to transfer files as binary data.

10. Type **hash** and then press Enter to have FTP print hash marks as the file is transferred.

11. Type **get releases.txt** and then press Enter to download the releases.txt file from the FTP site.

12. Type **close** when the file transfer is complete and then press Enter.

13. Type **quit** and then press Enter.

and the UNIX shell account command line programs to send and receive e-mail. You may also have to use the UNIX command line in order to manage World Wide Web files in this UNIX account if you are using the ISP to publish your Web pages to the Internet.

Windows NT comes with a telnet utility that is installed when you install the operating system. See Figure 9.7 for an example of telnet in use.

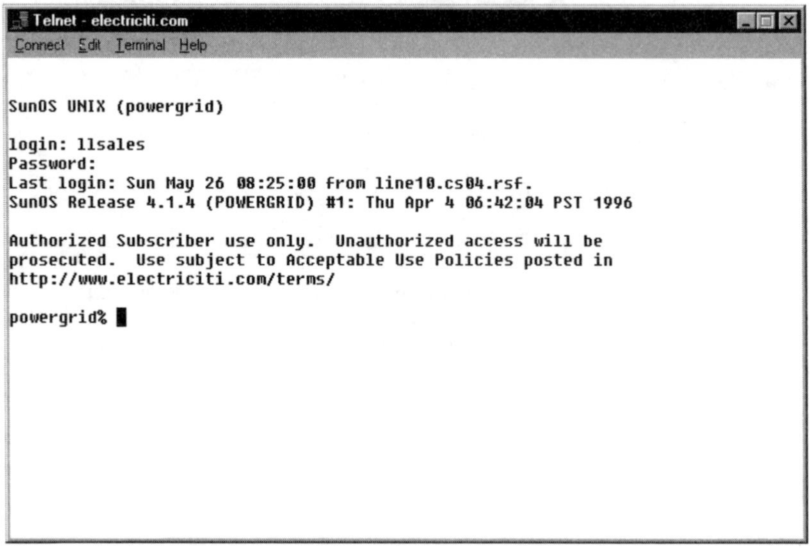

FIGURE 9.7
Telnet enables you
to access command
line accounts on
other computers.

```
Telnet - electriciti.com                                          _ □ ×
Connect  Edit  Terminal  Help

SunOS UNIX (powergrid)

login: llsales
Password:
Last login: Sun May 26 08:25:00 from line10.cs04.rsf.
SunOS Release 4.1.4 (POWERGRID) #1: Thu Apr 4 06:42:04 PST 1996

Authorized Subscriber use only.  Unauthorized access will be
prosecuted.  Use subject to Acceptable Use Policies posted in
http://www.electriciti.com/terms/

powergrid% █
```

FIGURE 9.7
Telnet enables you to access command line accounts on other computers.

UseNet News

UseNet News is a worldwide replicated bulletin board network with tens of thousands of topics that individuals around the world discuss constantly. You will find that it is an unparalleled resource for solving technical problems, especially computer and computer networking problems. For any problem you face, you can be assured that someone has probably already faced that problem—and found a solution to it. Many progressive companies also provide technical support in newsgroups.

Internet newsgroups are not limited to technical subjects. You will find newsgroups on topics ranging from boat building to politics. The subjects of newsgroups are only as limited as the imaginations of the individuals on the Internet.

In order to access Internet News, you will need to install a newsreader program and have access to a UseNet server supplied on your network or by your Internet provider (most UseNet servers are limited to subscriber access). Many newsreaders are available for Windows NT, and you may find other Internet tools that include a newsreader. Netscape, for instance, is a World Wide Web browser that has a built-in newsreader and an Internet e-mail package. See Figure 9.8 for an example of Internet News in use.

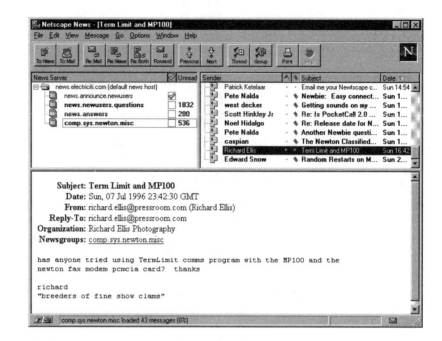

FIGURE 9.8
With Internet News you can communicate with other people interested in a topic.

Peer Web Services

WITH NT WORKSTATION 4.0 Microsoft has adapted many of the Internet tools and services for use in individual client computers. The Microsoft Internet Information Server makes organizational information accessible via Internet tools over your network and (if so configured) over the Internet. The Microsoft IIS is a set of Server services and is explained in the book *MCSE: NT Server Study Guide*. The IIS is designed to serve information simultaneously to a large number of locally connected (on your network) and remote (over the Internet) users.

Windows NT Workstation 4.0 includes a similar set of tools. This set of tools, called Peer Web Services, is not designed to serve organizational information; instead it is designed to publish (electronically) individual and personal information from your workstation computer. This service is much like NT Workstation's peer-to-peer directory sharing capability, which was designed to allow individual users to make files on their computer available to others over the network, rather than to provide network file storage.

The Internet services that Peer Web Services provides are

- **WWW:** Allows you to publish World Wide Web pages from your workstation to your network and (if your computer is configured appropriately) to the Internet.

- **Gopher:** Uses a textual Internet menuing system to present information in a less resource and bandwidth intensive manner than is required by the World Wide Web.

- **FTP:** Allows you to make files on your computer available to others using the Internet File Transfer Protocol.

The following Windows NT Workstation 4.0 tools help you manage your Peer Web Services:

- **Internet Services Manager:** Allows you to start and stop the Internet services as well as to configure their operation.

- **Key Manager:** Allows you to configure additional security measures.

- **Peer Web Services Install:** Allows you to add or remove Peer Web Services software.

Once you have installed Peer Web Services, these tools appear in the Start menu location: Start ➤ Programs ➤ Microsoft Peer Web Services (common).

Installing Peer Web Services

Peer Web Services require the TCP/IP protocol. If you installed TCP/IP earlier in this chapter or if you installed TCP/IP when you installed the operating system or if someone else has installed TCP/IP, then you may proceed with the following exercise. Others can access your Peer Web Services via RAS if you have installed RAS and are connected to the Internet, but RAS is not a requirement for installing Peer Web Services.

You install Peer Web Services from the Network icon in the Control Panel. Exercise 9.5 will walk you through the process of installing Peer Web Services.

EXERCISE 9.5

Installing Peer Web Services

1. Open the Network Control Panel icon (Start ➤ Settings ➤ Control Panel and then double-click the Network icon).

2. Click the Services tab and then click the Add button.

3. Select Microsoft Peer Web Services from the list and then click OK. You may be asked for the location of the Windows NT CD-ROM installation files.

4. Insert the Windows NT CD-ROM if necessary and then enter the location of the setup files. Press OK when you are ready to continue. The Peer Web Services setup program will then run.

5. Press OK at the bottom of the Microsoft Peer Web Services window. You will be presented with a number of service options to install.

6. Accept the default settings and press OK at the bottom of the screen. Next you will see a Publishing Directories window, with default settings for each of the Internet services.

7. Accept the default settings by clicking OK at the bottom of the screen.

8. Press Yes to confirm the creation of the directories.

9. Press OK if Peer Web Services tells you that you do not have an Internet Domain name configured. (The Gopher service will not operate properly without it.)

10. Click OK to accept the default selection if you are asked to select OBDC drivers from an Install Drivers window.

11. Press OK when you are informed that Microsoft Peer Web Services setup was completed successfully. Microsoft Peer Web Services should now appear in the Network window's Services tab.

12. Press Close.

Using Peer Web Services

Once you have installed Peer Web Services on your workstation, you can place information in three subdirectories of the `InetPub` directory created during the Peer Web Services install process. You will place World Wide Web pages in the `wwwroot` subdirectory, Gopher information in the `gophroot` subdirectory, and FTP files in the `ftproot` subdirectory.

If you are using Microsoft Internet Explorer in a network of Windows and Windows NT computers, you can access peer Web pages by typing **http://** followed by the computer name of the workstation you wish to access. Microsoft Explorer can translate Microsoft network UNC names into Internet addresses.

If information on your workstation will be accessed from the Internet or from computers that do not recognize UNC names, your computer's name must have an entry in the Domain Name Service that satisfies requests for Internet names for your network. You cannot configure this name from your workstation; the maintainer of your TCP/IP network is responsible for handling the entry.

Exercise 9.6 publishes an HTML document using Peer Web Services.

EXERCISE 9.6

Publishing an HTML Document Using Peer Web Services

1. Insert the CD-ROM that came with this book into the CD-ROM drive.

2. Copy the `hello.html` file from the CD-ROM to the `InetPub\wwwroot` directory.

3. Start Microsoft Internet Explorer (double-click the Explorer icon on the desktop).

4. Type the URL address of your computer followed by `/hello.html` in the Address: field of Explorer. (For example, if your computer's name is YOYO, type **http://yoyo/hello.html.**) Press Enter.

5. Notice the Web page that now exists on your computer. Close Explorer.

Web Security

You may wish to use Peer Web Services to publish information that only certain individuals or groups can view. You can restrict access to Web pages and FTP files in several ways.

Web accesses can either be made with a username and password, passed to your computer by the Web browser on the accessing computer, or they can be made anonymously. Similarly, FTP connections can be made with a username and password or with the anonymous username and a password consisting of an e-mail address. (This access method is the anonymous logon process for FTP.) When a Peer Web Service action is taken (that is, a Web page is transmitted or an FTP file is read or written), the action is performed using the account specified by the Web connection, the FTP connection, or the anonymous account (created during the installation of Peer Web Services).

When the `InetPub` resides on an NTFS partition, Windows NT applies NTFS security requirements to any accesses to the Peer Web Services data. This process, combined with the account information received from the Internet service request, gives you a powerful and flexible way of controlling the information that you present over the Internet.

You can allow anyone to view some files and allow only certain users and groups in your network to view other files by removing the ability of the Everyone group (of which the anonymous user is by default a member) to read the files and granting that right specifically to certain users or to a group of users. This method works for both FTP files and World Wide Web files if the user is browsing the files with a World Wide Web browser that transmits the username and password to a requesting (and trusted) Web service. Microsoft Internet Explorer works in this manner.

If you are concerned that passwords might be intercepted while traveling from the accessing computer to your Peer Web site, you should require the Microsoft challenge-and-response password-authentication option. This option protects the usernames and passwords from capture while they travel over an unsecured medium such as the Internet.

Chapter Summary

TCP/IP ORIGINATED AS THE native networking protocol of UNIX computers and is now the networking protocol of the Internet.

The TCP/IP protocols operate at the Network and Transport layers of the OSI model. Many Application layer networking programs that are traditionally a part of the Internet protocol suite are also a part of the TCP/IP package provided by Microsoft for Windows NT.

TCP/IP configuration can be automatic if you use DHCP, or you can specifically set the Internet address, subnet mask, name server address, gateway addresses, and WINS server address for the TCP/IP protocols.

Your workstation can connect to the Internet either directly and constantly over your LAN or temporarily via a dial-up connection through RAS whenever you need to access the Internet.

Once you have TCP/IP installed on your computer and you have an Internet connection, you will be able to use Internet tools. Internet e-mail will carry your messages around the world, the World Wide Web will deliver unimaginable amounts of information, and Internet News will connect you with colleagues everywhere.

Exercise Questions

1. TCP/IP is mostly used in its native realm of high-performance engineering workstations.

   A. True

   B. False

2. TCP/IP was designed as a local area network protocol, rather than as a protocol to link LANs together.

   A. True

   B. False

3. The Network layer in the TCP/IP protocol suite corresponds to the Data Link and Physical layers in the OSI model and to the device drivers in Windows NT architecture.

   A. True

   B. False

4. NDIS is a TCP/IP standard interface.

   A. True

   B. False

5. UDP guarantees that the data will arrive and will arrive in the order sent.

   A. True

   B. False

6. TCP guarantees that the data will arrive and will arrive in the order sent.

   A. True

   B. False

7. Windows NT does not support the DNS protocol.

   A. True

   B. False

8. The IP address for your computer must be unique.

    A. True

    B. False

9. If you do not have a valid default gateway setting in your TCP/IP configuration, you will not be able to communicate with computers beyond your local area network using TCP/IP.

    A. True

    B. False

10. `198.263.5.97` is a valid IP Address.

    A. True

    B. False

11. The native protocol for UNIX computers is _____.

12. The first TCP/IP specifications were circulated as _____ for _____.

13. The current open membership standards body for TCP/IP and the Internet is the _____ _____ _____ _____.

14. _____ and _____ operate at the Transport and Network layers of the OSI model.

15. IP is a part of the _____ layer in the TCP/IP protocol suite.

16. _____ uses IP to control the flow of data over TCP/IP networks.

17. DHCP stands for _____ _____ _____ _____.

18. TCP/IP provides two types of Transport layer services: _____ and _____.

19. IP addresses ending in _____ and _____ are special addresses in TCP/IP.

20. The _____ _____ is used to identify a message destination that is beyond your local network.

21. When a destination network ID is not the same as your network ID, then the message is sent to a _____.

22. DNS stands for _____ _____ _____.

23. The most compelling reason to configure your workstation to use the TCP/IP protocol suite is to connect you to the _____.

24. Match the Internet tool with the activity:

1. Internet News

A. Exchange messages with other individuals around the world

2. FTP

B. Browse information presented by others over the Internet in a graphical format

3. World Wide Web

C. Retrieve files from other computers using a command line interface

4. Telnet

D. Use a command line interface to access a UNIX shell account

5. Internet mail

E. Participate in discussion groups

NetWare
Connectivity

THE NETWARE INTEROPERABILITY network components for Windows NT were designed to make working in a NetWare environment and the migration from NetWare to Windows NT very smooth. Windows NT workstations can connect to NetWare servers as easily as can clients running any other operating system. Windows NT servers can function with and complement NetWare servers in the same network. Clients configured for NetWare access can log in to Windows NT servers and can run many NetWare-aware applications and utilities.

These capabilities are provided by two Windows NT networking components: NetWare Link (NWLink), a Transport Driver Interface (TDI)–compliant transport that is compatible with NetWare's IPX protocol, and Client Services for NetWare (CSNW), a NetWare compatible redirector that integrates NetWare servers into the Windows NT browsing paradigm as seamlessly as native Windows NT servers.

New to Windows NT 4.0 is the ability to browse the NetWare 4.x NetWare Directory Services (NDS) tree structure. Windows NT no longer requires NetWare 3.1x bindery emulation to attach to a NetWare 4.x server and is able to show the entire NDS tree structure in the Network Neighborhood browser.

NetWare Networks

MANY ORGANIZATIONS INSTALLED NetWare file servers in an attempt to downsize from expensive mainframes and minicomputers. NetWare is optimized for file and print services, and it performs these tasks faster than Windows NT does on comparable hardware.

However, the tradeoff for this optimization is the lack of protected memory features and cooperative multitasking, which means in essence that any application (called a *NetWare loadable module*, or NLM) running on a NetWare server that crashes will bring down the entire server. The reliability of a NetWare server is equal to the reliability of its least reliable component. For this reason, NetWare servers do not make very good application servers.

NetWare 4.1 has protected memory partitioning and is capable of running untrusted NLMs in a protected memory space that should make the server capable of surviving an application crash, but even that powerful technology does not approach the robust, protected, preemptive multitasking of Windows NT.

Rather than attempting to compete with NetWare's speed at file and print services, Microsoft wisely chose to build a well-rounded operating system that performs bulletproof file and print sharing with integral security and mainframe-class application service. The security features and the overhead of Windows NT's preemptive, multitasking architecture require more computing power than NetWare requires, so Microsoft recommends using a powerful Pentium-based computer when running Windows NT Server.

Microsoft has made a number of significant improvements in the CSN component by truly supporting NetWare 4.1 and the NDS.

NDS acts like the Windows NT domain paradigm and the browser name service, but it includes more robust enterprise management and more control over the interaction between organizational units (domains) than does Windows NT.

Windows NT 4.0 now includes support for logging on to NetWare 4.1 servers without the need to run bindery emulation on the NetWare server. NT also now supports running NetWare logon scripts.

Workstations and NetWare

Because Windows NT is a modular operating system designed with network interoperability in mind, every type of network appears the same to a Windows NT client. For instance, the Windows NT Explorer can browse NetWare file servers as easily as it can browse Windows NT servers. The user interface is the same for all supported network.

The multi-provider router (MPR) built into Windows NT shields the difference between NetWare servers and Windows NT servers from the Windows NT workstation. Users do not need to know or to care that the files or printers they are using are attached to a NetWare file server rather than to a Windows NT server.

Servers and NetWare

Windows NT servers can provide gateway services to NetWare file servers for workstations that do not have NWLink or CSNW installed, making network migrations very easy. Rather than installing CSNW and NWLink on every one of a thousand clients, a network administrator can provide the NetWare Gateway Service on a single Windows NT server to connect clients to file and print services on a NetWare server.

For most installations, using Gateway Services for NetWare on a single Windows NT server will be easier than installing client services on every workstation. Use this method unless operational speed is paramount.

Using Gateway Services for NetWare on a single Windows NT server also provides a convenient way to bridge NetWare networks in one department with Windows NT networks in another without changing client software on the Windows NT network. NetWare clients will be able to access the Windows NT server for application services, but because Windows NT Server does not respond to NetWare core protocol file and print requests, they will not be able to use Windows NT file and print services without installing Windows NT client software. Figure 10.1 shows a network diagram that illustrates these concepts.

NetWare Gateway Service is covered in more detail in the companion Network Press book *MCSE: NT Server Study Guide*, also published by Sybex.

FIGURE 10.1
Connecting networks with NetWare Gateway Service.

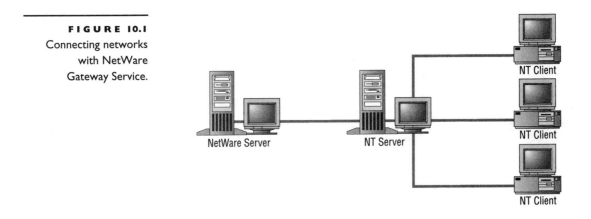

NetWare Compatibility Components

M AKING NETWARE FILE SERVICES visible to Windows NT clients requires two Windows NT components: NWLink and Client Services for NetWare. NWLink is the TDI-compliant implementation of the IPX/SPX transport protocol for Windows NT. CSNW is the NetWare redirector for Windows NT that generates NetWare Core Protocol requests for file and print services.

Application services are also available because NWLink supports the Windows Sockets and NetBIOS programming interfaces.

NetWare Link

NWLink implements Novell's IPX/SPX transport protocol for Windows NT by conforming to the TDI specification. Although NWLink was designed to provide an interface to NetWare file servers, it can be used to connect to any operating system implementing the IPX transport protocol such as OS/2, Windows, or MS-DOS.

Microsoft recommends TCP/IP as the default transport protocol for Windows NT because of its seamless Internet connectivity, but you may want to use NWLink as your default protocol instead—even if you do not intend to support NetWare.

Setting up NWLink is considerably easier than setting up TCP/IP. NWLink is also slightly faster than TCP/IP in the current implementation because it does not perform as much error correction for slow unreliable links.

Using NWLink as your default transport protocol also allows you to control access to and from the Internet by withholding the TCP/IP transport protocol. This method lets you use NWLink as a low-level security gateway. Machines not running the TCP/IP stack will not be able to access the Internet, nor will they be susceptible to intrusion from the Internet.

NWLink is routable through routers that support IPX, so you can create very large enterprise networks based upon it. Because NetWare has been around for a long time, most routers support the IPX protocol.

Like all Windows NT transport protocols, NWLink interfaces to network adapter drivers through the NDIS 3 specification, so it supports all network adapters supported by NDIS. This interface is shown in Figure 10.2.

FIGURE 10.2
NWLink in the
Windows NT Model.

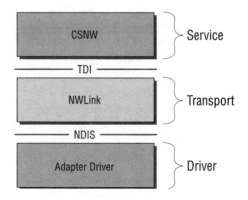

Sockets

NWLink supports the Windows Sockets API. Sockets are commonly used to communicate with NLMs, which implement the server side of client/server applications running on NetWare servers. The server side of client/server NLMs running on NetWare servers can be rewritten to Windows NT from NetWare without changing the client interface.

NetBIOS

NetBIOS over NWLink is fully compatible with Novell's implementation of NetBIOS over IPX. Microsoft's NetBIOS is enhanced to provide retransmission timers and sliding windows. These enhancements do not apply when communicating with a NetWare server.

Installing and Configuring NWLink

Installing NWLink is very similar to installing other Windows NT transports such as TCP/IP or NetBEUI. NWLink does have some setting information that can be changed after it is installed by double-clicking the NWLink protocol in the Protocols list box, but the default settings will work for most users. Exercise 10.1 takes you through the process of installing NWLink. Note that NWLink will be installed during the installation of CSNW if it is not already installed.

When you log back on to Windows NT Workstation, you will have a running IPX stack upon which to run CSNW. NWLink will also function as a capable transport for the Microsoft Windows NT Network, so you may chose to use it as your sole transport if you do not require TCP/IP or NetBEUI.

FRAME TYPES For most users, leaving the default frame type (auto) is the best choice. Unfortunately, some Ethernet adapters cannot properly detect frame types automatically and will therefore not work with this setting. For these adapters, you will need to set the frame type specifically. The Ethernet 802.2 setting is recommended for new installations. Your setting must match the frame type on the NetWare server to which you are going to connect.

Ethernet frame types control how Ethernet adapters communicate with each other. They include Ethernet source and destination information and a checksum. The different frame types handle this task in slightly different fashions and are therefore incompatible. The differences between them are esoteric and of little

---

EXERCISE 10.1

Installing and Configuring NWLink

1. Right-click on the Network Neighborhood icon on the Desktop.

2. Select Properties.

3. Select the Protocols tab.

4. Click the Add button.

5. Select the NWLink IPX/SPX Compatible Transport in the Network Protocols list box.

6. Click OK.

7. Enter the path to your Windows NT 4.0 Workstation CD-ROM in the Path field of the Windows NT Setup dialog box and click Continue. If you have RAS installed, a dialog box will ask whether you want to bind NWLink to RAS. Click OK to bind them or Cancel to leave them unbound.

8. Click the Close button.

9. Click Yes when asked if you want to restart.

---

importance. Novell NetWare 3.11 and earlier used Ethernet_802.3 as the default frame type. Novell 3.12 and later uses the Ethernet_802.2 frame type as the default setting. To avoid reconfiguring clients when new servers are added, many NetWare servers simply load the LAN driver once for each frame type. This method reduces performance a little and takes slightly more memory, but it is a good tradeoff to preclude frame incompatibility problems. Exercise 10.2 shows you how to change frame types.

You may add as many frame types as you like to the supported frames dialog box. Be aware that many early Ethernet adapters support only certain frame types. If your network adapter is not software configurable (if it uses jumper switches to set the port and interrupt), it probably does not support all four frame types.

Another way to set the network number is through the NWLink setting dialog box. You can use the default setting of zero to match any network number. If you set a network number, it must match the network number assigned to the adapter through which the NetWare server is communicating to your Windows NT

EXERCISE 10.2

Changing the Ethernet Frame Type and IPX Network Number

1. Right-click on the Network Neighborhood icon on the Desktop.

2. Select Properties.

3. Select the Protocols tab.

4. Double-click the NWLink IPX/SPX Compatible Transport item in the Network Protocols list box.

5. If you have more than one adapter in your computer, select the adapter that resides on the same network as your NetWare file server in the Adapter drop-down box.

6. Select the Manual Frame Type Detection radio button.

7. Click the Add button.

8. Select the Frame Type you wish to use. Frame type 802.2 is standard for NetWare versions 3.12 and above. Frame type 802.3 is standard for NetWare versions 3.11 and below. You will not be able to communicate with a NetWare server unless the frame type you enter here matches a frame type loaded on the server.

9. Enter the IPX network number to which the adapter is attached in the Network Number field. Use the number shown on the NetWare Server's LAN driver Information dialog box in the NetWare Monitor NLM.

10. Click the Add button.

11. Repeat steps 8, 9, and 10 for each additional frame type you wish to use.

12. Click OK.

13. Click the Close button.

14. Click Yes when asked if you want to restart.

workstation. If your NetWare server has only one network adapter, the matching number will be obvious. However, if your NetWare server has multiple adapters, you will need to determine which adapter is connected to the same network as your Windows NT workstation and use that network number.

Client Services for NetWare

CSNW implements a Windows NT-compatible file system redirector for NetWare servers. This redirector implements NetWare Core Protocol (NCP) requests for file and print services. NCP is roughly similar to server message blocks (SMB) used in the workstation and server redirectors native to Windows NT. Figure 10.3 shows how CSNW fits into the Windows NT architecture.

CSNW provides access to NetWare file and print servers. In addition, CSNW supports NetWare MS-DOS console applications like SYSCON and the various console programs used to control NetWare services. You'll find a complete list of supported applications at the end of this chapter.

CSNW also supports Burst mode, an enhancement for large data transfers, large Internet protocol (LIP), which allows routed connections to negotiate the largest possible packet size in order to improve bandwidth, and long filename (LFN) support when the NetWare server is running the OS/2 name space NLM.

FIGURE 10.3
The relationship of Client Services for NetWare to Windows NT.

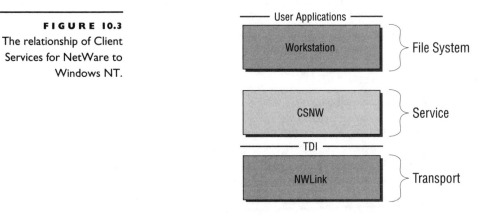

Bindery and NDS Support

Windows NT 4.0 supports both the bindery style logon used in NetWare versions prior to version 4 and the NDS supported in version 4 and later. Support for NDS is new to Windows NT 4.0. Prior to this release, NetWare 4.x servers had to run bindery emulation (which is on by default) to be seen by Windows NT clients.

NDS allows resources and account databases to be shared among a number of servers and managed from a central location, very much the way Windows NT domains allow the same facility. By supporting NDS directly, Windows NT now supports NDS tree browsing through the standard network browser.

By default, Windows will attach through the bindery emulation mechanism. Consequently, if you want a Windows NT workstation to see the NDS tree, you must disable bindery emulation on the NetWare file server with the following NetWare console command:

```
SET BINDERY CONTEXT = " "
```

Disabling bindery emulation may not work in your situation if you have client/server applications that need bindery services. Unless you need to be able to browse the NDS tree structure, you should leave the default settings in place.

Dependencies

Because CSNW uses the IPX transport, NWLink must be installed to use CSNW. Windows NT will automatically install NWLink when you install CSNW if it is not already installed. NWLink automatically installs the NetBIOS over IPX services.

CSNW also requires at least one network adapter driver and the Workstation service to be installed.

Installing CSNW

Installing CSNW is as straightforward as any other service in Windows NT. Unlike most services, however, CSNW installation does not require you to change any settings. All CSNW settings are changed via the CSNW control panel, which is installed along with the service. The procedure for installing CSNW is shown in Exercise 10.3.

LOGGING ON You will need to supply a NetWare account and password the first time you attach to a NetWare server. Windows NT will remember your NetWare account name and password from that point on and will automatically log you on to NetWare resources when you log on to your Windows NT workstation.

You may be able to log on to a NetWare server directly after you've restarted from installing CSNW because the default options of *No Preferred Server* and *Auto Frame Detection* and the absence of assigned network numbers will attach you to the first NetWare server with a bindery or bindery emulator. Although

---

EXERCISE 10.3

Installing and Configuring Client Services for NetWare

1. Right-click on the Network Neighborhood icon on the Desktop.

2. Select Properties.

3. Select the Services tab in the Network dialog box.

4. Click the Add button.

5. Select the Client Services for NetWare in the Network Service list box.

6. Click OK.

7. Enter the path to your Windows NT 4.0 Workstation CD-ROM in the Path field.

8. Click Continue to install the service.

9. Click Close.

10. Click Yes when asked if you want to restart.

---

the bindery-emulation technique works, you should change the settings for Net-Ware 4.*x* in order to take advantage of NDS tree browsing, as shown in the CSNW control panel section if you are running NetWare 4 or greater.

CHANGING THE REDIRECTOR SEARCH ORDER Redirectors are searched in the order they are shown in the Services Settings tab of the Network control panel. You can change the order by using the Network Access Order button below the Services list box. Exercise 10.4 shows the process for changing the network search order.

Windows NT will now search the Microsoft Windows Network for a resource before searching the NetWare network. Make these settings match the servers you use most often to optimize them for your specific installation.

CONNECTING TO NETWARE RESOURCES The Windows NT component networking system hides the differences between network types completely. Consequently, you can use the Network Neighborhood to attach to file and print resources on a NetWare file server in exactly the same way as you would use a Windows NT server or peer. This abstraction of very different networking

---

EXERCISE 10.4

Changing the Redirector Search Order

1. Right-click the Network Neighborhood icon.

2. Select Properties.

3. Select the Services tab.

4. Click the Network Access Order button.

5. Select Microsoft Windows Network.

6. Click the Move Up button.

7. Click OK to close the Access Order dialog box.

8. Click OK to close the Network Settings dialog box.

---

environments into the same user interface is the culmination of Microsoft's *component architecture philosophy*.

For example, you can double-click the Network Neighborhood to browse the Microsoft Windows network resources. NetWare resources also appear at the root of this tree. You can browse through them in exactly the same manner, mapping drives to NetWare volumes and attaching to NetWare printer servers just as you would if these resources were attached to a Windows NT server. Exercise 10.5 details the process of connecting to a NetWare shared directory.

NETWARE PRINTING NetWare printing is handled in the same manner as it is under Microsoft Windows Network. You simply browse the Network Neighborhood for the server and printer to which you wish to attach and right-click its icon to map a connection to that printer. You don't have to concern yourself with NetWare concepts like print servers and queues—simply use the familiar Windows interface and let the CSNW component handle the differences. Exercise 10.6 walks you through the process of connecting to a NetWare printer.

EXERCISE 10.5

Connecting to a NetWare Directory

1. Double-click the Network Neighborhood icon.

2. Double-click the NetWare server if it is shown. Otherwise, double-click Entire Network, NetWare or compatible Network, the directory tree icon, and down through the organizational units until the server to which you want to attach appears. Double-click that server.

3. Open one of the folders shown. If you are not logged on, a dialog box will ask for an account name and password. Enter a user account on the NetWare server that will allow you to open the directory.

4. Notice that you are now able to browse the contents of the NetWare server as if it were a Windows NT server.

EXERCISE 10.6

Connecting to a NetWare Printer Queue

1. Double-click the Network Neighborhood icon.

2. Double-click the NetWare server if it is shown. Otherwise, double-click Entire Network, NetWare or compatible Network, the directory tree icon, and down through the organizational units until the server to which you want to attach appears. Double-click that server.

3. Open one of the folders shown. If you are not logged on, a dialog box will ask for an account name and password. Enter a user account on the NetWare server that will allow you to open the directory.

4. Notice that you are now able to browse the contents of the NetWare server as if it were a Windows NT server.

5. NetWare Print Queues will be shown as printers. Right-click to install them the same way Windows NT network printers are installed.

The CSNW Control Panel

Microsoft chose to control the features of CSNW through its own control panel rather than through the Network control panel. When you double-click the CSNW service in the Network control panel, you will get an error message stating that the software component is not configurable. You can control all the CSNW settings through the CSNW control panel shown in Figure 10.4.

You can set the following CSNW options through this panel:

- Preferred server (for NetWare 3.1*x* servers)

- Default tree and context

- Print options

- Login script options

Novell NetWare refers to logging on as logging in. There is no difference between these terms. We use the Novell standard term logging in *when discussing a NetWare server, and we use* logging on *when discussing a Microsoft server.*

FIGURE 10.4
Selecting the CSNW
control panel.

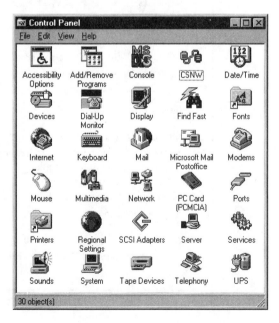

In Figure 10.5 you'll notice that the Preferred Server setting and the Default Tree and Context setting are radio buttons that are mutually exclusive. If you are connecting to a NetWare 3.1*x* server, you will use the Preferred Server setting and enter the name of the server to which you wish to attach by default. If you are connecting to a NetWare 4.*x* server, you will use the Default Tree and Context to enter the tree and context of the server to which you wish to attach by default.

Note that you can use the Preferred Server setting to attach to a NetWare 4.*x* server that is running bindery emulation, but you will lose the ability to browse the NDS tree if you attach this way. This setting treats a 4.*x* server as a 3.1*x* server and loses the richer NDS environment in the process.

SETTING AND CHANGING THE PREFERRED SERVER To assign a Default Tree and Context, follow the procedure detailed in Exercise 10.7. The procedure for setting a default NetWare 3.1*x* server is similar and should be obvious.

You do not have to assign a default NetWare 3.1*x* server. If you leave this setting in its default state of <None>, you will be attached to the first (closest) server that responds to your login attempt.

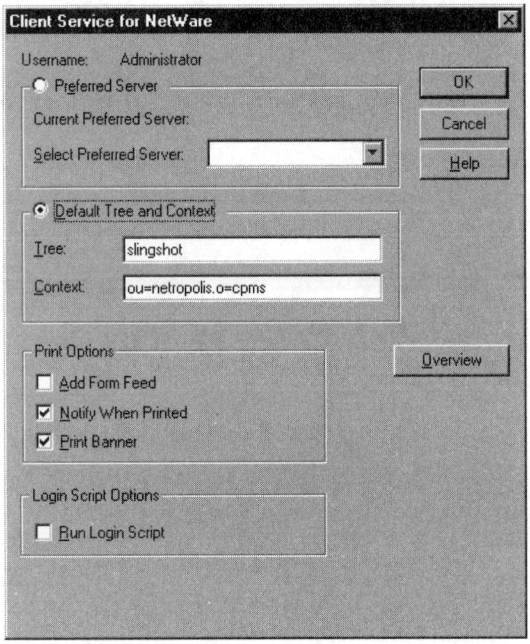

FIGURE 10.5
Client Services for
NetWare control panel.

EXERCISE 10.7

Assigning a Default Tree and Context

1. Select Settings ➤ Control Panel from the Start menu.

2. Double-click the CSNW control panel.

3. Select the Default Tree and Context radio button.

4. Type the name of the tree to which you wish to attach in the Tree input line.

5. Type the name of the context of the tree to which you wish to attach in the Context input line.

6. Click OK. If you have typed an incorrect tree name, a message will inform you that you cannot be authenticated on that tree. Type **No** to change it again or type **Yes** to accept the setting anyway.

7. Click OK to acknowledge the warning box that tells you that your changes will take effect next time you log in. The CSNW control panel closes.

8. Select Shutdown from the Start menu.

9. Select *Close all programs and log on as a different user.*

10. Click Yes.

11. Log in again. You will now be able to browse the NDS tree from the context you assigned in the control panel.

NetWare-Aware Programs

WINDOWS NT DOES NOT SUPPORT the full range of NetWare-aware applications or all of the utilities normally used to administer a NetWare file server. It instead allows you to use standard Windows NT utilities to perform NetWare utility functions. Many native NetWare utilities are supported, however. If a NetWare utility is not supported, and no

Windows surrogate is available to perform the same function, that function cannot be performed from a Windows NT Workstation.

NetWare-Aware Applications

Many MS-DOS and Windows-based NetWare-aware programs will run correctly under Windows NT Workstation 4.0. Generally, they will require the NetWare dynamic link libraries that are installed by the NetWare client for Windows installation.

In order to support these applications, you can run the NetWare client for Windows installation off the NetWare CD-ROM, copy these dynamic link library files from the directory created by the installation to your Windows NT System32 directory, and then delete the directory created by the NetWare client installation package.

Some applications require a connection to a NetWare server prior to the application being loaded. Many will run only on workstations that use the Intel $x86$ family of microprocessors.

Other applications will work but require workarounds that are beyond the scope of this book. Before installing NetWare-specific software, check with the manufacturer of the software you intend to use on your Windows NT workstation for problems and solutions. Better yet, check to see if a Windows NT native version of the same software exists. Many NetWare applications have been ported to run on Windows NT servers and workstations. In either case the manufacturer's technical support staff will be the best source of information on a specific product.

Unsupported NetWare Utilities

Some important NetWare commands are not supported, but their functionality is encapsulated in the NetWare command when using the DOS command prompt. Table 10.1 shows the NetWare equivalent commands that you should use when you are working from a Windows NT workstation. Note also that most of the functionality of the Net command is available from the Explorer Network Neighborhood. You should not have to use the command prompt during normal Windows NT sessions.

TABLE 10.1 NetWare Command Equivalents.	NETWARE COMMAND	NT EQUIVALENT
	Attach	Net Use
	Capture	Net Use
	Login	Net Logon
	Logout	Net Logoff
	Slist	Net View

Supported NetWare Utilities

The following NetWare commands are supported in Windows NT. Many have certain problems when running Windows NT, which are noted in Table 10.2. Be aware that these NetWare commands have not been tested under every possible circumstance and that some problems may not have been discovered yet. Table 10.2 shows the NetWare commands that are supported by Windows NT from the MS-DOS command prompt.

NetWare Troubleshooting

TROUBLESHOOTING NETWARE CONNECTIONS to a Windows NT workstation is straightforward. As with all troubleshooting, you should eliminate potential problems first and then isolate the location of the fault to a single component that can be repaired or replaced.

If you perform the following troubleshooting steps and are still unable to connect to a NetWare file server, you have a hardware problem or software conflict that is beyond the scope of this book. At that point, you should use network test equipment to verify that your link is good and to display the network traffic between your station and server. That step should allow you to isolate and fix the problem quickly.

UTILITY	PROBLEM
chkvol	No Known Problem
colorpal	No Known Problem
dspace	No Known Problem
flag	No Known Problem
flagdir	No Known Problem
fconsole	No Known Problem
filer	No Known Problem
grant	No Known Problem
help	No Known Problem
listdir	No Known Problem
map	No Known Problem
ncopy	No Known Problem
ndir	No Known Problem
pconsole	No Known Problem
psc	No Known Problem
pstat	No Known Problem
rconsole	No Known Problem*
remove	No Known Problem
revoke	No Known Problem
rights	No Known Problem
security	No Known Problem

*The Microsoft Help file NWDOC.HLP incorrectly notes that NetWare file servers are not visible from a 4.x server. In fact, you should have no problem running the rconsole from a Windows NT 4 workstation that is remotely controlling a NetWare 4.1 server.

	UTILITY	PROBLEM
T A B L E 10.2 (cont.) Windows NT-Supported NetWare Utilities.	send	No Known Problem
	session	Search mapping is not supported; will always map as root.
	setpass	No Known Problem
	settts	No Known Problem
	slist	No Known Problem
	syscon	No Known Problem
	tlist	No Known Problem
	userlist	No Known Problem
	volinfo	If update interval = 5, command executes very slowly.
	whoami	No Known Problem

Troubleshooting Steps

The following procedures will help you quickly isolate common problems encountered when connecting Windows NT workstations with NetWare file servers. Note that these steps assume at least one NT workstation, another Microsoft network peer or server, a NetWare server, and a NetWare client. They also presume that you are the NetWare supervisor or equivalent and that you have physical access to the NetWare file server. If this is not the case, you must have your NetWare supervisor assist you with troubleshooting your connection.

Bringing a NetWare file server online is beyond the scope of this book. You must have a running NetWare file server that is known to operate correctly with NetWare clients in order to attach a Windows NT workstation to its resources.

Troubleshooting Physical layer problems is also beyond the scope of this book. You should use network test equipment to verify that your cable plant, hubs, and network adapters are all working correctly. If you can establish network traffic of any sort between the two computers in question, then your Physical layer is not part of the problem.

If you do not have any NetWare clients on your network, you can create an MS-DOS boot disk and NetWare redirector by following the instructions included with NetWare. Boot this disk on your Windows NT workstation to use it as a NetWare client for testing.

To pin down a problem connecting to a NetWare server, you must first determine if the problem is with the NetWare server or with your workstation. If the NetWare server is working normally with NetWare clients, the problem is with the Windows NT workstation. This diagnostic procedure is outlined below:

- Verify that the NetWare server is working normally.

- Verify that the Windows NT Workstation can attach to Microsoft Windows Network Resources.

- Verify that NWLink and CSNW are installed.

- Verify that the CSNW Tree and Context settings are correct.

- Ensure that the frame types and network numbers match between the NetWare server adapter and the NWLink settings in the NT Workstation.

The following sections add the details to these NetWare connection troubleshooting steps.

Verify That the NetWare Server Is Working Normally

If the NetWare server is not working normally, it may not be attached to the network through a working cable, it may not be allowing logins, it may not have a LAN adapter loaded, or it may not be bound to the IPX protocol.

If the NetWare server is available to NetWare clients, you know that the server hardware and software is all functioning correctly and that the problem is on either the Windows NT Workstation client or its connection to the network.

If NetWare clients cannot connect to the NetWare server, check the server for possible problems. A short list of common NetWare server problems follows.

- **Is the NetWare server running?** The NetWare server will be showing a command prompt called the console or (usually) the NetWare Monitor NLM, which may be showing a snake screen saver moving around the screen. In any case, press Ctrl+Esc to get a list of screens and select the console screen. If this procedure does not work, the server is not running properly. Correct this problem before proceeding to the next steps.

- **Is the server's LAN adapter working correctly?** Check the LEDs on the LAN adapter for activity. Any network activity should cause the TX or RX lights to blink. Blinking lights indicate that the adapter is working correctly.

- **Is the LAN driver loaded and bound to IPX with the correct network number?** Use Ctrl+Esc to select the monitor screen. If monitor is not running, type **load monitor** at the console. Select the LAN information bar to display a list of adapters installed in the system. Determine which adapter is connected to the same network as your Windows NT Workstation and ensure that it has the same IPX network number and frame type as your Windows NT workstation. If there is a difference, change your Windows NT workstation to match the server.

Verify That the Windows NT Workstation Can Attach to Microsoft Windows Network Resources

When you click the Entire Network option in the Network Neighborhood, you should see two network branches:

- Microsoft Windows Network

- NetWare or Compatible Network

If you do not see NetWare or Compatible Network, you do not have CSNW installed correctly. Install it according to the instructions in the "Installing CSNW" section earlier in this chapter before continuing with the troubleshooting process.

If you can access resources on a Windows NT server or a peer workstation, then you can be sure that your basic network setup is working correctly. Test this feature by opening a shared directory and viewing its contents.

Verify That NWLink and CSNW Are Installed

In the Network Neighborhood, click Entire Network and then NetWare or Compatible Networks. If NetWare or Compatible Networks is not an option in this list, CSNW is not properly installed. Go through Exercise 10.3 to install CSNW correctly.

If you can click on NetWare Compatible Networks, then CSNW is installed. Unless you have removed NWLink, it is also installed. If you don't see anything in this list, your workstation is not communicating with a NetWare server.

Check the following:

CSNW AND NWLINK MAY NOT BE INSTALLED AND WORKING CORRECTLY Follow the instructions in Exercise 10.2 to ensure that the Windows NT Workstation and the NetWare server have at least one frame type in common and that they are on the same IPX network number.

YOU MAY NOT BE LOGGED ON CORRECTLY TO THE NETWARE FILE SERVER If the file server shows up in the NetWare or Compatible Networks tree, but you cannot access any resources, then you are not logged in to a valid account on the NetWare file server. Windows NT will open a dialog box and ask for a valid account and password for the NetWare file server. Follow the instructions under "Connecting to Netware Resources" earlier in this chapter for logging in to a NetWare server from a Windows NT Workstation correctly.

THE NETWARE SERVER MAY NOT BE RESPONDING ON THE NETWORK Verify that the NetWare server is reachable from the network you are on by creating an MS-DOS NetWare client boot disk and booting it on your Windows NT workstation. If the client network settings are correct and you still can't attach to a NetWare file server, you may have a network cable or device problem or the server may not be bound to an adapter communicating on the same network as your Windows NT workstation.

Verify That the CSNW Tree and Context Settings Are Correct

For Windows NT to attach to a NetWare server, it must have correct server name, context, and tree information. You can verify this information by checking settings on the NetWare file server. Perform the following procedure at the NetWare file server to which you wish to attach:

1. Press Ctrl+Esc at the NetWare console.

2. Select screen number 1, the System Console, and press Return.

3. Type **Set** and press Return.

4. Select option 13, Directory Services.

5. Press Return twice. The last setting is called Bindery Context. Record this string exactly as it appears. You will put this information in the Default Context setting in the CSNW control panel.

6. Type **load monitor** at the command prompt.

7. Record the information at the top of the screen labeled directory tree when the monitor loads. You will put this information in the tree input line of the CSNW.

8. Return to the Windows NT Workstation. Go through the steps shown in Exercise 10.7 using the information you recorded from the NetWare file server.

If you are using NetWare 3.1*x*, use the preceding procedure but skip the Set command and go straight to the Load Monitor command. The server name, which should be set in the Preferred Server input line, will be shown at the top banner of the monitor screen.

Ensure That the Frame Types and Network Numbers Match

In the NWLink settings control panel, you should set the Internal Network number to 0, the Network number to 0, and the frame type to auto. If you have performed all the troubleshooting steps to this point and everything passes, but you still cannot log into the NetWare file server, perform the following procedure to specifically match Ethernet frame types and network numbers. At the NetWare file server console:

1. Press Ctrl+Esc.

2. Select the screen named Console Monitor or words to that effect. If no screen matching this description appears, select the System Console and type **load monitor** and the command prompt.

3. Press the down arrow to select LAN information in the Available Options dialog box. If the Available Options dialog box is not visible, press Esc until it appears.

4. Record the frame type information listed in the Available LAN Drivers list of the adapter to which your network is attached.

5. Select the adapter driver and press Return. A dialog box will appear, showing the network address. Record this number.

6. Go through the procedures outlined in Exercise 10.2 to set the frame type and network number to these settings.

Chapter Summary

WINDOWS NT INCLUDES TWO COMPONENTS to provide seamless connectivity to Novell NetWare networks: CSNW and NWLink. NWLink is a TDI-compliant IPX/SPX-compatible protocol suite that will communicate with NetWare servers running IPX/SPX. NWLink supports all the configuration options supported by the Novell version of IPX. NWLink is robust and makes a good choice for a primary transport protocol, even without NetWare, if routing is required but Internet access is not.

CSNW provides a NetWare 4.*x* NDS-compatible NetWare redirector that integrates NetWare networks into the Windows NT domain browsing paradigm. Windows NT workstations can be configured with NWLink and CSNW to participate as full clients on NetWare networks.

Gateway Services for NetWare allows Windows NT servers to act as gateways to NetWare servers, precluding the necessity for CSNW and NWLink installations on every client on the Microsoft Windows Network.

Printing and file services provided by NetWare servers are available through the same mechanisms as Windows NT resources of the same type. You connect to printers and NetWare directories through the Network Neighborhood network browser.

By supporting Windows Sockets and NetBIOS over IPX, Windows NT supports a wide range of NetWare-aware client/server applications and utilities. Some applications may require special installation procedures to operate correctly on Windows NT, and a few may not work at all.

Windows NT provides very robust connectivity to NetWare servers to allow connections and interoperation between workstations and servers throughout a mixed-network operating system environment.

Exercise Questions

1. Windows NT 4.0 clients require bindery emulation on NetWare 4.*x* servers.

   A. True

   B. False

2. All versions of NetWare default to the Ethernet_802.2 frame type.

   A. True

   B. False

3. NDS allows resources and account databases to be shared among a number of servers and managed from a central location.

   A. True

   B. False

4. Because NetWare does not share security trusts with Windows NT, you must provide your password each time you attach to a NetWare server.

   A. True

   B. False

5. Windows NT searches the Microsoft Windows network before it searches the NetWare network.

   A. True

   B. False

6. NWLink is a good general purpose transport and should be considered as a primary transport even if you don't need connectivity to NetWare.

   A. True

   B. False

7. Windows NT supports only the NetBIOS client/server programming interface for NetWare.

   A. True

   B. False

8. Windows NT supports attaching to NDS trees, but it cannot browse them.

  A. True

  B. False

9. Windows NT is faster than NetWare at sharing files on equivalent hardware.

  A. True

  B. False

10. Changes to the CSNW setting are made in the _____ control panel.

11. Windows NT connectivity to NetWare file servers is provided by the _____ service.

12. CSNW is implemented as a NetWare-compatible _____ in the Windows NT architecture.

13. Which is the easiest way to allow access to a NetWare file server for a large group?

  A. Over the Internet

  B. Using GSNW

  C. Using CSNW

  D. Using NWLink

14. Which frame type setting is best for most network adapters?

  A. Ethernet_802.3

  B. Ethernet_802.2

  C. Ethernet_II

  D. Ethernet_SNAP

  E. Auto

15. Windows NT supports _____ standard NetWare utilities.

  A. all

  B. most

  C. some

  D. none

16. Which transport protocol is used by default on NetWare servers?

A. TCP/IP

B. IPX

C. NetBIOS

D. NetBEUI

Workgroups, Domains, and Network Browsing

I N THE THREE PRECEDING CHAPTERS ("Network Environment," "TCP/ IP," and "NetWare Connectivity"), you installed and configured the network components that allow your Windows NT workstation to join a LAN. This chapter introduces the concepts that govern a workstation's interaction with other computers on a LAN. Specifically, you will read about workgroups and domains in Microsoft networks, and you will find out how browsers work in Microsoft networks.

Workgroups and Domains

Y OU NEED TO BE AWARE of two networking models when you network Windows NT workstations. One model, workgroups, governs the interactions of Windows 95 and Windows NT computers in a peer network. The other model, domains, governs the interactions of Windows 95 and Windows NT computers in a server-based network with a Windows NT server (designated the primary domain controller) coordinating the actions of the computers on the network. Each networking model has its advantages and disadvantages, as you will learn in the following sections.

Working in a Workgroup

W INDOWS NT LOCAL AREA NETWORKS that are small and that do not need centralized network control or centralized data storage can be organized into workgroups. Workgroups are peer-to-peer networks, which means that the users of each workstation select and manage the resources on that workstation that are made available to other computers on the network. The user accounts and resources on the workstation are administered from that workstation, not from a network server. Figure 11.1 shows a typical workgroup.

FIGURE 11.1
A workgroup has a small number of computers with no computer dedicated to serving files for the other computers.

A workgroup is a good choice for your networking model if your organization is small (10 users or less), the workstation users have the ability to administer their own workstations, and central file storage and central control of network security are not important.

Because the user accounts for a workstation are independent of other workstations, a user on one workstation who accesses a resource on another workstation (other than simple directory sharing, which may not require an account and password) may need to have an account on the second workstation as well. In the extreme, you can have a workgroup in which each user in the workgroup has a separate account on each workstation in the workgroup. The same account name can be used on each workstation as well, adding to the confusion.

A workgroup is not a good choice for your networking model if you have a large number of users, if you need to centralize user account management and network security, if the users of your network cannot be relied upon to administer their own workstations, or if you need to store data centrally on your network.

Joining a Workgroup

Exercise 11.1 takes you through the steps of configuring your workstation to join a workgroup.

Working in a Domain

MOST NETWORKS WITH MORE THAN 10 workstations are server-based networks. In a server-based network, a central computer stores network files, enforces network security, and maintains network data such as user account information and trust relationships between computers.

EXERCISE 11.1

Configuring Your Workstation to Join a Workgroup

1. Log on as an administrator.

2. Open the Network icon in the Control Panel. The Network Settings dialog box will appear.

3. Click the Identification tab if it is not already the active tab.

4. Click the Change button to display the Identification Changes window.

5. Select the Workgroup option and enter the name of the workgroup your workstation will be a part of. If you wish to change your workstation's name, enter the new name at this time. The system will welcome you to the new workgroup.

6. Click OK.

7. Click the Close button in the Network window. You will be informed that you must restart your computer in order for the changes to take effect.

The Windows NT networking model that implements this type of network is the domain model. The primary domain controller is the controlling computer in a Windows NT domain and must be running the Windows NT Server operating system. Figure 11.2 shows a small domain with a primary domain controller, a server, and several client computers.

The domain model of networking is a good choice if you have a large number of computer users and workstations to network, central data storage is important, security is important, or your users cannot be relied upon to administer (install and configure software, maintain the network security, backup applications and data, etc.) their own computers.

Domain Overview

In a Windows NT domain, the user accounts, group accounts, account policies, and security information are controlled by the primary domain controller and can be administered from that server. All of the servers in the domain share the information controlled by the primary domain controller.

Because this information is centrally controlled, the task of managing a large network is easier for the network administrator than it would be if the information had

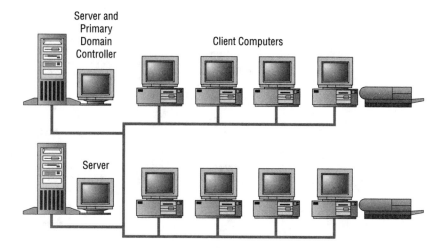

FIGURE 11.2
A domain consists of one or more servers, one of which must be a domain controller, and client computers that communicate with the server computers.

to be maintained individually on each computer in the network. Centralizing this information also means that users don't have to perform their own administration tasks for their workstations.

In a domain, one or more servers store the shared network files for all of the workstations in the domain. The primary domain controller controls workstation access to the files stored on the servers using account and security information it stores in a central database. With the network files stored in servers, the network administrator can more easily control who has access to the information. Backing up the data is also easier when it is centrally located.

Structuring Domains

A large network may have more than one domain. An organization that is divided into functional units, for instance a business that is split into marketing, finance, manufacturing, and research departments, may divide its domain-based network along those same functional lines. In this example, the network could have four domains, each providing resources specific to the needs of the department it serves. Figure 11.3 shows a larger network that has several domains.

Servers and Domain Controllers

Each domain has one or more servers to store the network files for workstations and to provide other network services such as network printing, e-mail routing, network faxing, etc.

FIGURE 11.3
A large network
may consist of
several domains.

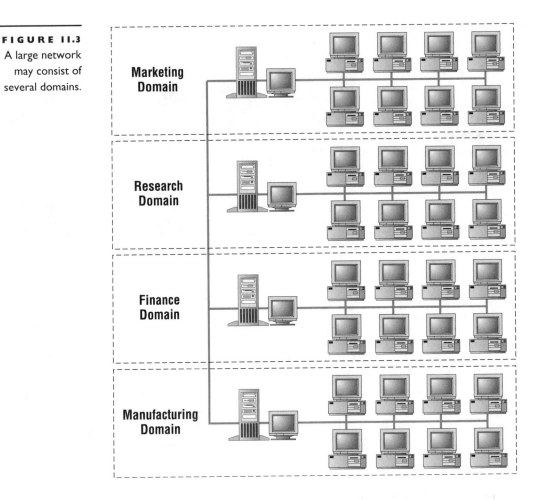

THE PRIMARY DOMAIN CONTROLLER One (and only one) server in the domain must be the primary domain controller for the domain. Only a computer running the Windows NT Server operating system can be a primary domain controller. The primary domain controller maintains a database that contains the user and group account information and the account and security policies.

BACKUP DOMAIN CONTROLLERS Other servers can be designated as backup domain controllers. The backup domain controllers maintain a copy of the primary domain controller's database. A backup domain controller can authenticate and log on domain users, and in the event that the network does not have a primary domain controller, it can be promoted to primary domain controller.

DESIGNATING DOMAIN CONTROLLERS You must designate a server as a primary or backup when you install Windows NT Server on the computer. If you designate a server to be a backup domain controller, you can later promote it to primary domain controller. If you do not designate a server to be a primary domain controller or backup domain controller, you cannot convert the server to a primary domain controller or backup domain controller later; instead, you will have to re-install the operating system.

You may wish to leave some of your Windows NT Server computers as simple servers. This decision will spare these servers the overhead of coordinating with the primary domain controller to maintain a copy of the domain database.

Joining a Domain

In order for your workstation to participate in a domain-based network, it must join the domain. Joining your workstation to the domain requires making changes in two places on the network: the primary domain controller must create an account for the workstation, and the workstation must be configured to join a domain and told which domain to join.

You can create an account for a workstation on a Windows NT Server from within the Server Manager program (found in the Administrative Tools part of the Start menu). You can also create the account from the workstation by supplying a valid administrator account name and password for the domain when you configure your workstation to join the domain.

To configure your Windows NT workstation to connect to a domain, follow the steps outlined in Exercise 11.2.

Workstation User Accounts and Domain User Accounts

When your Windows NT workstation joins a domain, domain user accounts in the domain Administrators group and the domain Users group are added to the local Administrators and Users groups. This arrangement allows individuals with domain user and domain administrator accounts to log on to the workstation and to the network using the workstation.

The domain user and administrator accounts cannot be administered with the User Manager program that comes with Windows NT Workstation. These accounts are administered by the User Manager for Domains program on the Windows NT Server. This program, along with other domain tools, can be installed on NT Workstation from the NT Server CD (in the \clients\srvtools\winnt directory).

EXERCISE 11.2

Configuring Your Workstation to Join a Domain

1. Log on as an administrator.

2. Open the Network icon in the Control Panel. The Network Settings dialog box will appear.

3. Click the Identification tab if it is not already the active tab.

4. Click the Change button to display the Identification Changes window.

5. Select the Domain option and enter the name of the domain your workstation will be a part of. If you want to change your workstation's name, enter the new name at this time.

6. Check *Create a Computer Account* in the Domain dialog box if the primary domain controller does not have an account set up for your computer. Your computer must have a computer account on the domain before it can join the domain. You can skip this step if the account has already been created by your domain administrator. Then enter the username and password for an Administrator account for the domain.

7. Click OK. A message welcoming you to the domain will be displayed. Click OK.

8. Click the Close button in the Network window. You will be informed that you must restart your computer in order for the changes to take effect.

Local user and group accounts are not added to the domain database. Local users and groups are still administered with the User Manager program. When you log on from the workstation, you have the choice of logging on to the domain (using an account in the domain user account database) or of logging on to the workstation computer (using an account in the workstation's local user account database). If you log on using a user account that is local to the workstation, you may not have access to resources on the domain.

Windows NT workstation manages its security information using information in both the local and domain accounts databases. For this reason, access rights and permissions can be set for resources on the workstation in relation to both local and domain users and groups.

Domain Logon

You must have a domain user account before you can log on to the domain. The domain administrator for your network can create a domain user account using the User Manager for Domains program on a Windows NT Server computer.

The network administrator will perform the steps outlined in Exercise 11.3 to create your user account.

EXERCISE 11.3

Creating a Domain User Account from the Primary Domain Controller

1. Log on to the primary domain controller using the Administrator account.

2. Run the User Manager for Domains program.

3. Select New User from the User menu.

4. Enter the username for the new domain user account into the Username field.

5. Enter the full name of the user into the Full Name field.

6. Enter a description into the Description field.

7. Enter a password into the Password field and into the Confirm Password field.

8. Click the Add button in the New User window.

9. Click the Close button in the New User window.

When your Windows NT workstation is joined to a domain, you have a choice of whether you will log on to the domain using a domain user account or log on using a user account from the account database local to the workstation. You choose whether you will log on to the domain or just to the workstation by selecting the domain name or the computer name (respectively) in the From input box in the initial logon screen.

If you log on to a workstation account instead of a domain account (by selecting the computer name instead of the domain name and presenting a valid username and password for the workstation), your access to resources in the domain will be limited because you will not be using an account that is recognized by the domain.

You will still be allowed to access any workstation and workgroup resources that your workstation account has permission to use.

If the username and password for a workstation are the same as the entered domain username and password, the domain user can access all resources granted to the local user through a process called pass-through authentication. For this reason, a good practice is to keep usernames and passwords consistent between the workstation and the domain (if they must exist in both places). Of course, it's even less confusing if the user is defined only at the domain level.

If you log on to a domain account (by selecting the domain name and presenting a valid username and password for the domain), you will still have access to the resources of the local computer. However, the access you have may not be the same as you would have using the local account. The domain account is not the same account as the local account, and different access permissions may have been established for resources in the computer for domain accounts.

If your workstation is a part of a domain, you should always use a domain account to log on. If a domain controller is not available, the workstation will still allow you to log on using the domain account. The workstation accepts your logon by validating your username and password, using information stored from a prior valid logon session. A workstation will allow you to log on using cached information only in the absence of a domain controller to verify your logon. If a domain controller becomes available later, you may be required to log on at that time before accessing information on the domain.

Exercise 11.4 shows the domain logon process.

EXERCISE 11.4

Domain Logon

1. Start your Windows NT Workstation computer.

2. Press Ctrl+Alt+Del. The logon window will appear.

3. Select the domain that you will log on to in the From field.

4. Enter a valid username for the domain.

5. Enter the password.

6. Press Enter or click OK in the window.

Network Browsers

YOUR WORKSTATION, WHETHER IT IS a part of a domain or a workgroup, must know what network resources are available before it can access those resources. The network browser maintains the list of currently available network resources for a workgroup or domain.

When a computer in a workgroup or domain joins the network, it announces its presence and provides a list of the resources it makes available on the network. If there were no central location to store network resource information, every computer would need to keep a list of all of the other computers on the network and record all of the resources available from those computers. In addition, every computer would need to be notified every time a change occurred in resource availability on the network. This notification process would produce unnecessary traffic on the network and reduce network performance.

Network browsers reduce the amount of traffic on the network by storing a list of network resources in a central location. Computers in a network with browsers can then request the list from a browser when they need to find a network resource.

Computers running Microsoft Windows for Workgroups, Windows 95, Windows NT Workstation, and Windows NT Server operating systems can all perform the role of browser in a Windows workgroup or domain.

We describe the various browser roles in a domain or workgroup in the following section and the manner in which the browser roles cooperate in the section "Browsing the Network." Figure 11.4 shows network computers configured as Master Browsers, backup browsers, potential browsers, and nonbrowsers.

Browser Roles

Computers in a workgroup or domain can be divided into four groups depending on how they support the browsing service: Master Browsers, backup browsers, potential browsers, and nonbrowsers. If the network has a primary domain controller, it is normally the Master Browser. Otherwise, any Microsoft operating system that supports network browsing can perform any of the browsing roles.

- The **Master Browser** is the computer that maintains the master list of resources available on the network. The list of resources is called the Browse

FIGURE 11.4
If the network has a
primary domain
controller, it is the
Master Browser.

Primary Domain Controller
(Master Browser)

Backup Domain Controller
(Backup Browser)

Windows NT Server
(Potential Browser)

Windows NT
Workstations
(Potential Browsers)

Windows 95 and
Windows for Workgroups
(Potential Browsers
and Nonbrowsers)

list. The Master Browser listens for announcements from computers and adds the computers and their shared resources to the Browse list. It distributes this list to the backup browsers and promotes potential browsers to be backup browsers when necessary. In the absence of backup browsers, the Master Browser also supplies the Browse list to computers that request it. Only one Master Browser can exist in a workgroup or domain.

- A **backup browser** receives a copy of the Browse list from the Master Browser and supplies the Browse list to computers requesting the list. The backup browser announces itself periodically to the Master Browser in the same way that any other computer participating in the workgroup or domain announces itself. It periodically requests the Browse list from the Master Browser, and if it cannot find the Master Browser, it forces an election on the network. (Elections are described later in the section called "Configuring Browsers and Browser Elections.")

- A **potential browser** does not receive a copy of the Browse list unless it is promoted by a Master Browser to be a backup browser or unless it becomes the Master Browser in the absence of another Master Browser or backup browser. A browser computer, like any other computer participating in a workgroup or domain, will periodically announce its presence and list the services it makes available.

- A **nonbrowser** does not maintain a Browse list for other computers or receive a Browse list from a Master Browser for other computers to request. A nonbrowser computer can still provide network services and request a Browse list from network browsers for its own use. A nonbrowser computer participating in a domain or workgroup will periodically announce its presence and list the services it makes available.

- You can designate a computer on the network to be the **preferred Master Browser**. When this computer joins the network, it will designate itself the Master Browser. If a Master Browser is already on the network, the preferred Master Browser will force an election that reevaluates the browser roles of computers in the network. The computer that has the preferred Master Browser setting will win the election unless another computer is the primary domain controller or more than one computer is designated as the preferred Master Browser.

Browsing the Network

Browsers exist to provide networked computers with a list of the resources that are available on the network. The steps that the requesting computer and the network browsers perform before and during a request are as follows:

1. When each computer starts up and connects to the network, the computer announces its existence to the Master Browser in the workgroup or domain. If the computer has resources to share—that is, the user has enabled file and print sharing and has selected local printers or files to share—it advertises them to the Master Browser.

2. When the computer attempts to locate network resources for the first time, the computer contacts the Master Browser and retrieves a list of backup browsers.

3. The computer contacts a backup browser and requests the network resource list.

4. The backup browser responds with the list of domains and workgroups and with the list of servers and client computers participating in the domain or workgroup that the computer is a part of.

Step 4 gives the computer a list of domains, workgroups, and server and client computers on the network, and browsing the resources of a particular domain, workgroup, server, or workstation continues.

5. The computer contacts the server, domain controller, or workstation to request the list of resources exported by that entity. The computer connects using the IPC$ share for this communication.

6. That computer returns a list of resources to the requesting computer.

7. An application or a user might then select a resource, such as a shared printer or file, and establish a session with that computer for the requesting computer to use the resource. This sequence of events describes what happens when you select a shared directory on another computer and map a local drive to that shared directory.

In Exercise 11.5 you will view the computers on your network and then view the resources of one of the computers. Your workstation will perform the steps described above in order to present the network information to you.

EXERCISE 11.5

Browsing the Network

1. Double-click the Network Neighborhood icon from the desktop. You will see a list of computers on your network, which the computer retrieves by performing steps 1 through 4.

2. Double-click on a computer in the list. Your network server is a good choice. You will see the list of resources that the computer makes available to the network. Your computer retrieves this list by performing steps 5 and 6 above.

3. Click on a resource to prompt your computer to perform step 7 above.

Configuring Browsers and Browser Elections

Every domain or workgroup must have one and only one Master (or network) Browser. Microsoft networks hold elections to determine which computer will be the Master Browser. Which computer is selected to be the Master Browser depends on the operating system of the computers on the network, the versions of the operating systems, and the designated role of the computer in network browsing.

The computer that is designated the preferred Master Browser will win the election unless a primary domain controller is present in the network. If the network has neither a preferred Master Browser nor a primary domain controller, the Master Browser will be selected by other criteria.

The following browser roles are presented in the order in which they will be selected as a Master Browser:

- Preferred master

- Master

- Backup browser

- Potential browser

When computers have different operating systems and share the same browsing role, the following systems will win an election in order of priority:

- A Windows NT server that is the primary domain controller

- Windows NT server

- Windows NT workstation

- Windows 95

- Windows for Workgroups

When Windows NT computers have the same role and the same operating system, the first computer in the list according to operating system version will win:

- 4.0

- 3.51

- 3.5

- 3.1

An election is held whenever the Master Browser is unavailable or more than one Master Browser is available. A client computer, a backup browser, or a preferred Master Browser can cause an election to occur by broadcasting a special packet called an *election packet* over the network. All of the browsers will receive the packet and evaluate their precedence in relation to the election packet. If any of the browsers determines that it has precedence over the browser that sent the election packet, it will broadcast its own election packet. A network in which election packets are being exchanged is in an *election-in-progress state*. When browsers cease to produce election packets, the last browser to produce an election packet is the new Master Browser.

By modifying the following setting the the Windows NT Registry, you can configure your Windows NT workstation to never be a browser, always be either the Master Browser or a backup browser, or be a potential browser. (Chapter 4 introduced the Registry and the Registry Editor program.)

```
\HKEY_LOCAL_MACHINE\SYSTEM\CurrentControlSet\Services\
   Browser\Parameters\MaintainServerList
```

This setting has three possible values:

- **No:** A workstation with this setting will not be a network browser.

- **Yes:** A workstation with this setting will be either a network browser or a backup browser. This setting is the default for Windows NT Server primary domain controller or backup domain controller computers.

- **Auto:** A workstation with this setting will either become the Master Browser, a backup browser, or a potential browser, depending on the number of currently active browsers on the network. Auto is the default for Windows NT workstation computers and Windows NT server computers that are not domain controllers.

You can configure your Windows NT workstation to be the Master Browser in the absence of a primary domain controller by changing the following setting in the Windows NT Registry of your workstation:

```
\HKEY_LOCAL_MACHINE\SYSTEM\CurrentControlSet\Services\
   Browser\Parameters\IsDomainMaster
```

The default of this setting is No or False, even if the computer is currently the Master Browser of the network. Changing the value to Yes or True will cause the workstation to win any election other than one with a primary domain controller.

You can configure your workstation to never be a browser, always be a browser, or be a potential browser by following the steps in Exercise 11.6. Exercise 11.7 shows you how to change the preferred Master Browser status of your computer.

EXERCISE 11.6

Configuring the Workstation's Browser Status

1. Start the Registry Editor program (REGEDIT.EXE).

2. Open the HKEY_LOCAL_MACHINE subtree by clicking on the plus sign beside HKEY_LOCAL_MACHINE.

3. Open the SYSTEM key.

4. Open the CurrentControlSet key.

5. Open the Services key.

6. Open the Browser key.

7. Open the Parameters key.

8. Select the MaintainServerList value by double-clicking it. You will see the Edit String dialog box.

9. Enter No, Yes, or Auto.

10. Press OK.

11. Exit the Registry Editor and restart your computer to activate the changes.

Browser Interactions

All browsers on the network cooperate to provide a browsing service to the users of the domain or workgroup. The browsers and the computers exchange information periodically, and each of the interactions follows specific timing constraints.

EXERCISE 11.7

Changing the Workstation's Preferred Master Browser Status

1. Start the Registry Editor program (REGEDIT.EXE).

2. Open the HKEY_LOCAL_MACHINE subtree by clicking on the plus sign beside HKEY_LOCAL_MACHINE.

3. Open the SYSTEM key.

4. Open the CurrentControlSet key.

5. Open the Services key.

6. Open the Browser key.

7. Open the Parameters key.

8. Select the IsDomainMaster value by double-clicking it. You will see the Edit String dialog box.

9. Enter True to make your workstation the Master Browser or enter False to leave it with its default setting.

10. Press OK.

11. Exit the Registry Editor and restart your computer to activate the changes.

All Domain Participants

Computers that provide services in the workgroup or domain (in Windows NT Workstation, a computer that runs the Server service) must inform the Master Browser that they are available when they start. These computers must broadcast their continued existence periodically. Initially, the computer must announce itself once a minute, but as the computer continues to run, the announcement interval increases until it reaches 12 minutes. If the Master Browser does not receive a message from the computer for longer than three announcement periods, it removes the computer from the Browse list.

Because of the delay between when a computer goes down and when the computer entry is removed from the Browse list, up to 36 minutes can elapse before the Master Browser's list reflects the computer's condition.

Backup Browsers

Backup browsers announce themselves on the networks like normal computers. They also poll the Master Browser at 15-minute intervals to retrieve the Browse list. The backup browser delay in combination with the delayed computer announcement to the Master Browser could result in a resource not being available for as long as 51 minutes while a backup browser list maintains the resource in its Browse list.

If the backup browser polls the Master Browser and the Master Browser does not respond, the backup browser will force an election on the network.

Master Browser

The Master Browser periodically broadcasts updated Master Browser information to all of the backup browsers.

The size of the Browse list that the Master Browser maintains is limited to 64K, which limits the number of computers on a single workgroup or domain to 2,000 or 3,000 computers. In practice, this limitation is not likely to be serious, as a network of this size will likely be divided into much smaller domains or workgroups simply for easier management.

The Master Browser can broadcast a *Request Announcement packet,* which requires all computers participating in the domain or workgroup to respond within 30 seconds. If during the response to a Request Announcement packet (or at any other time) the Master Browser receives an announcement from another computer claiming to be a Master Browser, it forces an election on the network.

Number of Browsers

A workgroup or domain always has one Master Browser. The maximum number of backup browsers in a domain is three, regardless of the size of the domain, but it can have any number of potential browsers. In a workgroup with workstations that have their MaintainServerList parameter set to Auto, the Master Browser will select one potential browser to be a backup browser for every 32 computers that are a part of the workgroup.

Browsing Other Workgroups and Domains

In addition to maintaining a list of computers in its own domain or workgroup, the Master Browser is also responsible for maintaining a list of other domains and workgroups. When a computer becomes the Master Browser, it broadcasts a Domain Announcement message to each workgroup or domain. It performs this routine every minute for 5 minutes and then every 15 minutes thereafter.

The Master Browser listens for broadcasts from other Master Browsers, and if another domain has not sent an announcement message for three times its announcement delay, the Master Browser removes that domain or workgroup from its list. With a waiting period of three times the default 15-minute delay, a domain or workgroup can be down for as long as 45 minutes before it is removed from the Browse list. This list of other workgroups and domains is given to the backup browsers with the list of computers in the Master Browsers domain.

The Master Browser can force other domains to announce themselves in the same manner that it can force all computers in a domain to announce themselves. However, a Master Browser will force other domains to announce themselves only if it has an empty domain list.

Chapter Summary

THIS CHAPTER INTRODUCES THE CONCEPTS of workgroups, domains, and network browsing.

Workgroups are peer-to-peer networks that function without a server to centralize data storage and network administration. Each computer can share data on the network, and the users of the workstations determine which resources to share over the network. Workgroups are best used in small networks where the computer users will administer their own workstations.

Domains centralize data storage and network security in central computers called servers. One server is designated the primary domain controller and is responsible for maintaining user accounts, group accounts, user and security policies, and other network control information. Backup domain controllers replicate these databases, can perform domain authentication and logons, and can take over as the primary domain controller in the absence of a primary domain controller.

A user can choose to log on to the domain or to the workstation, but logging on to the workstation will limit the user's access to network resources. A workstation can allow a user to log on to the workstation using a cached domain logon account if a domain controller is not present.

Network browsers provide computers on the workstation or domain with a list of computers that provide resources on the network. Every computer periodically announces its presence to the Master Browser. The Master Browser listens for computer announcements and periodically presents the Browse list to the backup browsers. The backup browsers also poll the Master Browser for the list.

The Master Browser will provide computers with a list of backup browsers, and the backup browsers will provide computers with the Browse list. The Master Browser announces the workgroup or domain it is a member of to other workgroups and domains, and it maintains a list of workgroups and domains that it also gives to the backup browsers to give to other computers.

Exercise Questions

1. The workgroup model governs the interactions of Windows 95 and Windows NT computers in a peer network.

   A. True

   B. False

2. In a workgroup the user accounts and resources on the workstation are administered from a network server.

   A. True

   B. False

3. In a server-based network a central computer stores network files, enforces network security, and maintains network data such as user account information and trust relationships between computers.

   A. True

   B. False

4. Each domain has one and only one server to store the network files for workstations.

   A. True

   B. False

5. A domain can have several primary domain controllers.

   A. True

   B. False

6. Only a computer running the Windows NT Server operating system can be a primary domain controller.

   A. True

   B. False

7. A backup domain controller can authenticate and log on domain users.

   A. True

   B. False

8. If you do not designate a server to be a primary domain controller or backup domain controller when you install the Windows NT Server operating system, you can change your mind later and promote the server to primary domain controller or backup domain controller status.

A. True

B. False

9. When your Windows NT workstation joins a domain, user accounts in the local Administrators and Users groups are added to the domain Administrators group and to the domain Users group that the primary domain controller maintains.

A. True

B. False

10. The User Manager program that comes with Windows NT Workstation cannot administer the domain user and administrator accounts.

A. True

B. False

11. If no domain controller is available, you can still log on to the workstation using the domain account.

A. True

B. False

12. Computers running the Windows for Workgroups operating system cannot perform the function of network browsers.

A. True

B. False

13. A Windows NT workstation will win an election between a workstation and a server, all other considerations being equal.

A. True

B. False

14. The computer with the more recent operating system version will win an election, all other considerations being equal.

A. True

B. False

15. A Master Browser can promote a nonbrowser to backup or potential browser.

A. True

B. False

16. Owing to the delay between the time when a computer goes down and when the computer entry is removed from the Browse list, up to 36 minutes can elapse before the Master Browser's list reflects the computer's condition.

A. True

B. False

17. The backup browser delay in combination with the delayed computer announcement to the Master Browser could result in a resource not being available for as long as 90 minutes while a backup browser maintains the resource in its Browse list.

A. True

B. False

18. The Master Browser can force other domains to announce themselves.

A. True

B. False

19. A domain or workgroup can be down for as long as 45 minutes before it is removed from the Browse list.

A. True

B. False

20. The _____ model governs the interactions of Windows 95 and Windows NT computers in a server-based network with a Windows NT Server (designated the primary domain controller) coordinating the actions of the computers on the network.

21. The controlling computer in a Windows NT domain is called the _____ _____ _____.

22. The _____ _____ _____ maintains a copy of the primary domain controller's database.

23. The network _____ maintains the list of currently available network resources for a workgroup or domain.

24. A _____ browser does not receive a copy of the Browse list unless it is promoted by a Master Browser to be a backup browser.

25. A _____ does not maintain a Browse list for other computers or receive a Browse list from a Master Browser.

26. Microsoft networks hold _____ to determine which computer will be the Master Browser.

27. A client computer, a backup browser, or a preferred Master Browser can cause an election to occur by broadcasting a special packet called an _____ packet.

28. If the Master Browser does not receive a message from the computer for longer than _____ announcement periods, it removes the computer from the Browse list.

29. Backup browsers poll the Master Browser at _____ minute intervals.

30. The size of the browse list that the Master Browser maintains is limited to _____K.

31. The _____ _____ packet requires all computers participating in the domain or workgroup to respond within 30 seconds.

32. When a computer becomes the Master Browser, it broadcasts a _____ _____ message to each workgroup or domain.

Internetworking with Remote Access Service

REMOTE ACCESS SERVICE (RAS) allows a client computer to communicate over a low-speed dial-up telephone line to a server as if they were both on the same local area network. Once a RAS session has been established, speed is the only difference in operation between a RAS attached computer and a computer on the same local area network.

RAS can be implemented as a gateway or packet router, so a RAS host on a Network can provide access to the resources of the entire network, not just the resources on the host to which you are attached.

This chapter will focus on the client side of a RAS connection. Setting up and administering multiple-line RAS servers is covered in the companion to this book, *MCSE: NT Server Study Guide*.

Understanding Remote Access Service

RAS PROVIDES A SEAMLESS CONNECTION to networks over low-speed public telephone lines. RAS works by controlling the dialing and protocol negotiation required to establish a connection and then by routing packets or gating NetBIOS calls as appropriate through the host (answering) machine on the network.

The terms host *and* RAS server *are synonymous. The term* host *is used so as not to confuse an NT workstation running a RAS server with a Windows NT server.*

RAS is capable of not only connecting Windows Network clients to Windows NT servers but also connecting to any server answering the SLIP or PPP serial protocols and capable of communicating with the IPX, TCP/IP, or NetBEUI transport protocols. Consequently, RAS is capable of establishing sessions with any Internet server, as well as with most UNIX hosts, NetWare servers, and many others. Figure 12.1 shows a basic RAS workstation connection to a network. Study it to understand the various devices involved with a RAS session.

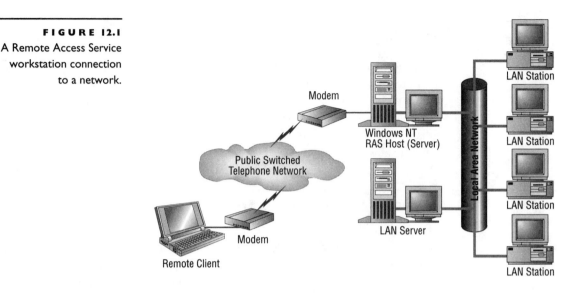

FIGURE 12.1
A Remote Access Service
workstation connection
to a network.

Remote Access versus Remote Control

Many remote link software packages implement *remote control,* rather than *remote access.* Remote control uses the local computer (the one you are using) as a dumb terminal for the remote computer (the one to which you are attaching). Keystrokes and mouse events are sent to the remote computer to drive its user interface. All computing operations are performed on the remote computer, and the output (video) is sent back over the low-speed line to the terminal computer.

Remote control is entirely different from remote access, which attaches the local computer to the remote computer as a LAN client. In remote access all compute operations take place on the local computer. The local computer reads data from the remote computer and writes data back to it.

Remote control trades a general feel of "sluggishness" for the sporadic periods of "hurry up and wait" that occur with remote access. The World Wide Web is implemented with the remote access paradigm, not the remote control paradigm.

Because of Windows NT's mandatory logon security architecture, a remote control package could not be used to perform the WinLogon process as required for operation.

To perform a remote control session, the remote computer would have to remain logged on at all times, a clear violation of the purpose of security systems.

Remote Access Service Capabilities

RAS performs both the dial-out client service and the dial-in host service. RAS can host clients from a wide variety of operating systems and can support all Windows NT Interprocess communications mechanisms. RAS supports all TDI-compliant protocols loaded on your machine and is capable of operating over any dial-up public network medium. RAS supports software compression to maximize bandwidth over low-speed connections.

Supported Dial-In Operating Systems

RAS is capable of hosting any computer running the following operating systems. Note that RAS can support any computer using a TCP/IP protocol stack and capable of dialing in via Point-to-Point Protocol (PPP), but these clients will not be able to use many domain resources such as print and file services.

- LAN Manager

- Windows For Work groups

- Windows NT 3.1 and higher

- Windows 95

- Serial Line Internet Protocol (SLIP) and PPP based TCP/IP clients

Although Windows NT can dial out to SLIP servers, it will only answer PPP.

Supported Network Interfaces

RAS supports all Windows NT interprocess communications mechanisms. Therefore, the client side of any client/server application capable of running under Windows NT can run over a RAS connection. These mechanisms include

- Windows Sockets

- NetBIOS

- Mailslots

- Named pipes

- Remote Procedure Calls (RPC)

- Win32 and LAN Manager APIs

Supported Protocols

RAS supports all TDI-compliant protocols via the PPP serial protocol. Dialing out to SLIP servers is supported, but Windows NT RAS hosts will only answer PPP.

- SLIP

- PPP

- TCP/IP

- NetBEUI

- IPX

Supported WAN Connections

RAS currently supports wide area network connections over the following media:

- PSTN (public switched telephone network; regular modems)

- ISDN (integrated services digital network)

- X.25 (leased-line frame relay)

ISDN and X.25 interfaces are treated as network adapters rather than as modems.

Support for other wide area network interfaces such as asynchronous transfer mode (ATM) will be added when those products become available. The ability to support future products is one of the benefits of Windows NT's modular component-based architecture.

Remote Access Service Limitations

RAS for Windows NT Workstation is limited to hosting one inbound connection. RAS for Windows NT Server supports up to 256 simultaneous inbound sessions.

Setting RAS to receive calls will lock the COM port and modem you are using. The port will not be available for non-RAS communication software such as terminal emulators or FAX software.

Point-to-Point Tunneling Protocol

P OINT-TO-POINT TUNNELING PROTOCOL (PPTP) is a protocol layer on top of the PPP protocol that allows the secure "tunneling" of encrypted data directly between any computers attached to a TCP/IP network. This protocol allows the creation of "virtual private networks" over public networks such as the Internet. For example, remote users can connect via PPP to an Internet service provider and then connect to a corporate network through the secure PPTP layer to communicate as if they were dialed in directly to the corporate network—thus simulating a local area network connection over an encrypted public link.

Point-to-Point Tunneling Protocol works by simulating NDIS LAN adapters that provide an encrypted bidirectional data channel directly to the TCP/IP computers on each end of the connection. Since it works as a LAN adapter, other protocols such as IPX and NetBEUI can be used within the secure tunnel, thus allowing the operation of any NT networking protocol or service through the secure tunnel.

Perhaps more important is the ability to create a RAS server that answers PPTP through an X.25 link to the Internet. This technique allows you to connect an NT server to a network through a single high speed connection like a T1 leased line and have it act as a remote server, thus obviating the need for modem banks, multiport serial boards, and the attendant cables and hardware required to set up a RAS server. Remote users with PPTP configured can simply dial the closest local Internet service provider to reach your RAS server.

PPTP RAS connections are covered in detail in the companion book *MCSE: NT Server Study Guide*.

Using Remote Access Service

NSTALLING RAS IS NO MORE or less difficult than installing any other service. Since the purpose of RAS is to connect (at least) two computers over a low-speed dial-up line, you should have access to another computer running RAS with the same protocols or a dial-up PPP Internet account.

Without access to another computer to which you can attach, you will have difficulty understanding the operational nuances of RAS. You really need to use the software in order to understand it.

Remote Access Service Requirements

RAS requires either a modem, an ISDN adapter, or an X.25 interface in your workstation. All the exercises in this chapter presume the use of a modem, since you are more likely to have a modem than an ISDN or X.25 connection. Connections through ISDN adapters and X.25 interfaces are covered in the volume *MCSE: NT Server Study Guide*.

The first step is to identify a free COM port in your computer and configure the modem to use that port. Use Exercise 12.1 to perform this step if you have an internal modem. You should have your modem documentation available to show you how to change the COM and IRQ settings for that device. If you are using an external modem, you will only need to know the COM port to which it is attached. If you are using an external modem or if your modem is already installed in the Windows NT system, you won't need to perform Exercise 12.2. If you have a modem, but have not installed it through the Modem control panel, do so now. Exercise 12.2 will walk you through the steps.

Once your modem has been physically installed in your computer, you need to tell Windows NT about it. Unlike Windows 95, Windows NT is not capable of automatically detecting new equipment and installing drivers for it. Windows NT will not risk crashing the machine to run the hardware-probing routines used in Windows 95.

Your modem is now available to Windows NT programs such as RAS.

EXERCISE 12.1

Finding an Available COM Port

1. Select Programs ➤ Administrative Tools ➤ Windows NT Diagnostics from the Start menu.

2. Select the Resources tab.

3. Click the IRQ button.

4. Note the state of interrupt requests (IRQ) 03 and 04. If either does not appear in the list, you will configure your modem to use that IRQ.

5. Select a free IRQ and COM port.

- If IRQ 04 is available (not in the resource list), set your modem to use IRQ 04 and COM 1.

- If IRQ 03 is available, set your modem to use IRQ 03 and COM 2.

- If both are in use, you will need to set your modem to use another unused IRQ and COM port. Check your modem documentation to see if IRQ 05, 07, or 09 are supported. Set the modem IRQ to any IRQ your modem supports that is not shown in the resource list. Set the COM port to a free COM port that your modem and computer support.

6. Shut down your Windows NT Workstation and physically install the modem. When you restart, your modem should be available for use. If you have any difficulties or encounter new error messages, call the technical support number provided by your modem manufacturer for assistance.

WARNING

IRQ conflicts can appear as a number of different problems under Windows NT. If you suddenly begin having problems with your Windows NT installation, remove your modem and verify that the COM port and IRQ are indeed free. Check that no other service (for instance, a fax monitor) is attempting to use the same modem. Check the Event Viewer for Serial events occurring during startup.

EXERCISE 12.2

Modem Installation

1. Double-click the My Computer icon on the Desktop.

2. Double-click Control Panel.

3. Double-click the Modems control panel.

4. Click the Next button to detect your modem. Letting Windows NT automatically detect will allow you to confirm that your modem is answering as it should. Detecting will take up to five minutes depending upon the speed of your computer.

5. Accept the settings shown in the detected modem window by clicking the Next button unless you are absolutely certain they will not work with your modem. Windows NT will usually work correctly with a modem it has identified even if the model shown in the window doesn't match the brand name of the modem.

6. Click Finish to complete the installation process.

7. Click the Dialing Properties button in the Modem Properties dialog box.

8. Enter the country and area code information that is appropriate for you.

9. Enter the appropriate information if you need to add outside line access or disable call waiting. If you have call waiting and someone calls while a RAS session is active, your RAS connection can be abruptly disconnected.

10. Click OK.

11. Click Close.

Installing Remote Access Service

Installing the RAS client is similar to installing all other network services. If you are using a leased line (X.25) or an ISDN connection, install those adapters first with the procedures provided by the manufacture of that device before proceeding with the RAS installation. Rather than selecting the Modem settings, you will use the X.25 PAD button in the RAS Setup dialog box. Exercise 12.3 shows the standard procedure for installing a RAS client with a regular modem.

You should already have installed your modem to work with Windows NT through the Modems control panel before proceeding with this exercise.

EXERCISE 12.3

Installing the Remote Access Client

1. Right-click on the Network Neighborhood icon on the desktop.

2. Select the Properties menu item to open the Network control panel.

3. Click the Services tab.

4. Click the Add button.

5. Select Remote Access Service from the Services list.

6. Click OK.

7. Enter the path to your Windows NT Workstation CD Intel 386 directory. Generally, this path is D:\I386, where D: is the drive letter of your CD-ROM.

8. Select the modem you wish to use for RAS and click OK in the Add RAS Device dialog box. If your modem does not appear in the Modem list, click the Install Modem button and follow the prompts to install your modem.

9. Click Configure.

10. Select the Dial Out Only option and click OK. Receiving RAS calls is covered in the companion book *MCSE: NT Server Study Guide*.

11. Click Add and then repeat steps 8 through 11 if you have another modem or serial port you would like to configure for RAS.

12. Click Continue when you are finished adding your modem(s).

13. Close the Network dialog box.

14. Answer Yes when asked if you want to restart your computer.

Creating a Dial-Up Connection

After installing RAS, you will need to create a dial-up network connection in the RAS phone book that contains the dialing and network information for each different dial-up server to which you will attach. This process is basically the same for Windows RAS servers and UNIX/Internet servers. Follow Exercise 12.4 to create a dial-up networking connection. Repeat this process for each dial-up server to which you need access. The RAS Phonebook Entry screen is shown in Figure 12.2.

If you don't know the name of your RAS server, ask your network administrator. Without a computer acting as a RAS server, you will not be able to complete this exercise. If you are installing RAS just to connect to the Internet, skip to Exercise 12.11.

Testing a Remote Access Service Installation

Testing a RAS installation requires running either a Microsoft RAS server or a UNIX server configured to answer PPP. If you are going to attach to a UNIX or Internet server to test your RAS installation, skip to the "Connecting to the Internet" section. If you have a Microsoft RAS server for testing, proceed with

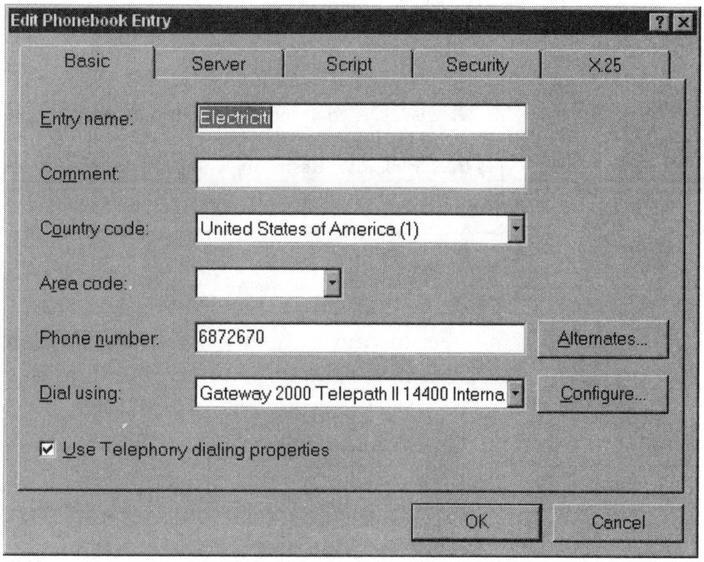

FIGURE 12.2
The Remote Access Service Edit Phonebook Entry screen.

EXERCISE 12.4

Creating a Dial-Up Networking Connection

1. Double-click the My Computer icon on the Desktop.

2. Double-click the Dial-Up Networking icon.

3. Click OK to pass *The phonebook is empty* notice if it appears. If it does not appear, you already have at least one RAS entry. Click New.

4. The New Phonebook Entry Wizard dialog box appears. Type the name of the new phonebook entry, check the *I know all about phonebook entries* box and click Next. (Once you choose to enter the phonebook information without the Wizard, you must select More ➤ User Preferences ➤ Appearance ➤ Use Wizard to use the Wizard again.) Enter the name of the server to which you will be attaching in the Entry name input line.

5. Select your modem in the *Dial using* drop-down box. If you are using a Null modem cable to connect two computers, select the *Dial-Up Networking Serial Cable between 2 PCs* on the appropriate COM port.

6. Click *Use Telephony dialing properties*.

7. Enter the area code and phone number of your RAS server in the Phone number input line. If you are using a Null modem cable, leave these lines blank.

8. Click the Alternates button if your RAS server has alternate phone numbers. Add the other phone numbers.

9. Click OK to accept your settings.

10. Click Close. Restarting your computer is not necessary after adding dial-up servers.

Exercise 12.5. You may need to ask your network administrator for the phone number of your company's RAS server and what protocols it supports. Configuring RAS to support dial-in connections is covered in the Network Press book *MCSE: NT Server Study Guide*.

After running this procedure, you are connected to the remote RAS host. If they have packet routing or NetBIOS Gateway enabled, you will have access to all the resources on the remote network that your security permissions allow.

EXERCISE 12.5

Testing a Remote Access Service Connection

1. Double-click the My Computer icon on the Desktop.

2. Double-click the Dial-Up Networking icon.

3. Check whether the server or service provider you entered in the previous section appears as the default phonebook entry. If the name does appear, select the entry from the list box. If it does not appear, repeat Exercise 12.4.

4. Click the Dial button.

5. Enter your username, password, and domain for the remote server in the Connect to window. (If you are connecting to a non-Windows NT server and no script is attached to this connection, this information may not matter because you will be entering your logon information for that server in a post-connect terminal window.) Click the Save password checkbox.

6. Click OK.

7. Listen for the modem to dial and connect. If you enabled post dial-up terminal window, a terminal window will appear allowing you to log on to the non-Windows server.

8. Enter your logon information for the service provider now.

9. Click done. RAS will beep if the connection went through correctly.

The Remote Access Service Monitor

The RAS monitor is a useful way to keep track of the occasionally unreliable status of modem connections over the public network. The RAS monitor is shown by default in the task bar. This can be changed to a window that constantly shows the connection status. If you use Exercise 12.6 to change the RAS monitor icon into a window, remember that clicking on the window has the same effect as clicking on the icon. Figure 12.3 shows the Dial-Up Networking Monitor screen.

EXERCISE 12.6

Checking the Status of a Remote Access Service Connection

1. Double-click the RAS monitor icon next to Time on the task bar.

2. Notice the count of incoming bytes and frames in the status page.

3. Select the Preferences tab.

4. Select the *As a window on the desktop* in the *Show status lights* control group.

5. Check *Display the windows title bar.*

6. Check *Always on top.*

7. Click OK.

8. Notice the RAS monitor now shows up as a window on the desktop.

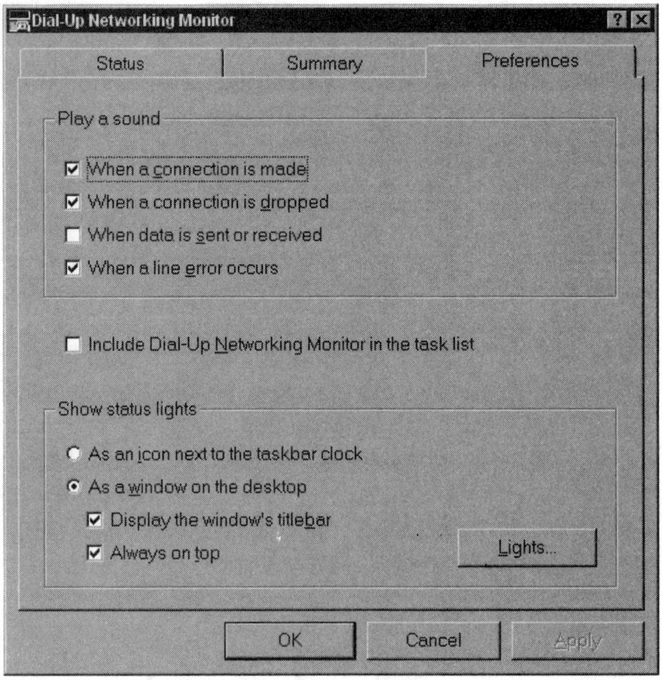

FIGURE 12.3
The Dial-Up Networking
Monitor screen controls
the Remote Access
Service monitor.

Disconnecting a Remote Access Service Session

You can disconnect a RAS session through the RAS session dialog box. Exercise 12.7 shows this simple procedure.

EXERCISE 12.7

Disconnecting a Remote Access Service Session

1. Right-click on the RAS monitor next to the Time in the task bar. (If you already changed the icon into a status window, right-click on the window.)

2. Select the Hang up connection option.

3. Select the name of the server or service provider from which you wish to disconnect.

4. Answer Yes to the Disconnect dialog box.

5. Listen for a beep to confirm the disconnect.

Configuration

You can configure most RAS options through the RAS in the Networking control panel. RAS can be configured to use any or all installed transport protocols and can be set up with SLIP connections for older UNIX servers and Internet service providers. RAS can also be configured to support either hardware or software compression between the client and the host.

Serial Protocols

RAS supports two serial protocols: PPP and SLIP. PPP replaces the older and less efficient SLIP. Both function as virtual network interface adapters in that they establish a two-party network between computers on each end of a serial link that looks the same as any other type of network (for example, Ethernet) to the transport protocol. The computers on each end of the serial link must be communicating with the same serial protocol, either PPP or SLIP.

POINT-TO-POINT PROTOCOL PPP knows not to transmit certain header information that is redundant when only two computers are participating in a network and supports the dynamic assignment of IP address, name server addresses, and gateways. PPP supports multiple protocols, such as AppleTalk, IPX, TCP/IP, and NetBEUI.

PPP is the serial transport of choice for all applications and operating systems. You should use PPP if your RAS server supports it.

SERIAL LINE INTERNET PROTOCOL SLIP was the original serial framing transport for TCP/IP. SLIP is the Internet Protocol specially adapted to full-duplex low-speed serial transmissions. SLIP was first developed to connect UNIX computers over low-speed telephone lines and became the standard for dial-up access to the Internet before the advent of the World Wide Web. SLIP can transmit only TCP/IP packets.

Since SLIP does not support dynamic assignment, SLIP users must enter their IP address each time they make a SLIP connection or write a complicated dialing script to set the IP address. And since SLIP does not support dynamic name server or gateway addresses, these addresses must be set permanently in your TCP/IP stack settings. SLIP does not support encrypted authentication and is therefore less secure than PPP.

Windows NT supports different IP settings for each dial-up server primarily to make SLIP easier to use. Note that SLIP is supported only on the client side of RAS. Windows NT will not answer SLIP when acting as a RAS server.

Transports

RAS will work with all TDI-compliant network transports installed in Windows NT. RAS creates a "virtual" NDIS-compatible network interface called the remote access WAN wrapper that allows you to treat your modem or serial interface as a network adapter when enabling or disabling bindings.

The WAN wrapper can be bound to any of the protocols available to Windows NT. Each transport differs slightly in its setup because of the different features and options provided.

When you install RAS, you will be required to enter some information for each protocol you have installed and enabled for remote access. In the simplest case, you will need to set whether or not you want to enable the network gateway service.

NETBEUI NetBEUI is the easiest protocol to configure for RAS. Since NetBEUI cannot be routed, you do not have to enter the network routing information required by TCP/IP and IPX. If you are going to use RAS only to connect two computers, consider using NetBEUI. If you enable the RAS gateway option, you will have access to all NetBIOS network resources to which the serving computer has access, even if they are not accessible to the NetBEUI protocol.

- **NetBEUI over PPP:** NetBEUI is generally the fastest of the transports over RAS because it does not transport routing information with each packet. When you enable NetBEUI in RAS, the only question you will be asked is whether or not to enable the RAS gateway service. You will generally enable this service unless your security policy prohibits it.

- **NetBIOS Gateway:** Prior to Windows NT 3.5, RAS supported only a NetBIOS gateway. Therefore, applications could function remotely only if they used the NetBIOS interprocess communication protocol. You are enabling the NetBIOS gateway when you allow access to the entire network in the NetBEUI dialog box of the RAS installation.

The Windows NT 4.0 PPP architecture is fundamentally different from the PPP architecture used by RAS in Windows NT 3.5 and earlier. The versions after RAS 3.5 support the full spectrum of interprocess communications mechanisms and all TDI-compliant transports. However, the transport must be installed on both the host and client side of the serial link if you intend to use Windows Sockets, Remote Procedure Calls, or IPX/SPX interfaces. The PPP architecture does not replace the functionality of the NetBIOS gateway, which remains useful as a way to access NetBIOS resources when you don't have a protocol in common with the service provider.

TCP/IP Internet connectivity requires the TCP/IP protocol because all Internet client packages, such as the Internet Explorer, use the Windows Sockets interface and IP routing to reach their destinations. Many network installations also use TCP/IP for the primary transport protocol. Many Windows utilities, such as Ping, telnet, and FTP, require the TCP/IP transport running at both ends of the connection.

Although TCP/IP can be used to perform all network functions, NetBEUI and NetBIOS are faster when performing browse requests to a remote Windows NT network. You should make NetBEUI your primary protocol for RAS connections, and use TCP/IP only for applications that require the Windows Sockets interface.

- **TCP/IP over PPP:** When you dial into a PPP TCP/IP RAS server, your IP address, name resolution server, and gateway information will be automatically negotiated. You will not have to provide any of this information. Your IP address will either be assigned by a DHCP server or by a static range of addresses configured on the RAS server.

- **TCP/IP over SLIP:** When dialing into a SLIP TCP/IP UNIX host, you must provide an IP address, the address to a name resolution server, and the address to your gateway. The SLIP logon interface may provide an IP address, or your administrator or Internet provider may assign them to you permanently.

IPX IPX is supported over RAS through the PPP serial protocol, which allows NetWare compatibility software such as Client Services for NetWare to run over a remote link. IPX routing is also supported, allowing full access to all IPX resources on the remote network if the IPX gateway option is enabled when the RAS service is installed.

Software Compression

RAS supports software compression very similar to the compression used in the NTFS file system, which typically affords greater compression than the International Telephony Union (ITU) V.42 hardware compression built into most modern modems.

If you enable both software and hardware compression on V.42/MNP 5 modems, they will attempt to compress data streams already compressed in software, which will actually result in data expansion. If you enable software compression, then disable V.42 or Microcom Network Protocol (MNP) 5 hardware compression to prevent data expansion.

Most Internet servers do not support software compression. Dial-up connections that attach to the Internet should use ITU V.42/MNP 5 modem compression, rather than software compression, to maximize your bandwidth. Software compression is used primarily for remote access to Windows NT networks.

Depending upon the type of data being transmitted, you can expect compression ratios between 2 and 4 to 1. Exercise 12.8 shows the process for enabling software compression and disabling hardware compression.

Routing

RAS functions as an IP and IPX router for clients attached through the PPP protocol, giving them full access to attached network resources, including interprocess communications interfaces like Windows Sockets, remote procedure calls, and named pipes.

EXERCISE 12.8

Enabling Remote Access Service Compression

1. Double-click the My Computer icon on the desktop.

2. Double-click the Dial-Up Networking icon in the My Computer window.

3. Select the connection on which you wish to enable compression in the Connection drop-down list. If you have only created one connection, it will be showing.

4. Click the More button.

5. Select Edit Entry ➤ Modem Properties.

6. Click the Configure button in the Basic Properties tab.

7. Disable *Enable modem compression*.

8. Click OK.

9. Select the Server tab.

10. Check *Enable software compression*.

11. Click OK.

12. Click Close.

IPX broadcasts are forwarded through an IPX router, so remote clients will be able to attach to NetBIOS resources like file and print services. IP broadcasts are not forwarded, so some other method of NetBIOS name resolution must exist. You can use WINS or LMHOSTS to connect NetBIOS resources over the TCP/IP protocol when using RAS.

In summary, when you enable the Entire network option in the NetBEUI protocol, you are enabling the original RAS gateway service called NetBIOS gateway. Since NetBIOS is implemented over NetBEUI, IPX, and TCP/IP, a NetBEUI client attached through RAS can access network resources over any protocol loaded on the RAS server. The NetBIOS gateway is protocol independent.

When you enable the Entire network options under NWLink or TCP/IP, you are enabling a packet router. Therefore both the RAS server and the network resources you want access to must support the connection protocol.

Multilink

Multilink allows the combination of multiple serial data streams into one aggregate bundle. The most common use of Multilink is to combine the multiple ISDN channels into one aggregate total, but it can also be used to combine regular modems. For instance, if you have two 14.4Kbps modems with Multilink enabled, your bandwidth will be 28.8Kbps.

The Multilink protocol supported in Windows NT 4.0 enables you to combine data streams regardless of the physical type of the connection. For example, if you have two analog modems and an ISDN modem with two digital channels, you can combine all four data streams into one aggregate channel. The number of devices determines the number of links.

To use Multilink, both the server and client must be Windows NT computers and both must have Multilink enabled.

RAS Scripts

When you are connecting to non-Windows NT RAS servers, you may have to enter plain text logon information. This step is especially true when you use UNIX servers and Internet service providers, and it is required when using SLIP.

Fortunately, Windows NT provides an easy automation mechanism called *dial-up scripting*. You can create a dial-up script for each of your dial-up connections. Before attempting to write a script, use the *Pop up a terminal window* option. Log on and record all the data provided by your service provider and the responses you are expected to return. The Script tab of the RAS Edit Phonebook Entry screen is shown in Figure 12.4.

Creating a Connection Script

The Windows NT connection script language has many unusual characteristics based on different combinations of keywords and macros. Your best bet when creating a connection script is to consult the help files and the SWITCH.INF file provided with Windows NT. Copy the example shown in step 11 of Exercise 12.9 as closely as you can, replacing the final command line with the text required by your provider. Because connection scripts vary widely, you may have to work with your script for a while to get it working correctly; we did!

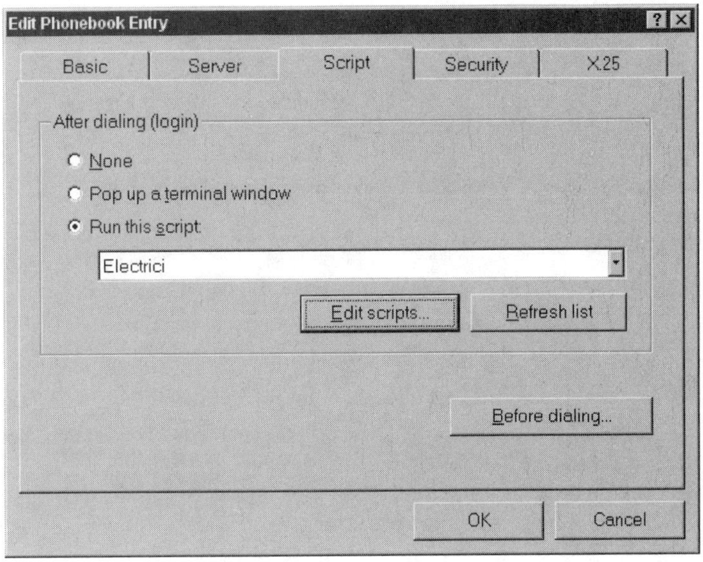

FIGURE 12.4
Adding scripts to Remote
Access Service
phonebook entries.

FIGURE 12.4
Adding scripts to Remote Access Service phonebook entries.

EXERCISE 12.9

Creating a Connection Script

1. Double-click the My Computer icon on the Desktop.

2. Double-click the Dial-up Networking icon in the My Computer window.

3. Select the phonebook entry you want to add a script to in the *Phonebook entry to dial* drop-down list.

4. Click the More button.

5. Select *Edit entry and modem properties*.

6. Select the Script tab in the Edit Phonebook Entry screen.

7. Select *Run this script.*

8. Click the Edit scripts button. Notepad will open the SWITCH.INF RAS script file. Read through the instructions and sample script for detailed instructions on creating a script file. You may wish to print this file. This exercise will assume you are connecting to our Internet service provider in San Diego, which is probably not the case, but it represents a pretty typical logon process.

9. Move to the end of the file by dragging the vertical scroll bar to the bottom of the scroll track.

10. Set the cursor at the end of the file.

11. Type the following lines into Notepad:

```
;name of service provider enclosed in []
[Electrici]
; send an initial carriage return—required by some service
  providers
COMMAND=<cr>
; wait for the colon after username: or logon:
OK=<match>":"
LOOP=<ignore>
; send the user name entered in the connect dialog
COMMAND=<username><cr>
; wait for the colon after password:
OK=<match>":"
LOOP=<ignore>
; send the password entered in the connect dialog
COMMAND=<password><cr>
; required by COMMAND= if passwords are not echoed
NoResponse
; send the start ppp command to the remote computer.
COMMAND=ppp default<cr>
; ignore everything else sent by the remote computer.
OK=<ignore>
```

12. Select Exit in the File menu of Notepad.

13. Answer Yes when asked to save changes.

14. Click the Refresh List button. This will cause the dialog box to search the SWITCH.INF file for new connection scripts.

15. Select Electriciti (or your service provider's name) from the script drop-down list.

16. Click OK.

17. Close RAS. New scripts are not loaded until RAS is restarted.

Although you can include your plain text username and password, you are better off using the <username> and <password> macros. These provide the name and password typed into the Connect to Dialog box. If you don't want to enter them every time, enter them once and check the Save password option in the Connect to Dialog box. This method has two advantages over simply putting your password in the connection script. First, it stores your password in the encrypted password list rather than in the text file where it can be read by anyone. Second, it allows other users who may log on to your computer to connect to the remote computer using your script but with their user-name and password.

Debugging a Connection Script

The Windows NT RAS script language is barely adequate and very finicky. (For instance, this script language cannot deal with any sort of variation in echoed text at all, which will cause random connection failures when in fact nothing is wrong.) Often a connection script will not work correctly on the first attempt. To debug a connection script, Windows NT provides connection logging. Windows NT will record all the communication that occurs on a serial port to a file, which you can review for errors. This file is called DEVICE.LOG, and it is stored in your system directory.

Connection logging is enabled by editing the Registry as shown in Exercise 12.10.

Viewing the Connection Log

Once you've enabled connection logging, each connection attempt you make through RAS will be written to the DEVICE.LOG file in the \SYSTEM32\RAS\ directory subtree in your windows system directory. On my computer, this file is C:\WINNT\SYSTEM32\RAS\DEVICE.LOG.

You can open this file using Notepad. Windows NT will record each command sent to the remote computer, the echo sent back, and the responses received from the remote computer. Read through the following example:

```
Remote Access Service Device Log 07/24/1996 13:04:48
------------------------------------------------------------


Port: Command to Device:

Port: Echo from Device :
```

EXERCISE 12.10

Enabling Command Logging

1. Select Run from the Start menu.

2. Type **regedit** in the input box.

3. Press OK.

4. Double-click HKEY_LOCAL_MACHINE.

5. Double-click SYSTEM.

6. Double-click CurrentControlSet.

7. Double-click Services.

8. Double-click RasMan.

9. Click Parameters.

10. Double-click *Logging in the Values* drop-down list.

11. Enter 1 in the Value Data input box.

12. Click OK.

13. Close the Registry Editor by clicking the Close box.

14. Restart the computer for the logging setting to take effect.

```
Port: Response from Device:
CS6 Welcome to ElectriCiti. Authorized subscriber access only.
CS line 9


User Access Verification

Username:
Port: Command to Device:llsales

Port: Echo from Device :llsales

Port: Response from Device:
```

```
Password:
Port: Command to Device:protect!

Port: Command to Device:ppp default

Port: Echo from Device :
CS>ppp default
Port: Response from Device:
Entering PPP mode.
Async interface address is unnumbered (Ethernet0)
Your IP address is 198.5.212.54. MTU is 1500 bytes
Header compression will match your system.


Header compression will match your system.


~
```

Each dial-up session replaces the file, and the file is held open (and so cannot be deleted) while the RAS Automatic Connection Manager service is started. Compare the contents of this file with your script to locate your connection problems. When your script is working properly, you can turn off connection logging by following the procedure shown in Exercise 12.10 and setting the logging value to 0.

Administering Remote Access Service

Windows NT computers that receive calls can administer the permissions assigned to dial-in users. Windows NT Workstation allows only one dial-in session, so actual administration is not usually necessary. RAS permissions are administered using the Remote Access Admin tool, shown in Figure 12.5. To access this screen, select Programs ➤ Administrative Tools ➤ Remote Access Admin from the Start menu.

You can use this tool to assign dial-in permissions to various users, but remember that the Workstation version of RAS supports only one connection at a time. This tool can also be used to start and stop the RAS server (answer) service. You will need to stop this service before you can use your modem for non-RAS functions such as faxing or connecting to a bulletin board service. The RAS Administration tool is covered in detail in the companion to this book, MCSE: NT Server Study Guide.

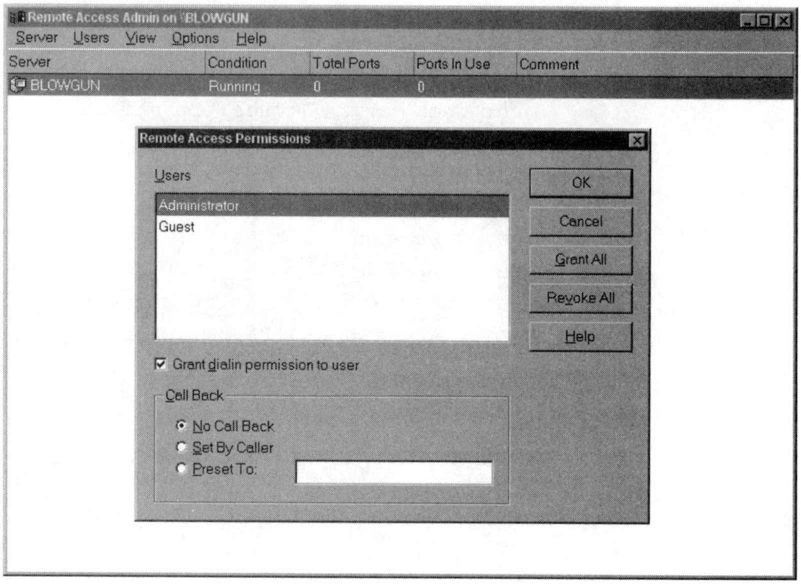

FIGURE 12.5
The Remote Access
Admin tool.

Remote Access Service Security

RAS IMPLEMENTS A NUMBER OF security methods to limit the possibility of unauthorized access and/or eavesdropping. Windows NT RAS clients and hosts negotiate passwords through sophisticated challenge and reply authentication protocols. Communication stream encryption is supported to thwart attempts at wiretapping and eavesdropping.

Encrypted Authentication

RAS supports a number of authentication protocols to support a wide range of remote servers and clients. RAS will automatically select the protocol appropriate for the host and client relationship you establish. When dialing into a Windows NT host from a Windows NT client (versions 3.5 and above), the MS-CHAP protocol is used.

Remote Access Service Client Authentication Settings

When you change the security settings in the RAS phonebook, you are selecting the authentication protocols your client will attempt to use. Be advised that allowing less secure authentication from clients can create a hole in your security policy. If the client requires greater security than the host can provide, the RAS connection will fail. Figure 12.6 shows the Security tab in the RAS phonebook.

FIGURE 12.6
Use the Security tab in the Edit Phonebook Entry window to set the RAS authentication and encryption options.

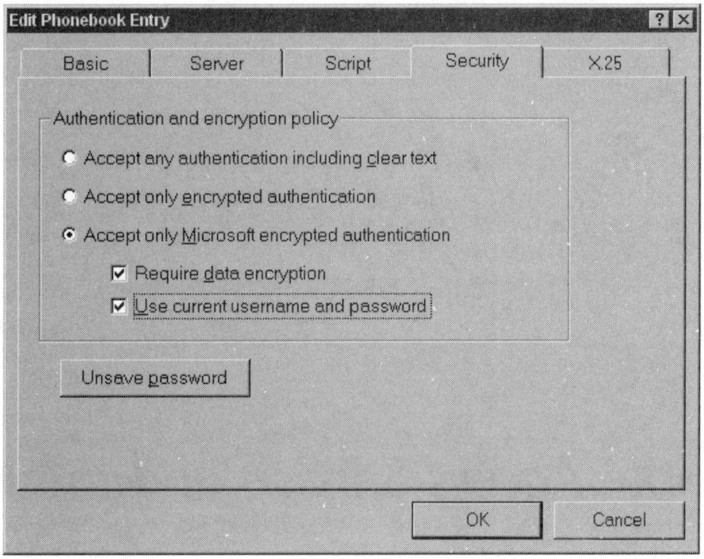

Remote Access Service Server Authentication Settings

Authentication security settings for RAS hosts are set in the Network control panel under the RAS service in the Services page. Server Authentication settings are covered in *MCSE: NT Server Study Guide*.

Authentication Methods

RAS supports the following authentication methods:

- **CHAP (MD5):** Challenge Handshake Authentication Protocol. Windows NT supports CHAP for outbound PPP dialing, allowing Windows NT clients to connect to most non-Microsoft hosts.

- **MS-CHAP (MD4):** A Microsoft version of RSA Message Digest 4 is the default RAS server challenge and reply protocol. This authentication protocol can negotiate encryption and use the RC4 algorithm to encrypt communications between the host and client.

- **DES:** Data Encryption Standard is the encryption protocol designed by the National Bureau of Standards. DES supports compatibility with older clients and servers like LAN Manager-based systems.

- **PAP:** Password Authentication Protocol is a nonsecure plain text password authentication protocol. It is included for compatibility with non-Microsoft applications that require it, but it is disabled by default. You may need to use PAP for older UNIX-based SLIP Internet servers.

- **SPAP:** Shiva PAP is a version of PAP implemented by Shiva in its remote client software. Windows NT RAS Server (only) supports SPAP so Shiva clients can dial in. SPAP does not send the password in plain text.

Most of these protocols are included for backward compatibility to older servers. You should use MS-CHAP if you are setting up your own RAS hosts.

Remote Access Service and the Internet

MANY USERS WILL USE RAS primarily as an on-ramp to the Internet. With the Internet Explorer provided free with Windows NT 4.0 and RAS, you have all the software you need to browse the World Wide Web, use Internet e-mail, and download files from FTP servers. You will need to establish an Internet account with an Internet service provider if you do not already have one.

Connecting to the Internet

Install RAS according to Exercise 12.3. Make certain you've installed the TCP/IP protocol stack as shown in Exercise 9.1 before continuing. Assuming you've installed RAS and TCP/IP and you have an Internet service provider, continue with Exercise 12.11.

EXERCISE 12.11

Establishing a Dial-Up Configuration

1. Double-click the My Computer icon on your Desktop.

2. Double-click the Dial-Up Networking icon in the My Computer window. If this is the first entry you are creating, a window will appear stating that the phonebook is empty.

3. Click OK. If you've already created one or more entries, click the New button. For this exercise, we'll use the Phonebook Entry Wizard. If the Wizard doesn't appear (after being disabled previously), choose More ➤ User Preferences ➤ Appearance ➤ Use wizard to create new phonebook entries.

4. Type the name of the server or service provider to which you will be attaching in the *Name the new phonebook entry* input box.

5. Click Next.

6. Check the *I am calling the Internet* option if you are connecting to an Internet or a UNIX server.

7. Check the *Send my plain text password* option if this Internet service provider requires a plain text logon.

8. Check the *Type logon information* option if you need to enter logon information after dialing. (This may be the case for many Internet service providers.)

9. Click Next.

10. Check *Use Telephony dialing properties*. This setting will ensure that your outside line and call waiting preferences are migrated to this dial-up networking connection.

11. Enter the telephone number of the server or service provider. If you can use alternate phone numbers to connect, click the Alternates button and add the additional numbers.

12. Click Next.

13. Select the protocol you will be using to connect. Unless your service provider does not allow PPP access, leave PPP checked. This exercise assumes PPP access.

14. Click Next.

EXERCISE 12.11 (CONTINUED)

15. Select *Use a terminal window* if your service provider requires a manual logon. Otherwise, select none. (Automation scripts were covered earlier in this chapter.)

16. If you checked the logon information option earlier in the process, a dialog box will ask for your IP address. If you did not check this option, skip to step 18. If the server or service provider can provide an IP address, leave the defaults (0.0.0.0) in place. Otherwise, enter a valid IP address. All PPP servers provide an IP address. Click Next when finished.

17. If you checked the logon information option earlier in the process, a dialog box will ask for the DNS server address. If you did not check this option, skip to step 19. Many PPP servers will provide this information. If not, enter the DNS server IP address in the DNS server box. This information will be in the documentation from your Internet service provider. (Note that only one DNS and WINS server number can be entered here. Secondary entries, which many providers supply, can be added to the Server-TCP/IP Settings portion of the phonebook entry.)

18. Click Finish.

19. Close the Dial-Up Networking window.

Once you've established a connection to your Internet service provider through RAS, you are connected to the Internet. At this point, you will be able to use any of the standard Internet tools like FTP or the Internet Explorer.

Running Internet Explorer with Remote Access Service

Running the Internet Explorer with RAS is quite simple. Simply establish a RAS connection and then launch the Internet Explorer following the steps explained in Exercise 12.12.

Using other Internet tools such as telnet or FTP is as easy under Windows NT as using any UNIX operating system. These tools are used from the command

---

EXERCISE 12.12

Running Internet Explorer with Remote Access Service

1. Double-click the My Computer icon on the Desktop.

2. Double-click the Dial-Up Networking icon.

3. Select your Internet service provider from the list of RAS servers in the Connection drop-down list.

4. Click Dial.

5. Perform any post-dial logon procedures necessary for your connection. If you have written a script or your Internet server is capable of logging you on with supported authentication, you may not need to do anything. RAS will beep to indicate connection success.

6. Double-click the Internet Explorer icon on the Desktop.

7. Type **www.microsoft.com** in the Address text box and press return. In a moment you will see the Microsoft home page.

---

prompt. They are not covered here because their functionality is encapsulated within the Internet Explorer. Figure 12.7 shows the Internet Explorer browsing the Web.

Chapter Summary

REMOTE ACCESS SERVICE (RAS) provides the powerful capability of extending your network to any location in the world through the public telephone networks. RAS allows you to attach to any RAS-configured Windows NT host or to many third-party remote access servers including the global Internet.

RAS allows clients running all recent Microsoft operating systems and any computer running the TCP/IP and PPP protocols to attach. RAS supports all TDI-compliant transport protocols, including NetBEUI, NWLink, and TCP/IP. It will

FIGURE 12.7
Use the Internet Explorer to browse the Web.

function as a NetBIOS gateway and as an IPX and TCP/IP router to allow the client computer to access any network resources available to the host. RAS also supports hardware and software compression to maximize bandwidth by eliminating data redundancy and the combination of multiple serial streams into one aggregate connection to fully utilize available communications resources.

RAS supports all Windows NT IPC mechanisms, allowing client computers to operate as full network clients and run the client side of client/server applications remotely.

RAS will run over the standard public switched telephone network, the integrated services digital network, or X.25 frame relay leased lines. The modular network component architecture of RAS will automatically support all future wide area network links as they become available.

RAS is easy to install and use. RAS provides a scripting language to automate attaching to plain text, authenticating SLIP and PPP servers. RAS provides a full suite of debugging and monitoring facilities to allow the rapid resolution of RAS related problems. RAS can log all negotiations between the host and client. Using the RAS monitor, you can determine the error rate of a dial-up connection.

RAS implements a suite of authentication protocols to ensure the most secure authentication of client passwords possible. RAS authentication is backward compatible with many older, less secure authentication schemes. You can use the RAS administrator to control the use of these authentication methods. RAS can also support fully encrypted links if both the client and host are capable of negotiating under the MS-CHAP protocol.

Finally, RAS serves as the Windows NT springboard to the Internet. RAS is the foundation of Microsoft's Internet strategy. All Windows NT Internet tools can use RAS as their connection to the Web. With RAS and Internet Explorer, Windows NT now ships with complete access to the Internet and the World Wide Web.

Exercise Questions

1. RAS can use more than one modem simultaneously to make a connection to a RAS host.

   A. True

   B. False

2. RAS allows computers to communicate over a local area network.

   A. True

   B. False

3. RAS allows seamless remote access by controlling the functions of the host computer from the remote client.

   A. True

   B. False

4. Using the RAS monitor will not slow down your RAS connection.

   A. True

   B. False

5. RAS server does not support the SLIP protocol.

   A. True

   B. False

6. Internet connectivity requires the TCP/IP protocol.

   A. True

   B. False

7. RAS supports either hardware or software compression, but not both.

   A. True

   B. False

8. RAS supports _____ Windows NT interprocess communication mechanisms.

9. The RAS _____ is used to check the status of a RAS connection.

10. RAS scripts can be debugged by enabling logging and checking the _____ file.

11. You can use the _____ to browse the World Wide Web after establishing a remote access session with an Internet service provider.

    A. Internet Explorer

    B. Windows NT Explorer

    C. FTP

    D. telnet

12. Which protocol is RAS not capable of routing?

    A. TCP/IP

    B. IPX

    C. NetBEUI

13. Which of the following protocols does SLIP support?

    A. IPX

    B. NetBEUI

    C. NetBIOS

    D. TCP/IP

14. RAS does not yet support which of the following WAN connections?

    A. PSTN

    B. ISDN

    C. X.25

    D. ATM

15. RAS on Windows NT Workstation is limited to how many inbound connections?

  A. 1

  B. 4

  C. 10

  D. 256

16. You should use the following serial protocol with RAS whenever possible:

  A. SLIP

  B. TCP/IP

  C. NetBEUI

  D. PPP

17. Which transport protocol is recommended for connecting Windows NT computers via RAS?

  A. TCP/IP

  B. NWLink

  C. NetBEUI

  D. Any TDI-compliant protocol

18. Which is the slowest RAS transport between Windows NT computers?

  A. NetBEUI

  B. NWLink

  C. TCP/IP

19. Which authentication protocol is used by default?

  A. CHAP

  B. MS-CHAP

  C. DES

  D. MS-DES

  E. PAP

20. The connection device log is cleared

    A. When the user clears it in the RAS administrator

    B. Every time a new connection is made

    C. When it hits the size limit stored in the Registry

    D. Never

Printing

WINDOWS NT WORKSTATION gives you flexible and powerful printing support. You can attach printers directly to your computer, or you can print to printers over the network. Windows NT supports many different types of printers from many different printer manufacturers. Some of the printing features of Windows NT include local and remote printing, print spooling with print job monitoring and forwarding, printer security, and foreign client support for operating systems such as Macintosh and UNIX.

This chapter will introduce the basic concepts of local and network printing, describe the Windows NT print model, show you how to use the print manager, set up printers, and troubleshoot common printer problems.

Introduction to Printing

MANY COMPANIES MANUFACTURE PRINTERS, and each manufacturer makes printers that are a little different from all of the others. There are many ways of making marks on paper, which is, after all, what printers do. Some manufacturers introduce new technology to increase the resolution, color capacity, or pages per minute of their printers. Other manufacturers wait a while to see which technologies will prove to be popular and then implement the features that are most cost effective in their niche of the printer market. The end result is that almost any printing technology is implemented on some manufacturer's printer.

Any operating system's printing system has three components—the printing devices themselves and how they are attached to the computers, the printing software that translates print requests from application software into a form the printing devices will understand, and the way the operating system accomplishes printing over networks.

Printing Devices

The printing devices are the physical parts of the printing system, the components that actually make the black or colored marks on the paper. These units are commonly called *printers,* but in Windows NT terminology they are called *printing devices* because application software never directly communicates with a printing device. The "printer" that a Windows application sees is a software construct that translates print requests and forwards the resulting print job to the appropriate printing device.

A printing device is usually connected to a computer via a serial or parallel cable, but printing devices can be connected to computers in other ways, such as directly via the computer's expansion bus or through a SCSI interface. Sometimes printers are connected directly to a network without an intervening general-purpose computer.

Some printing devices do not print directly to paper. For instance, a Post-Script slide maker will print directly to 35mm slides for use in presentations. A fax modem, connected via a serial cable or installed in an expansion slot in your computer, can be configured as a printer, making it possible for you to print directly from your word processor or other application to a fax machine anywhere in the world. If the device you are "printing to" is actually a fax modem, the document may never actually be printed. Figure 13.1 illustrates several printing devices.

FIGURE 13.1
Laser printers, ink-jet printers, fax modems, slide makers, and plotters are all printing devices.

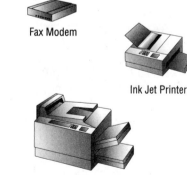

Fax Modem

Ink Jet Printer

Slide Maker

Laser Printer

Plotter

Printing Software

You cannot expect your word processor or spreadsheet to understand the printing languages and features of every printing device you can attach to your computer—the variety of printing devices and printing languages is too great. If the routines for accessing printing devices were contained in the applications, you would have to update your applications whenever you attach a new printer with new options to your computer. (This unwieldy technology was used in early operating systems such as MS-DOS.)

Windows NT, like many other modern operating systems, frees the application from having to speak the printer's native printing language. A layer of software between the printing device and the application software converts the application's print requests into a form that the user's printer can understand. This middle layer in Windows NT is the set of software components described in the "NT Print Model" section later in this chapter.

The printer, in Windows NT terminology, is a software component, not the physical device that produces documents on paper. When you select a printer from within an application, you are selecting the software component that will translate the application's print requests into a form that the printing device can understand. If your printing device is versatile, you might have several printer software components for one device, one for each mode of printing that the device supports. For instance, if you have a printer that supports both the HPGL/2 printing language and the PostScript printing language, you might have two printer icons and two printer options within your application but only one physical printer. Or if you have two printers that are the same, you might have just one printer (software component) that operates both of the printing devices; whichever one is free will print the current document.

When one printer services more than one printing device, the printing devices form a *printer pool*. All the printing devices in the printer pool must be of the same type, and the printer will assign documents to be printed to whichever printing device is free in the printer pool.

Some network operating systems (NetWare, for example) use the term queue to refer to what Windows NT calls printers.

Figure 13.2 shows the relationship between applications, printers, and printing devices.

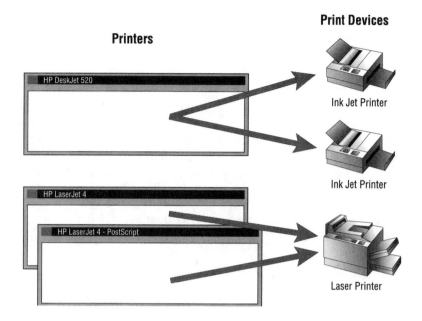

FIGURE 13.2
A printing device may be associated with more than one printer (application visible software component), and a printer may be associated with more than one printing device.

Printing and Networks

One of the most common uses of a network is to share a printer. In the Windows NT print model, an application program doesn't care whether a printing device is connected directly to the computer the application is running on or resides elsewhere on the network.

If the printing device is attached to another computer over the network, the networking software will redirect the print request to the computer to which the printing device is attached. That computer will present the print request to its printing device.

One computer can provide printing services for many different types of computers. For instance, Windows NT Workstation can provide printing services for Windows, UNIX, Apple Macintosh, and MS-DOS computers.

NT Print Model

Windows NT has a modular print architecture. Each portion of the Windows NT printing system has a specific purpose and well-defined interfaces to other components of the system. The modular architecture makes Windows NT printing flexible; different versions of the modules can be installed for different purposes, and only the versions of the modules that are needed must be loaded. The software and hardware components that make up the print model are as follows:

- Graphics device interface (GDI)

- Print driver

- Print router

- Print provider (spooler)

- Print processor

- Print monitor

- Network printing devices

Figure 13.3 illustrates the Windows NT print model.

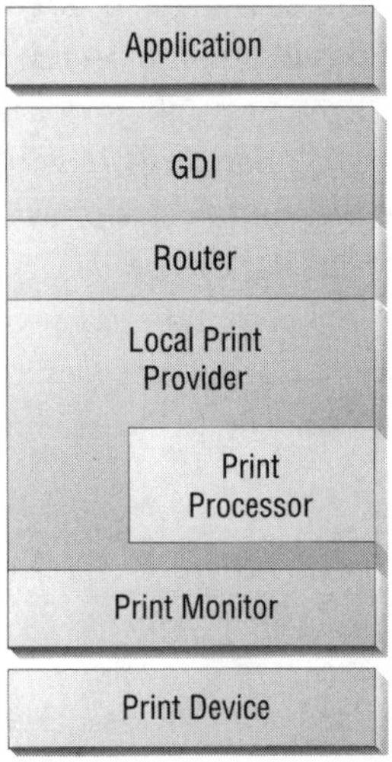

FIGURE 13.3
Software components in the Windows NT print model cooperate to provide a sophisticated and powerful printing system.

Application

GDI

Router

Local Print Provider

Print Processor

Print Monitor

Print Device

Graphics Device Interface

The graphics device interface (GDI) provides Windows programs with a single unified system for presenting graphical information to the user. Therefore, the program can ignore the specific details of a device's resolution, color depth, coordinate system, bits per pixel, available fonts, and so on. The GDI will translate the generic print requests of the application into device driver requests that are specific to the printing characteristics of that device.

The GDI does not make a special case of either drawing on the screen or printing to a printer; both are merely graphical devices that vary somewhat in characteristics. The screen, for instance, is usually a much lower-resolution printing device than is a printer, but the screen usually supports many more colors.

The GDI takes application print requests and translates them into device driver interface (DDI) calls. DDI calls are specific to the drawing characteristics of a printer, but are not specific to an individual printing device.

When an application prints a document using the GDI interface and the device driver for the printer, the GDI and device driver produce a file called a print job. The *print job* contains either the sequence of instructions for the printer that will produce the printed document, in which case it is called a *raw print job,* or a list of the DDI calls that will produce a raw print job, in which case the print job is called a *journal file print job*.

The GDI produces a journal file print job when the printing device is local (directly connected to the computer instead of over the network). GDI produces a journal file more quickly than it produces a raw print job, which means that the GDI can return control to the application more quickly. The DDI calls stored in the print job must still be performed in order for the document to be printed. However, the print processor (see "Print Processor") will perform each DDI call in order, in the background, producing the raw print job that will be sent to the printing device.

Print Driver

The print driver is the software component that translates the printer-generic DDI calls into the printer-specific commands that will be passed on to the actual printer. You must have a print driver for the type of printer your workstation is connected to when you print. The print driver may be downloaded from a remote print server automatically. The printer manufacturer usually supplies the printer driver software.

The printer driver consists of three parts:

- **Printer Graphics Driver:** This part of the printer driver does the actual DDI-to-printer-language conversion. Three printer graphics drivers included with Windows NT are PSCRIPT.DLL (for PostScript printers), RASDD.DLL (for raster-based printers), and PLOTTER.DLL (for HPGL/2-based printers).

- **Printer Interface Driver:** This component provides the Print Manager user interface in which you configure the printer. The printer interface for the above-mentioned printer graphics drivers are PSCRIPTUI.DLL, RASDDUI.DLL, and PLOTUI.DLL.

- **Characterization Data File or Minidriver:** This file isolates the make- and model-specific characteristics of a printer for the printer graphics driver.

Printer manufacturers can supply all three components of the printer driver; however, often the only part that the manufacturer needs to provide is a mini-driver for one of the three Microsoft-supplied printer graphics and printer interface drivers.

Print Router

The print router directs the print job to the appropriate print provider. The router can also download a printer driver for the printer if the printer is on a remote computer and the remote computer is configured to provide a printer driver for the type of computer the router is running on.

Print Provider (Spooler)

Each printing device configured for use in your Windows NT workstation has a print provider. A print provider may accept print jobs from the router for a local printer, or it may accept print jobs to be printed on a remote printer. An application sees this printer when it prints.

A print provider for a local printer accepts print jobs from the router, calls the print processor to perform any final modifications to the print jobs, and then transfers the jobs one by one to the print monitor. Print providers can accept print jobs while a print job is printing; print jobs that are waiting to be printed are stored in memory or on disk as spool files.

The print provider also adds separator pages to print jobs if the user has requested them in the Print Manager.

A print provider for remote printers locates the network print server that is the destination of the print job and transfers the print job to that print server. Remote print providers do not spool the print job—they transfer the print job to the destination where it may be spooled.

Print Processor

The print processor performs any modifications to the print job before passing the print job to the print monitor. Windows NT supplies two print processors: the Windows print processor and the Macintosh print processor.

In the Windows print processor, if the print job is a journal file, the print processor creates the raw type of print job by performing each of the DDI print driver calls.

The print processor may perform print processing on a raw print job if it is of one of two types: Raw FF Auto or Raw FF Appended. In the first case the print processor always appends a form feed to the print job, which will cause the printer to eject the printed page. The second case appends a form feed if one is not already present. These two options are useful for older programs that send ASCII text to the printer, never or seldom appending a form-feed character.

The print processor does not change a normal raw print job (the kind of print job produced by Windows programs when they do not produce journal files).

The Windows print processor handles all print jobs from Macintosh computers to PostScript printers attached to a Windows NT computer and from UNIX, Windows 95, older versions of Windows, and DOS.

The Macintosh print processor processes print jobs that a Macintosh computer sends to a non-PostScript printer connected to a Windows NT computer. The Macintosh print processor interprets the PostScript language in the Macintosh Postscript print job and prepares a raw print job for non-Postscript printers.

Print Monitor

The print monitor is the software component that transmits the print job (by now transformed into the language of the printer) to the printing device. Windows NT supplies several print monitors, the most important of which are LOCALMON.DLL, HPMON.DLL, and LPRMON.DLL.

The local print monitor communicates with the printing device through serial and parallel ports, remote print shares, and named pipes and can store the print job in a file instead of sending it to a printer.

The HP print monitor sends the print jobs to an HP printer that is connected directly to the network instead of attached through a computer.

The LPR (line printer) print monitor sends the print job to a UNIX LPD (line printer Daemon) print server.

The print monitor can also report the condition of the printing device (busy, off-line, ready, out of paper or toner, etc.), detect printing errors, and restart a print job if necessary.

Managing Printers

FROM THE PRINTERS WINDOW (opened by selecting Start ➤ Settings ➤ Printers), you can perform local and network printer administrative tasks, such as creating and attaching to printers; configuring printers; setting print permissions; starting, stopping, and redirecting print jobs; and auditing printer use.

This section will show you how to

- Manage print jobs

- Create local printers

- Attach to remote printers

Configuring printers is a complex task and is covered in the "Printer Configuration" section later in this chapter.

Managing Print Jobs

Within the Printers folder is an icon for each of the printers you have installed or connected to your workstation. Opening the icon for a printer (double-clicking on the icon) shows you the status of the printer. (See Figure 13.4.) Each printer has a separate window, showing only print jobs for that printer.

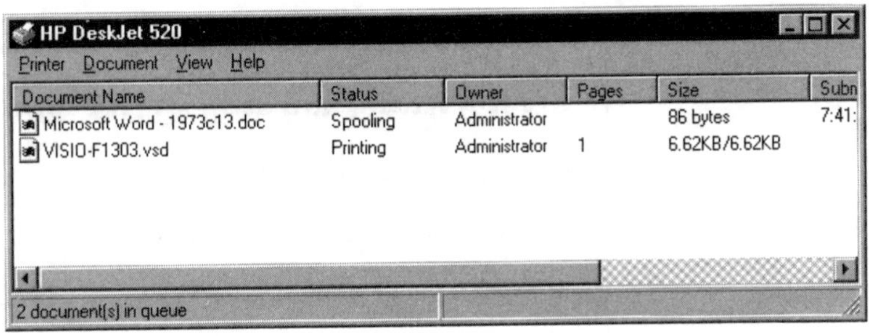

FIGURE 13.4
Opening the Printer icon will show you the jobs in that printer's queue and allow you to control the printer and manage those jobs.

Print job entries will appear in the list in the middle of the window and will persist until the document is printed or until the print job is removed from the queue. You can modify a print job's status while it is in the queue.

If you have sufficient permission, you can pause, resume, restart, and cancel print jobs. You perform any of these actions by clicking once on the print job name and then selecting the operation (pause, etc.) from the Document menu in the Printers window.

From the Printer menu in the Printers window you can pause all printing for that printer, cancel all of the print jobs on that printer, set the printer to be the default printer, start and stop sharing of the printer, select the default document properties (page size, paper tray, and so on), and reach the Properties window for that printer. (The Properties window is described in the "Printer Configuration" section later in this chapter.)

Follow the steps in Exercise 13.1 to create a print job, pause the job, and then cancel the job.

Creating a Local Printer

Before you can use a printer that is directly attached to your computer, you must create a printer within Print Manager. Exercise 13.2 outlines the steps for creating a printer.

EXERCISE 13.1

Create, Pause, and Stop a Print Job

1. Log on as an administrator.

2. Select Start ➤ Settings ➤ Printers.

3. Double-click on a printer installed in your computer.

4. Select Properties from the Printer menu.

5. Position the Properties window so that you can see both the Properties window and the Printers window.

6. Click the Print Test Page button in the Properties window. As soon as the test page appears in the Printers window, click once on the test page print job (highlighting the test page print job) and then select Document ➤ Pause.

The test document is small and your printer may be quick, so you may need several tries to do this step. If you are quick enough, the status of the test print job will change to paused.

7. Select Document ➤ Cancel. The print job will disappear from the list.

EXERCISE 13.2

Creating a Local Printer

1. Log on as an administrator.

2. Select Start ➤ Settings ➤ Printers to display the Printers window (see Figure 13.5).

3. Open the Add Printer icon by double-clicking on it. This step will start the Add Printer Wizard.

4. Make sure that the My Computer option is checked.

5. Click the Next button at the bottom of the window. The Add Printer Wizard window will now show you a list of available ports (see Figure 13.6).

6. Select the port that the printer is attached to (a parallel printer will most likely be attached to LPT1:) and then click the Next button at the bottom of the window.

EXERCISE 13.2 (CONTINUED)

7. Select the manufacturer of your printer from the first list and then select your printer model from the other list. Click Next.

8. Enter a name for the printer. If you wish this printer to be the default printer for use with Windows programs, select the Yes option; otherwise, select No. Click Next when you are ready to continue.

9. Select the Shared option and enter a name for the printer to be recognized by on the network if you wish to allow other computers on the network to print to this printer. If it will be a shared printer, also select the types of clients that will connect to the printer. Click Next when you are ready to continue. (See Figure 13.7).

10. The Add Printer Wizard window will allow you to print a test page. Select Yes to print a test page and then click Finish.

11. Insert the operating system installation media (the Windows NT CD-ROM) if you are asked to do so. Follow the instructions in the dialog boxes so Windows NT can load the drivers it needs to control the printer.

12. Notice that a new icon appears in the Printers window. In addition the Properties window for the icon will open in order for you to configure the printer you have just installed. Click OK to close the window.

FIGURE 13.5
The Printers window shows you the printers you have configured in your workstation.

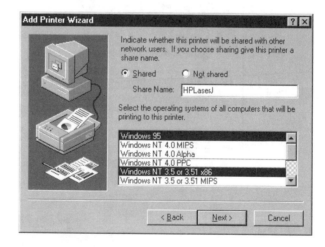

Creating a printer installs the printer driver for the printer and configures Windows NT applications and the Windows NT operating system to be able to print to the printer.

When you install the printer, you can also select the drivers for other operating systems that your computer can download to a remote printer so that it can print your job.

Connecting to a Remote Printer

When a printer is not directly attached to your computer, but is instead attached to another computer over the network, you must connect your workstation to that printer before you can print to it. The printer attached to a computer over the network is called a *remote printer*. To the other computer, however, the remote printer is a local printer. (Refer to Exercise 13.2 to create a local printer for the remote computer.) Exercise 13.3 shows you how to connect to a remote printer.

Exercise 13.3 explains the preferred method of connecting to a remote printer. You can also connect to a remote printer by creating a local printer of the same type as the remote printer and then changing the port setting of the printer to point to the remote location, rather than to LPT1, as follows: `\\remote_computer_name\printer_name`. *This statement will cause the print job to be spooled locally as well as on the remote computer.*

EXERCISE 13.3

Connecting to a Remote Printer

1. Log on as an administrator.

2. Select Start ➤ Settings ➤ Printers to display the Printers window.

3. Open the Add Printer icon by double-clicking on it. This step will start the Add Printer Wizard and display a network browse window.

4. Make sure that the Network printer server option is checked.

5. Browse the network to find the printer that you wish to attach to. Figure 13.8 shows a remote printer being selected.

6. Select the printer you want to attach to and click OK in the Connect to Printer window. You will be asked if this printer should be the default printer for use with Windows programs.

7. Select the Yes option to make it the default printer; otherwise, select No. Click Next when you are ready to continue.

8. Click Finish to allow Windows NT to complete the installation of the remote printer in your workstation.

FIGURE 13.8
The Add Printer Wizard
will help you connect to
remote printers.

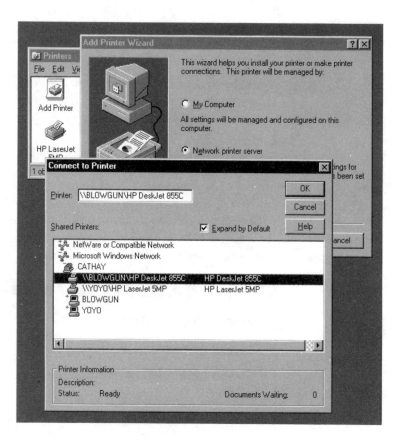

Printer Configuration

YOU CONFIGURE THE PRINTER from the Properties window for that printer. You can reach the Properties window from the Printers window. (Right-click the Printer icon and then select Properties, or click the Printer icon and then select File ➤ Properties.)

The printer's Properties window has six tabs across the top. Each tab allows you to modify one aspect of the printer's operation. The tabs are

- General
- Ports
- Scheduling

- Sharing

- Security

- Device Settings

General

From this tab you can enter a comment about the printer, describe the location of the printer, and select the print driver for the printer. (See Figure 13.9.) Across the bottom of the General tab are three buttons:

- **Separator Page…:** Allows you to place a separator page between each document printed on the printer. Exercise 13.4 outlines the steps of selecting a separator page for a printer.

- **Print Processor…:** Allows you to select a print processor for this printer. When a printer has a print processor, it can accept print jobs from other operating systems such as UNIX or Macintosh. (Refer to the section on Windows NT printing architecture earlier in this chapter.)

- **Print Test Page:** Prints a test page so that you can be sure the settings for the printer are correct.

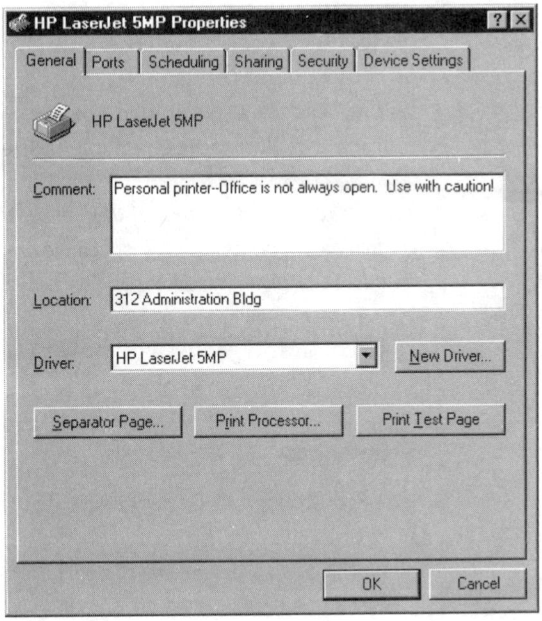

FIGURE 13.9
The Properties window for your printer has six tabs. The general tab allows you to describe the printer to network users, print a test page, and set the separator page and print processor options.

HP LaserJet 5MP Properties

General | Ports | Scheduling | Sharing | Security | Device Settings

HP LaserJet 5MP

Comment: Personal printer--Office is not always open. Use with caution!

Location: 312 Administration Bldg

Driver: HP LaserJet 5MP ▼   New Driver...

Separator Page...   Print Processor...   Print Test Page

OK   Cancel

EXERCISE 13.4

Selecting a Separator Page

1. Log on as an administrator.

2. Select the printer from the Printers window (click the printer one time).

3. Select File ➤ Properties from the Printers window.

4. Make sure that the General tab is selected and then click the Separator Page button.

5. Click Browse....

6. Select the file SYSPRINT.SEP and then click Open.

7. Click OK.

8. Click OK to close the printer's Properties window.

Ports

The Ports tab shows you a list of ports that this printer selection can print to. If you can have more than one printing device attached to your computer, configure this printer selection to print to whichever is not busy. Several printing devices that work together are called a *print pool*. All of the printers in a print pool must be of the same type.

The buttons at the bottom of the window allow you to add, delete, and configure ports. You can also enable bidirectional printing if your printer supports it.

You can redirect the output of the printer to a file, which you might do if you needed a file containing the printing-device specific commands, for example, to send output for printing on a large or high-resolution printing device.

Exercise 13.5 shows you how to redirect printer output to a file.

Scheduling

The Scheduling tab (see Figure 13.10) controls when the printer is available and how print jobs are presented to the printer. You can set the printer to be always available or to be available for certain hours of the day. If you limit the availability

EXERCISE 13.5

Redirecting Printer Output to a File

1. Log on as an administrator.

2. Select the printer from the Printers window (click the printer one time).

3. Select File ➤ Properties from the Printers window.

4. Select the Ports tab.

5. Remove the check mark from the currently checked ports.

6. Click Add Port… and then select Local Port from the Printer Ports window.

7. Click the OK button at the bottom of the window. In the Port Name window, enter the path and filename that this printer will print to. Click OK and then click Close. The name you entered will appear in the Ports list.

8. Click the checkbox for that entry to enable printing to the file.

9. Click the OK button at the bottom of the window.

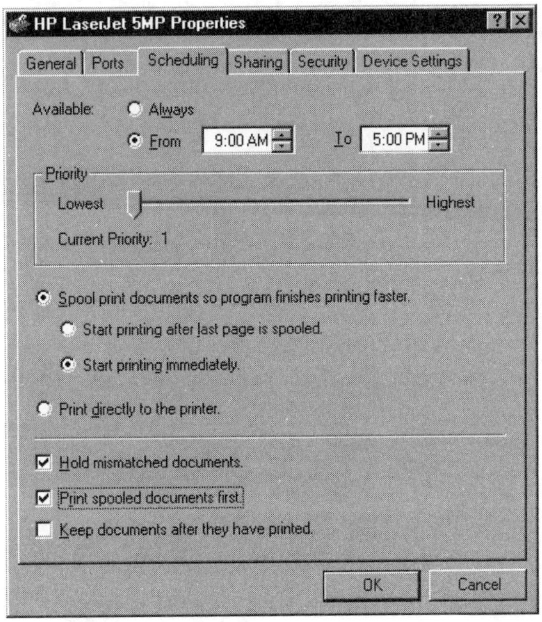

FIGURE 13.10
The Scheduling tab governs the availability of the printer and its print spooling characteristics.

of the printer, you must enter the start time and stop time of the printer's operation. Exercise 13.6 shows you how to limit the hours of operation of a printer.

EXERCISE 13.6

Limit the Hours of Operation of a Printer

1. Log on as an administrator.

2. Select the printer from the Printers window.

3. Select File ➤ Properties from the Printers window.

4. Select the Scheduling tab.

5. Go to the top of the window. After Available: select the From: option. Enter the start time (9:00 AM, for example) and the end time (5:00 PM).

6. Click the OK button at the bottom of the screen.

You can set the priority of print jobs from this printer (represented by an icon) in the Priority section of the window. If you have created more than one printer icon for one printing device, and therefore more than one logical printer, the print jobs from the printer with the highest priority print first. The priority for this printer can be set to any number from 1 to 99.

The Spooling Options in the middle of the window allow you to set the printer either

- Not to spool (store jobs on the hard disk until the print monitor is ready to accept them)

- To spool the jobs to disk

If you enable spooling, you can set the spooler either

- To begin sending the print job to the print monitor immediately

- To send the print job when the whole job has been received by the spooler

The three checkboxes at the bottom of the window allow you to

- Specify that the spooler hold mismatched jobs (which checks to ensure that the type of print job matches the type of printer, or holds the document otherwise)

- Print spooled jobs first (which gives documents that have been spooled to disk priority)

- Keep documents after they have been printed (which you might enable if you needed an electronic copy of every document printed on a printer)

Sharing

From the Sharing tab you control the availability of your printer on the network. By selecting the Not Shared option, you restrict printing to that printer to your computer.

If you enable sharing by selecting the Shared option, you must give a network name for the printer in the Share Name field.

You may also wish to configure your workstation to automatically download print drivers to computers that access your printer over the network. The remainder of the window allows you to select the client operating systems for which your workstation will provide print drivers.

Security

The Security tab contains three buttons: Permissions, Auditing, and Ownership.

Clicking the Permissions button displays a window from which you set user permissions for printing and managing documents. Exercise 13.7 leads you through the process of restricting a printer so that only administrators can print to it.

The Auditing button displays an auditing window, which allows you to track the printing activities of users and groups for this printer.

With the Ownership button, you can take ownership of the printer, although we do not recommend this step.

EXERCISE 13.7

Restricting Access to a Printer

1. Log on as an administrator.

2. Select the printer from the Printers window.

3. Select File ➤ Properties from the Printers window.

4. Select the Security tab and then click the Permissions button to display the Printer Permissions window.

5. Click once on the Everyone item in the Name: list.

6. Click Remove.

7. Click once on the Power Users item in the Name: list.

8. Click Remove.

9. Click the OK button in the Printer Permissions window and then click OK in the printer's Properties window.

Device Settings

The Device Settings tab contains a hierarchical view of device-specific settings such as the default tray assignment, loaded printer fonts, available printer memory, and so on. Although you can change device settings from this tab, the printer's Properties window (available from within the Print dialog box by clicking Properties when you print from an application) is a better place from which to change these settings.

Printer Troubleshooting

THE MANY DIFFERENT PRINTER TYPES and configurations make the job of troubleshooting printing problems difficult. No set of guidelines can solve every printing problem. However, you can resolve many printing problems by checking a few basic failure points of printers and printing systems.

Follow the steps outlined in Exercise 13.8 if you have difficulty printing to your printer. Each of the steps checks a potential printing problem.

EXERCISE 13.8

Resolving Simple Printing Problems

1. Make sure that the printer is plugged in to the wall and that the printer is turned on.

2. Make sure that the printer is online. If the printer is not online and is reporting an error condition, consult the printer manual to determine the cause of the error and then fix the problem.

3. Make sure that the printer cable is attached securely to both the printer and the computer.

4. Check the print driver. Is it installed properly, and is it the correct version for the printer? If not, install the correct print driver.

5. Make sure that when you attempt to print, you are selecting the print driver you verified in step 4.

6. Check to see if you have sufficient hard disk space for the print driver to create temporary print files. Without sufficient space, the print driver will not be able to create a print job to send to the printer. If space is low, delete some files, archive some files to floppy or backup tape, or add hard disk space.

7. Check to see if you can print from other applications within Windows NT. If so, you may have to troubleshoot the printing options of the application you are using. If you can print from Win32 based applications but not from a DOS, Win16, or POSIX application, you may have to troubleshoot that subsystem of your Windows NT operating system configuration.

8. Print to a file (see Exercise 13.4) and then copy the output of the file to the printer port. If you get a printed document using this method, then the problem may lie with the spooler or data transmission. Otherwise, the problem probably lies with the driver or application.

Printing Problems

Occasionally, the print jobs are transferred to the spooler but fail to print. You can usually solve this problem by stopping and starting the print spooler as shown in Exercise 13.9.

EXERCISE 13.9

Stopping and Restarting the Print Spooler

1. Select Start ➤ Settings ➤ Control Panel.

2. Double-click the Services control panel.

3. Select Spooler in the Services list box.

4. Click Stop.

5. Answer Yes to confirm.

6. Click Start. Your stuck print jobs should print.

Chapter Summary

WINDOWS NT PROVIDES Windows programs with a flexible and powerful printing system. Windows NT supports local and remote printers, print pools, sophisticated printer and print job management, and sharing printers attached to a Windows NT computer with computers of other operating systems such as UNIX and Macintosh.

In Windows NT terminology, the printing device is the physical machine that produces the document. A printer is the software component that the application sends print jobs to. You may have more than one printer for a single printing device and more than one printing device for a single printer. In the latter case, the several printing devices are called a printing pool.

The Windows NT print model splits the software that provides the printing services to the applications into several components: the GDI, the printer driver, the router, the print provider (or spooler), the print processor, and the print monitor.

An icon in the Printers window represents each printer. Opening the icon shows the print jobs in that printer's queue and allows you to manage those print jobs. It also allows you to start and stop that printer.

Opening the properties of that icon allows you to modify the settings for that printer. Settings that you can change include the destination port, user permissions, hours of operation, spooling characteristics, separator pages, print processor, and default tray settings.

Troubleshooting printing problems requires patience and experience, but common printing problems can be resolved by carefully confirming the correct operation of each hardware component (such as the cables and print mechanism) and of each software component (such as the print drivers loaded and the printer selected) of the printing system.

Exercise Questions

1. In Windows terminology a printer is the physical device that produces printed pages.

   A. True

   B. False

2. Some printers are not attached to a computer, but are instead connected directly to the network.

   A. True

   B. False

3. In Windows NT all printing devices print directly on paper.

   A. True

   B. False

4. Every printer is connected to one and only one printing device.

   A. True

   B. False

5. Windows NT Workstation can provide printing services for Windows, UNIX, Apple Macintosh, and MS-DOS computers.

   A. True

   B. False

6. The GDI translates application print requests into DDI calls to the print driver.

   A. True

   B. False

7. DDI calls are not specific to the drawing characteristics of a printer.

   A. True

   B. False

8. A journal file print job contains DDI calls that must be made to the device driver to produce a raw print job.

A. True

B. False

9. The GDI will produce a journal file for a print job destined for a remote printer.

A. True

B. False

10. You must have a print driver for the type of printer your workstation is connected to when you print.

A. True

B. False

11. Windows NT can send print jobs to HP network printers and to UNIX printers.

A. True

B. False

12. The print provider is also known as the spooler.

A. True

B. False

13. Windows NT does not support printing Macintosh PostScript files to non-PostScript printing devices attached to the Windows NT computer.

A. True

B. False

14. You can schedule several times during the day when a printer is and is not available from within the printer's Properties window.

A. True

B. False

15. The _____, in Windows terminology, is a software construct that will translate print requests from applications and forward the resulting print job to the appropriate printing device.

16. A _____ consists of several printing devices fed by one printer.

17. GDI stands for _____ _____ _____.

18. DDI stands for _____ _____ _____.

19. A _____ print job contains the sequence of instructions for the printer that will produce the printed document.

20. The _____ _____ is the software component that translates the printer-generic DDI calls generated by the GDI system into the printer-specific commands that will be passed on to the actual printer

21. The _____ _____ performs modifications to the print job before it passes the print job to the print monitor.

22. The _____ _____ is the software component that transmits the print job (by now transformed into the language of the printer) to the printing device.

Performance
Tuning

WINDOWS NT IMPLEMENTS a number of automatic performance optimizations to ensure that any Windows NT workstation will operate very well. However, as with an automobile, understanding how and why resources of the system function (and knowing how to measure their performance) will help you tune your system for optimal performance.

Performance tuning is finding the resource that slows your system the most, speeding it up until something else has the most impact on speed, and then starting over by finding the new slowest resource. This cycle of finding the speed-limiting factor, eliminating it, and starting over will allow you to reach the natural performance limit of your computer in a simple, methodical way.

In this chapter we first cover the automatic optimizations that Windows NT performs to ensure that a system will operate smoothly and respond quickly to user requests at almost any load level. Then we dig into performance-tuning theory and definitions, explaining how the different software and hardware resources interact to achieve the smooth, responsive system performance you expect from Windows NT.

Next we cover the performance monitor, the tool that implements most performance-tuning procedures in Windows NT. After you understand how the performance monitor works, we show you how to ferret out processor, memory, and hard disk bottlenecks. Finally, we discuss how to speed up specific applications in order to improve system responsiveness for your specific needs.

Bottlenecks

BOTTLENECKS ARE FACTORS THAT LIMIT performance in a computer. For instance, slow memory limits the speed at which a processor can manipulate data—thus limiting the computer's processing performance to the speed at which the processor can access memory. If the memory can respond faster than the processor, the processor is the bottleneck.

The terms processor, microprocessor, *and* central processing unit (CPU) *are synonymous throughout this book.*

There is always a bottleneck in system performance. You may not notice it because your computer may be quite a bit faster than you actually need for the work you perform. Chances are, if you use your computer only for word processing, the speed of your machine has never slowed you down. On the other hand, if you use your computer as a CAD workstation or to compute missile trajectories, chances are you've spent a lot of time waiting for your computer.

There is always a bottleneck that limits system performance when you use your computer. Ideally, it's you.

Performance tuning is the systematic process of finding the resource experiencing the most load and then relieving that load. You can almost always optimize a machine to make it work better for you. Although tuning a server for maximum network performance is more crucial (and more difficult) than tuning a workstation, understanding how Windows NT Workstation achieves its performance and how you can increase its performance is important. Even if you don't need to make your computer any faster, understanding performance tuning can help you diagnose problems when they arise.

Before we get too far into our discussion of computer performance, you should understand a few of the terms we will be using in the context of performance tuning.

- **Resources** are hardware components that provide some quantifiable work capacity in the context of performance tuning. Software processes load down hardware resources.

- **Bottlenecks** are resources with performance limitations that affect the responsiveness of a computer. When used singularly, bottleneck refers to the most limiting component of the system.

- **Load** is the amount of work that a resource has to perform. For example, the microprocessor is "under heavy load" if it is performing a number of complex math operations. The disk drive is under load any time files are read from or written to it.

- **Optimizations** are the measures taken to reduce the impact of a bottleneck on performance. Optimizations may include eliminating unnecessary loading, sharing loads across devices, or finding ways to increase the speed of a resource.

- **Throughput** is the measure of information flow through a resource. For instance, disk I/O throughput is the measure of how much data can be read from or written to a disk in a given time period, usually one second.

- **Processes** are software services running concurrently on your computer that perform a certain function. Drivers and file systems are processes. A process has its own address space and is therefore protected from other processes in Windows NT. Refer to Chapter 15 for more information on processes.

- **Threads** are software chains of execution that run concurrently to perform the functionality of a process within the address space of that process. A process is one or more threads. Threads are the basic unit of division among processors in a multiprocessing environment.

The term bottleneck *comes from the observation that the neck of a bottle limits the flow of water through it. To visualize a bottleneck, imagine the difference between turning over a cup of water and turning over a bottle of water.*

Exercise 14.1 will help you see the difference between threads and processes by introducing you to the Task Manager. If you are running any other applications, you can leave them running, but the Task Manager will display more information than the exercise describes.

Now that you understand the terms used in performance tuning, we can discuss how performance tuning works. A slow hardware resource, such as a hard disk drive, causes the microprocessor and system RAM (both fast) to wait for it to complete I/O requests. Thus during disk I/O the speed of the hard disk is the speed of the computer.

Although you cannot make your hard disk faster (unless you replace it with a faster one), you may be able to reduce the number of times the computer needs to access it or limit the amount of information transferred. You may also be able to spread the load across many hard disk drives, thus dividing the time you spend waiting for drive access by the number of drives available.

You will reach a point when you have a limitation you cannot overcome. This point is the natural limit of your machine and the ultimate goal of performance tuning. If you find you need speed beyond the natural limit of your machine, you will need to upgrade the hardware resource causing the limitation.

EXERCISE 14.1

Viewing Applications, Processes, and Threads

1. Select Programs ➤ Accessories ➤ Paint from the Start menu.

2. Select Programs ➤ Accessories ➤ WordPad from the Start menu.

3. Press Ctrl+Alt+Del.

4. Click Task Manager.

5. Select the Applications tab.

6. Notice the number of applications running. You should see Paint and WordPad listed in the Task list box.

7. Select the Processes tab.

8. Notice how many processes are running. Find the `MSPAINT.EXE` and `WORDPAD.EXE` processes in the list. In this case each application has only one process. The other processes you see are system processes that run all the time.

9. Select the Performance tab.

10. Notice how many threads are running in the Totals box.

11. Close the Windows NT Task Manager.

Finding Bottlenecks

Ferreting out bottlenecks involves a little understanding of how computers work, and it requires some software. Without proper monitoring tools, even the best system engineers can only guess at what causes a complex system to run slowly. Windows NT provides a comprehensive set of tools for finding and eliminating bottlenecks.

To find a bottleneck, you must be able to measure the speed of the different resources in your system. Measurements enable you to find the one resource that is performing at its peak and therefore causing the bottleneck.

The hardware resource that is operating at its maximum performance level is the bottleneck.

The measurements you will need to make differ among resources. For instance, disk throughput is measured in megabytes per second, whereas interrupt activity is measured in interrupts per second. To compare resources you must use measurements that are equal. In most cases Windows NT provides a basic "percentage of processor time spent doing this" metric that you can use to compare very different resources.

The first step to finding a bottleneck is to run the performance monitor application. You then have to put your computer under the load that causes it to perform more slowly than you want. Run your CAD program and import a file from another format. Attach to your network file server and start copying a lot of files. Run that graphic-intensive game. Run whatever software you want to make run faster.

Using the performance monitor, you will then look at a few broad measures that will show you where to search more deeply to find the exact bottleneck. For example, if after showing processor time and disk time, you see that the disk is running at its peak, you know to concentrate on disk-related measurements to find the bottleneck.

Make certain you've found the bottleneck before concentrating on detailed performance monitoring. Since performance-limited resources hide behind other, slower resources, you won't be able to see the difference if you make changes to objects that are not truly the bottleneck.

Eliminating Bottlenecks

Finding a bottleneck is only half the battle. Eliminating it (making it fast enough that something else is now the primary bottleneck) may involve changing a Control Panel setting or replacing an old, slow hard disk. You will have to determine how to relieve the load placed on the resource.

Most of the time you will be able to look at more detailed measurements to determine the specific activity that is loading your system down. For instance, if you determine that your microprocessor is the bottleneck, you can look at the time spent in each process to determine exactly which process is causing the most load. Discontinuing the use of the application that relies on that process or replacing it with equivalent software that creates less load will relieve your bottleneck.

When troubleshooting, make only one change at a time. Otherwise, you will not be able to tell which change fixed the problem.

The Perpetual Cycle

You can achieve maximum performance from your hardware through a continuous cycle of improvement. Once you've eliminated the major bottleneck in your system, start over and eliminate the next new bottleneck. There will always be a bottleneck in your system because one resource will always cause other resources to wait for it.

Keep eliminating bottlenecks until you either make your computer so fast that you never need to wait for it, find the component to replace or upgrade, or realize that you can't afford to buy any new components and settle for what you have, knowing that your system is running as fast as it can.

Windows NT Self-Tuning Mechanisms

YOU MAY NEVER HAVE TO deal with manual performance tuning because Windows NT tunes itself very well for most users and for most situations. Unlike many operating systems, you will not have to manually adjust arcane environment variables to improve Windows NT performance. Windows NT takes care of that for you. The tuning you will do to optimize Windows NT performance involves determining which hardware resources are under the greatest load and then relieving that load. Windows NT comes with some very powerful tools to assist you, but because of the system's self-tuning nature, you may never have to use them.

Windows NT implements a number of automatic performance optimizations. They are

- Multiprocessing

- Avoiding physical memory fragmentation

- Swapping across multiple disks

- Prioritizing threads and processes

- Caching disk requests

Multiprocessing

Multiprocessing divides the processing load across several microprocessors. Windows NT uses *symmetric multiprocessing*, a technique in which the total processor load is split evenly among processors. Simpler operating systems use *asymmetric processing*, which splits the processing load based upon some non-load-based metric. Those operating systems usually put all system tasks on one processor and all user tasks on the remaining processors.

Windows NT Workstation ships with support for two microprocessors. If you have a computer that uses more than two microprocessors, contact your OEM vendor for the support files for your computer.

Scheduling and resource assignment between processors takes computing time. Because of this load, two processors are not twice as fast as one. Windows NT with two processors generally runs at about 150 percent of the speed of one, depending upon the type of programs run. An application that has only one thread cannot run on more than one processor.

In many computing problems the result of one thread depends upon the results of other threads. This circumstance is like a baton race in which a runner (thread) must wait for the baton (results) before taking off. Obviously, splitting these threads among processors will not make the application faster. Multiprocessing works best with large computing data sets that can be broken into chunks and solved independently.

Symmetric Multiprocessing

Symmetric multiprocessing shares the total processing load among all available processors as equally as possible. When processor time becomes available, a routine determines which thread gets that processing time, depending upon its priority in the thread queue. Figure 14.1 shows a hypothetical four-processor computer running two multithreaded applications. The height of the bars indicates the total computing capacity of the processors. The shaded areas indicate how much of that load a process uses.

Asymmetric Multiprocessing

Asymmetric multiprocessing dedicates certain threads to certain processors. For instance, all system threads and drivers might be run on one processor, and user

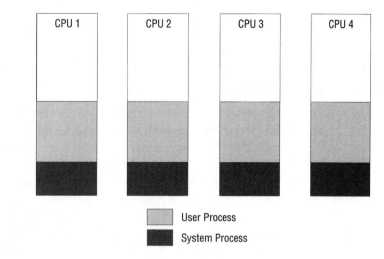

FIGURE 14.1
Symmetric
multiprocessing.

threads may be run on another. Asymmetric processing does not allow the operating system to make the most effective use of processor time. Figure 14.2 shows another hypothetical four-processor computer running two multithreaded applications. Compare Figures 14.1 and 14.2 to see why symmetric multiprocessing works better. Notice that in Figure 14.2 the second CPU is at maximum performance (making it the bottleneck), while the third and fourth CPUs are not working at all.

Computer designers often use asymmetric multiprocessing to give the system processor hardware-level access to input/output devices and deny that access to

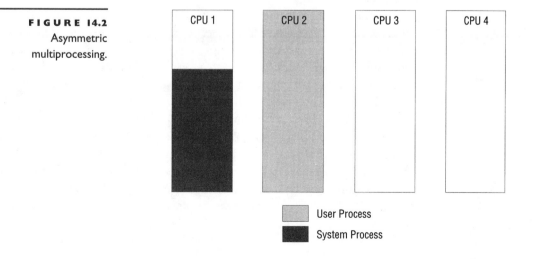

FIGURE 14.2
Asymmetric
multiprocessing.

the user processor(s), thus protecting system resources and reducing the need for security in the operating system.

Memory Optimizations

Windows NT performs a number of optimizations to make the most effective use of random access memory (RAM). In Windows NT, memory is divided into 4KB chunks called pages. Each page can be used by only one thread. A thread may be stored in any number of pages. Therefore, a 13KB thread will actually take 16KB of physical RAM because the remaining 3KB in the last page cannot be used by anything else.

Some operating systems use 64KB page files in order to maximize swapping speed (64KB is the maximum size of a single block transfer to SCSI and IDE hard disks). Unfortunately, this optimization forces each thread to use a minimum of 64KB. If the average size of an executing thread is 96KB, 25 percent of physical RAM would be wasted on unusable excess storage. Windows NT loses the performance benefit of 64KB page sizes in favor of leaving more physical memory available to reduce the necessity for swapping.

The system must have enough memory to store all the executing threads. If the amount of memory is insufficient, Windows NT uses a portion of the hard disk to simulate memory by swapping memory pages not currently in use to a special system file called the *virtual memory swap file* (PAGEFILE.SYS). When the system needs the pages that were swapped to disk, Windows NT trades pages in RAM for pages on the hard disk. This process is completely hidden from the threads, which do not need to know anything about the memory swapping process.

The more memory you have, the less time the system spends on page swapping. Windows NT systems having less than 32MB of memory will spend a significant amount of time swapping pages to the virtual memory page file, especially if they are running more than one application at a time. This swapping activity slows the computer dramatically, since hard disks are very slow (but very cheap) compared to physical RAM.

The faster page swapping can be made, the lower its impact on system responsiveness. To speed this process, Windows NT supports simultaneous writing to more than one hard disk for its virtual memory paging file. Since physical drives can perform simultaneously, splitting the virtual memory swap file among different disks allows Windows NT to divide the time spent processing virtual memory swaps by the number of physical disks. Exercise 14.2

shows you how to split your swap file among more than one disk. (You must have more than one hard disk drive to perform this exercise.)

EXERCISE 14.2

Splitting the Swap File among Disks

1. Select Settings ➤ Control Panel from the Start menu.

2. Double-click the System control panel.

3. Select the Performance tab.

4. Click Change in the virtual memory area.

5. Select the primary volume on the first physical disk.

6. Set the Page file Initial size to 16MB.

7. Set the Page file Maximum size to 48MB.

8. Click set.

9. Repeat steps 5 through 8 for the primary volume on each physical disk.

10. Click OK.

11. Click Close.

12. Answer Yes to restart your computer.

Windows NT allows you to split your swap file among volumes on the same physical disk, but doing so will not improve disk performance. In fact, splitting the files increases swap time by forcing the drive head to move a great deal more than normal during swapping. You should set only one swap file per physical disk.

Prioritizing Threads and Processes

In a multitasking operating system, if each thread of each process got equal processor time round-robin fashion, the computer would respond to user requests very slowly. Some system processes, such as moving the mouse cursor or updating the screen, must happen all the time—far more often than most other system processes.

Windows NT prioritizes each thread based upon its importance to system responsiveness or any requirements it may have to respond to external (real-time) events in a timely fashion. Windows NT does a good job of setting thread priorities by default. However, Microsoft cannot predict exactly how you will use your computer, so it leaves you some ability to tune priorities.

Processes start with a base priority of 7 on a scale of 0 to 31. Each thread of a process inherits the base priority of the process. Windows NT can automatically vary priority levels up to two priorities higher or lower as the system runs, allowing the system to prioritize as it sees fit. Users can also start processes with higher than normal priorities. Figure 14.3 shows the Windows NT thread priority scale.

Real-time applications start with priorities higher than 15. These real-time processes require processor time quite frequently to ensure that they can respond to external real-time events. Drivers, which must respond to hardware events very close to the time the device demands attention, run in these priority levels.

Only administrators may start processes with a priority higher than 23. These processes demand so much processor time that they can make all other processes run very slowly. Starting a regular application with a priority this high will make even moving the cursor slow and laborious. Starting processes with other than normal priorities is shown in Exercise 14.15 in the "Application Performance" section of this chapter.

You can also use the Task Manager to increase the priority of an already running program. This step will normally not be necessary, but it is a good way to test the demands a process will make on the system at different priority levels.

FIGURE 14.3
Thread priorities in
Windows NT.

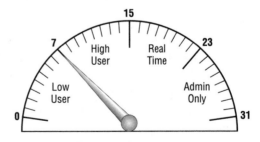

Caching Disk Requests

Windows NT uses disk caching to reduce the amount of input/output traffic to the hard disk drive. Caching works by reserving a portion of memory as a staging area for hard disk reads and writes. When data is read from the disk, it is stored in the cache. If the same data needs to be read again, it is retrieved from the very fast memory cache, rather than from the disk.

In this book, the term memory *is synonymous with* random access memory (RAM), *not with hard disk space.*

Actually, disk read operations don't just bring in the data requested. Entire clusters are transferred from the hard disk to the memory cache because read and write operations are most efficient at the cluster size. Consequently, a good portion of the data on the hard disk located immediately after the data that is requested also comes into the memory cache. Since read accesses tend to be sequential, chances are good that the next read request will also be in the cache.

The disk cache is also used for write operations. The Windows NT file system (NTFS) doesn't write data to the hard disk immediately. It waits for system idle time so as not to impact the responsiveness of the system. Data writes are stored in the memory cache until they are written to disk. Often, especially in transaction-oriented systems like databases, write data in the cache will be superseded by new changes before being written from the cache to the hard disk—meaning that the write cache has completely eliminated the need to write that data to disk.

Data writes waiting in the cache can also be read back if they are subsequently requested, which allows yet another cache-related optimization. The type of caching used in Windows NT is called *write-back caching,* as opposed to *write-through caching,* which immediately writes data to the disk while preserving it in the cache for subsequent rereads. Write-through caching is used in operating systems that cannot otherwise guarantee the integrity of data on the disk if power is lost while data is in the cache waiting to be written to disk.

Caching is analogous to using your refrigerator to store food rather than going to the grocery store each time you need an egg or a glass of milk. By estimating your future needs, you are able to make one trip out to the slow resource (the grocery store) and store the data (food) you need very close to you in the cache (refrigerator). (Don't try to extend this analogy to write-back caching though.)

The caching schemes used in hardware to make your microprocessor run faster operate on exactly the same cache theory as presented here.

Windows NT uses all the memory that remains free after the running processes have the memory they need. Windows NT dynamically changes the amount of memory assigned to the disk cache as new processes are started to ensure the optimal performance boost from caching. Windows NT balances the amount of disk cache and the amount of virtual memory page swapping to optimize the use of physical memory.

Although you cannot change any software parameters to impact caching performance, you can add more memory, up to the limit your motherboard will support. Windows NT Workstation runs best when used with 24MB of RAM or more. Windows NT can make good use of all the RAM you give it.

Performance Monitoring

THE WINDOWS NT PERFORMANCE MONITOR is an amazing tool, unique to the Windows NT operating system, that provides the ability to inspect the performance of just about every process and resource that occurs in your computer. The performance monitor allows you to determine the exact cause of every performance-related problem your computer experiences. Figure 14.4 shows the performance monitor running with some processor and disk activity showing.

Performance and the performance monitor are broad topics. An entire book could be dedicated to the various features and the work flow theory used to discern where and why bottlenecks occur. Windows NT automatically makes most

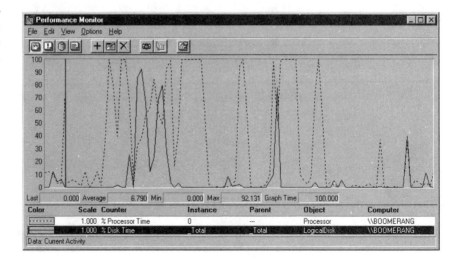

FIGURE 14.4
The performance monitor.

adjustments for you though, so that level of detail is not required to make your computer run well for most tasks.

This section explains how the performance monitor works and tells you which indicators to watch in order to quickly narrow down performance problems. You should feel free to play with the performance monitor to see the effect of the different low-level indicators. You cannot harm your system by experimenting with the performance monitor.

Heisenberg's uncertainty principle states that to measure quantum phenomenon is to change it. This principle is also true of performance monitoring. Running the performance monitor takes a small amount of CPU time, and enabling disk monitoring will slow input/output requests slightly. Therefore, you cannot measure system performance without causing the performance to change slightly. In almost every case, this change in performance is slight and will have no real effect on your measurements or the validity of your conclusions, but you should be aware that it is happening.

Be sure to let your computer finish the various logon processes before using the performance monitor to measure performance. A number of services are started in the background after logging on that will affect performance measurements taken right after booting.

Exercise 14.3 shows how to start the performance monitor. The remaining exercises in this chapter will assume you have the performance monitor loaded before beginning the exercise.

EXERCISE 14.3

Starting the Performance Monitor

1. Select Programs ➤ Administrative Tools ➤ Performance Monitor in the Start menu.

2. Size the Performance Monitor window so that it takes up about one-quarter of your screen.

3. Select Add to Chart in the Edit menu.

4. Click Add when the drop-down box opens with %Processor Time selected.

This value is the measure of how busy the microprocessor is. Leave this measurement running throughout the remaining exercises.

Object Counters

The performance monitor doesn't actually measure anything. It is only a graphical tool used to inspect the measurements that occur constantly throughout the running processes in Windows NT.

Counters associated with each Windows NT software object are incremented every time that object performs a function. For instance, each time a network device driver reads a packet, the device driver increments the packet read counter by one and the byte read counter by the size of the packet. Or each time the processor switches threads, it updates the time spent in that thread in a counter used for that purpose.

These counters permeate all Windows NT objects, and they allow meaningful measurement to occur by accounting for everything that happens that may be of interest. Windows NT uses many of these counters to measure performance for its own automatic optimizations and is the first PC operating system to include this level of support for performance monitoring. Table 14.1 shows the built-in objects that you can monitor with the performance monitor.

In addition to these, you will see objects for each network service you have installed. Actually, any software can be written to register performance monitor counters with the system, so you may see even more counters than are shown here.

TABLE 14.1
Windows NT
Object Counters.

OBJECT	PURPOSE
Cache	Microprocessor level 2 cache performance
Logical disk	Mass storage performance, including network storage
Memory	Memory performance and usage
Objects	Process and thread counts
Paging file	Virtual memory usage
Physical disk	Hard disk drive performance
Process	Process performance
Processor	Microprocessor performance
System	Windows NT performance
Thread	Individual thread performance

Processor Performance

The microprocessor is generally the fastest component in a computer. In Pentium class and higher computers, the microprocessor is rarely the cause of a bottleneck unless you are running scientific, mathematical, or graphical software that puts a heavy load on the floating point unit of the microprocessor.

Windows NT was designed to run on fast microprocessors. If you are using a computer with a processor slower than a Pentium, you may be experiencing processor bottlenecks routinely.

Monitoring Processor Performance

Monitoring processor performance is simple in Windows NT. As with all performance objects, a few measurements will give you a good idea of whether the processor is a bottleneck in your system. Important processor-related counters are

- Processor: %Processor Time

- Processor: Interrupts/sec

- System: Processor Queue Length

PROCESSOR: %PROCESSOR TIME The microprocessor does not become a bottleneck until you see a sustained 80 percent or better level of utilization when watching the Processor: %Processor Time counter in the performance monitor. If after tuning your computer to eliminate processor bottlenecks, your computer still runs in this zone, you need to upgrade to a faster (or another) microprocessor. This counter shows how busy the microprocessor is. The processor will spike to 100 percent at times—this spike is normal and does not indicate a bottleneck. As long as the processor normally runs somewhere between 0 and 80 percent, your processor is sufficient for the work load. Exercise 14.4 shows you how to add this counter to the performance monitor.

After adding this counter, let the computer sit idle for a moment. Now move your mouse around on the screen and notice the effect on the Processor: %Processor Time measure. Dramatic, isn't it?

PROCESSOR: INTERRUPTS/SEC Processor: Interrupts/sec measures the rate of service requests from peripheral devices. An unusual amount of activity on this counter without a corresponding increase in activity indicates that a hardware component is malfunctioning and is sending spurious interrupts. This

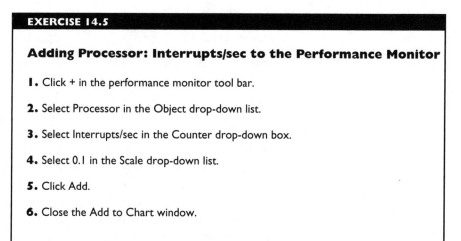

Adding Processor: %Processor Time to the Performance Monitor

1. Click + in the Performance Monitor tool bar.

2. Select Processor in the Object drop-down list.

3. Select %Processor Time in the Counter drop-down box.

4. Click Add.

5. Close the Add to Chart window.

counter should operate continuously between 100 and 1,000, but spikes up to 2,000 are acceptable. Exercise 14.5 shows you how to add this counter to your system.

EXERCISE 14.5

Adding Processor: Interrupts/sec to the Performance Monitor

1. Click + in the performance monitor tool bar.

2. Select Processor in the Object drop-down list.

3. Select Interrupts/sec in the Counter drop-down box.

4. Select 0.1 in the Scale drop-down list.

5. Click Add.

6. Close the Add to Chart window.

SYSTEM: PROCESSOR QUEUE LENGTH System: Processor Queue Length counts the number of threads waiting for attention from the processor. Each thread requires a bit of microprocessor time. A large number of running threads may exceed the supply of processor time, causing the microprocessor to become a bottleneck. A sustained thread queue greater than two indicates a processor bottleneck; too many threads are standing in line awaiting execution, which bogs down the processes that rely upon those threads.

If you try to watch only the processor queue length indicator, you will notice that it always sits at zero. This reading occurs because the performance monitor must be monitoring a thread-related counter in order to determine how many threads are awaiting execution. To see the true value of the processor queue length counter, you must also be monitoring a thread counter of some sort. Exercise 14.6 shows how to monitor the processor queue length.

EXERCISE 14.6

Adding System: Processor Queue Length to the Performance Monitor

1. Click + in the Performance Monitor tool bar.

2. Select System in the Object drop-down list.

3. Select Processor Queue Length in the Counter drop-down box.

4. Click Add.

5. Select Thread in the Object drop-down list.

6. Select Context Switches/sec in the Counter drop-down box.

7. Leave Total selected in the Instance drop-down box.

8. Close the Add to Chart window.

Remember that in order to monitor the processor queue length, you must also be monitoring a thread-specific counter. Context Switches/sec shows how many thread switches occur each second.

Troubleshooting Processor Performance

If you have determined that your processor is truly a bottleneck, you may not be able to find an inexpensive way to fix your problem. Before you run out and buy a new processor though, check your computer for the following common problems:

- Do you have sufficient external processor cache?

- Are your internal and external caches enabled?

- Is the BIOS processor startup speed set to Fast?

SUFFICIENT PROCESSOR CACHE Do you have sufficient level 2 cache? Reboot your computer and enter the BIOS. Find the area that describes the amount of external cache your computer uses. Your system should have at least 256K external cache. Some Pentium-class computers ship with less than this amount. If your computer does not have at least this much cache memory, you need to increase it at least to this amount.

Some computers ship with EDO RAM (which is faster than normal memory) in order to eliminate the necessity for an external cache. Unfortunately, EDO RAM does not speed your computer as much as a 256K external cache. Even if you have EDO RAM in your computer, you should add an external cache if you can.

ENABLING CACHES Are your processor level 1 and level 2 caches enabled? Using the manual that came with your computer or motherboard, enter the BIOS settings when you reboot your computer and verify that the CPU internal cache is enabled and that the external (or level 2) cache is enabled. If they are not, enable them.

Changing settings in your BIOS without knowing exactly what the setting does may cause your computer to become erratic or fail to work. If you are not an absolute computer genius, have an experienced PC technician make these changes for you.

DECIDING WHAT TO UPGRADE If after checking both of these things your processor is still a bottleneck, you will need to upgrade to a newer micropro-cessor or computer. If you can't get a microprocessor that is twice as fast to work in your computer, don't bother upgrading the microprocessor. Upgrade the entire computer.

Disk Performance

Disks are the biggest single bottleneck in your computer. Booting, application loading, data storage and retrieval, and swap file performance are all tied to the speed of your disk because disks are so much slower than the processor or memory. For these reasons, the speed of your disk(s) impacts the overall speed of your computer.

As with all performance monitoring in Windows NT Workstation, you can use the disk monitor to profile your disk activity. However, your computer also comes with a performance indicator that works in any operating system: the hard disk drive light. If your disk light is on most of the time under normal working conditions, you need to add RAM. You can't avoid this solution, and all the performance monitoring on the planet isn't going to uncover a different answer.

Physical versus Logical Disk Performance

In Table 14.1 you'll notice two disk-related objects: logical disk and physical disk. Logical disk is used to measure performance at a higher level than physical disk.

The logical disk object can measure the performance of network connections that are mapped as drives and the performance of volume sets and stripe sets that cross physical disks. You will use the logical disk object to uncover bottlenecks initially and then move to the physical disk object to uncover the reasons why that bottleneck is occurring.

Physical disk measures only real transfers to and from actual hard disk drives (or a RAID set in the case of RAID controllers, discussed later in this chapter). This object is used only when you want to isolate performance differences between disks in your system or when you want detailed information about the specific performance of a certain disk.

High-Impact Counters

Disk counters cause a measurable performance degradation by distracting the processor at critical input/output periods. These counters are disabled by default. If you attempt to monitor physical or logical disk performance without enabling these counters, you will not see any disk data.

On Intel i386-based computers, the disk counters cause about a 2 percent degradation in overall performance. You should enable them only when you need to monitor disk performance and disable them when you are finished. Enabling the disk counters is shown in Exercise 14.7.

When you have finished monitoring disk performance, remember to disable the disk performance monitors. Leaving them enabled serves no purpose and slows down your machine. Exercise 14.8 shows how to disable them.

Enabling the Disk Performance Counters

1. Type **diskperf-y** in the input line and press Return. A message will indicate that disk performance counters on the system are set to start at boot time.

2. Restart your system.

Disabling the Disk Performance Counters

1. Choose Programs and Command Prompt from the Start menu.

2. Type **diskperf-n** in the input line and press Return. A message will confirm the change.

3. Restart the system.

Monitoring Disk Performance

Once you've enabled the disk performance monitors as shown in Exercise 14.7, you'll be able to make meaningful disk throughput measurements.

Important counters you'll want to watch are

- Memory: Pages/sec
- %Disk Time
- Disk Bytes/Transfer
- Current Disk Queue Length

MEMORY: PAGES/SEC Why a memory indicator in the disk performance section? Because the pages swapped in this indicator are written to disk. Leave this counter showing in the performance monitor while watching the % Disk Time to see how dramatically page file performance affects your overall performance. Add Memory: Pages/sec to your performance monitor graph using Exercise 14.9.

EXERCISE 14.9

Adding Memory: Pages/sec to the Performance Monitor

1. Select Programs ➤ Administrative Tools ➤ Performance Monitor from the Start menu.

2. Click + in the Performance Monitor tool bar.

3. Select Memory in the Object drop-down list.

4. Select Pages/sec in the Counter drop-down box.

5. Click Add.

6. Close the Add to Chart window.

%DISK TIME This counter shows how much processor time is spent servicing disk requests. It is a good broad indicator for determining whether or not your hard disk drive is a bottleneck during activities when you would not normally expect to wait for it. Note that this counter is a processor metric, not a physical disk metric. Measure this counter against Processor: %Processor Time to see if disk requests are eating up all your processor time. Use Exercise 14.10 to measure the amount of time used servicing disk requests.

EXERCISE 14.10

Adding Logical Disk: %Disk Time to the Performance Monitor

1. Click + in the Performance Monitor tool bar.

2. Select Logical Disk in the Object drop-down list.

3. Select %Disk Time in the Counter drop-down box.

4. Click Add.

5. Close the Add to Chart window.

DISK BYTES/SECOND This counter shows how fast your hard disks are transferring data. Turn this counter on and then copy a large directory of files between disks to get a good baseline of the speed at which your disk(s) runs. Exercise 14.11 shows how to monitor this counter.

EXERCISE 14.11

Adding Logical Disk: Disk Bytes/sec to the Performance Monitor

1. Click + in the Performance Monitor tool bar.

2. Select Logical Disk in the Object drop-down list.

3. Select Disk Bytes/sec in the Counter drop-down box.

4. Click Add.

5. Close the Add to Chart window.

AVERAGE DISK BYTES/TRANSFER This metric shows how large the average transfer is. Larger average transfers make more efficient use of disk hardware and execute faster. Looking at this metric will tell you if small transfer sizes are causing your computer to work too hard to write them to disk. Perform Exercise 14.12 to monitor this counter.

EXERCISE 14.12

Adding Logical Disk: Average Disk Bytes/Transfer to the Performance Monitor

1. Click + in the Performance Monitor tool bar.

2. Select Logical Disk in the Object drop-down list.

3. Select Avg Disk Bytes/Transfer in the Counter drop-down box.

4. Click Add.

5. Close the Add to Chart window.

CURRENT DISK QUEUE LENGTH The Current Disk Queue Length shows how much data is waiting to be transferred to the disk. Many processes must wait for disk requests to be serviced before they can continue. A long disk queue indicates that many processes are being delayed by disk speed. Exercise 14.13 shows how to monitor this counter.

EXERCISE 14.13

Adding Logical Disk: Current Disk Queue Length to the Performance Monitor

1. Click + in the Performance Monitor tool bar.

2. Select Logical Disk in the Object drop-down list.

3. Select Current Disk Queue Length in the Counter drop-down box.

4. Click Add.

5. Close the Add to Chart window.

Troubleshooting Disk Performance

The best way to eliminate disks as bottlenecks is to use them as little as possible. Add a lot of RAM to your computer to increase the size of your disk cache and reduce the need for swapping pages to disk. This improvement will increase the performance of your computer more than any other.

If you cannot add more memory or if your computer already has all it can use, you will need to take other measures to improve disk performance. Your options are

- Use a newer, faster, or higher capacity hard disk

- Move to a faster hard disk controller interface

- Create stripe sets across multiple disks

- Use a redundant array of inexpensive disks (RAID)

UPGRADING YOUR DISK If your hard disk is more than two years old, you can probably increase your performance by upgrading it. New hard disk drives, especially hard disks larger than 1GB, transfer data quite a bit faster than the drives of just a few years ago. However, if your disk is relatively new, replacing it won't speed up you system much. Good, fast hard disk drives can transfer data at between 1.5 and 2 MB per second. This speed is generally faster than a single hard disk controller, but two or more fast hard disks running on a slow controller can easily swamp it, causing the controller to become the bottleneck.

FASTER HARD DISK CONTROLLERS Hard disk controllers impact the speed at which data can be transferred from your hard disk. Original SCSI and IDE both have a maximum limit of 5MB per second per controller bus. New hard disks can exceed this limit. Synchronous SCSI runs at 10MB per second for devices that support it.

Hard disk controllers running in ISA slots also have a hard limit of about 8MB per second. Also, since ISA controllers can address only the bottom 16MB of RAM, disk requests from regions higher in memory must be moved by the processor, creating an additional load.

If you have a SCSI or IDE controller running in an ISA slot and you have a PCI slot available, you should replace the ISA controller with a PCI controller.

Finally, if you are using a PCI controller and you need more speed, consider moving to wide or ultra SCSI. These technologies transfer more data by increasing the width of the SCSI bus from 8 bits to 16 or 32, which doubles the amount of data that can be transferred on the bus. Your disk must support wide or ultra SCSI, or upgrading the controller will have no effect. Table 14.2 shows the performance maximums for various types of hard disk controllers. Note that in all cases the hard disk drives run slower than the maximum speed of the controller but that the controller can be loaded at the sum of the sustained transfer rates of all attached drives.

STRIPE SETS Stripe sets increase the speed of a logical disk by splitting it across many physical disks. Since disks can operate simultaneously, striping allows you to multiply the speed of a logical drive by the number of physical drives it comprises up to the maximum speed of a shared bus. For example, Figure 14.5 shows how Windows NT splits data across physical drives to improve performance. Creating stripe sets is covered in detail in Chapter 5 under the section on the disk administrator utility.

RAID Redundant arrays of inexpensive disks (RAID) works on the same theory as stripe sets. The difference is that a RAID controller replaces your regular SCSI controller and makes the stripe set look like one physical disk to Windows NT.

TABLE 14.2 Hard Disk Controller Technologies.	CONTROLLER TECHNOLOGY	MAX TRANSFER RATE	DEVICES
	BIOS Hard disk (MFM, RLL, ESDI)	8MB/s*	2
	IDE	5MB/s	2
	SCSI	5MB/s	7
	SCSI-2 Fast	10MB/s	7
	SCSI-2 Wide	20MB/s	7
	SCSI-2 F/W	40MB/s	7
	Ultra SCSI	80MB/s	15

*This rate is the theoretical maximum for a BIOS-controlled hard disk running in an ISA slot. In practice, you will not achieve this result. Controllers running in local bus slots may achieve higher burst throughput, but these types of drives will have sustained transfer rates less than 1MB/s.

FIGURE 14.5
A stripe volume
across three disks.

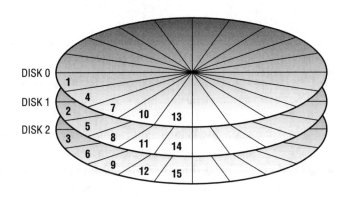

RAID controllers include a microprocessor that handles breaking up and recombining the disk data so that the computer's microprocessor doesn't have to. Most RAID controllers also have some RAM used as a cache to increase the speed of transfers to and from the controller. This cache works the same way as the Windows NT cache described in the memory optimization section.

RAID controllers essentially perform the same service as stripe sets, but because they relieve the computing burden of stripe sets from the processor and add a memory cache dedicated to disk transfers, they can help relieve processor bottlenecks. Unfortunately, they are very expensive. RAID controllers are generally used only in servers. RAID is covered in depth in the companion book *MCSE: NT Server Study Guide*.

Application Performance

You can change the performance of applications running in Windows NT to optimize the responsiveness of applications for your situation. Windows NT automatically changes priorities for processes (and therefore, their descendant threads) based upon what the user is doing. When you bring an application to the forefront, Windows NT automatically raises the priority levels of its processes to ensure a quick response to your requests.

Remember that boosting priorities changes only the way the processor divides time among running processes. If you are using only one application, you are competing for processor time with system processes that must be serviced in a timely manner. Raising priorities when you are running only one application will not make the application run faster because the processor is already dedicating all of its free time to the application.

Changing Default Application Responsiveness

If you normally run many different applications and you need them to all operate simultaneously with the same speed regardless of which one is in the forefront, you can change Windows NT Workstation's default behavior. You can also manually launch applications with higher than normal priority if you need to increase the time spent in that process.

The performance boost slider has three settings. Maximum boost provides the best foreground application responsiveness by increasing the foreground application's processes by two priorities. The middle setting makes foreground applications somewhat more responsive than background applications by increasing the priority level by one. None (No boost) makes foreground and background applications run with the same priority. Exercise 14.14 shows how to change default application responsiveness.

Remember to slide this Performance tab back to maximum when you are working under normal circumstances.

EXERCISE 14.14

Changing the Default Application Responsiveness

1. Select Settings ➤ Control Panel in the Start menu.

2. Double-click the System control panel.

3. Select the Performance tab.

4. Slide the Performance slider from Maximum Boost to None.

5. Click OK or Apply.

6. Answer Yes when asked if you want to restart your computer.

Launching a High-Priority Process

You can launch an application with a higher-than-normal priority using the Start command at the Command prompt or in the Run dialog box. Start also allows you to run Win16 applications in their own memory spaces so that if one 16-bit application crashes, it does not affect other 16-bit applications. Exercise 14.15 shows how to start processing with other-than-normal priority.

EXERCISE 14.15

Starting Processes with Other Than Normal Priority

1. Select Programs ➤ Command Prompt from the Start menu.

2. Insert the CD-ROM that came with this book into the CD-ROM drive. Change drives to the CD-ROM drive. (For example, if your CD-ROM shows up as drive F: you would type **F:** and then press Enter at the command prompt.)

3. Type **start /low /exercise/globe32.exe**.

4. Select the command prompt window and type **start /normal /exercise/ globe32.exe**.

5. Select the command prompt window and type **start /high /exercise/globe32.exe**.

EXERCISE 14.15 (CONTINUED)

6. Select the command prompt window and type **start /realtime /exercise/ globe32.exe**.

7. Select the command prompt window. Notice the difference in execution speed among the four instances of the program.

8. Close each instance of PROGXX.EXE.

Chapter Summary

WINDOWS NT PROVIDES low-level support for performance monitoring by including counters in every object that can be meaningfully measured. Windows NT uses these counters to perform a number of automatic optimizations, such as multiprocessing, spreading virtual memory swap files across multiple disks, prioritizing threads, and caching disk requests.

Windows NT also provides a performance monitor tool to allow you to measure system performance through object counters. You can use the performance monitor to find bottlenecks, or performance-limiting resources, in your computer. The performance monitor allows you to inspect the value of the object counters in real time so you can watch the effect that various activities have on the resources of your computer.

Tuning a computer's performance is a perpetual cycle of finding performance bottlenecks, eliminating them, and starting over with the next most limiting factor. When a computer can no longer be tuned for greater performance, it is at its natural performance limit for the software being used.

To effectively find bottlenecks, you must look at the overall performance of your computer under a typical load. Using more general counters and averages will give a good indication of where to look for specific bottlenecks. Processor performance, memory performance, and disk performance are the three major capacities that should be checked for performance.

You can use the System control panel's Performance tab to change application performance to meet your specific software requirements. This tab allows you to change the priority of foreground applications to more effectively share processor time for your specific needs.

Exercise Questions

1. Running the performance monitor does not affect the performance of the computer.

    A. True

    B. False

2. The performance monitor measures system performance.

    A. True

    B. False

3. Upgrading your hardware is one way to eliminate bottlenecks.

    A. True

    B. False

4. Bottlenecks are components that are not operating at peak performance.

    A. True

    B. False

5. Even the fastest computers have bottlenecks.

    A. True

    B. False

6. Windows NT can vary priority levels up to _____ priorities higher or lower automatically.

7. _____ performance counters are disabled by default to increase overall operating speed.

8. _____ are the measures taken to reduce the impact of a bottleneck on performance.

9. _____ are the basic units of division among processors in a multiprocessing environment.

10. Windows NT supports which type of multiprocessing?

    A. Symmetrical

    B. Asymmetrical

    C. Both symmetrical and asymmetrical

    D. Neither

11. Windows NT provides this tool for optimizing Windows NT performance:

   A. Microsoft Diagnostic tool (WinMSD)

   B. Performance tuner

   C. Windows NT Diagnostics (NTD)

   D. Performance monitor

   E. Task Manager

12. Which performance optimization is not implemented in the Windows NT operating system?

   A. Symmetric multiprocessing

   B. Swapping across multiple disks to increase performance

   C. Prioritizing threads and processes

   D. Caching RAM in the external processor cache

   E. Caching disk requests

13. In Windows NT, memory is divided into pages of what size?

   A. 4KB

   B. 16KB

   C. 64KB

   D. 256KB

14. NTFS uses which type of caching to improve performance?

   A. Write through

   B. Write back

   C. Write now

   D. Write optimization

   E. Buffered

15. The biggest single bottleneck in most computers is

    A. The processor

    B. Memory

    C. Disks

    D. Networks

16. The best way to eliminate disks as bottlenecks is to

    A. Create a stripe set

    B. Use them as little as possible

    C. Install a RAID controller

    D. Use ultra SCSI drives and controllers

Windows NT Application Support

WINDOWS NT PROVIDES a flexible, powerful, and robust environment for 32-bit Windows programs. It also supports applications written for 16-bit versions of Windows as well as for MS-DOS, OS/2 version 1.*x*, and POSIX programs. Windows NT satisfies the requirements of these applications through its application subsystem architecture, which adapts the services provided by the Windows NT kernel for each of the other operating environments.

This chapter describes the Windows NT application subsystem architecture and shows you how it supports each of the various application subsystems:

- Win32

- Win16

- DOS (VDM)

- OS/2

- POSIX

Windows NT Application Subsystem Architecture

WINDOWS NT WAS DESIGNED to support several different environments for running users' applications. Each type of application (16-bit Windows or OS/2, for example) requires a different operating environment, or Application Programming Interface (API). OS/2 applications, for instance, may require thread support, whereas 16-bit Windows applications require a 16-bit version of the Windows graphical environment.

Although each application subsystem has a different API, the functionality of the various subsystems has much in common. MS-DOS and Win32 open files in different ways, for example, but their basic operations are the same (both read, write, and seek along a file, both open and close files, and so on). Windows NT provides a subsystem-neutral implementation of operating system services in a part of NT called Executive Services, which encapsulates the common functionality that the different subsystems need. The subsystems for each type of application provide the environment that the applications expect by adapting the functionality that Executive Services provides.

The Win32 subsystem plays a special role in the Windows NT subsystem architecture. Windows NT channels all graphics requests to the Win32 subsystem for presentation to the user and funnels mouse and keyboard events back through the Win32 subsystem. Figure 15.1 shows the relationships between the application subsystems and Executive Services.

FIGURE 15.1
The application subsystems adapt the functionality provided by Executive Services to the different application environments.

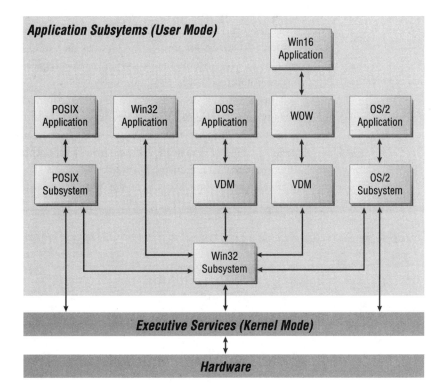

Windows NT provides several different environments for application support:

- Win32
- VDM
- Win16
- OS/2
- POSIX

Win32

THE WIN32 SUBSYSTEM GIVES application programmers the most flexible environment for developing Windows applications. The Win32 environment supports 32-bit applications, multithreading, large address spaces (each application runs in its own 2GB address space), memory protection between applications, and advanced application services such as OpenGL. These features are not immediately discernible to the user except perhaps as faster execution or a more sophisticated or reliable program.

A program written to use the Win16 environment may look the same as a program written to use the Win32 environment, but programs written to use the more sophisticated features of Windows NT (such as multithreading or OpenGL) must use Win32. Figure 15.2 shows how Win32 applications relate to the Win32 subsystem and to Executive Services.

Several important aspects of the Win32 subsystem are

- 32 bits
- Threads
- Large address space
- Memory protection
- OpenGL

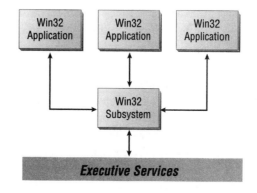

32 Bits

Win32 programs are developed for 32-bit processors such as the 386, 486, Pentium, MIPS, PowerPC, and Alpha (which also supports 64-bit processing). This environment is unlike the MS-DOS and Win16 environments, which were designed for 16-bit processing.

A processor works by manipulating values in memory that may represent numbers, text, images, or anything else that a computer can store.

A 32-bit processor can work directly with larger values than can a 16-bit processor. For example, 32 bits can represent the numbers from 0 to 4,294,967,295 whereas 16 bits can only represent the numbers from 0 to 65,535. A 16-bit processor can, of course, work with (add, multiply, divide, move, etc.) larger values, but it has to work on parts of the value at a time. This piecework arrangement takes more time than working on the large value directly.

Modern processors are able to manipulate the larger values, but if the program is not written to use the capabilities of the processor, the work will still be done the slow way, bit by bit. A program must be written for a 32-bit environment in order to take advantage of the 32-bit capabilities. Win32 programs are written to use the capabilities of 32-bit processors.

Threads and Scheduling

Win32 allows applications to have multiple threads of execution. A *thread of execution* is a task (defined as a sequence of instructions) for the processor to perform. If you compare the tasks that a processor performs in an application to the tasks an office staff performs in a business, the threads are like the job positions in the office. In this example the microprocessors in the computer are equivalent to the people who fill the job positions.

When jobs outnumber people, one person can fill more than one job position by switching from one task to another according to the workload. Similarly, when threads outnumber processors (which is most commonly the case because single-processor computers outnumber multiprocessor computers), then one processor switches between tasks according to the workload.

The application writer should make an application multithreaded even when the application will execute on only one processor because a multithreaded application can more easily switch between the tasks that it must perform. Multithreading makes the application more responsive to the user. Multithreading also facilitates the writing of programs that deal with multiple simultaneous events and processing that must happen in the background (while the application still responds to user requests). An example of multithreading is a graphics program that renders complex images in the background while allowing the user to modify parameters on the fly. Another example is a word processor that spell-checks your document as you type.

A multithreaded application will automatically take advantage of a computer with more than one microprocessor, which is not the case with single-threaded applications.

Win32 threads are *scheduled preemptively*. In other words, a thread receives a specific amount of time for execution, and when that time is up, Windows NT stops executing that thread and begins executing another thread. A thread may voluntarily give up its time, but a thread cannot execute for longer than its assigned period because a hardware timer will interrupt the task, allowing the operating system to regain control and switch execution to the next task.

Large Address Space

The Win32 application subsystem gives each program 2GB of continuous, unsegmented address space. This large address space allows programs to grow in size without using complex mechanisms such as segments and overlays to overcome the limitations of smaller address spaces.

The larger address space also allows programs to work with larger data sets than would be possible with smaller address spaces.

The address space that Windows NT supports is different from the RAM in the computer. Windows NT allows an application to allocate more memory for use in its address space than the computer may physically contain. For example, a graphics program may request 64MB of memory, and an NT computer that has only 32MB of RAM may still grant the request. The Windows NT virtual memory manager ensures that the sections of memory that the application uses are present in RAM, while inactive sections of that program's address space are swapped out to disk.

Memory Protection

Each application in the Win32 subsystem is protected from other applications. Because each application has its own address space, it cannot modify data belonging to another application without the cooperation of the other application.

Memory protection stops program errors and crashes caused by data that was changed by another application. It also protects applications from program crashes of other applications. (When a program crashes, it sometimes modifies random locations of memory accessible to it.)

Memory protection also enhances data security. A program may not make unauthorized modifications to other executing programs or to the operating system. This restriction prevents the most common virus propagation methods, making Windows NT a much safer operating environment than operating systems that do not support memory protection between applications.

Individual Input Queues

When the user interacts with the Windows NT GUI (icons, windows, menus, controls, mouse pointers, etc.), the user's actions are placed into queues depending on which application is responsible for interpreting the action. Each application has its own queue. For example, if a user moves the mouse pointer into a word processor's window, clicks on the title bar, and then types on the keyboard, several events will be placed in the word processor's queue: mouse motion events, mouse click events, and keyboard events.

The application that owns the queue handles the events in the queue. Because Windows NT maintains several queues, instead of one large queue, if one application stops processing events, other applications will still receive events that they are responsible for handling. This concept is important because if there were only one queue, an application could stop responding to events and allow the queue to fill up, thereby stopping other applications because they would no longer be able to receive events.

OpenGL

OpenGL is an industry standard software interface for 2-D and 3-D graphics display. It defines graphics operations independent of hardware and operating system types, making it easier to write and port graphics programs between machines and operating systems.

The exercises in this chapter will show you which components are active and how they interoperate as you run programs in each of the application subsystems.

Exercise 15.1 shows you which services are started when you run a Win32 program.

EXERCISE 15.1

Viewing the Processes in NT as You Run a Win32 Program

1. Log on as an administrator.

2. Run the Windows NT Task Manager by right-clicking on an empty space in the Task Bar and then selecting Task Manager.

3. Click on the Processes tab. Note the processes that are currently executing.

4. Start Notepad Win32. (Select Start ➤ Programs ➤ Accessories ➤ Notepad.)

5. Note that Notepad is the only new process in the process list. (No other subsystem components are required to support the Win32 program.)

6. Close Notepad.

7. Close the Windows NT Task Manager.

DOS (VDM)

WINDOWS NT SUPPORTS running MS-DOS programs in a component of the Win32 subsystem called a virtual DOS machine or VDM. VDMs recreate the hardware and software environment that DOS mode programs expect.

Every DOS program executes as a single thread in a separate VDM. Each DOS program thinks that it has the entire computer to itself. Figure 15.3 illustrates the relationship between DOS applications, VDMs, and the Win32 subsystem.

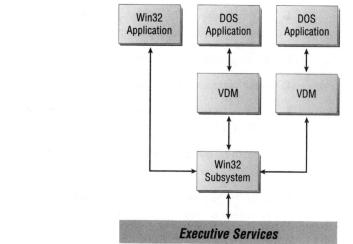

Software Environment

The following VDM components recreate the software environment that DOS programs expect:

- **NTVDM.EXE** is the portion of the VDM that runs in protected mode. It translates MS-DOS calls into Win32 calls that it forwards to the Win32 subsystem.

- **NTIO.SYS** and **NTDOS.SYS** are the equivalent of the IO.SYS and MSDOS.SYS component in regular MS-DOS. NTDOS.SYS runs in the real mode of the 386-compatible processor (or emulated processor on RISC computers).

- **VDMREDIR.DLL** is the component of the VDM that redirects file system and input/output requests to the Win32 subsystem.

Exercise 15.2 shows you which services are started when you run a DOS program under Windows NT.

EXERCISE 15.2

Viewing the Processes in NT as You Run a DOS Program

1. Log on as an administrator.

2. Run the Windows NT Task Manager by right-clicking on an empty space in the Task Bar and then selecting Task Manager.

3. Click on the Processes tab. Note the processes that are currently executing.

4. Open a command prompt. (Select Start ➤ Programs ➤ Command Prompt.)

5. Note that CMD.EXE is the only new process in the process list. (CMD.EXE is a Win32 program.)

6. Within the Command Prompt window, run the EDIT program. (Type **edit** and then press Enter.)

7. Note that the process NTVDM.EXE starts. (Since EDIT is a DOS program, it must execute within the NTVDM process.)

8. Exit the EDIT program (press Alt, select File, and Exit).

9. Type **exit** to close the command prompt window.

10. Note that both the NTVDM.EXE and CMD.EXE processes go away.

11. Close the Windows NT Task Manager.

Hardware Environment

The hardware environment that MS-DOS programs expect is created with virtual device drivers (VDDs). A VDD intercepts requests to hardware devices such as the mouse, keyboard, and serial ports and redirects those requests through the Win32 subsystem.

Configuration

Like earlier versions of DOS, a VDM reads from two configuration files when it starts. CONFIG.NT performs the same function as CONFIG.SYS in earlier versions of DOS, and AUTOEXEC.NT does the same for AUTOEXEC.BAT.

Win16

S INCE THE INTRODUCTION OF Windows 3 in 1990, Microsoft Windows has been the most popular operating system for personal computers. Programs have been written for Windows that perform almost any computer task. Not all of these programs have been implemented for the 32-bit Windows environment. The Win16 subsystem allows your Windows NT computer to run programs written for these earlier versions of Windows. Figure 15.4 illustrates the Win16 subsystem.

FIGURE 15.4
One VDM and WOW
pair can provide the
execution environment
for several Win16
applications.

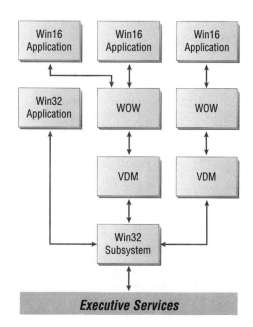

VDM and WOW

Earlier implementations of Microsoft Windows were designed to run on top of MS-DOS. For this reason 16-bit Windows programs expect the DOS environment to be available in addition to the Windows environment. Windows NT provides the combined environment to 16-bit Windows programs with a Windows-on-

Windows (WOW) environment in addition to a VDM (described in the previous section).

Each DOS program gets its own VDM, but Win16 programs work differently. Because 16-bit Windows applications are programmed to interact with other 16-bit Windows programs, (unless you specify otherwise) each additional Win16 application that is started is loaded into the same VDM and WOW that was established for the first 16-bit Windows application.

Because the Win16 programs are run together in the same VDM and WOW, as in earlier versions of Windows, the applications can interfere with each other and cause each other to fail. This arrangement will not, however, cause NT to fail.

To Windows NT and the Win32 subsystem, the VDM, WOW, and all of the Win16 applications executing within them all appear to be just one application.

WOW Components

The Win16 environment includes the components of the VDM environment—
NTVDM.EXE, VDMREDIR.DLL, NTIO.SYS, and NTDOS.SYS. In addition, WOW has the following components:

- **KRNL386.EXE** is a version of the Windows 3.1 operating system that has been modified to run under Windows NT. Many of the Windows kernel operations are not performed by this kernel. They are passed to the Win32 environment instead.

- **USER.EXE** is a modified version of the Windows 3.1 USER.EXE, which translates user API calls into Win32 calls.

- **GDI.EXE** is a modified version of Windows 3.1 GDI.EXE, which translates Windows graphics calls into Win32 graphics calls.

- **WOWEXEC.EXE** is the component that provides Windows 3.1 emulation for the VDM.

When a 16-bit program makes a call that will be satisfied by the Win32 subsystem, the 16-bit call must be transformed into a 32-bit call. The reverse is true when the Win-32 subsystem returns data to a 16-bit application. This translation incurs some overhead, but that overhead is usually offset by the greater speed of the 32-bit version of the service.

Exercise 15.3 shows you the processes that are involved in the execution of a 16-bit Windows program.

EXERCISE 15.3

Viewing the Processes in NT as You Run Win16 Programs

1. Log on as an administrator.

2. Run the Windows NT Task Manager by right-clicking on an empty space in the Task Bar and then selecting Task Manager.

3. Click on the Processes tab. Note the processes that are currently executing.

4. Run the WIN16APP.EXE 16-bit Windows application. (Select Start ➤ Run; type **<CDROM** Drive Letter**>:\exercise\win16app.exe** in the entry box and then press Enter.)

5. Note that one NTVDM.EXE process starts, one WOWEXEC.EXE process starts within the NTVDM process, and the WIN16APP.EXE process also starts within the NTVDM process.

6. Start another WIN16APP.EXE process (repeat step 4).

7. Note that the only additional entry in the list is another WIN16APP.EXE program. (Subsequent Win16 programs will be started within the existing NTVDM and WOWEXEC process area.)

8. Exit both WIN16APP programs by clicking the Close button in the program's menu bar.

9. Note that NTVDM.EXE and WOWEXEC.EXE continue to execute.

10. Close the Windows NT Task Manager.

The WOW Input Queue

Windows versions 3.11 and earlier had only one input queue for all of the user interface events for all of the applications. (See "Individual Input Queues" earlier in this chapter.) The Win16 subsystem recreates this environment, so each VDM and WOW pair has one input queue for all of the Win16 applications running in that VDM and WOW.

Since only one queue is available, a Win16 application can interfere with other Win16 applications in the same VDM and WOW by not responding to events. This arrangement will not interfere with applications running in other subsystems or with Win16 applications running in another VDM and WOW.

Scheduling within WOW

Windows versions 3.11 and earlier distributed execution time among applications by a method known as *cooperative multitasking.* In this form of multitasking, the applications share the microprocessor, each application performing a sequence of operations and then returning control to the operating system, which then selects another application to execute.

Cooperative multitasking is nonpreemptive, that is, an application does not have a set amount of time in which to execute—and no timer will return control to the operating system. Consequently, one application can monopolize execution time, or crash, interfering with all other applications in the cooperative execution environment.

Win16 programs within a VDM and WOW multitask cooperatively. The Win32 environment, however, multitasks in a preemptive manner with other applications and subsystems in the Windows NT operating system. Therefore, a Win16 application that crashes or monopolizes execution time affects only other Win16 applications within its VDM and WOW.

Starting Win16 Applications

You can start Win16 applications from the command prompt, from the Run menu item in the Start menu, or from an application icon in the Windows NT Explorer. When you start an application, you can cause it to execute either in the same VDM and WOW as other Win16 applications, or you can cause it to execute in its own VDM and WOW. The methods of starting Win16 applications are as follows:

- **From the Command prompt:** Type the name of the Win16 application in order to start it in the same VDM and WOW as other Win16 applications or type a command of the form: **start /separate [path] application_executable.**

- **From the Start menu:** Select Run and then type the program name in the Run window. If you wish the Win16 program to execute in its own VDM and WOW, check the *Run in separate memory space* option. Then press OK.

- **From the Windows NT Explorer:** Double-click the icon that represents the Win16 application. If you wish the application to execute in its own memory space, you must create a shortcut to the program with modified settings so that when you double-click the icon, it will use its own VDM and WOW. Exercise 15.4 shows you how to make the shortcut.

EXERCISE 15.4

Creating a Shortcut for a Win16 Application That Will Execute Separately

1. Open the window in the Windows NT Explorer that contains the Win16 program's icon.

2. Drag the program's icon with the right mouse button to a new location. Release the right mouse button.

3. Select Create Shortcut.

4. Click once on the newly created shortcut to highlight it and then select Properties from the File menu.

5. Click the Shortcut tab and then check the *Run in separate memory space* option. Click the OK button at the bottom of the window.

OS/2 Version 1.x

THE OS/2 SUBSYSTEM SUPPORTS many programs written for version 1.x of the OS/2 operating system. Windows NT does not support programs written for OS/2 version 2 or greater, programs that use APIs that would violate Windows NT security (such as the Vio video API and the Dev device driver API), or programs that use the OS/2 Presentation Manager unless you install the Windows NT add-on subsystem for Presentation Manager. Figure 15.5 illustrates the OS/2 subsystem.

FIGURE 15.5
The OS/2 subsystem
communicates with the
Win32 subsystem and
with Executive Services.

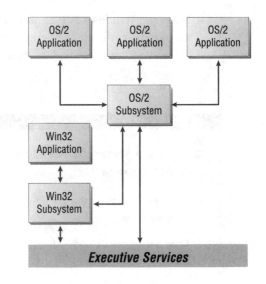

OS/2 Subsystem Components

As in the other application subsystems, several software components make up the OS/2 subsystem.

- **OS2SS.EXE** and **OS2SRV.EXE:** The main components of the OS/2 subsystem. They adapt services provided by Win32 and Executive Services to the environment that OS/2 applications expect. Only one instance of OS2SRV.EXE runs regardless of how many OS/2 programs are executing.

- **OS2.EXE:** One instance of OS2.EXE runs for every OS/2 program that is executing under NT and manages program-specific aspects of the OS/2 environment.

- **NETAPI.DLL** and **DOSCALLS.DLL:** These files contain Windows NT versions of APIs that OS/2 programs are written to.

Exercise 15.5 shows you the processes involved in executing an OS/2 version 1.*x* program.

EXERCISE 15.5

Viewing the Processes in NT as You Run OS/2 1.x Programs

1. Log on as an administrator.

2. Run the Windows NT Task Manager by right-clicking on an empty space in the Task Bar and then selecting Task Manager.

3. Click the Processes tab. Note the processes that are currently executing.

4. Run the OS/2 application by selecting Start ➤ Programs ➤ Command Prompt.

5. At the command prompt, type **<CDROM** drive letter>: and then press Enter.

6. At the command prompt, **type CD \exercise** and then press Enter.

7. At the command prompt, type **OS2APP.BAT** and then press Enter.

8. Note that one OS2SS.EXE process starts, one OS2.EXE process starts, and the OS2SRV.EXE process also starts. A window appears on your desktop with the program running in it.

9. Start another OS2APP process (repeat steps 4–7).

10. Note that the only additional entry in the list is another OS2.EXE program. (Subsequent OS/2 programs will start using the services of the existing OS2SS and OS2SRV processes.)

11. Exit both OS/2 programs by clicking the Close button in the program's title bar.

12. Note that OS2SS.EXE and OS2SRV.EXE continue to execute.

13. Close the Windows NT Task Manager.

Bound Applications

Some programs are compiled to run under either DOS or OS/2. These programs are called *bound programs*. When a bound program is started under Windows NT, NT will run it in the OS/2 subsystem unless you use the FORCEDOS.EXE program to force Windows NT to run the bound program in a VDM. You may be required to use FORCEDOS.EXE to run a bound program in a VDM if the bound program makes calls to the Presentation Manager and you do not have the Presentation Manager subsystem loaded.

POSIX

UNLIKE THE WIN16, VDM, and OS/2 subsystems, the Windows NT POSIX subsystem was not designed to allow you to run programs compiled for another operating system. Instead, the Windows NT POSIX subsystem was designed to make it easier to compile programs that were written to the POSIX specification (which is not operating-system specific) to run under Windows NT.

POSIX (which stands for Portable Open Systems Interface for computing environments) is a set of specifications that originated with the IEEE. The International Standards Organization (ISO) has also adopted some of the POSIX specifications as international standards. Windows NT implements the POSIX.1 standard (also an ISO standard), which defines a systems API for the C programming language. Figure 15.6 illustrates the POSIX subsystem.

FIGURE 15.6
The POSIX subsystem communicates with both the Win32 subsystem and Executive Services.

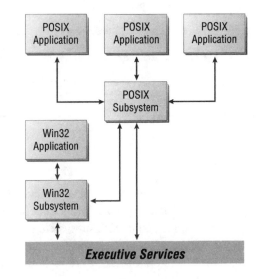

The POSIX Environment

An operating system must satisfy certain requirements in order to be POSIX compliant. The criteria, which are fully specified in the POSIX documents, include the following:

- **Case-sensitive naming:** The operating system's file system must support case-sensitive names. In such a file system, different files with the names Test, test, and TEST can all reside in the same directory. Also, in a directory that held only a file named Test, attempting to open test or TEST would not succeed because the case in the filename must match exactly. NTFS supports case-sensitive naming in the POSIX subsystem, as is described in Chapter 5.

- **Hard links:** The operating system's file system must allow one file to have two different names. Hard links allow this feature, and Windows NT supports hard links.

- **POSIX.1 library compliance:** A program written for the POSIX environment expects a library of C routines to be present to perform many operating system and environmental functions. Windows NT provides the library PSXDLL.DLL to fill this function.

POSIX Subsystem Components

Three components in the Windows NT POSIX subsystem maintain the environment that a POSIX program expects:

- **PSXSS.EXE** is the main POSIX subsystem component. It is loaded when the first POSIX program is started and remains in memory until explicitly unloaded by the user. Only one instance of PSXSS.EXE executes regardless of the number of POSIX programs executing.

- **POSIX.EXE** is the portion of the POSIX subsystem that handles communications between the POSIX subsystem and Executive Services. One instance of POSIX.EXE is loaded for each POSIX program that is run.

- **PSXDLL.DLL** is the dynamic link library that contains the POSIX library routines that POSIX specifies must be present in a conforming operating system.

Chapter Summary

THIS CHAPTER DESCRIBED each of the application subsystems supported by Windows NT. All of the application subsystems use the Executive Services, some (such as the Win32 subsystem, OS/2 subsystem, and POSIX subsystem) access Executive Services directly, while others (the Win16 and DOS subsystems) access Executive Services indirectly through the Win32 subsystem.

The Win32 subsystem is the native application environment for Windows NT. Applications developed to use the full potential of Windows NT will be written for the Win32 subsystem. Win32 provides applications with a 32-bit environment, a large address space, memory protection, multithreading and preemptive scheduling, separate input queues, and advanced resources such as the OpenGL graphic environment.

The DOS (VDM) subsystem makes it appear to DOS programs that each has complete control of a DOS environment. DOS system calls are handled by a version of DOS that redirects user interface calls directly to the Win32 subsystem and redirects hardware device calls through virtual device drivers to the Win32 subsystem.

The developers of Windows NT included the Win16 subsystem to allow you to run applications written for earlier implementations of Windows. The Win16 environment builds on the DOS (VDM) environment by providing a 16-bit Windows kernel on top of the emulated DOS environment. Many Win16 programs can execute within a single VDM/WOWEXEC pair, and multiple VDM/WOWEXEC pairs can run at once. All WOW applications share a single input queue, execute in the same address space, and execute cooperatively, rather than preemptively.

The OS/2 subsystem supports applications written for the OS/2 version 1.x environment. It does not support applications that use the Presentation Manager unless you have a Presentation Manager subsystem loaded.

The POSIX subsystem supports applications written to the POSIX specification and compiled for the POSIX subsystem of Windows NT. POSIX applications expect an environment that supports case sensitivity and hard links in the file system, as well as a library that implements standard POSIX calls.

Exercise Questions

1. Windows NT channels all graphics requests to the Win32 subsystem for presentation to the user.

   A. True

   B. False

2. Windows NT funnels all mouse and keyboard events back through the POSIX subsystem.

   A. True

   B. False

3. The DOS (VDM) subsystem gives application programmers the most flexible environment for developing Windows applications.

   A. True

   B. False

4. Win32 programs are developed for 32-bit processors such as the 386, 486, Pentium, MIPS, PowerPC, and Alpha.

   A. True

   B. False

5. A 32-bit processor can work directly with larger values than a 16-bit processor can.

   A. True

   B. False

6. Win32 programs, like Win16 programs, can have only one thread of execution.

   A. True

   B. False

7. Win32 threads are scheduled cooperatively.

   A. True

   B. False

8. Win32 applications all run within one shared memory space.

A. True

B. False

9. Each Win32 application receives its own input queue.

A. True

B. False

10. Every DOS program executes multiple threads within a single VDM.

A. True

B. False

11. Within a VDM, MS-DOS calls are translated into Win32 calls that are forwarded to the Win32 subsystem.

A. True

B. False

12. Earlier implementations of Microsoft Windows were designed to run on top of MS-DOS.

A. True

B. False

13. Each Win16 program that you run is executed in a separate VDM and WOW.

A. True

B. False

14. Each VDM and WOW pair has one input queue for all of the Win16 applications running in that VDM and WOW.

A. True

B. False

15. Win16 programs within a VDM and WOW multitask preemptively.

A. True

B. False

16. The OS/2 subsystem supports many programs written for version 2 of the OS/2 operating system.

    A. True

    B. False

17. The Windows NT POSIX subsystem allows you to run programs compiled for another operating system.

    A. True

    B. False

18. The POSIX.1 standard is also an ISO standard.

    A. True

    B. False

19. With case-sensitive naming, Test, test, and TEST all designate the same file.

    A. True

    B. False

20. With hard links, Test, test, and TEST could all refer to the same file.

    A. True

    B. False

21. Windows NT provides a subsystem-neutral implementation of operating system services in a part of NT called _____ _____.

22. The Win32 application subsystem gives each program _____ GB of continuous, unsegmented address space.

23. _____ is an industry standard software interface for 2-D and 3-D graphics display.

24. _____ stands for virtual DOS machine.

25. The hardware environment that MS-DOS programs expect is created with _____ _____ _____ (VDDs).

26. One instance of _____ runs for every OS/2 program that is executing under NT.

27. _____ programs are compiled to run under either DOS or OS/2.

28. POSIX stands for _____ _____ _____ _____ for computing environments.

Booting
Windows NT

B Y NOW YOU HAVE INSTALLED and booted Windows NT Workstation many times. You are familiar with the NT boot loader, know how to select an operating system to boot, and know how to select which operating system will boot by default. You even know what the boot components are.

This chapter will show you what the boot components do and how you can customize the boot process for your computer. You will learn the basic principles of booting and then step through the NT boot process on Intel-based and RISC-based computers. Then you will learn about the Windows NT load phases, and finally you will see how to view and customize your workstation's boot configuration.

How to Boot an Operating System

U SER PROGRAMS REQUIRE an operating system in which to run. The act of turning on the computer does not itself start the operating system; the computer must find and load the operating system from its disk drives. The process of finding, loading, and initializing the operating system is called *booting*.

Some operating systems (but not Windows NT) can also be loaded from other media (e.g., ROM) or over a network.

Before we show you how Windows NT boots, you should first understand the general principles of how any operating system boots. And you will better understand how and why a computer boots if you first understand how a computer stores information—both in memory and on its hard drives. This section takes you on a brief tour through your computer, explaining how parts of the hardware and software cooperate to boot an operating system.

The Microprocessor, RAM, CMOS, and ROM

Every time you turn on your computer, it starts fresh. A computer retains very little data in its memory from previous computing sessions; it does not even store the identity of the operating system you ran before. In fact, about all a computer can keep track of is the current date, what types of hard drives are attached, and a few more bits of very hardware-specific information about the computer itself.

The computer does not keep any information from previous computing sessions because the microprocessor and the RAM are volatile—that is, they lose any information stored in them whenever power is turned off.

Computers preserve some data from session to session, but that data is stored in ROM and cannot be modified during a session. The ROM gives the microprocessor a program to execute; otherwise, the microprocessor could do nothing, because RAM that has just been turned on does not hold any valid data or programs. IBM PC compatible computers call the program stored in ROM the basic input/output system (BIOS).

The BIOS contains routines for accessing the computer's hardware devices, such as the keyboard, hard disks, floppy disks, and video display. The BIOS is small compared to the size of most operating systems today—a BIOS can be 128K in size or even smaller, which is tiny in comparison with the many megabytes in Windows NT. The BIOS must be small because ROM costs much more per megabyte than hard disk storage costs and because IBM PC compatible computers contain only a small amount of ROM.

The CMOS is the one part of the computer that can contain information that changes from one computing session to the next. The CMOS can hold only a little bit of information, however, such as the types of hard drives, floppy drives, and IRQ settings for serial ports that the BIOS needs to know in order to talk to the hardware devices attached to the computers.

The BIOS provides an operating system with routines to access the computer's hardware, but the BIOS is not an operating system itself. The primary function of the BIOS, after it initializes the computer's hardware, is to find an operating system and load it.

Hard Disks, Floppy Disks, and File Systems

Hard disks and floppy disks store data. One significant advantage of both hard disks and floppy disks is that they maintain information stored on them even when the power is off. Another advantage of hard disk drives is that the cost of hard disk space is much less per megabyte than the cost of RAM. Another advantage of floppy disks is that you can take them (and thus the data stored on them) to different computers.

Disk drives do not interpret the data they store. They only store data to and retrieve data from sectors on the disk. The computer's operating system has the job of assigning meaning and structure to the information stored on a disk drive.

The operating system imposed arrangement of data on a disk is called a file system. Not all operating systems use the same file systems, and some operating systems (such as Windows NT) support several file systems. For an explanation of file systems, see Chapter 5.

The operating system itself is usually stored somewhere in the file system. Windows NT stores its operating system by default in the subdirectories under the directory Winnt.

Bootstrapping: From BIOS to Operating System

The BIOS does not know anything about file systems. It can, however, read sectors from hard disk drives. The BIOS uses this capability to load a small program (the master boot record program) that does understand file systems; that small program loads a larger program (the operating system loader program), which itself loads the operating system. This multistep process of loading more sophisticated programs that can then load other programs that load the operating system is called *bootstrapping,* or *booting.* The term *bootstrapping* is derived from the phrase "pull yourself up by your own boot straps."

The BIOS begins the boot process by loading a sector from the hard disk drive that is reserved for booting. That sector is usually called the *boot block,* or *master boot record.* IBM PC compatible computers reserve the first block on the hard disk (or floppy disk) for this purpose. Within the boot block sector is a very small program (a sector is not very large) that can find a larger program. The small program does not usually interact with the user. This program will either load the larger program or it will discontinue the boot and display an error message. If you see one of the following two messages, the master boot record program cannot find the operating system loader program.

```
Non-System disk or disk error
Replace and press any key when ready
```

The message above indicates that you are attempting to boot a DOS-formatted disk or hard drive that does not have the files necessary to run DOS.

```
Boot: Couldn't find NTLDR
Please insert another disk
```

The preceding message indicates that you are trying to boot an NT formatted disk or hard drive that does not have the files necessary to run Windows NT. (See the next chapter, "Troubleshooting Windows NT," to resolve this boot problem.) Exercise 16.1 shows you what happens when the boot sector cannot find the boot loader.

EXERCISE 16.1

Attempting a Boot without the Boot Loader (Format a Floppy Disk and Attempt to Boot It without the Boot Loader Installed)

1. Place a blank floppy disk in the A: drive.

2. Open the My Computer icon on the Desktop.

3. Select the A: icon in the My Computer window. (Click once on the icon.)

4. Select the Format menu item from the File menu.

5. Select Start in the Formatting A:\ window. The computer will warn you that you will destroy all data on the A: drive.

6. Click OK to continue.

7. Click OK when the format is complete and then close the Formatting A:\ window.

8. Leave the floppy disk in the drive. From the Start menu select Shut Down.

9. Click on the Restart button in the Shutdown window. Your computer will restart.

10. Note that when your computer restarts (with the floppy disk in the drive), you see the *Boot: Couldn't find NTLDR* message. This message is different from the one you would see if you attempted to boot a DOS-formatted floppy that had no operating system because the NT-formatted floppy and a DOS-formatted floppy do not have the same boot sector.

11. Remove the floppy disk from the drive and restart your computer.

The larger program that the boot block loads on a DOS-formatted disk is IO.SYS. This program is a major part of the MS-DOS operating system. The boot block may also load MSDOS.SYS or IO.SYS. Once these files are loaded, the boot block passes control to IO.SYS and the operating system is running.

MS-DOS is a simple operating system. Other operating systems often require a boot loader to prepare the computer's memory, CPU, and I/O devices before the operating system can run. Windows NT, for example, is a 32-bit operating system and executes only in the Intel microprocessor's 32-bit mode. One of the responsibilities of the Windows NT boot loader is to put the microprocessor into 32-bit mode.

A boot loader may also allow you to select between several operating systems. The Windows NT boot loader gives you the option of booting Windows NT in one of several configurations or of booting Windows 95 or DOS (if you have those operating systems installed on your computer).

Once the operating system is loaded, control passes to it, and the operating system prepares itself to run user programs. The operating system must initialize itself and adapt itself to the hardware configuration at that time. For instance, it may recognize the addition of a hard drive or the removal of a fax modem board. After initialization the operating system must load the services necessary to control the computer hardware and support user programs. Finally, when the operating system is ready, it allows the user to access the system.

Some advanced operating systems, such as Windows NT, can give users access to the system before all operating system services are started. If the user attempts to use a service before it is started, the user must wait until that service is ready.

Booting NT on Intel and on RISC Processors

THE WINDOWS NT BOOT PROCESS follows the sequence outlined in the previous section ("How to Boot an Operating System"), but the details of the boot process are different for Intel-based computers and RISC-based computers.

The files required for loading Windows NT on an Intel-based machine are as follows:

- **NTLDR:** This program is the Windows NT boot loader. The boot sector routine loads this program, which then finds and loads the Windows NT operating system.

- **BOOT.INI:** NTLDR reads the boot configuration options for Windows NT installations from this file. BOOT.INI contains the boot selection menu you see when the computer starts up.

- **BOOTSECT.DOS:** This MS-DOS boot sector is used if another operating system such as DOS or Windows 95 is selected from the boot selection menu.

- **NTDETECT.COM:** This program determines the current hardware configuration of the computer and returns the configuration information to NTLDR so that it can pass the information to the Windows NT operating system.

- **NTOSKRNL.EXE:** This program is the kernel of the Windows NT operating system.

- **NTBOOTDD.SYS:** This driver is used during the boot process only if the operating system is stored on a SCSI device attached to a SCSI adapter in the computer that does not have a SCSI BIOS.

The files required for loading Windows NT on a RISC-based machine are as follows:

- **OSLOADER.EXE:** The boot loader for RISC-based machines performs the same functions as NTLDR for Intel-based machines.

- **NTOSKRNL.EXE:** This file is the kernel of the Windows NT operating system.

- **NTBOOTDD.SYS:** This driver is used during the boot process only if the operating system is stored on a SCSI device attached to a SCSI adapter in the computer that does not have a SCSI BIOS.

The portion of the Windows NT boot process before the operating system itself begins to execute is called the pre-boot sequence. The *pre-boot sequence* is the portion of the boot process that shows the most difference between Intel-based and RISC-based computers. Table 16.1 shows the Intel and RISC pre-boot sequences.

TABLE 16.1 Intel and RISC Pre-Boot Sequences.	**INTEL PRE-BOOT SEQUENCE**	**RISC PRE-BOOT SEQUENCE**
	The BIOS power-on self-test (POST) routines check the state of the computer's hardware.	ROM firmware checks the state of the computer's hardware.
	The BIOS checks the floppy disk and the first hard disk for valid media. If the BIOS can read from the floppy disk or hard disk, the BIOS loads the boot sector (for a floppy disk) or the master boot record (MBR; for a hard disk) from the first sector of the disk.	The firmware loads the precedence of boot devices from nonvolatile memory (CMOS).
	Hard disks only: The BIOS executes the software routine in the MBR. The MBR routine scans the partition boot record in the MBR for the partition that has been marked active. The MBR routine loads the partition's boot sector (the first sector of the partition) and then passes control to the routine in the boot sector.	The first sector of each boot device is checked in turn to see if it contains a bootable partition with a file system that the firmware recognizes.
	The boot sector finds and loads the NTLDR program and then passes control to it.	When the firmware finds a bootable partition with a file system that it understands, it finds and loads OSLOADER.EXE and then passes control to it.
	NTLDR finds and loads NTDETECT.COM, which determines the current configuration of the computer, and then passes control back to NTLDR. NTLDR then finds and loads the operating system kernel, after which it passes control to the operating system along with configuration information from NTDETECT.COM.	OSLOADER.EXE finds and loads the operating system kernel and passes control and configuration information from the firmware to it.

The pre-boot sequence for RISC-based computers is simpler than the sequence for Intel-based computers because the firmware in RISC-based computers contains much of the functionality that is contained in external programs such as the boot sector routines and NTDETECT.COM in Intel-based computers.

Windows NT Load Phases

WHEN NTOSKRNL.EXE IS LOADED and takes control, the Windows NT kernel goes through five load phases. The phases are

- Kernel load
- Kernel initialization
- Services load
- Windows system start
- User log on

Kernel Load

In the kernel load phase, the Hardware Abstraction Layer (HAL) is loaded. Each computer platform that runs Windows NT has a HAL. Like the device drivers that insulate the operating system from differences between peripheral devices such as printers and video cards, the HAL insulates the operating system from differences in the way the computers themselves work, such as how they service interrupts and how memory caches operate.

After the HAL is loaded, the system loads the system hive. From the system hive the operating system determines which device drivers and services must be loaded during the kernel load phase. Some drivers and services are then loaded, but not initialized.

Kernel Initialization

The kernel initialization phase initializes the kernel and the drivers that were loaded in the kernel load phase. Then the operating system scans the system hive again for the rest of the drivers to load. It loads and initializes these drivers and then creates and saves two Registry areas—the CurrentControlSet and the CloneControlSet. The CurrentControlSet is saved. The operating system then creates the hardware list in the Registry, which contains the information passed to the operating system by NTLDR or OSLOADER.

As each driver is loaded, it can report an error condition to the kernel.

- **Ignore:** If a device driver returns this error condition to the kernel, the error is ignored and no message is displayed to the user.

- **Normal:** If a device driver returns this error condition to the kernel, the error message is displayed to the user, but the boot process continues.

- **Severe:** If a device driver returns this error condition to the kernel and if the LastKnownGood configuration is not being used, a message is displayed to the user and the boot process is restarted using the LastKnownGood configuration. If the LastKnownGood configuration is being used, the error message is displayed to the user and the boot process continues.

- **Critical:** If a device driver returns this error condition to the kernel and if the LastKnownGood configuration is not being used, a message is displayed to the user and the boot process is restarted using the LastKnownGood configuration. If the LastKnownGood configuration is being used, the error message is displayed to the user and the boot process fails.

Services Load

The Services load phase, in which the kernel starts the Session Manager, follows the kernel initialization phase. The Session Manager reads the entries stored in the following Registry key and starts the programs corresponding to the key's entries.

```
HKEY_LOCAL_MACHINE\SYSTEM\CurrentControlSet\Control\
    Session Manager\BootExecute
```

The default entry stored in the above key is

```
autocheck autochk *
```

Autocheck ensures that the files stored on your hard disk drive are always in a consistent state. Autocheck will detect and attempt to repair damage to files and directories, but Autocheck cannot guarantee that no information will be lost from a file system that has been damaged by an errant program or power failure, for instance.

After the file systems have been checked, the Session Manager sets up the paging files that are defined under

```
HKEY_LOCAL_MACHINE\SYSTEM\CurrentControlSet\Control\
    Session Manager\Memory Management
```

Next, the Session Manager writes the CurrentControlSet and the Clone control set to the Registry.

Finally, the Session Manager loads the subsystems defined in the Registry. The default subsystem is the Win32 subsystem. The Registry key containing the subsystems to be loaded is

```
HKEY_LOCAL_MACHINE\SYSTEM\CurrentControlSet\Control\
    Session Manager\Subsystems
```

Exercise 16.2 shows the Registry settings in your Windows NT workstation for the Session Manager.

EXERCISE 16.2

Viewing the Session Manager Registry Settings

1. Logon as an administrator.

2. Start the Registry Editor program (from the Start menu, select Run and then type **regedit** in the Open field). Click OK.

3. Open the HKEY_LOCAL_MACHINE key (click on the plus sign in front of the HKEY_LOCAL_MACHINE entry).

4. Open the System key.

5. Open the CurrentControlSet key.

6. Open the Control key.

7. Open the Session Manager key.

EXERCISE 16.2 (CONTINUED)

8. Double-click on the BootExecute entry in the window on the right. An Edit Binary Value window that contains the text of the BootExecute entry will appear (see Figure 16.1).

9. Select OK in the Edit Binary Value window.

10. Open the Memory Management key in the left side of the Registry window (click once on its folder icon).

11. Double-click on the PagingFiles entry in the window on the right. An Edit Binary Value window that contains the text of the PagingFiles entry will appear.

12. Select OK in the Edit Binary Value window.

13. Open the Subsystems key in the left side of the Registry window (click once on its folder icon).

14. Double-click on the Required entry in the window on the right. An Edit Binary Value window that contains the text of the Required entry will appear. Note that Debug and Windows are required.

15. Select OK in the Edit Binary Value window. An Edit Binary Value window that contains the text of the Windows entry will appear. Note that Debug and Windows are required.

16. Select OK in the Edit Binary Value window.

17. Close the Registry Editor by selecting Registry ➤ Exit.

Windows System Start

In this phase, the Win32 subsystem automatically starts the Windows logon process; it displays the logon screen, and allows the user to press Ctrl+Alt+Del to log on.

At the same time, the Service Controller looks through the Registry for services that are set to load automatically. It loads these services as well as the services they depend on.

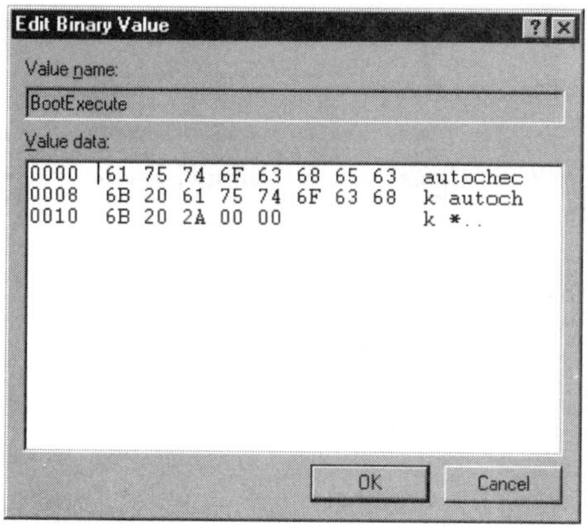

Boot Configuration

FIGURE 16.1
This Registry Editor Edit
Binary Value window
contains the text of the
BootExecute entry/

User Logon

The boot process is not complete until a user successfully logs on to the workstation. Once a user logs on, the Clone control set is copied to the LastKnownGood control set and the boot process is complete.

Boot Configuration

BOOT CONFIGURATION INFORMATION is stored in two places: in the BOOT.INI file and in the LastKnownGood key in the Registry. This section explains the meanings of the various entries and describes how to modify the settings to control the boot process.

BOOT.INI Entries

The BOOT.INI file is arranged like other INI files; each section begins with a section name in brackets and each of the entries following the section name. BOOT.INI has two sections:

- [boot loader]

- [operating systems]

Within each section is a list of entries; an equal sign and the entry's value follow each entry in the list. See Figure 16.2 for a view of a typical BOOT.INI file.

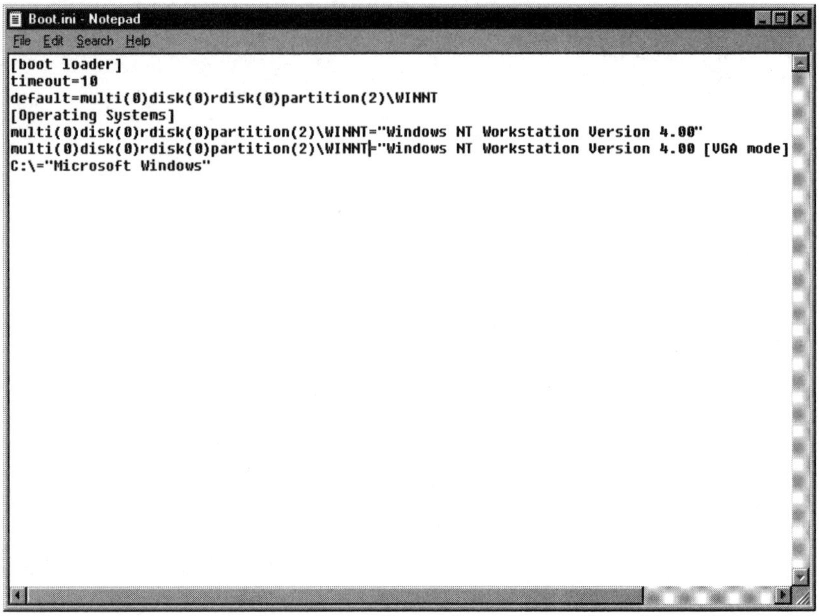

FIGURE 16.2

The BOOT.INI file has a section for the boot loader and a section for each of the operating systems that the boot loader can load.

```
Boot.ini - Notepad
File  Edit  Search  Help
[boot loader]
timeout=10
default=multi(0)disk(0)rdisk(0)partition(2)\WINNT
[Operating Systems]
multi(0)disk(0)rdisk(0)partition(2)\WINNT="Windows NT Workstation Version 4.00"
multi(0)disk(0)rdisk(0)partition(2)\WINNT="Windows NT Workstation Version 4.00 [VGA mode]
C:\="Microsoft Windows"
```

[boot loader]

The boot loader section contains information about the operation of the boot loader itself. Specifically, it contains the timeout (in seconds) before the default operating system is loaded, and it contains the path to the default operating system to load.

```
timeout=30
```

The timeout statement specifies the time in seconds that the boot loader will wait before loading the default operating system. The default is 30 seconds.

```
default=multi(0)disk(0)rdisk(0)partition(2)\WINNT
```

The next statement specifies the path to the default operating system. The path must match one of the entries stored in the [operating systems] section discussed next.

[operating systems]

This section contains the path to each of the operating systems that the boot loader can load. Each entry in the BOOT.INI file will be displayed in the boot menu when the computer first starts up. The entry name (the part before the equal sign) describes the path to the operating system, using the ARC naming convention (described below, in the "ARC Naming Convention" section). The entry value section (the part after the equal sign) contains the text to display on the boot menu screen and the operating system load options. Two examples of entries in the [operating systems] section follow.

```
multi(0)disk(0)rdisk(0)partition(2)\WINNT="Windows NT
    Workstation Version 4.00" /SOS
```

This entry loads the Windows NT operating system from the second partition of the boot hard drive. The text entry in the boot menu identifies it as Windows NT, and the option to list the device drivers as they are loaded has been selected.

```
C:\="Microsoft Windows"
```

This entry instructs the boot loader to load the bootsect.dos file for the C: drive and pass execution to it, thereby resuming the normal DOS boot process instead of continuing with a Windows NT boot. The text to display on the boot menu screen is Microsoft Windows, and the boot process has no configuration options for the DOS boot process.

Configuration Options

You can use several configuration options to load NT. The boot options are as follows:

■ /NOSERIALMICE=[COMx|COMx,y,z…] allows you to disable the serial mouse detection on one, several, or all of the COM ports in your workstation. Sometimes the serial mouse detection on a COM port can cause a non-mouse serial device attached to that serial port to fail; this boot option circumvents that problem.

- /BASEVIDEO causes Windows NT to load in standard VGA mode. When you install NT, this NT boot option is one of two that are installed by default. This option is useful when your video settings are inappropriate for your monitor or video card, but you need to boot NT to change the settings.

- /CRASHDEBUG enables the automatic recovery and restart features of Windows NT. (These features can also be set from the Control Panel.)

- /SOS displays the names of the device drivers as they are loaded during the boot process.

- /NODEBUG causes debugging information not to be monitored. This option may give the operating system a slight performance enhancement in an environment where debugging information is not needed, such as with unsophisticated users of Windows NT.

- /MAXMEM:n limits the amount of memory that Windows NT will use.

- /SCSIORDINAL:n selects which SCSI controller will be used to boot the operating system when two identical controllers are in the computer.

ARC Naming Conventions

In the [boot loader] section and in the [operating systems] section outlined previously, the path to the Windows NT operating system appeared in several places. That path has a structure, and each part of the path has significance to the boot loader. The ARC naming conventions describe the meanings of each of the parts of the path. The parts of the path are as follows:

- scsi(n) or multi(n) indicates the type of device that the operating system is on. SCSI is used only if the hard disk drive is connected to a SCSI adapter that does not include a SCSI BIOS. All other disk drives, including SCSI with a BIOS, IDE, and EIDE use multi. The (n), in which *n* is replaced with a number, indicates which hardware adapter to boot from.

- disk(n) indicates which SCSI bus number is to be used. If the adapter is a multi-adapter, the *n* is always zero.

- rdisk(n) indicates the SCSI LUN number or selects which of the disks attached to the adapter is the disk with the operating system.

- `partition(n)` selects which partition on the disk contains the operating system files.

- `\path` indicates the directory on the partition that contains the operating system files. The default path is `\Winnt`.

Viewing and Editing `BOOT.INI`

You can view and modify the information contained in the `BOOT.INI` file in several ways. The safest way to do so is through the Control Panel. If the boot configuration is incorrect, you can use the LastKnownGood boot option to use a boot configuration that worked before. Finally, you can edit `BOOT.INI` with a text editor to change the settings directly.

Using the System Option in the Control Panel

The System option in the Control Panel (described in Chapter 4) provides a safe way for you to change some of the boot options of Windows NT. In particular, System allows you to set the delay before the default boot selection is automatically started, and it allows you to choose the default boot selection.

Using the LastKnownGood Boot Option

If the boot configuration for Windows NT is incorrect, Windows NT may fail to load properly. You can use the LastKnownGood boot option to use a boot configuration that worked previously.

After you select an operating system to boot from the boot menu, a message will appear on the workstation screen saying that you can press the space bar to use the LastKnownGood configuration. This option appears only for a few seconds, so you must be ready to press the space bar as soon as it appears.

Editing `BOOT.INI` with a Text Editor

You can edit `BOOT.INI` with a text editor such as Notepad or `EDIT.COM`. You cannot modify the file, however, until you disable the file's read-only attribute. After you save an updated version of the file to the root directory of the boot drive, be sure to reenable the read-only attribute. Exercise 16.3 shows you how to edit the BOOT.INI file with a text editor.

EXERCISE 16.3

Edit the BOOT.INI **File**

1. Logon as an administrator.

2. Open the My Computer icon on the desktop.

3. Open the icon corresponding to the boot drive on your computer (most likely the C: drive).

4. Select view ➤ Options if the BOOT.INI file is not visible anywhere in the window. Then select the View tab ➤ Show All Files. Click OK to continue.

5. Find the BOOT.INI file and then select it.

6. Select Properties from the File menu (a BOOT.INI Properties window will appear).

7. Remove the check marks for Read-Only and Hidden if they are present.

8. Select OK.

9. Open the BOOT.INI file.

10. Find the entry in [operating systems] that you select or that is selected by default when you boot Windows NT on your computer.

11. Edit the menu text portion of the entry to reflect your name or your organization's name. For example, you could edit this boot selection **multi(0)disk(0)rdisk(0)partition(2)\WINNT="Windows NT Workstation Version 4.00"/SOS** to read instead **multi(0)disk(0)rdisk(0)partition(2)\WINNT="NT boot for Charles"/SOS**.

12. Save the BOOT.INI file and exit the editor program.

13. Select the BOOT.INI icon from the File menu, select Properties, and then check the Read-Only option. Click OK.

14. Restart your computer and observe that the text of the boot menu option has changed.

Be careful when you edit the BOOT.INI *file directly. You can cause Windows NT to fail to boot by modifying the file incorrectly. You should create a boot disk and an emergency repair disk (see Chapter 17 for information about boot disks and emergency repair disks) before you attempt to modify the* BOOT.INI *file.*

Booting Several Operating Systems (Multiboot)

YOU CAN INSTALL SEVERAL DIFFERENT operating systems on your computer and use the Windows NT boot loader to select which operating system you wish to boot at boot time. When you install Windows NT, it creates a boot menu with at least two operating system options. As you install operating systems on your computer, the new boot menu options are added to the menu automatically. (If you prefer, you can edit the BOOT.INI file to ask you whether to load new operating systems.)

Two new boot menu options are added to the BOOT.INI file every time you install Windows NT in a directory different from any previous installations (rather than upgrade Windows NT). The first new boot menu option loads the newly installed operating system with the working settings (screen size, drivers loaded, etc.). The second new boot menu option loads the operating system with basic VGA settings (640x480x16 resolution).

If you installed Windows NT on a computer that already had DOS or Windows installed and you did not overwrite the preexisting Windows directory, then you already have a multiboot setup. The third boot menu option presented is either DOS or Windows 95. Selecting that option will boot your computer to DOS or Windows 95 instead of booting it to Windows NT.

To create a computer environment in which you can boot either Windows NT Workstation or Windows NT server, first install one operating system (it doesn't matter which one) and then install the other. When you are asked if you wish to upgrade the current operating system or to install a new one, choose to install to a different directory. When you are done with the installation, the boot menu will have four Windows NT boot menu options—one each for conventional booting and one each for booting into basic VGA mode. In addition, you may have the option of booting to DOS or Windows.

You can edit the BOOT.INI file (in the same manner as explained earlier in this chapter) to add and remove operating system boot menu options.

Some other operating systems also come with boot managers. OS/2, for instance, comes with a boot manager that allows you to select between OS/2 and MS-DOS or Windows. Installing Windows NT on your computer will disable the OS/2 boot manager. It will also disable many other boot managers. You can reenable the OS/2 boot manager from the Windows NT partition manager by making the small partition that contains the OS/2 boot manager the active partition. When you start your computer, you are first presented with the OS/2 boot manager; then if you pick DOS or Windows, you are presented with the Windows NT boot loader. At this point you can pick Windows NT.

When you remove an operating system from your computer, you may need to edit the BOOT.INI file to remove the corresponding entry in the boot menu. Otherwise, you would have a boot menu option that would not load an operating system. (If you subsequently selected that menu choice, you would see one of the boot loader error messages described in the next chapter, "Troubleshooting.")

Chapter Summary

A COMPUTER POWERS UP with only a BIOS or ROM firmware to provide instructions for the microprocessor, but user programs cannot run without an operating system. Every computer goes through a boot process to load the operating system.

In a PC compatible computer, the BIOS loads the master boot record of the booting hard disk, which then loads the boot record of the booting partition, which then loads the boot loader, which then loads the operating system. In a RISC-based computer, the firmware finds a bootable drive and partition. The firmware then finds the boot loader in the file system on the partition, which, in turn, loads the operating system.

Once the kernel of the operating system is loaded, the operating system goes through five load phases.

1. Kernel loads the HAL and some drivers and services.

2. Kernel initializes itself and the drivers and services it loaded in step 1. Drivers and services may report error conditions that can cause error messages to be displayed to the user or cause the boot process to restart or even fail.

3. Session Manager starts, checks the file systems, sets up paging, and loads the Win32 subsystem.

4. Win32 subsystem starts up and starts the Winlogon process.

5. User successfully logs on, and the boot process is complete.

You can change the way Windows NT boots by changing entries in the System part of the Control Panel or by editing the BOOT.INI file on the hard drive. The BOOT.INI has two parts: [boot loader], which allows you to change the boot timeout and the default boot entry, and [operating systems], which contains an entry for each of the operating systems that the Windows NT boot loader can load. The first part of each operating system entry is an ARC path to the operating system. The second part is the text that will be displayed in the boot menu when the computer starts. The boot options for the boot loader and for the operating system for that boot option follow.

When Windows NT boots successfully (a user logs on), the current boot configuration is written to the LastKnownGood entry in the Windows NT Registry. During the boot process, you can instruct Windows NT to use the LastKnown-Good configuration instead of the current configuration. Windows NT will restart the boot process itself and select the LastKnownGood configuration if it detects a severe or critical error during the boot process.

Exercise Questions

1. BIOS stands for built-in operating system and refers to the operating system that is present in the computer when it is turned on.

   A. True

   B. False

2. ROM costs much less per megabyte than hard disk storage costs.

   A. True

   B. False

3. The BIOS provides an operating system with routines to access the computer's hardware.

   A. True

   B. False

4. The primary function of the BIOS, after it initializes the computer's hardware, is to find an operating system and then load it.

   A. True

   B. False

5. The BIOS does not know anything about file systems.

   A. True

   B. False

6. PC compatible computers reserve the first block of a hard disk for the hard disk directory.

   A. True

   B. False

7. The Windows NT boot loader allows you to select from several operating systems to boot.

   A. True

   B. False

8. Intel-based and RISC-based computers use NTLDR to load the Windows NT operating system.

    A. True

    B. False

9. The boot loader uses BOOTSECT.DOS when you boot Windows NT.

    A. True

    B. False

10. NTBOOTDD.SYS is used only when your workstation is booting an NT operating system residing on a SCSI partition that is connected to a SCSI controller without a SCSI BIOS.

    A. True

    B. False

11. NTOSKRNL.EXE is the Windows NT kernel on RISC-based computers.

    A. True

    B. False

12. The firmware on a RISC-based computer contains much of the functionality that is found in other programs on an Intel-based computer.

    A. True

    B. False

13. The boot process loads all drivers and services during the kernel load phase.

    A. True

    B. False

14. If the operating system path in the BOOT.INI file points to an operating system on a SCSI disk drive, the path will start with SCSI instead of multi.

    A. True

    B. False

15. The process of finding, loading, and initializing the operating system is called _____.

16. The microprocessor and the RAM are _____, which means that they loose any information stored in them whenever power is turned off.

17. IBM PC compatible computers call the program stored in the ROM the _____.

18. The operating system-imposed arrangement of data on a disk is called a _____ _____.

19. In the _____ _____ phase, the HAL is loaded.

20. The _____ _____ phase initializes the drivers and services loaded during the kernel load phase.

21. The Session Manager is started in the _____ _____ phase.

22. The Win32 subsystem starts the windows logon process in the _____ _____ _____ phase.

23. The phase in which the user logs on is called the _____ _____ phase.

24. The boot loader timeout value is stored in the [_____ _____] section of the BOOT.INI file.

25. Each operating system has an entry in the [_____ _____] section of the BOOT.INI file.

26. The _____ boot option will cause Windows NT to load in standard VGA mode.

27. The _____ boot option will cause the names of the device drivers to be displayed as they are loaded.

28. The _____ _____ conventions describe the meaning of each part of the path to the operating system in the BOOT.INI file.

29. If the boot configuration is incorrect, you can use the _____ boot option to implement a boot configuration that worked before.

Troubleshooting

COMPUTERS ARE INCREDIBLY complicated devices. Computer software is even more complex than computer hardware, and operating systems are the most sophisticated pieces of software that programmers can create. Making such complex and sophisticated things foolproof is virtually impossible, so although NT is as robust an operating system as you will encounter, you will occasionally need to fix problems with the operating system, its installation, or the hardware it runs on.

Troubleshooting is a skill like any other. You can apply certain general principles to any troubleshooting situation, but you must know how the specific system you are troubleshooting works if you want to be able to diagnose faults. As with any other skill, you get better at troubleshooting with practice.

This chapter introduces you to some general computer-troubleshooting principles and then shows you how to troubleshoot computer hardware and the Windows NT operating system software.

Principles of Troubleshooting

TROUBLESHOOTING IS THE METHODICAL PROCESS of eliminating faults from a system. Although troubleshooting a computer is difficult, you can quickly isolate the fault by following a few basic rules that allow you to focus your troubleshooting efforts on the components that are most likely at fault.

Troubleshooting a computer involves changing the hardware or software configuration of different components and then testing to see whether the configuration change has eliminated the fault.

If a hardware failure caused the fault, you will have to find and replace the failed component. If a software configuration caused the fault, you will have to reconfigure your system to eliminate the fault. You might not always be able to reconfigure your system; for example, reconfiguring the faulty component could mean the denial of some service that is required to reconfigure that component. If you run into this Catch 22, you will have to reinstall the operating system.

Working on electronic devices like computers can be dangerous. You should only attempt to troubleshoot a computer if you are very familiar with electrical safety, electronic equipment, and computer hardware.

Microsoft has done a thorough job of debugging Windows NT software. However, bugs exist in all nontrivial software, especially in the less frequently used areas. Nonetheless, Windows NT runs, and it runs well. All of its services operate properly. If you have a persistent problem with a Windows NT server, the cause of the problem may be less-than-compatible hardware or improperly configured software. Bugs are most likely to exist in rarely executed code.

Windows NT is very specific about which hardware it will work with. Early in NT's design cycle, Microsoft chose not to support all hardware devices that can be added to a PC because of the security holes DOS mode drivers allow—and because Microsoft could not possibly write drivers for all the PC compatible hardware that exists. If you are having a problem with a new Windows NT installation, chances are good that you are using hardware that does not appear on the Windows NT Hardware Compatibility List (HCL).

Bugs are more likely the fault of a third-party driver than of Windows NT standard components. Consider these drivers primary suspects when troubleshooting.

Focus is important in troubleshooting. Making changes randomly in a system, hoping something will work, is a good way to waste a lot of time and to create more problems with untracked changes. Focus on a specific component. Test it thoroughly. If you are not able to correct the fault, restore the original configuration before moving on to another component.

Troubleshooting is relatively easy when you are dealing with only one fault, as is generally the case with a hardware failure. Software failures, however, are usually a lot more complicated. You may face a situation in which two or more simultaneous problems are causing a fault. Correcting only one fault at a time will change the symptoms, but will not correct the problem. For instance, suppose your modem doesn't work. You have a hardware conflict because your modem is set to the same IRQ as your LAN adapter, which caused your modem software to automatically detect the wrong modem. You will have two problems (a hardware setting and a software configuration) to fix before you can operate your modem. Correcting one or the other problem will not allow you to use your modem.

Rotating between symptoms is usually a sign that more than one problem is present in the system.

Troubleshooting is either quick and easy, as in the case of a simple failure when you are pretty certain what is wrong, or long and complex, for example, when you return to work to find a computer that went down during the night and refuses to reboot. Often you will have to resolve one fault before you can progress to the next fault. This sequence is the natural cycle of troubleshooting.

Partial success usually indicates a complex failure involving two or more faults.

The rest of this section covers the general principles of troubleshooting that apply to any system. Following these guidelines will help you quickly determine what is at fault in your system. However, no book or set of rules will really help you find a problem unless you understand the system you are troubleshooting. That's why we put this section at the end of the book. We hope that by performing the exercises and taking the tests in the first 16 chapters you've gained the requisite knowledge to effectively troubleshoot Windows NT Workstation 4.0.

New Computers

The troubleshooting procedures presented here presume that the computer you are troubleshooting has operated correctly under Windows NT in the past. Troubleshooting a newly built computer is beyond the scope of this book.

If you are building a computer from scratch, save yourself a lot of time by getting it to work correctly under MS-DOS or Windows 95 before trying to install Windows NT. Better yet, save yourself even more time by buying a complete computer with Windows NT factory installed. If you can't buy Windows NT preinstalled, check the Microsoft Web site (www.microsoft.com) for computers listed on the Windows NT hardware compatibility list. Microsoft has certified that these computers will run Windows NT properly.

Microsoft will not certify individual components for use with Windows NT—it certifies complete computers only. Therefore, you can't be sure that all your hardware will work correctly under Windows NT if you have your computer custom built. For these reasons, even the most experienced PC technician should think twice before building a Windows NT machine from components.

If you are determined to build your own computer, study the Windows NT knowledge base on the Microsoft Web site so that you can avoid buying hardware that is known to cause problems under Windows NT. Pay special attention to the specific type of SCSI adapter and motherboard you purchase.

New Windows NT Installations

Make absolutely certain you don't have any interrupt, DMA channel, or memory port conflicts before attempting a Windows NT installation. Many Windows NT drivers do not allow interrupt sharing, which DOS uses in serial ports and can be set up under many PCI motherboard BIOS settings. Modems and sound cards are especially likely to share interrupts under less sophisticated operating systems like MS-DOS or Windows 95.

If you have a hardware conflict, turn off PCI Plug-and-Play compatibility, if your BIOS allows it, and manually assign interrupt settings to hardware. Record these settings so you know what they are. Remove any hardware that is not necessary for the operation of the computer, such as modems, sound cards, and (if possible) your network adapter. This step reduces possible sources of conflict when you install Windows NT. You can add these components one at a time to be certain they are configured correctly once the operating system is running.

If you are using SCSI devices, be aware that many common SCSI adapters have compatibility issues running under Windows NT. Check the Windows NT knowledge base using the search key "SCSI Adapters" for a run down of the compatibility issues of certain controllers. Also, the NT loader can have a hard time finding your boot drive if you have an active IDE bus and SCSI devices set on ID 0 with some SCSI controllers.

Axioms of Troubleshooting

Finding the component at fault is the primary purpose of troubleshooting. Once you know exactly what is wrong, fixing the problem is usually trivial. We've compiled a list of axioms for general troubleshooting that will help you quickly isolate and repair hardware and software faults in Windows NT.

- Be patient.

- Know the system.

- Isolate the fault.

- Check the most recent change.

- Check the most common failure point.

- Check things that have failed before.

- Perform easy tests first.

- Make assumptions to guide your troubleshooting.

- Use what you know.

- Change only one setting at a time.

- Track the changes you make.

- Try to make transient failures repeatable.

- Try to isolate individual faults in multiple fault malfunctions.

- Resort to permanent changes last.

Be Patient

Patience is not just a virtue when troubleshooting; it's an absolute necessity. If you are under pressure to get a system working, you are better off using another computer if possible. If you can't, you will just have to forget about your deadline because rushing through the troubleshooting process usually doesn't work. You will save yourself more time in the long run by taking the time now to troubleshoot properly, rather than by frustrating yourself with rushed efforts that don't work and may introduce additional faults. Most troubleshooting efforts will take hours.

Know the System

You can't troubleshoot unless you know your system. Troubleshooting is the process of diagnosing symptoms, postulating causes, and testing your hunch by making configuration changes. If you don't understand the symptoms you see, the rest of the troubleshooting process breaks down, and you will be unable to make a reasonable diagnosis.

If you are reading this chapter first because you have a Windows NT computer that isn't working, you should turn back to page one and start reading there. The knowledge you gain about the inner workings of NT from the rest of this book will help you diagnose your problem.

Isolate the Fault

The fastest way to determine fault in a malfunctioning computer is to remove what you know works from the list of suspect components. Narrowing your search will help you focus on components that could be at fault and keep you from making changes in other working portions of the system. For instance, if you can reliably see information on the screen, most of the hardware in your computer is working properly. You can eliminate the processor, motherboard, RAM, video card, and monitor from your list of suspect components.

In many cases, you will be able to isolate a component quickly by validating many components at a time. For instance, a computer that boots completely probably does not have any failed hardware components.

Check the Most Recent Change

If you've just changed something and your computer no longer works properly, it doesn't take a rocket scientist to figure out that the most recent change caused the problem (or exacerbated an existing unexpressed problem). This logic would normally go without saying, but when you are frustrated by a malfunctioning computer, it's easy to forget.

In addition, a fault might not show up immediately, and you may have to think about what you changed last. Or someone else might have changed something on the computer that you are not aware of.

Users sometimes break something accidentally when they try to make a change to their system and then pretend not to know what is wrong to avoid embarrassment or liability. You should try to foster an environment that encourages users to come clean with this information because ultimately you will spend a lot more time trying to get to the bottom of a fault if you don't know the history of the machine.

Here are some suggestions to facilitate troubleshooting in a corporate environment.

- Implement security on workstations to prevent users from being able to incorrectly configure a system.

- Try to change policies that hold your coworkers liable in some way for accidental damage to a computer, or they will never help you trouble-shoot anything.

- Make sure that the person who signs the checks understands that your ability to work quickly will save the company money.

Check the Most Common Failure Point

Checking the most common failure point is a rather obvious point, but it is an important axiom in troubleshooting. Hard disks have become very reliable lately, but they are still the third most-likely-to-fail component in a computer, after the monitor and the floppy disk drive. Unlike monitors and floppy disk drives, a crashed hard disk will probably make your computer useless. Hard disks are also complicated enough that the failure might not be obvious. A hard disk fault can also be a software problem that looks like a hardware problem.

Connectors and cables are also common failure points. Cables inside computers can become loose if a computer is moved or subject to vibration. PCI bus card edge connectors are very sensitive to movement compared to ISA bus cards, and single in-line memory modules can also come loose easily. Check all these components when you have a mysterious hardware failure that keeps your computer from booting.

Peripherals that rely on jumpers for option settings are susceptible to loose jumpers. Check to make sure no jumpers are missing and that they are firmly seated in their correct positions if you suspect a component is faulty.

Check Things That Have Failed Before

If you have a component that has failed or disconnected in the past, chances are it will do so again. If you are experiencing the same sort of failure symptoms as you have in the past, the first thing to check is a component that has a history of failure.

If you find that a recently replaced component has failed again, some other component may be causing that component to fail.

Perform Easy Tests First

If you don't have any idea what might be wrong, you should start by checking components that are easy to test. The easiest way to accomplish this process is to have a known working computer configured similarly. You can swap easily removable components between the two computers to see if the fault moves with a component.

Check BIOS settings if you have a problem with any hardware embedded on the motherboard.

You should perform quick software reconfigurations before resorting to more lengthy or sweeping changes like reinstalling the operating system or swapping out a hard disk.

Make Assumptions to Guide Your Troubleshooting

When troubleshooting, you will refine or redefine your initial diagnosis as you work. This diagnosis will lead in the direction of failed components. For instance, if your computer boots but does not come up on the network, you can assume that (1) the network software is configured incorrectly, (2) another piece of hardware conflicts with that network adapter, (3) the network adapter has failed, (4) the network adapter cannot reach the network because of a cable fault, or (5) the server is down and not responding.

Use What You Know

You might know the events that precipitated a failure without realizing it. For example, in the network scenario described above, you can use your knowledge of the computer's environment to guide your troubleshooting.

- If the computer used to work fine on the LAN but stopped networking after a new sound card was installed, the LAN adapter and the sound card might be in conflict.

- If the computer stopped networking after a recent remodel, perhaps a cable was broken or unplugged during the construction.

- If a network administrator has been reading this book and performing the exercises, the networking software might no longer be configured correctly for your network.

Change Only One Setting at a Time

This axiom is very important. Often, especially with software configuration troubleshooting, you are tempted to try something, see if it works, then try something else, and see if that works. Unfortunately, this haphazard process causes you to unwittingly change configuration information that may, in turn, produce another fault. You can easily and inadvertently introduce a new fault while you are fixing the original fault.

Each time you make a change, restore the original settings—if the change didn't correct your problem—*before* continuing to your next test.

Track the Changes You Make

Write down each change you make in a *change log*. Be sure to keep track of the multiple changes you implement simultaneously in an effort to solve a complex problem. A change log also allows you to update the computer configuration report you keep on all your computers.

Try to Make Transient Failures Repeatable

Transient failures indicate either an environmental variable failure, such as a loose connection, or conflicting software that causes the faulty condition when certain states occur.

If you suspect an environmental fault, try to exacerbate the condition to make the fault stable. If you suspect a software fault, try stopping services and unloading running applications until the fault disappears. Then begin restarting services until you can get the fault to reappear.

Try to Isolate Individual Faults in Multiple-Fault Malfunctions

Unusual symptoms (those you don't see in this chapter) usually occur because more than one fault is present. To get a computer up in a multiple-fault malfunction, you may have to correct the faults simultaneously if the faulty components depend on each other. This domino effect makes troubleshooting exponentially more difficult. If you can isolate a fault by removing a hardware component or stopping a software service that allows you to identify one of the factors in the malfunction, you will be able to concentrate on that factor until it works correctly.

If you cannot isolate an individual fault in a multiple-fault situation, you should start with the basic troubleshooting procedures of validating the proper performance of your hardware and then reducing the complexity of your software by stopping unnecessary services and unloading software that is running. This process reduces the complexity of the environment and narrows down the list of suspect components. When you have reduced the software environment to the minimum level required to operate, reintroduce components—one at a time—until the fault reappears.

Resort to Permanent Changes Last

Permanent changes, such as replacing hard disk drives, reinstalling the operating system, or deleting files should be your last resort. All of these repairs will take a long time to implement and will reset your security permissions, shares, and network names. Be certain that you are replacing the component at fault before making these drastic repairs.

Troubleshooting Computer Hardware

N ORDER FOR YOUR SOFTWARE to run correctly, the hardware in your computer must be operating correctly. Whenever a hardware component is possibly at fault in a malfunctioning computer, you should validate its correct operation before attempting to correct software faults.

The few simple troubleshooting techniques presented here help you isolate common hardware problems quickly. These techniques are not all inclusive, nor do they in any way replace the general techniques presented in the previous section. These techniques are simply the culmination of a great deal of troubleshooting experience.

Night of the Living DOS

Windows NT requires a completely functional hardware and software environment just to boot. Windows NT probes hardware and exercises the entire system as it comes online. Consequently, any number of faults will prevent Windows NT from starting at all. Simpler operating systems, like MS-DOS, can operate on a computer that is significantly degraded. A floppy disk that boots a simple operating system can be an invaluable troubleshooting tool.

In addition, quite a few DOS-based hardware validation tools are available. You can use these tools to inspect hardware, check for hardware conflicts, and validate the proper operation of a number of computer components. You can run these tools from a floppy disk on a system that doesn't boot Windows NT at all.

Remember, however, that MS-DOS will not have access to NTFS file system partitions. The DOS partition and format tools will not be able to modify an NTFS partition. Because NTFS creates partitions in larger boundaries than the FAT file system, you are likely to find 1 or 2MB of free space after the end of an NTFS partition that you can partition and format for MS-DOS. You can use this area to verify the physical operation of a hard disk drive by checking to see if you can read and write to it. You can also store MS-DOS utilities and Plug-and-Play software configuration tools for the hardware in your computer.

Finding Hardware Faults

The following is a short list of components to consider suspect under a range of troubleshooting issues. Check these in order to progressively narrow your search. Remember that complex faults (those involving more than one specific failure) may not fit into any one category. Also, many software problems can look like hardware faults until you test the component under a different operating system like MS-DOS.

Power

If nothing happens when you turn the computer on, check the power cords and switches. Even in the worst failure situation, you should at least hear the fan spinning in the power supply. If you hear the fan in the power supply, check to see if the microprocessor fan is spinning. If it is, you probably don't have a power supply problem. See if you can hear hard disks spinning.

Never install or remove anything while your computer is powered on. Dropping a screw onto a powered motherboard will probably destroy it and some of your peripheral cards.

Motherboard, Processor, RAM, and Video

The computer's motherboard, processor, RAM, and video adapter must all be operating correctly for the computer to complete the power on self-test (POST) performed by the BIOS each time you turn it on. If after turning on your computer you see the normal boot screen, these components are probably all working correctly. If they are not, you may hear a few beeps (POST codes) or there may be no activity at all. Some computers can operate with a bit of failed RAM. These computers will either display an error message while testing RAM or will not count up to the entire compliment of memory.

If you suspect a problem with any of these components, remove and reseat the video card and memory modules. Processor failures are very rare. The only way to test for a processor failure is to swap in a known good processor of the same brand, model, and speed rating. Motherboard failures are also rare and very difficult to validate. Verifying the processor, RAM, and video adapter in another computer of exactly the same make is usually easier than swapping out the motherboard.

BIOS Configuration Problems

Many computers allow you to set the BIOS information incorrectly. The BIOS determines such critical parameters as how fast the computer can access its RAM memory, what type of hard disk drive is attached, and how interrupts are assigned to PCI slots. Incorrectly configuring your BIOS can very likely degrade its performance or keep it from working at all.

If you don't understand a BIOS setting's purpose, don't change it without recording its present value so you can change it back.

When you suspect a hardware conflict or a problem with the video, memory, processor, or the motherboard, check your BIOS parameter settings before you replace anything. The manual that came with your computer or motherboard should show the proper settings for your computer. If it does not, check with the manufacturer's technical support.

Failing all else, you can usually use a "BIOS default settings" option to get your computer working, although generally at a lower-than-optimal speed. Use this setting to verify whether or not you are having a BIOS configuration problem and then tune parameters to increase the speed.

Hardware Conflicts

Hardware conflicts are by far the most common problem in PCs running any operating system. Hardware conflicts occur when two peripherals are configured to use the same interrupt, DMA channel, port address, or buffer memory. Windows NT is especially sensitive to hardware conflicts because it does not allow devices to share resources, as MS-DOS and Windows 95 do. For this reason, a computer that worked fine under MS-DOS or Windows 95 may malfunction under Windows NT.

You troubleshoot these problems by removing all peripheral cards that are not absolutely essential to boot the computer, such as modems, LAN adapters, sound cards, I/O controllers, secondary hard disk controllers, CD-ROM controllers, and any other peripheral cards except video and your primary (boot) hard disk controller.

If your computer goes through a normal start up process, reintroduce each peripheral card, starting with the secondary hard disk controller and adding each additional card in order of its importance to you. Power off the computer, install the card, and then check for a normal boot. If you have a diagnostic tool that will show you interrupt, DMA channel, and port assignments, use it to make sure a hardware conflict has not occurred. Repeat this process with each card until the problem reappears. When the problem reappears, the most recent card installed is either conflicting with an installed device, incorrectly configured, or has failed.

Hard Disk Controllers and Drives

Hard disk failures are the most damaging of all computer component failures because they contain the most recent set of all the data you store on your computer. Their loss means the loss of irreplaceable data. Hard disk problems fall into just a few categories:

- Power or connection problems
- Hardware configuration problems

- Failed mechanisms

- Failed hard disk controllers

- Bad sectors

- Corrupted boot sectors

- Corrupted partition tables

- Corrupted file systems

Symptoms and solutions for each of these problems appear in the following sections.

Backing up your data to other media, usually tape or magneto-optical disk, is the only way to recover completely from a total hard disk failure. If your data is important, you need to back it up daily.

POWER OR CONNECTION PROBLEMS Power or connection problems are easy to find. Check to make sure each hard disk drive is receiving power. If the hard disk is spinning, it is powered up correctly. On IDE drives, check to make sure the cables are securely and correctly installed. If you can't tell which way the cable should fit and the connector isn't keyed to prevent incorrect insertion, the side of the connector with two notches mates to the side of the hard disk port that has a notch in the center. Make sure the cable is attached to the motherboard/hard disk controller correctly by matching the red striped side of the cable to the pin labeled *1* on the circuit board.

SCSI is slightly more difficult. A SCSI bus must be properly terminated and the total cable length should be as short as possible. Proper SCSI termination is set when the devices at each end of the SCSI bus have termination enabled or a physical terminator is installed at the end of the bus. No device, including the controller card, should have termination enabled if it is not at the end of the SCSI bus. Often, one SCSI bus will have some internal components and some external components. In this case the last drive attached to the internal bus should be terminated, the SCSI controller should not be terminated, and the last device on the external bus should be terminated. Refer to your SCSI adapter manual for more information on SCSI termination.

HARDWARE CONFIGURATION PROBLEMS Drives can be incorrectly configured in ways that will prevent them from operating. Make sure that you don't have two devices on a SCSI bus with the same SCSI identification number. Make sure that you don't have two IDE devices both set to master or slave. If you have only one IDE device, you should set it to master. If you have an IDE CD-ROM and an IDE hard disk on the same bus, the CD-ROM should be set to slave.

Some SCSI drives must be set to have the SCSI controller issue a startup command before the disk will spin up. Make sure the controller is set to issue a startup command to these disks. If your controller can't issue startup commands, jumper the drive to start up at power on.

INCORRECT BIOS INFORMATION In the past you had to set the specific drive parameters for each hard disk in the BIOS so that operating systems knew how to partition and format the disk. Most modern controllers and motherboards are capable of automatically detecting hard disk geometry. Some computers have BIOS programs that are too old to recognize new large disks. In these cases you should upgrade to a hard disk controller that can recognize the full capacity of your disk.

Use the automatic hard disk geometry detection setting if it is available.

Many IDE and SCSI disks provide sector translation so that operating systems with a 1,024 cylinder limit can access an entire large disk. You may need to turn on this feature to complete the MS-DOS portion of the Windows NT installation if your primary disk has more than 1,024 cylinders. Once you turn on sector translation, it must remain enabled for that drive.

FAILED MECHANISMS A failed mechanism is the worst hard disk problem that you can have. A hard disk spindle or head assembly that physically breaks is the cause of this problem. Unfortunately, you cannot recover from this situation, and you will lose the data on that hard disk.

Because you cannot prevent hard disk failures, you should back up regularly to another mass storage device to keep from losing your data.

Strange noises coming from your hard disk signal this fault. If your disk is "knocking" when you try to access it or if you hear strange grinding or scraping noises, it is usually too late. Sometimes the disk will bind and fail to spin at all. This symptom can make a physical disk failure seem like a power problem.

FAILED HARD DISK CONTROLLERS Hard disk controllers rarely fail, but they can conflict with other devices in your computer. Check these cards the same way you would check any other hardware conflict. If you seem to have no access whatsoever to your hard disk, or if during the BIOS phase of the boot process your computer tells you that you have a hard disk controller failure, check the seating and settings of your hard disk controller. Swap it with another hard disk of the same type if necessary. If your hard disk controller is embedded on your motherboard, disable it and install a peripheral card hard disk controller set to the same interrupt, port, and DMA channel.

BAD SECTORS Bad sectors are a fact of life in hard disks. As hard disks age, they gradually lose their ability to store information. This gradual loss shows up as bad sectors. Hard disks typically ship from the factory with bad sectors, so all operating systems are capable of marking sectors bad. Sectors will usually fail on a write operation rather than a read operation, so the NTFS hot-fixing feature described in Chapter 5 will usually keep you from having to worry about them.

When many sectors fail suddenly, you are about to experience a failed hard disk mechanism. The unexplained loss of hard disk space during the normal operation of Windows NT, as NTFS marks more and more sectors out of use, signals this failure. You may also experience unrecoverable read errors. Transfer data off the disk as soon as possible and replace the hard disk.

CORRUPTED BOOT SECTORS Corrupted boot sectors can occur during a file system installation when a power fluctuation interrupts the computer. Sometimes the cause is the installation of another operating system over Windows NT. You can correct this problem by using the MS-DOS fdisk utility and issuing the following command at the C:\> prompt:

fdisk /mbr

The /mbr switch tells fdisk to write a new master boot record to the hard disk. You may also see this problem if you turn off sector translation in the BIOS of your hard disk controller. Try changing the sector translation setting before issuing the fdisk command. If you are unable to correct the problem by changing sector translation, change the translation setting back to its original setting and issue the fdisk /mbr command.

This command will not have an adverse effect on your system—even if it doesn't correct the problem—unless you have sector translation in a different state than when the disk was originally formatted.

CORRUPTED PARTITION TABLES Corrupted partition tables usually do not happen unless you have tried to use a different operating system to set a partition on your hard disk that is not compatible with the IBM/Microsoft partitioning scheme. Some UNIX operating systems fall into this category. Unfortunately, this problem will probably result in a data loss.

If you have not written anything to the disk since the partition problem occurred and you know how your disks were partitioned before this problem occurred, you may be able to set the partition tables exactly as they were and recover the data on your hard disks. Probably, though, you will have to create new partitions, format the partitions, and reinstall Windows NT if you have this problem.

CORRUPTED FILE SYSTEMS NTFS has a number of built-in mechanisms to keep it from becoming corrupt. However, some problems, especially hardware configuration, can cause NTFS to become corrupted. NTFS will check for hard disk corruption each time you reboot your computer.

FAT file system volumes are very likely to become corrupt over time with normal usage. You should use the Microsoft Scandisk utility frequently, at least once a month, to detect and correct file system corruption.

VIRUSES Viruses are insidious programs that intentionally cause computer malfunctions and are capable of self-replicating among computers that share media. These programs can look like any sort of real malfunction. They may advertise their presence on your machine through some sort of message, usually during boot time.

So far no Windows NT viruses have appeared because the security permissions structure of Windows NT prevents User mode programs from writing to system files.

However, a boot sector virus may exist on your disk if you used an operating system older than Windows NT, such as MS-DOS, on that computer. If you have any reason to suspect a virus infestation, run one of the many available virus detection software kits under MS-DOS to detect and eliminate the virus.

Troubleshooting the Windows NT Boot Process

AFTER YOU HAVE DETERMINED that the computer hardware is operating properly, you must be sure that Windows NT is being loaded correctly. The previous chapter ("Booting Windows NT") described the booting process. This section will show you some of the boot sequence errors and what they mean, teach you how to diagnose BOOT.INI problems, and explain how to use Windows NT boot disks and emergency repair disks to repair the Windows NT boot process.

Boot Sequence Errors

The boot sequence, as described in Chapter 16, is a complicated process. If one of the boot components is damaged or removed or if your BOOT.INI file is incorrectly configured, you may see one of the following messages (in which case you need to use a boot disk or an emergency repair disk to fix the boot sequence).

- The following message indicates that the NTLDR file is missing or corrupt:

    ```
    BOOT: Couldn't find NTLDR
    Please insert another disk
    ```

- If this message repeats after you have selected the Windows NT operating system on the boot menu, then NTDETECT.COM is damaged or missing:

    ```
    NTDETECT V1.0 Checking Hardware ...
    NTDETECT V1.0 Checking Hardware ...
    ```

- The following message indicates that the Windows NT operating system is damaged or missing, that the BOOT.INI file is missing and that Windows NT was installed in a directory other than \WINNT, or that BOOT.INI directs the operating system loader to a location that does not contain a valid NTOSKRNL.EXE:

    ```
    Windows NT could not start because the following file is
    missing or corrupt:
    \<winnt root>\system32\ntoskrnl.exe
    Please re-install a copy of the above file.
    ```

    The problem can occur when you partition free space on your hard disk if the partition number that contains Windows NT changes. Edit the BOOT.INI file to reflect the new partition number for the partition that contains Windows NT.

- The following message indicates that the boot sector is missing or corrupt:

    ```
    I/O Error accessing boot sector file
    multi(0)disk(0)rdisk(0)partition(1):\bootsect.dos
    ```

- The next message indicates that the Windows NT entry in `BOOT.INI` points to a missing or malfunctioning device or to a disk partition that does not contain a file system recognized by the Windows NT boot loader:

```
OS Loader V4.00
Windows NT could not start because of a computer disk
hardware configuration problem.
Could not read from the selected boot disk. Check boot
path and disk hardware.
Please check the Windows NT™ documentation about hardware
disk configuration and your hardware reference manuals
for additional information.
```

- This error occurs when the NT loader cannot access the hard disk upon which your Windows NT partition is stored or when NT loader is confused about which hard disk controller to consider the primary device:

```
STOP: 0x000007E: Inaccessible Boot Device
```

Because a number of SCSI adapters do not conform to the complete SCSI standard, they may cause this problem. If you have just added a SCSI controller to a Windows NT computer that boots from an IDE hard disk, make sure that no SCSI device is set to id 0 (or otherwise disable bootable SCSI hard disks). This setting will prevent the SCSI controller from attempting to boot the disk and will prevent the NT DETECT portion of the boot loader from assigning the SCSI adapter a bus number of zero, thereby causing `BOOT.INI` to refer to the wrong partition.

The STOP message is also heralded by the (in)famous "blue screen" of Windows NT crash fame. These screens indicate a serious failure from which Windows NT cannot recover. Blue screen problems are usually related to I/O, and the bug that crashed the computer probably resides in a driver. If you have a problem with a STOP message blue screen, log on to the Windows NT knowledge base and use search key "STOP:" to find the bugs that Microsoft knows how to correct.

The Windows NT Boot Disk

Your Windows NT Workstation will normally boot from a hard disk drive. You may have installed NT into the boot partition of your hard drive, in which case the boot files and the operating system all reside in the same volume, or you may have installed Windows NT on another partition, in which case the boot files will reside in the boot partition separate from the operating system.

A third boot configuration is possible for Windows NT. You can create a floppy boot disk that contains the boot files necessary to start the Windows NT operating system. Booting from a floppy is slower than booting from a hard disk, but a floppy boot disk can be very useful when your computer is not booting properly. Exercise 17.1 will walk you through the steps of creating a boot floppy.

EXERCISE 17.1

Creating a Windows NT Boot Floppy

1. Open My Computer and select the floppy icon.

2. Place a blank floppy disk in the disk drive.

3. Select File ➤ Format; press Start. You will be warned that formatting the floppy disk will destroy all data on the disk.

4. Press OK to continue.

5. Press OK when the format is complete and then close the Format window.

6. Open the icon for your boot drive (probably your C: drive) in the My Computer window.

7. Position the boot drive window (C: drive) so that you can also see the floppy disk icon in the My Computer window. (You will need to copy some files from your boot disk to your floppy disk.)

8. Copy the BOOT.INI, NTLDR, and NTDETECT.COM files to your floppy drive. If NTBOOTDD.SYS also resides in the root directory of your boot drive, copy that file as well.

9. Close the boot drive window and the My Computer window.

10. Reboot the computer with the floppy disk still in the disk drive.

If the problem you are experiencing booting NT is because one of the boot files (BOOT.INI, NTLDR, NTDETECT.COM, or NTBOOTDD.SYS) is missing or corrupt, you can boot NT with the boot floppy disk you have just created and then copy the files from the floppy disk to your boot drive (C: drive). This process will restore the missing or corrupted files and allow the boot process to proceed normally.

The Emergency Repair Disk

The trouble you are experiencing may be more severe than simply missing or corrupted boot files. If a file that contains Windows NT Registry information becomes corrupt, Windows NT itself can become unstable, even to the point of making it impossible to fix the problem from within NT.

You can create an emergency repair disk to restore the Registry from the last time you performed an emergency repair disk update. The emergency repair disk includes the security account manager (SAM) database, disk configuration, and numerous other system parameters.

You can use the Windows NT RDISK.EXE utility to create or update your emergency repair disk. This utility has two options—Update the repair information or Create a new repair disk.

When you choose Update repair information, RDISK.EXE copies the system hive, the security accounts manager, the security hive, the software hive, the default hive, and copies of the CONFIG.NT and AUTOEXEC.NT files used when initializing a Windows NT virtual DOS machine (see Chapter 15 for an explanation of NTVDMs) into a directory off the Windows NT root directory called \REPAIR. The utility then asks if you want to create an emergency repair disk containing this information.

> *The emergency repair disk is not a replacement for regular backups. The emergency repair disk stores only Registry configuration information, not your data.*

WARNING

The Create emergency repair disk option simply formats a floppy disk and copies the contents of the repair directory on to it. Exercise 17.2 shows you how to run the rdisk utility. You should create a new repair disk each time you make a major change to security policy, add new users, or change the configuration of your Windows NT Workstation.

EXERCISE 17.2

Creating an Emergency Repair Disk

1. Click the Start menu and select Programs ➤ Command prompt.

2. Type **rdisk** at the command prompt and then press Enter.

3. Click Update Repair Info.

4. Click Yes to overwrite the current repair information.

5. Click Yes to create an emergency repair disk.

6. Insert a new floppy disk into your A: drive and click OK.

7. Remove the emergency repair floppy for safekeeping.

8. Click Exit to close the rdisk program. Close the command prompt window.

Restoring Windows NT

The process of restoring a Windows NT installation that has somehow become damaged or corrupt is similar to reinstalling the operating system. In fact, you are reinstalling the operating system, but rather than using default information, you are restoring security and account information in the Registry from the emergency repair disk.

The restoration process checks the hard disk for errors and can verify the Windows NT system files. It restores some or all of the Registry information if you want it to.

You will need your Windows NT Setup boot disks, Workstation 4 CD-ROM, and the emergency repair disk for this specific computer. The repair process will reinstall the security database from the last time you updated your repair disk. If your repair disk is very old or you don't remember the administrator password from the time the disk was made, you will be better off not reinstalling the Registry from the emergency repair disk.

Exercise 17.3 shows the process of restoring a Windows NT Workstation installation. *Do not run this exercise on a computer you use for work.* The purpose of this exercise is merely to illustrate the process.

EXERCISE 17.3

Restoring Windows NT Workstation

1. Boot the Windows NT Workstation Setup boot disk.

2. Insert Setup Disk #2 when prompted and press Enter.

3. Press **R** for restore when prompted for which type of installation you want to perform.

4. Press Enter on each option you want repaired.

5. Move to Continue and press Enter.

6. At the detect devices screen, press Enter.

7. Insert Setup Disk #3.

8. Add additional drivers as necessary using the Other disk option. When finished, re-insert Setup Disk #3.

9. Press Enter if you have a recent emergency disk created by the rdisk utility, otherwise press Esc.

10. Insert the emergency disk and press Enter.

11. Press Enter to select each registry hive you would like restored.

12. Select Continue and press Enter.

13. Press **A** to replace all non-original files.

14. Insert any third-party driver disks requested by the Setup program.

15. Press Esc to skip using the Windows NT Workstation DRVLIB diskette if you do not have it.

16. When the repair process completes, reboot your computer.

Troubleshooting a Running Windows NT Environment

I F YOU ARE SURE THAT YOU HAVE no hardware problems and your Windows NT Workstation boots properly, but you are still experiencing difficulties, you will need to troubleshoot the running operating system. Windows NT provides an excellent environment for troubleshooting—you can view almost any aspect of the operating system with tools provided by Microsoft. The tools you will most often use are the Event Viewer, which records problems detected by Windows NT, and the Windows NT diagnostic tool, which shows you how Windows NT is configured. You can also use the performance monitor to find programs that are using more resources that you might expect and degrading the performance of your machine. Use of the performance monitor is covered in Chapter 14, "Performance Tuning."

Troubleshooting with the Event Viewer

Rather than reporting nonfatal error messages on screen during operation, Windows NT adds a record to the Event log. This system eliminates the display of annoying messages that users may not have the permissions to fix, and more important, keeps a written log of all error messages for you to review. If you've ever had a user call you to fix an error and then not remember what the error was, you'll appreciate the Event log. You can review the Event log with a program called the Event Viewer. Figure 17.1 shows the Event Viewer.

You should begin all troubleshooting sessions by reviewing the Event log with the Event Viewer. Quite often the log will tell you exactly what is wrong. You can save yourself a lot of time by checking this log often. The Event Viewer allows you to view three different types of events:

- System events are recorded by the Windows NT Kernel and drivers.

- Security events are recorded when security events as set by your audit and user policies occur.

- Application events are recorded by Windows NT User mode applications that are designed to use the Event log.

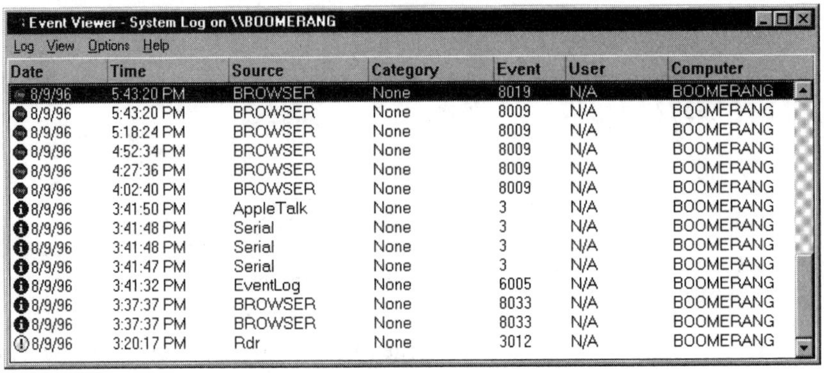

FIGURE 17.1
The Windows NT
Event Viewer.

Date	Time	Source	Category	Event	User	Computer
8/9/96	5:43:20 PM	BROWSER	None	8019	N/A	BOOMERANG
8/9/96	5:43:20 PM	BROWSER	None	8009	N/A	BOOMERANG
8/9/96	5:18:24 PM	BROWSER	None	8009	N/A	BOOMERANG
8/9/96	4:52:34 PM	BROWSER	None	8009	N/A	BOOMERANG
8/9/96	4:27:36 PM	BROWSER	None	8009	N/A	BOOMERANG
8/9/96	4:02:40 PM	BROWSER	None	8009	N/A	BOOMERANG
8/9/96	3:41:50 PM	AppleTalk	None	3	N/A	BOOMERANG
8/9/96	3:41:48 PM	Serial	None	3	N/A	BOOMERANG
8/9/96	3:41:48 PM	Serial	None	3	N/A	BOOMERANG
8/9/96	3:41:47 PM	Serial	None	3	N/A	BOOMERANG
8/9/96	3:41:32 PM	EventLog	None	6005	N/A	BOOMERANG
8/9/96	3:37:37 PM	BROWSER	None	8033	N/A	BOOMERANG
8/9/96	3:37:37 PM	BROWSER	None	8033	N/A	BOOMERANG
8/9/96	3:20:17 PM	Rdr	None	3012	N/A	BOOMERANG

Event Viewer - System Log on \\BOOMERANG

NT assigns one of three priorities to events in the Event log. Informative messages are marked with a blue icon containing the letter *i*. Informative messages are for your information only. They do not affect the operation of your computer.

Alerts are recorded with a yellow icon containing an exclamation mark (!). Alerts indicate that your computer is operating in a degraded condition or that some noncritical resource is not operating correctly.

A red stop sign indicates a critical warning. Something serious is wrong with your computer or configuration that will cause denial of a service.

The Security section of the Event log has two event icons. A key indicates that an audit policy event was passed. A padlock indicates that the system blocked an audit policy event.

Exercise 17.4 will show you how to run the Event Viewer and how to view the different event types.

You should check your Event log any time you suspect something isn't working correctly in your system. You should check it periodically (at least once a month) even when things are working fine.

You will generally want to clear your Event log before a troubleshooting session (after you've reviewed it, of course) to make events that relate to the problem you are currently experiencing easier to find.

Application Troubleshooting

Ill-behaved applications, and applications written specifically for MS-DOS or Windows that violate Windows NT security, may hang or cease to function

EXERCISE 17.4

Using the Event Viewer

1. Click the Start menu and select Programs ➤ Administrative Tools ➤ Event Viewer.

2. Notice the events in your log. System events are shown by default when you first run the Event Viewer.

3. Double-click on any event to see the entire event message. Click Close when you are finished viewing that event.

4. Select security in the Log menu. If you don't have any audit policies set up, it's quite likely you won't see anything here.

5. Select application in the Log menu. Again, if you haven't run any Event log-enabled applications, you may not see anything recorded here.

6. Select Clear All Events in the Log menu.

7. Answer No—you don't want to save the log.

8. Answer Yes—you are sure you want to clear the log.

normally. While this situation does not usually present a problem for other running programs, these hung programs still use CPU cycles and may lock resources such as communication ports.

You can use the Task Manager to shut down troublesome processes. Of course, any shutdown of a program other than its normal exit routine can result in lost data, so you should use this procedure only when you have to.

Ending a 32-bit application is easy—you simply shut down the executing thread. Ending a DOS or Win16 application involves shutting down the virtual DOS machine in which the application ran. This step ensures that the VDM and WOW environments are reinitialized for the next DOS or Win16 application you run. Exercise 17.5 explains how to end a task in Windows NT.

Shutting Down a Task with Task Manager

1. Right-click the empty area of the task bar.

2. Select Task Manager.

3. Select the Image name list for the name of the hung process. For MS-DOS or Win16 applications, this process is always the NTVDM.EXE program.

4. Click End Process.

5. Click Yes.

6. Close Task Manager.

The Windows NT Diagnostic Tool

WinMSD is also called the Windows NT diagnostic tool. This tool enables you to inspect everything Windows NT knows about your computer and verify that it works correctly. WinMSD is split into the following sections accessed by the tabs near the top of the WinMSD window.

- Version
- System
- Display
- Drives
- Memory
- Services
- Resources
- Environment
- Network

Exercise 17.6 shows how to load and use the Windows NT diagnostic tool. As you read through the rest of this section, move through the diagnostic tool to see the specific information it reports about your machine.

EXERCISE 17.6

Using the Windows NT Diagnostic Tool

1. Click Start and select Programs ➤ Administrative Tools ➤ Windows NT Diagnostics.

2. Click the Resources tab.

3. Click IRQ. Note the interrupt level of each device.

4. Click I/O Port. Note the I/O ports used by each device.

5. Click DMA. Note the DMA status of each device.

6. Click Memory. Note the memory ranges used by each device.

7. Click Devices. Note the device drivers installed in your system.

8. Double-click on the serial device driver.

9. Note how many serial device interrupts and port address are used in your system. Click OK to close the Serial Properties window.

10. Click Print.

11. Click OK to print.

12. Click OK to close the Windows NT diagnostic tool.

The following sections describe how to use each Windows NT Diagnostic tab for troubleshooting. Figure 17.2 shows the Windows NT Diagnostic screen and its many options.

Version

Version tells you what version of Windows NT you are running, what build of the operating system you have, how many processors are installed, and who this copy is registered to. This information is not of much value when troubleshooting.

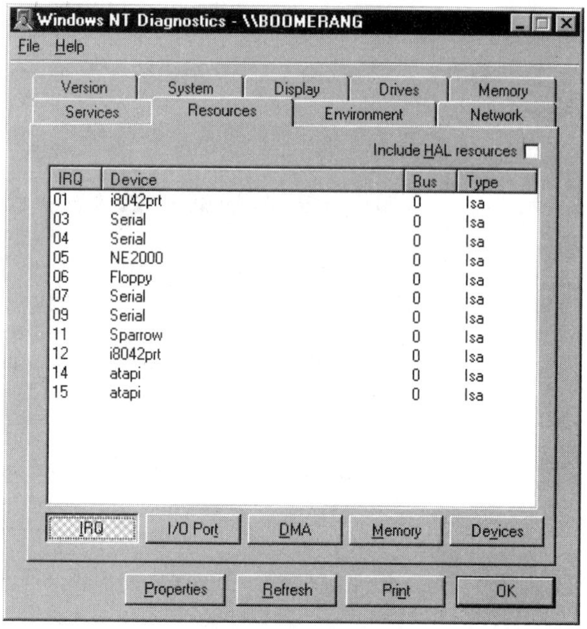

FIGURE 17.2
The Windows NT
Diagnostic screen.

The Windows NT Diagnostic screen showing the Resources tab.

System

System will identify what sort of motherboard and microprocessor you are using and show you the BIOS date and manufacturer. This information is not of much value when troubleshooting.

Display

Display shows the BIOS date and revision for your video adapter, as well as the current settings. You should see the manufacturer of your video adapter and the type of digital-to-analog converter used. This information is not of much value when troubleshooting.

Drives

Drives shows all of the currently installed volumes, grouped by type such as removable drives, hard drives, CD-ROM, and network drives. Clicking on individual drives will give you information about that drive, such as the file system time and how much data is stored on it. This tab is not available when viewing diagnostic information on a remote computer.

Memory

The Memory tab shows how memory is being used in the system. In addition to showing the amount of physical RAM, this tab shows how much is being used by the Kernel and how much is being used by the page file. At the bottom of this screen, you can see how the page file is distributed across your physical disks.

The Memory tab also shows the number of heap handles allocated, how many threads are running, and how many processes are currently executing. This tab is not available when viewing diagnostic information on a remote computer.

Services

The Services tab shows the state of all loaded services and drivers. Services are shown when you click the Services button at the bottom of the screen, and devices are shown when you click the Devices button.

When you double-click on a service or device driver, a window will appear showing the start type of the service or device driver and some other less useful information. You can click the Dependencies tab to show what services must be running for this service or device driver to operate.

Resources

The Resources tab is the most important part of the Windows NT Diagnostic screen. This tab shows the state of all hardware in the computer that Windows NT knows about. This tab will help you iron out hardware conflicts by showing the resource use for all devices installed in Windows NT.

You select the resource type you want to see by clicking the IRQ, I/O port, DMA, Memory, or Devices buttons located at the bottom of the Resource pane.

When you double-click a resource item in the display drop-down box, a window displays information about that resource line item. For the most part, useful information is shown only when viewing devices. Then the window will show all the resources that a device is using.

Before installing a new device in your computer, review the Resources tab of the Windows NT diagnostic tool to be certain other devices aren't already using the interrupt, DMA channel, and I/O port settings you intend to use for the new device. This step will prevent hardware conflicts and keep you from having to troubleshoot new hardware installations.

Environment

The Environment tab shows the environment variables that Windows NT uses to communicate simple information to applications about the Windows NT environment. Environment variables in Windows NT appear to applications the same way DOS environment variables do, so older applications can use them to find information or change their state based on the current system settings. You will probably not need to change or inspect any of these settings.

Network

The Network tab shows information about the current network session. Use this tab to determine which workgroup or domain you are logged into and under which account. This tab also shows the name of the logon domain and server.

Troubleshooting Security Problems

If a user cannot access a program or some data on a computer that he or she knows is there or can see, chances are the user does not have sufficient permissions to perform the action in question. To troubleshoot security problems, log on as the administrator and attempt the same operation. If you can perform the operation, the problem is a security problem. You can either assign the user permissions to use the resource, or you can move the resource to an area where the user has sufficient permissions.

Sometimes even the administrator can't use or delete a resource that is visible. The reason is that the resource was created and assigned permissions under a previous installation of Windows NT that has been overwritten. Now the old administrator account that no longer exists is the owner. Because Windows NT assigns a new security ID to the new administrator during the new installation, no current user has permission to use or delete the resource.

Fortunately, Windows NT has a way around this problem. For any resource, the administrator can take ownership of the resource and then reassign permissions as necessary. Exercise 17.7 shows how to take ownership of a resource. Under normal circumstances, you would not take ownership of every resource on the computer as shown below. You would take ownership only of the specific files or subdirectories that had this security problem.

EXERCISE 17.7

Taking Ownership of a Resource

1. Log on as an administrator.

2. Double-click the My Computer icon on the desktop.

3. Right-click on the C: drive (or any other NTFS volume) and select Properties and then the Security tab.

4. Click Ownership.

5. Click Take Ownership.

6. Click Yes to take ownership of all files and subdirectories.

7. Click Yes to continue if a file in use error occurs.

8. Wait while the security manager assigns each resource in the drive.

9. Click OK to close the window.

Memory Dumps

If you are having a problem with crashes ("blue screens"), a Microsoft support technician may ask you to make a memory dump. *Memory dumps* are copies of the information in RAM when the computer crashed, written to your boot partition when the computer crashes. Memory dumps assist Microsoft in assessing the reason for your crash. Memory dumps require disk space equal to the amount of memory in your computer plus 1MB.

Enabling memory dumps is set through the system Control Panel as shown in Exercise 17.8.

EXERCISE 17.8

Configuring for Memory Dumps

1. Select Start ➤ Settings ➤ Control Panel.

2. Double-click System.

3. Select the Startup/Shutdown tab.

4. Check the *Write debugging information to* and *Overwrite any existing file* checkboxes. Leave the path shown in its default state.

5. Click Close.

6. Answer Yes if the system raises any alerts about page file size.

7. Answer Yes when asked to reboot your computer.

Troubleshooting Resources

ONCE YOU HAVE EXHAUSTED your own knowledge and skills and the diagnostic utilities provided by Microsoft give you no more useful information, you will need to turn to other resources for help. One of the best resources, the Windows NT Help files, exists right on your local hard drive. If you do not find the solution there, you can turn to the TechNET CD or the Microsoft Knowledge Base Library for more information. You can also ask for help on the Internet or an online service such as CompuServe and America Online.

Windows Help Files

The Windows NT Help files are an excellent troubleshooting resource. These Help files are based upon Microsoft's experience with customer support, so they include specific troubleshooting help for the problems reported to Microsoft most often. You stand a good chance of finding a Help file that can walk you through the steps for fixing software configuration problems.

Sometimes you may not be able to find the specific help you need. Use Exercise 17.9 to find specific Help files when you don't know the correct context.

EXERCISE 17.9

Opening Help Files

1. Click Start and select Find ➤ Files or Folders.

2. Type ***.hlp** in the Named input line.

3. Check the Include subfolders option.

4. Make sure the root directory of the volume containing the Windows NT directory is showing in the Look In drop-down list.

5. Click Find now.

6. Double-click the `REGEDIT.HLP` file in the resulting list of help files.

7. Double-click the book titled *Changing keys and values*.

8. Read the topic by double-clicking on each subtopic; then double-click on the Help Topics button to return to the list of topics.

9. Close the Registry Editor Help file and the Find Files window.

TechNET

Microsoft distributes the TechNET CD-ROM to technical support professionals who subscribe. The TechNET CD-ROM contains much of the same information that you can find on the Microsoft Web site, but it is far faster because your searches are not limited to the speed of your modem. The TechNet CD-ROM also includes the complete MS Download Library—Windows NT Service Packs (which are now about 30MB each!), Resource Kits, the complete text of several Microsoft training courses, and many informative white papers detailing the technical background or implementation of Windows NT products. Since it is updated monthly, a subscription to TechNet is an invaluable resource for Windows NT professionals and an efficient way of keeping an installation up-to-date. A Windows NT professional will find his/her answer on TechNet more reliably than by using the Internet or the manuals. The TechNET CD is especially useful for larger organizations that can absorb the cost of the subscription. You can subscribe to the TechNET CD-ROM service by calling 1-800-344-2121.

Internet

The Internet is by far the best troubleshooting resource for any computer problem. The cumulative experience of thousands of Windows NT experts is available through both Microsoft-sanctioned and private resources. Unless you are working with an experimental release of Windows NT, you can presume that other people have already experienced your problem. There's a good chance they posted a question on a news group that was answered by someone who knew how to fix the problem.

Most hardware manufacturers also maintain Web sites that contain current versions of their Windows NT drivers. If you are having a problem with a third-party driver, check the vendor's Web site for an updated driver. If you can't find the site, use AltaVista to search for it.

The Microsoft Knowledge Base

The Microsoft knowledge base is the official repository for support information about all Microsoft products including Windows NT. The knowledge base is an accumulation of answers to technical support questions received by Microsoft since Windows NT was first released. Figure 17.3 shows the Microsoft Web site.

You can access this database at URL http://www.microsoft.com. You will need to have set up RAS to connect to an Internet account. This process is shown in Chapter 12, "Internetworking with Remote Access Service." Exercise 17.10 shows how to access and navigate the knowledge base.

Web sites change quickly. The exact steps to access the knowledge base may change, but you should be able to access the site easily from Microsoft Explorer.

FIGURE 17.3
The Microsoft Web site
at www.microsoft.com.

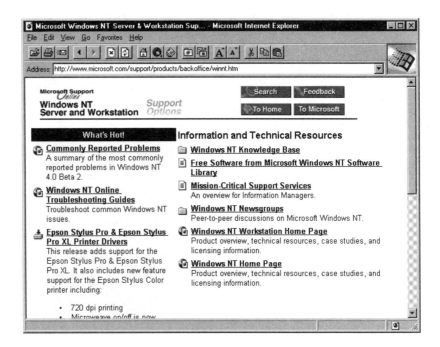

EXERCISE 17.10

The Microsoft Knowledge Base

1. Double-click the My Computer icon on the desktop.

2. Double-click the Dial-up Networking icon.

3. Select your Internet service provider in the Dial-up service drop-down list.

4. Click Dial. Perform any postconnection logon procedures necessary to establish an Internet connection to your service provider.

5. Double-click the Internet Explorer Icon on the desktop.

6. Type **http://www.microsoft.com** in the address input box and press Return.

7. Click the Support link when the Microsoft home page appears.

EXERCISE 17.10 (CONTINUED)

8. Click the Search the Knowledge Base link.

9. Select Windows NT in the Microsoft Product list.

10. Type **SCSI Adapter** in the word search input line.

11. Click Go.

12. Select one of the articles and review it.

13. Leave Internet Explorer and the dial-up connection active for the next exercises.

World Wide Web Indexes and Search Engines

You can use many of the Web search engines and indexes to locate information about Windows NT and troubleshooting. Corporations that want to further the development of the Internet and the World Wide Web provide these search engines without charge. Many others exist, and you will find links to them through these providers.

YAHOO! Yahoo! is an Internet index. When you pull up the Yahoo home page, you will see a menu of general topics covering the spectrum of Web pages. You can also enter a search term at Yahoo's opening screen, rather than drilling down through the various categories—a very efficient method if, for example, you know the company name you're looking for. You will successively narrow your search through Yahoo by choosing more specific links through each page. Figure 17.4 shows the Windows NT index at Yahoo!

You can use Yahoo! when you can't think of a specific search phrase for a search engine or when your problem is a little too broad to express in a single search phrase. Exercise 17.11 shows how to use the Yahoo! Internet index to find troubleshooting support for Windows NT.

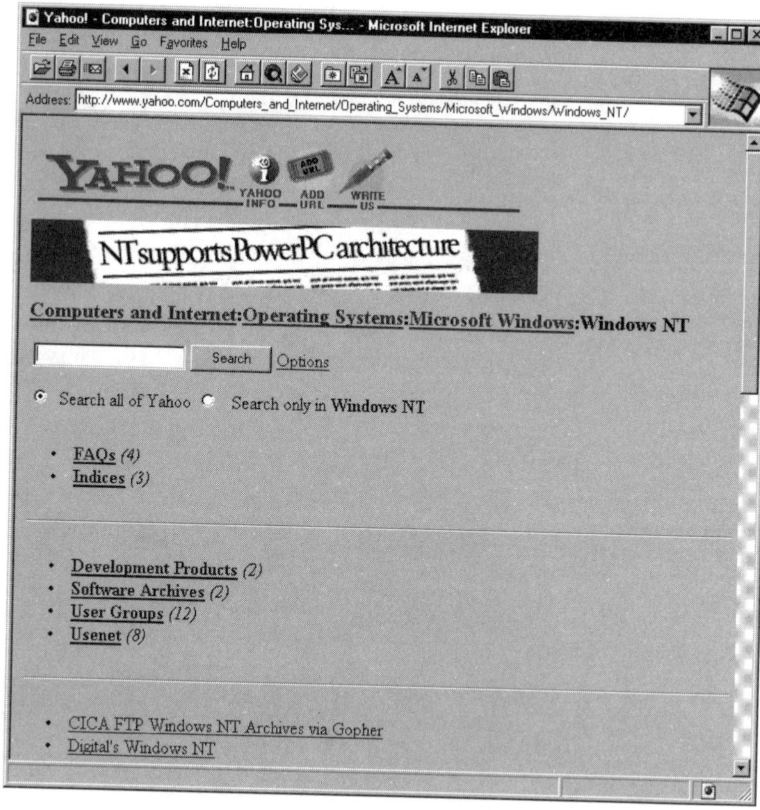

FIGURE 17.4
Yahoo!

Yahoo! - Computers and Internet:Operating Sys... - Microsoft Internet Explorer

File   Edit   View   Go   Favorites   Help

Address: http://www.yahoo.com/Computers_and_Internet/Operating_Systems/Microsoft_Windows/Windows_NT/

YAHOO!   YAHOO   ADD   WRITE
                    INFO   URL   US

NT supports PowerPC architecture

Computers and Internet:Operating Systems:Microsoft Windows:Windows NT

[Search]   Options

○ Search all of Yahoo   ○ Search only in **Windows NT**

- FAQs *(4)*
- Indices *(3)*

- Development Products *(2)*
- Software Archives *(2)*
- User Groups *(12)*
- Usenet *(8)*

- CICA FTP Windows NT Archives via Gopher
- Digital's Windows NT

EXERCISE 17.11

Using Yahoo to Find Troubleshooting Support

1. Type **http://www.yahoo.com** in the address input line of the Internet Explorer and press Return.

2. Click the Computers and Internet link.

3. Click the Operating Systems link.

4. Click the Microsoft Windows link.

5. Click the Windows NT link.

6. Review the resources available to you at this site.

ALTAVISTA The AltaVista Web and Usenet search engines are services provided by Digital Equipment Corporation. AltaVista works by constantly searching the World Wide Web for new Web pages. When the search engine finds new content, it sends the content back to the AltaVista site where it is indexed and stored in a huge database of indexed key words. When you enter a search phrase into the AltaVista main page, the engine searches the database of indexed key words and reports the results of your search on a new Web page. You can select any link in the Web page simply by clicking on the corresponding link. Figure 17.5 shows AltaVista during a Windows NT specific search.

Use AltaVista when you have a specific problem and you think you can narrow down a search with a single phrase. The AltaVista Web site has instructions on how to narrow down your searches. Exercise 17.12 shows how to use AltaVista as a Windows NT troubleshooting resource.

FIGURE 17.5
The AltaVista Web site.

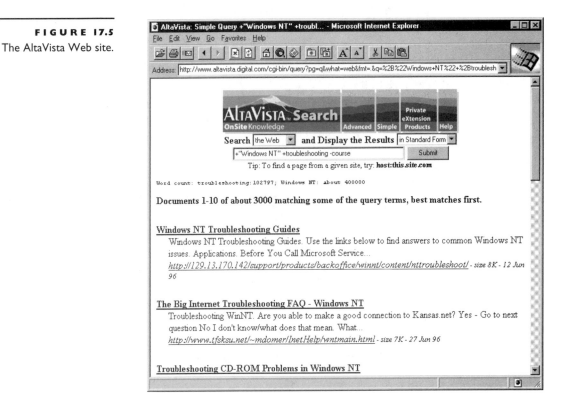

EXERCISE 17.12

Using AltaVista to Find Troubleshooting Support

1. Type **http://www.altavista.digital.com** in the address input line of the Internet Explorer and press Return.

2. Type **+"Windows NT"+troubleshooting-course** in the search input line.

3. Click Submit.

4. Review the Web sites available from this search query.

5. Select Usenet in the Search type list.

6. Type **+"Windows NT"+troubleshooting-jobs** in the search input line.

7. Review the Usenet information available from this search query.

Online Services

The major online services sponsor forums that provide support for most popular software, including Windows NT. Microsoft has moved its official support from online services to the Web, but many resources still exist in these communities. America Online has an active Windows NT forum. Exercise 17.13 shows how to use America Online as a troubleshooting resource. (Similar facilities exist on CompuServe.)

EXERCISE 17.13

Using America Online Support Forums

1. Log on to your America Online account.

2. Click Channels.

3. Click Computers & Software.

4. Click Support Forums.

5. Select Windows Forum in the forums drop-down list.

EXERCISE 17.13 (CONTINUED)

6. Select Windows Forum in the forums drop-down list.

7. Click Message Boards.

8. Select Windows NT Forum.

9. Click Browse folders.

10. Click NT Workstation.

11. Browse through the questions and answers posted on these boards.

Chapter Summary

THE BASIC PRINCIPLES YOU USE to troubleshoot Windows NT are universal and apply to any malfunction.

Hardware problems are common in personal computers, and Windows NT is especially sensitive to them. For this reason, you must resolve hardware problems before attempting to troubleshoot software problems. MS-DOS is a valuable troubleshooting tool that can be used when a hardware problem prevents Windows NT from being booted.

In this chapter you learned how to create a Windows NT boot disk to direct the NT boot loader to a partition containing Windows NT in the event that your master boot record or boot files become damaged. You also learned how to create an emergency repair disk and how to perform an emergency restoration.

Windows NT provides a number of tools to assist in troubleshooting, including the Event Viewer, the Windows NT diagnostic tool, and the Performance Monitor. These tools will guide you to the source of a software configuration problem and help you prevent future hardware malfunctions.

The Internet is a powerful troubleshooting resource. Microsoft provides free support for customers via its World Wide Web site, which includes the Microsoft knowledge base. Internet indexes like Yahoo! and search engines like AltaVista can help you find third-party sources of information. You can also find updated Windows NT drivers via the Web. Finally, online service like America Online and CompuServe also sponsor Windows NT support forums.

Conclusion and Note from the Authors

E'VE ENJOYED PREPARING you on this tour through the Windows NT Workstation operating system. We hope we've conveyed the sophistication and power of Windows NT and sparked your enthusiasm for this amazing operating system. If we've succeeded, you'll be throwing your NetWare server out the 15th floor of your office building right about...now.

You'll find the material in this book useful as you prepare for Microsoft's Certified System Engineer tests. Now that you understand Windows NT from a single computer perspective, you'll want to understand server-based networking and how to use Windows NT to build local and wide area networks. The companion book in this series, *MCSE: NT Server Study Guide,* will take you there.

Thanks for reading!

Charles Perkins & Matthew Strebe, 11 August 1996.

Exercise Questions

1. Release versions of Windows NT are bug free.

    A. True

    B. False

2. Windows NT runs on all computers capable of running Windows 95.

    A. True

    B. False

3. Microsoft maintains all Internet troubleshooting resources for Windows NT in the Windows NT knowledge base at the Microsoft Web site.

    A. True

    B. False

4. Microsoft does not certify hardware components as compatible with NT.

    A. True

    B. False

5. Recent changes to your computer system are likely to be the cause of new malfunctions.

    A. True

    B. False

6. If you use Windows NT, you no longer have any reason to use MS-DOS.

    A. True

    B. False

7. The Microsoft knowledge base is the official repository for support information about all Microsoft products, including Windows NT.

    A. True

    B. False

8. With MS-DOS you cannot access _____ volumes.

9. To create an emergency repair disk, use the _____ utility.

10. The _____ section of the Windows NT diagnostic tool is the most useful for troubleshooting.

11. The _____ is by far the best troubleshooting resource for any computer problem.

12. Which of the following is not good practice when troubleshooting?

A. Be patient.

B. Perform easy tests first.

C. Change only one setting at a time.

D. Make as many changes as possible.

13. The most common hardware problem in PCs is

A. Bad memory

B. Hardware conflicts

C. Loose cables

D. Power supply failure

14. Which of these failures is the most damaging of all computer component failures?

A. Processor

B. Memory

C. Motherboard

D. Hard disk

15. An emergency repair disk can restore

A. Missing Windows NT system user files

B. Damaged user files

C. Back up tapes

D. Registry information

16. To view the Event log, use the

    A. Event Monitor

    B. User Manager

    C. Notepad

    D. Event Viewer

Exercise
Answers

APPENDIX

A

his appendix contains the answers to the exercise questions that appear in Chapters 1 through 17.

Chapter 1

1. Windows NT Workstation is another name for Windows 95.

   A. True
   B. False

   Answer: B

2. Windows NT 4 uses the same graphical user interface as Windows and Windows for Workgroups.

   A. True
   B. False

   Answer: B

3. Windows NT Server can run the same software as Windows NT Workstation.

   A. True
   B. False

   Answer: A

4. The _____ allows Windows NT to run on many different platforms with only minor changes.

   Answer: Hardware Abstraction Layer (HAL)

5. Multiprocessing is

   A. Running more than one process at a time on one microprocessor
   B. Using more than one microprocessor in the same computer

   Answer: B

6. Windows NT divides memory into_____.

    A. user and protected

    B. conventional and expanded

    C. conventional and extended

    D. Windows NT does not segment memory

    Answer: A

7. Windows NT is not available for which of the following computers:

    A. Intel 386 class machines

    B. Digital Alpha based computers

    C. MIPS based computers

    D. PowerPC based computers

    E. VAX minicomputers

    Answer: E

8. Which of the following does Windows NT support?

    A. Asymmetrical Multiprocessing

    B. Symmetrical Multiprocessing

    C. Coherent Multiprocessing

    D. Incoherent Multiprocessing

    Answer: B

9. Which of the following network protocols does Windows NT not support?

    A. TCP/IP

    B. NWLink (IPX/SPX)

    C. NetBEUI

    D. AppleTalk

    E. XNS

    Answer: E

10. The core of the Windows NT operating system is called

    A. the Kernel

    B. Executive mode

    C. Privileged mode

    D. Process Manager

    Answer: A

Chapter 2

1. Windows NT will run on any computer system.

   A. True

   B. False

   Answer: B

2. A computer with an 80486 processor running at 33MHz with 120MB of disk space, a VGA video adapter, and 12MB of memory can run Windows NT Workstation 4.0.

   A. True

   B. False

   Answer: A

3. A Sparc RISC-based computer running at 100MHz with 500MB of hard disk space and 64MB of memory will run Windows NT Workstation 4.0.

   A. True

   B. False

   Answer: B

4. You must have a CD-ROM drive supported by the Windows NT installation program in order to install Windows NT from CD-ROM to your computer.

   A. True

   B. False

   Answer: B

5. Windows NT requires more processing power than does Windows 95 to achieve the same level of responsiveness to the computer user.

   A. True

   B. False

   Answer: A

6. Windows NT can automatically detect devices installed in your computer.

   A. True

   B. False

   Answer: A

7. Windows NT Workstation 4.0 supports the Plug-and-Play standard.

A. True

B. False

Answer: B

8. Upgrading from some previous versions of Windows or Windows NT will transfer some of the configuration information of the operating system to the Windows NT installation.

A. True

B. False

Answer: A

9. If you install Windows NT Workstation on your computer, you will not be able to run other operating systems, such as Windows 95 or OS/2.

A. True

B. False

Answer: B

10. If Windows NT is used only with a FAT partition, the advanced features of NTFS will not be available.

A. True

B. False

Answer: A

11. You must have three installation boot floppy disks in order to install Windows NT Workstation 4.0.

A. True

B. False

Answer: B

12. The graphical screens in the second portion of the installation process examine your computer's hardware; allow you to select the partition, file system, and directory for the installation; and copy essential files to your hard disk drive.

A. True

B. False

Answer: B

13. You can install Windows NT into unpartitioned hard disk space.

A. True

B. False

Answer: A

14. Windows NT can convert an existing FAT partition to NTFS.

A. True

B. False

Answer: A

15. If you select an installation directory that already contains a Windows or Windows NT operating system, you have the option of overwriting or upgrading the previously installed operating system.

A. True

B. False

Answer: A

16. The exhaustive hard disk examination examines only operating system files on the hard disk drive.

A. True

B. False

Answer: B

17. Your computer's name can be up to 31 characters long.

A. True

B. False

Answer: B

18. Windows NT will not function without an administrator password.

A. True

B. False

Answer: B

19. You cannot install the networking components if you do not have a network card in your computer.

A. True

B. False

Answer: B

20. AppleTalk is a default protocol for Windows NT Workstation 4.0.

A. True

B. False

Answer: B

21. AppleTalk is a protocol included with Windows NT Workstation 4.0.

    A. True

    B. False

    Answer: A

22. HCL stands for _____ _____ _____.

    Answer: Hardware Compatibility List

23. For running Windows NT on Intel-based computers, you should partition your computer's hard disk space into at least _____ partitions.

    Answer: two

24. You can use the DOS _____ program to partition your hard disk.

    Answer: FDISK

25. Under DOS and versions of Windows including Windows 95, you can use the _____ program to start the installation process.

    Answer: Winnt

26. Under Windows NT, you can use the _____ program to start the installation process.

    Answer: Winnt32

27. The _____ option instructs the installation program that you wish to perform a floppy-less install.

    Answer: /B

28. The _____ option will re-create the Windows NT installation boot floppies.

    Answer: /OX

29. In a _____ installation of Windows NT, the installation files reside in a shared directory on a file server.

    Answer: network

30. The installation files for Intel-based computers reside in the _____ subdirectory of the CD-ROM.

    Answer: i386

31. Windows NT 4.0 supports two file systems: _____ and _____.

Answer: FAT, NTFS

32. The _____ installation option allows you to select for yourself what software provided with Windows NT to install on your workstation.

Answer: custom

33. The _____ installation option installs the most used software that comes with Windows NT in the most common configuration.

Answer: typical

34. The _____ _____ adapter is a software driver that pretends to be a network adapter but that does not really control a hardware device.

Answer: MS Loopback

35. The default workgroup name is _____.

Answer: WORKGROUP

36. The default domain name is _____.

Answer: DOMAIN

Chapter 3

1. Windows NT 4 Workstation creates two default user accounts.
   A. True
   B. False

   Answer: A

2. In NT 4 you can add new users in two ways.
   A. True
   B. False

   Answer: A

3. The Administrator account cannot be renamed.
   A. True
   B. False

   Answer: B

4. The Username, Full Name, and Description fields are left blank when copying user accounts.

    A. True
    B. False

    Answer: B

5. Copying user accounts can save you time when you have many user accounts to create.

    A. True
    B. False

    Answer: A

6. Since account permissions are based on the username, you will have to reassign permissions if you change an account username.

    A. True
    B. False

    Answer: B

7. You should audit most system activities.

    A. True
    B. False

    Answer: B

8. Deleting and disabling accounts are the same thing.

    A. True
    B. False

    Answer: B

9. The default Administrator account can never be locked out.

    A. True
    B. False

    Answer: A

10. Policies should usually be set by group, not by user.

    A. True
    B. False

    Answer: A

11. Deleting an account removes information, but permissions can be restored by creating a new account with the same name.

    A. True

    B. False

    Answer: B

12. A good administrative practice is to assign permissions to groups rather than to users.

    A. True

    B. False

    Answer: A

13. Only administrators can create groups and assign permissions.

    A. True

    B. False

    Answer: B

14. Only administrators can manage policies.

    A. True

    B. False

    Answer: A

15. Windows NT does not ensure that permissions are the same across local groups with the same name on different workstations.

    A. True

    B. False

    Answer: A

16. Policy changes are effective only after the current users log off.

    A. True

    B. False

    Answer: A

17. The _____ account provides limited access to the computer for users with low or no security access.

    Answer: Guest

18. The _____ account has the highest level of permissions of any user.

    Answer: Administrator

19. Windows NT provides _____ to make assigning permissions easier among a large number of users.

Answer: Groups

20. _____ policy controls passwords.

Answer: Account

21. All user and group administration functions are performed through the _____ utility.

Answer: User Manager

22. The _____ utility is used to view the Security log.

Answer: Event Viewer

23. The _____ checkbox prevents users from using an account when checked.

Answer: Account Disabled

24. A Windows NT Workstation installation contains _____ default groups.

Answer: six

25. When a user leaves your organization, you should _____ that account.

Answer: disable

26. Which of the following is not a default group?
   A. Power Users
   B. Backup Operators
   C. Administrative Assistants
   D. Users

Answer: C

27. When copying user accounts, which of the following fields is not copied into the New Account dialog box?
   A. Profile Settings
   B. Description
   C. Group Memberships
   D. User Must Change Password at Next Logon

Answer: D

28. Account policy governs the use of what?

    A. User account permissions

    B. Passwords

    C. Accounting practices

    D. Security identification

    Answer: B

29. Which of the following is not a user right?

    A. Change system time

    B. Load and unload device drivers

    C. Add/remove software

    D. Shutdown the system

    E. Access this computer from network

    Answer: C

30. A user has been reassigned from sales to marketing. You should

    A. Change his user permissions

    B. Change her group assignment from sales to marketing

    C. Delete this account and then create a new one with new permissions

    D. Do nothing

    Answer: B

31. You suspect someone may be attempt to gain unauthorized access to the system. To verify your suspicion, you should:

    A. Lock out all accounts and then grant access to people who show photo identification

    B. Force all users to change their passwords at the next logon.

    C. Audit failed logon attempts

    D. Audit use of shared resources

    E. Change the Administrator account password

    Answer: C

Chapter 4

1. All Windows NT Workstation computers have the same icons visible in the Control Panel.

    A. True

    B. False

    Answer: B

2. The Network settings are an example of system settings that all users share.

A. True

B. False

Answer: A

3. You can use icons in the Control Panel to modify system settings or to modify user profile settings, but not to modify both.

A. True

B. False

Answer: B

4. Windows NT can use only one page file at a time.

A. True

B. False

Answer: B

5. A user profile is created for a user from the default user profile the first time the user logs on.

A. True

B. False

Answer: A

6. Screen saver settings are stored in the user's profile.

A. True

B. False

Answer: A

7. Paging file settings are stored in the user's profile.

A. True

B. False

Answer: B

8. You can add programs to the start menu that will appear only when you log on under your username.

A. True

B. False

Answer: A

9. The system maintains certain environment variables for Windows NT to use, but users can also set up environment variables to customize their own user accounts.

A. True

B. False

Answer: A

10. The Registry stores device configuration data only. Security information and user settings are stored in INI files.

A. True

B. False

Answer: B

11. You can easily render your Windows NT system unusable by making inappropriate changes to the Windows NT Registry.

A. True

B. False

Answer: A

12. Six keys are located directly below HKEY_LOCAL_MACHINE in the Registry.

A. True

B. False

Answer: B

13. The HARDWARE key is generated automatically every time the computer boots. The HARDWARE key does not have a hive.

A. True

B. False

Answer: A

14. The SYSTEM key is generated automatically every time the computer boots. The SYSTEM key does not have a hive.

A. True

B. False

Answer: B

15. Anything that has to do with the appearance or function of your workstation will most likely be controlled from the _____ _____.

Answer: Control Panel

16. Settings that affect every user of the system can only be modified by members of the _____ group.

Answer: Administrators

17. Windows NT uses a technique called _____ to allow your computer to run more programs and larger programs than the physical memory in your computer would allow.

Answer: paging

18. The process that performs the paging function is called the _____ _____ Manager.

Answer: Virtual Memory

19. The paging data, when it is stored on the disk, is stored in a virtual memory page file called _____.SYS.

Answer: PAGEFILE

20. When Setup calculates how big to make your initial page file, it chooses a size that is _____ MB bigger than you physical memory size.

Answer: 11

21. The _____ loader appears while your computer boots and allows you to choose between Windows NT and other operating systems you may have installed on your computer.

Answer: boot

22. The _____ _____ section of the System Properties window is where you can set several hardware configurations for your Windows NT workstation.

Answer: Hardware Profiles

23. UPS stands for _____ _____ _____.

Answer: Uninterruptible Power Supply

24. The UPS communicates with Windows NT through a standard _____ cable.

Answer: RS-232

25. User preferences are stored in a _____ _____.

Answer: user profile

26. _____ profiles are normally stored on a Windows NT server.

Answer: Roaming

27. The recommended method of configuring Windows NT settings is through the _____ _____.

Answer: Control Panel

28. You can directly modify the data in the Registry that the Control Panel items change by using a program called _____.EXE.

Answer: REGEDIT

29. The _____ is where Windows NT stores all of its important configuration information.

Answer: Registry

30. In order to organize the information in the Registry, it is structured in a _____ manner, much like the file system on your computer's hard drive.

Answer: hierarchical

31. A _____ is a set of keys, subkeys, and values from the Registry that is stored in its own file in the location \<winnt_root>\SYSTEM32\CONFIG.

Answer: hive

32. The values in the Registry can have one of three value types: _____, _____, and _____.

Answer: DWORD, String, and Binary.

33. Fill in the Control Panel item that performs the described function:
   A. _____ allows you to start and stop hardware devices.
   B. _____ allows you to install and configure network components.
   C. _____ contains the system fonts available to programs on the workstation.
   D. _____ allows you to start and stop system services such as the Remote Access Server and simple TCP/IP services.
   E. _____ allows you to set the time and date of the computer's clock.
   F. _____ allows you to modify system settings such as the default startup parameters, system environment variables, and paging options.

Answers:
   A. Devices
   B. Network
   C. Fonts
   D. Services
   E. Date/Time
   F. System

34. From where can you delete user profiles?
  A. The Services Control Panel
  B. The Server Control Panel
  C. The User Manager program
  D. The System Control Panel

  Answer: D

35. Match the UPS condition to the control line:

  A. Power failure   **1.** DCD
  B. Low battery   **2.** DTR
  C. Remote UPS shutdown   **3.** CTS

  Answer: A-3, B-1, C-2

36. Match the Registry subtree with the information stored in it:

A. HKEY_CURRENT_USER	**1.** Contains information for use with OLE and file associations
B. HKEY_CLASSES_ROOT	**2.** Contains information about the user currently logged in
C. HKEY_LOCAL_MACHINE	**3.** Contains the hardware and software configuration that does not change between user logons
D. HKEY_CURRENT_CONFIG	**4.** Contains the subkey DEFAULT and the subkey corresponding to the SID of the current user
E. HKEY_USERS	**5.** Contains additional information about the current configuration of the system

  Answer: A-2, B-1, C-3, D-5, E-4

Chapter 5

1. Files on a hard disk that contain programs are stored differently than normal data files because the program files contain instructions for the computer to execute.
  A. True
  B. False

  Answer: B

2. Directories can contain both subdirectories and files.

A. True
B. False

Answer: A

3. The DOS FAT file system was introduced with the CPM operating system.

A. True
B. False

Answer: B

4. The DOS FAT file system is the most widely supported file system type.

A. True
B. False

Answer: A

5. The DOS FAT file sytem does not record security information such as the owner or file-sharing access permissions of a file or directory.

A. True
B. False

Answer: A

6. The DOS FAT file sytem has more overhead for small volumes than NTFS does.

A. True
B. False

Answer: B

7. The primary difference between the DOS FAT file sytem and VFAT has to do with file-sharing access permissions.

A. True
B. False

Answer: B

8. Under VFAT names are not case sensitive, but they do preserve case.

A. True
B. False

Answer: A

9. You must be careful not to create a new partition in the same space as an existing partition.

A. True

B. False

Answer: B

10. Windows NT assigns a drive letter to each partition as you create it.

A. True

B. False

Answer: A

11. Windows NT must reside in a primary partition.

A. True

B. False

Answer: B

12. The Windows NT boot loader must reside in the primary partition that has been set to be the boot partition.

A. True

B. False

Answer: A

13. The partitions combined into a volume set must be the same size and on the same drive.

A. True

B. False

Answer: B

14. The system and boot partitions cannot be a part of a volume set.

A. True

B. False

Answer: A

15. Volume sets provide fault tolerance to your file storage.

A. True

B. False

Answer: B

16. Because of the way data is stored to a stripe set, stripe sets can retrieve files much faster than volume sets can.

A. True
B. False

Answer: A

17. The system and boot partitions cannot be a part of a stripe set.

A. True
B. False

Answer: A

18. Windows NT always assigns the letter C to the active system partition unless you have selected another letter for the drive.

A. True
B. False

Answer: A

19. Formatting a volume will cause any data stored on that volume to be lost.

A. True
B. False

Answer: A

20. NTFS favors size over speed when compressing and decompressing files.

A. True
B. False

Answer: B

21. The memory in your computer is _____, which means that it goes away when the power is turned off.

Answer: volatile

22. Hard disks and floppy disks (and increasingly, CD-ROMs) are the most popular form of nonvolatile (or _____) storage in personal computers.

Answer: persistent

23. The two file systems for hard disks that Windows NT supports are _____, and _____.

Answer: FAT, NTFS

24. Hard disks are subdivided into _____.

Answer: partitions

25. The _____ _____ _____ is the first portion of data on a hard disk and is reserved for the BIOS bootstrap routine.

Answer: master boot record

26. Windows NT supports converting _____ to NTFS for the purpose of easing the migration of a computer from OS/2 to Windows NT.

Answer: HPFS

27. Filenames under NTFS are limited to _____ characters.

Answer: 255

28. _____ is the preferred file system for use with Windows NT.

Answer: NTFS

29. A disk with no partitions set up on it is completely given over to _____ _____.

Answer: free space

30. There can be only _____ primary partitions on a hard disk.

Answer: four

31. The partition that your computer boots when it is turned on is the _____ partition.

Answer: active

32. In Windows NT terminology, the partition that contains the startup files is called the _____ partition.

Answer: system

33. A _____ is one or more partitions treated as a single unit and given a single drive letter.

Answer: volume

34. In a stripe set, the data is stored evenly across all of the disks, one row at a time in _____ K blocks.

Answer: 64

35. Once you have created a partition, whether it be a single partition, volume set, or stripe set, you must _____ the partition to make it usable by Windows NT.

Answer: format

36. The recommended minimum partition size for NTFS is _____ MB.

Answer: 50

37. File _____ removes redundancy from files, thereby decreasing their physical size.

Answer: compression

Chapter 6

1. Anyone can create a shared directory.
   A. True
   B. False

   Answer: B

2. The user attempting to view the shared directory must have at least List permissions for that directory if it is on an NTFS partition.
   A. True
   B. False

   Answer: A

3. You can only share directories that are on NTFS partitions.
   A. True
   B. False

   Answer: B

4. The share name must be the same as the directory name.
   A. True
   B. False

   Answer: B

5. You can use the CACLS.EXE program to change the access control list of an administrative share that was creaed automatically by the system.
   A. True
   B. False

   Answer: B

6. When shared directory permissions and NTFS permissions differ, the shared directory permissions take precedence.
   A. True
   B. False

   Answer: B

7. Shared directory permissions do not depend on the partition type and are the same for DOS FAT and NTFS partitions.
   A. True
   B. False

   Answer: A

8. A user with No Access to a shared directory cannot connect to a shared directory.
   A. True
   B. False

   Answer: B

9. A user with Read access to a directory can execute files in that directory.
   A. True
   B. False

   Answer: A

10. A user with change access can delete files in a directory.
   A. True
   B. False

   Answer: A

11. NTFS gives you many security options that you do not have with a DOS FAT file system.
   A. True
   B. False

   Answer: A

12. An Administrator always has the permission to take ownership of a file or directory.
   A. True
   B. False

   Answer: A

13. You can give ownership of a file or directory to another user only if you have the Owner Transfer permission.

A. True

B. False

Answer: B

14. You can use the Windows NT backup utility to back up files on DOS FAT, or NTFS partitions.

A. True

B. False

Answer: A

15. You must restore to the same type of partition (DOS FAT or NTFS) from which you backed up the data.

A. True

B. False

Answer: B

16. Using the backup tool, you can back up only drives that you have permission to access.

A. True

B. False

Answer: A

17. Incremental, daily copy, and differential backups take more time and require more storage space than do normal and copy backups.

A. True

B. False

Answer: B

18. When you restore data from backup tape, you must restore the data to its original location.

A. True

B. False

Answer: B

19. You cannot schedule a tape backup to happen at a certain time through the graphical interface of the Windows NT backup utility.

A. True

B. False

Answer: A

20. All of the tape backup utility functions are available from the command line.

    A. True

    B. False

    Answer: A

21. In a network environment, you will often need to share information that resides on your Windows NT Workstation. You do this by creating _____ directories.

    Answer: shared

22. The default groups that permit creating shares are _____, _____ _____, and _____ _____.

    Answer: Administrators, Power Users, Server Operators

23. Windows NT Workstation has a limit of _____ simultaneous users accessing a shared directory.

    Answer: ten

24. _____ is a special administrative share that always points to the Windows NT directory.

    Answer: Admin$

25. You can make a permanent connection by mapping a _____ letter to the shared directory.

    Answer: drive

26. _____.EXE is a command line utility that allows you to edit the access control lists of files and directories.

    Answer: CACLS

27. ACL stands for _____ _____ _____.

    Answer: access control list

28. By default, the creator of a file or directory has _____ of that file or directory.

    Answer: ownership

29. NTFS supports the _____ of files and directories, which allows you to track the successful or unsuccessful attempts to access selected resources on your computer.

    Answer: auditing

30. With auditing you can specify which access attempts will be written to the _____ log of the Event Viewer.

Answer: Security

31. Auditing must be enabled via the _____ Manager in order for auditing to be performed.

Answer: User

32. Each file system supports an _____ bit that can be asserted to indicate that the utility should back up the file.

Answer: archive

33. A _____ _____ is the group of files, directories, and drives stored together on a backup tape.

Answer: backup set

34. The set of tapes that contain backup sets spanning multiple tapes is called a _____ _____.

Answer: family set

35. The _____ for a family set is stored on the last tape of the set.

Answer: catalog

36. If you do not have rights to a file or directory, you may still be able to back them up if you belong to the _____ _____ group.

Answer: Backup Operators

37. The default shares have the following at the end of the share name:
   A. Default Administrative Share
   B. (hidden)
   C. $
   D. Nothing

Answer: C

38. Which of the following is not a permission for shared directories?
   A. No Access
   B. Read
   C. Full Control
   D. Change Ownership

Answer: D

39. Match the NTFS feature with its description:

A. Auditing	**1.** Keeps track of which users and groups can access certain files and directories.
B. Permissions	**2.** Records security-related events to a log file.
C. Ownership	**3.** Records changes to files and directories as they happen and also records how to undo or redo the changes in case of a system failure.
D. Transaction logging	**4.** Tracks the individual who has full rights to a file or directory regardless of permissions.

Answer: A-2, B-1, C-4, D-3

40. Which of the following access permissions apply only to directories?

A. No Access

B. List

C. Read

D. Add

E. Add & Read

F. Change

G. Full Control

H. Special Access

Answer: B, D, and E

41. Match the backup method with its description:

A. Normal	**1.** Backs up the files if they have changed since the last backup. Does not mark those files as having been marked up.
B. Copy	**2.** Backs up the files that have changed that day. Does not mark those files as having been backed up.
C. Incremental	**3.** Backs up the files if they have changed since the last backup. Marks those files as having been backed up.
D. Daily copy	**4.** Backs up and does not mark the files as having been backed up.
E. Differential copy	**5.** Backs up and marks the files as having been backed up.

Answer: A-5, B-4, C-3, D-2, E-1

Chapter 7

1. Security is control of a system to prevent what?(Choose the best selection.)

A. Intrusion

B. Theft

C. Loss of any nature

Answer: C

2. The _____ process implements the security user interface when the computer is booted.

Answer: WinLogon

3. If you delete a user account and then add it again, the permissions will remain the same because the name has not changed.

A. True

B. False

Answer: B

4. Permissions changed while a user is logged on do not take effect until the user has logged out and back on again.

A. True

B. False

Answer: A

5. Windows NT allows access to objects by default.

A. True

B. False

Answer: B

6. The Windows NT logon process can be eliminated by adding default user information and an AutoAdminLogon value to the Windows NT Registry.

A. True

B. False

Answer: B

7. The Windows NT logon process is useful for more than just security.

A. True

B. False

Answer: A

8. All Windows NT resources are represented as objects in the system.
   A. True
   B. False

   Answer: A

9. All Windows NT objects have access control lists to implement security.
   A. True
   B. False

   Answer: A

10. The _____ _____ is created by the Security Access Manager process and identifies the current user to all subsequent processes.

   Answer: access token

11. Objects are composed of _____ that contain data and of _____ that are functions that operate on that data.

   Answer: attributes, services

12. An access token is a Windows NT object.

   A. True
   B. False

   Answer: A

13. Your access token is attached to each object you open after you log on.
   A. True
   B. False

   Answer: A

14. You should never change the default behavior of the WinLogon process.
   A. True
   B. False

   Answer: B

15. The account lockout policy applies to all accounts.
   A. True
   B. False

   Answer: B

Chapter 8

1. The NDIS boundary layer allows any number of adapters to be bound to any number of transport protocols.

   A. True
   B. False

   Answer: A

2. Microsoft added networking support after Windows NT was already finished.

   A. True
   B. False

   Answer: B

3. Programming interfaces are the boundary between the Application layer and user applications.

   A. True
   B. False

   Answer: A

4. All Windows NT adapter drivers are written by Microsoft and included on the Windows NT CD-ROM.

   A. True
   B. False

   Answer: B

5. IPC mechanisms are the protocols used to support client/server applications.

   A. True
   B. False

   Answer: A

6. IPC components are required only if you intend to support client/server applications.

   A. True
   B. False

   Answer: B

7. More than one redirector can be active in Windows NT.

   A. True
   B. False

   Answer: A

8. NWLink provides all necessary functions for Windows NT computers to share files and printers with NetWare servers.
   A. True
   B. False

   Answer: B

9. The Mailslots file system is not required if you do not install Microsoft Exchange.
   A. True
   B. False

   Answer: B

10. The Multi-Provider Router determines which redirector should handle Win32 API calls.
    A. True
    B. False

    Answer: A

11. The TDI is a required software component.
    A. True
    B. False

    Answer: B

12. NetBIOS can communicate over any TDI-compliant transport.
    A. True
    B. False

    Answer: A

13. Windows NT installs the NetDDE services by default.
    A. True
    B. False

    Answer: A

14. Windows NT automatically determines the best bindings between components, which should not be changed.
    A. True
    B. False

    Answer: B

15. Local area networking was developed primarily to support file sharing and print sharing.
    A. True
    B. False

    Answer: A

16. Once a software component is installed in Windows NT, it must be removed before it can be reconfigured.

    A. True

    B. False

    Answer: B

17. NWLink can be used only to attach to NetWare file servers.

    A. True

    B. False

    Answer: B

18. Windows NT components match the OSI model exactly.

    A. True

    B. False

    Answer: B

19. The _____ layer provides a reliable connection between computers.

    Answer: transport

20. The _____ allows Windows NT to run several transport protocols at once.

    Answer: transport driver interface (TDI)

21. The Windows NT version of _____ includes a security feature called impersonation.

    Answer: named pipes

22. Remote procedure calls allow both the client and the server portion of a client/server program to reside on the same machine through the _____ mechanism.

    Answer: local procedure call (LPC)

23. The _____ service includes the Windows networking redirector.

    Answer: Workstation.

24. In Windows NT the unified interface to all network resources is called

    A. The redirector

    B. The Workstation service

    C. The I/O Manager

    D. The Multiple Universal Naming Convention Provider

    Answer: D

25. Which type of component is named pipes?

    A. Programming interface

    B. File system

    C. Transport protocol

    D. Transport driver interface

    Answer: B

26. Which of the following is not installed by default in Windows NT?

    A. TCP/IP

    B. NetBIOS

    C. NWLink

    D. Workstation

    Answer: C

27. Which networking component is required for printer sharing?

    A. Workstation

    B. Server

    C. TCP/IP

    D. DLC

    Answer: A

28. Which of the following is not an IPC mechanism in Windows NT?

    A. NetBIOS

    B. NetDDE

    C. Windows Sockets

    D. TDI

    Answer: D

29. Which of the following transports cannot be routed?

    A. TCP/IP

    B. NWLink

    C. NetBEUI

    Answer: C

30. Which of the following is not a feature of TCP/IP?

    A. Routable across wide area networks

    B. Broad support across hardware and software systems

    C. Faster than NetBEUI

    D. Support for Internet protocols like SNMP

    Answer: C

Chapter 9

1. TCP/IP is mostly used in its native realm of high-performance engineering workstations.
   A. True
   B. False

   Answer: B

2. TCP/IP was designed as a local area network protocol, rather than as a protocol to link LANs together.
   A. True
   B. False

   Answer: B

3. The Network layer in the TCP/IP protocol suite corresponds to the Data Link and Physical layers in the OSI model and to the device drivers in Windows NT architecture.
   A. True
   B. False

   Answer: A

4. NDIS is a TCP/IP standard interface.
   A. True
   B. False

   Answer: B

5. UDP guarantees that the data will arrive and will arrive in the order sent.
   A. True
   B. False

   Answer: B

6. TCP guarantees that the data will arrive and will arrive in the order sent.
   A. True
   B. False

   Answer: A

7. Windows NT does not support the DNS protocol.
   A. True
   B. False

   Answer: B

8. The IP address for your computer must be unique.

   A. True

   B. False

   Answer: A

9. If you do not have a valid default gateway setting in your TCP/IP configuration, you will not be able to communicate with computers beyond your local area network using TCP/IP.

   A. True

   B. False

   Answer: A

10. 198.263.5.97 is a valid IP Address.

   A. True

   B. False

   Answer: B

11. The native protocol for UNIX computers is _____.

   Answer: TCP/IP

12. The first TCP/IP specifications were circulated as _____ for _____.

   Answer: Requests, Comments

13. The current open membership standards body for TCP/IP and the Internet is the

   _____ _____ _____ _____.

   Answer: Internet engineering task force

14. _____ and _____ operate at the Transport and Network layers of the OSI model.

   Answer: TCP, IP

15. IP is a part of the _____ layer in the TCP/IP protocol suite.

   Answer: Internet

16. _____ uses IP to control the flow of data over TCP/IP networks.

   Answer: ICMP

17. DHCP stands for _____ _____ _____ _____.

   Answer: Dynamic Host Configuration Protocol

18. TCP/IP provides two types of Transport layer services: _____ and _____.

Answer: TCP and UDP

19. IP addresses ending in _____ and _____ are special addresses in TCP/IP.

Answer: 0, 255

20. The _____ is used to identify a message destination that is beyond your local network.

Answer: subnet mask

21. When a destination network ID is not the same as your network ID, then the message is sent to a _____.

Answer: gateway

22. DNS stands for _____ _____ _____.

Answer: Domain Name Service

23. The most compelling reason to configure your workstation to use the TCP/IP protocol suite is to connect you to the _____.

Answer: Internet

24. Match the Internet tool with the activity:

1. Internet News	**A.** Exchange messages with other individuals around the world
2. FTP	**B.** Browse information presented by others over the Internet in a graphical format
3. World Wide Web	**C.** Retrieve files from other computers using a command line interface
4. Telnet	**D.** Use a command line interface to access a UNIX shell account
5. Internet mail	**E.** Participate in discussion groups

Answers: A-5, B-3, C-2, D-4, E-1

Chapter 10

1. Windows NT 4.0 clients require bindery emulation on NetWare 4.*x* servers.

A. True

B. False

Answer: B

2. All versions of NetWare default to the Ethernet_802.2 frame type.

A. True

B. False

Answer: B

3. NDS allows resources and account databases to be shared among a number of servers and managed from a central location.

A. True

B. False

Answer: A

4. Because NetWare does not share security trusts with Windows NT, you must provide your password each time you attach to a NetWare server.

A. True

B. False

Answer: B

5. Windows NT searches the Microsoft Windows network before it searches the NetWare network.

A. True

B. False

Answer: B

6. NWLink is a good general purpose transport and should be considered as a primary transport even if you don't need connectivity to NetWare.

A. True

B. False

Answer: A

7. Windows NT supports only the NetBIOS client/server programming interface for NetWare.

A. True

B. False

Answer: B

8. Windows NT supports attaching to NDS trees, but it cannot browse them.
   A. True
   B. False

   Answer: B

9. Windows NT is faster than NetWare at sharing files on equivalent hardware.
   A. True
   B. False

   Answer: B

10. Changes to the CSNW setting are made in the _____ control panel.

    Answer: CSNW

11. Windows NT connectivity to NetWare file servers is provided by the _____ service.

    Answer: CSNW

12. CSNW is implemented as a NetWare-compatible _____ in the Windows NT architecture.

    Answer: redirector

13. Which is the easiest way to allow access to a NetWare file server for a large group?
    A. Over the Internet
    B. Using GSNW
    C. Using CSNW
    D. Using NWLink

    Answer: B

14. Which frame type setting is best for most network adapters?
    A. Ethernet_802.3
    B. Ethernet_802.2
    C. Ethernet_II
    D. Ethernet_SNAP
    E. Auto

    Answer: E

15. Windows NT supports _____ standard NetWare utilities.
    A. all
    B. most
    C. some
    D. none

    Answer: B

16. Which transport protocol is used by default on NetWare servers?

    A. TCP/IP
    B. IPX
    C. NetBIOS
    D. NetBEUI

    Answer: B

Chapter 11

1. The workgroup model governs the interactions of Windows 95 and Windows NT computers in a peer network.

    A. True
    B. False

    Answer: A

2. In a workgroup the user accounts and resources on the workstation are administered from a network server.

    A. True
    B. False

    Answer: B

3. In a server-based network a central computer stores network files, enforces network security, and maintains network data such as user account information and trust relationships between computers.

    A. True
    B. False

    Answer: A

4. Each domain has one and only one server to store the network files for workstations.

    A. True
    B. False

    Answer: B

5. A domain can have several primary domain controllers.

    A. True
    B. False

    Answer: B

6. Only a computer running the Windows NT Server operating system can be a primary domain controller.

A. True

B. False

Answer: A

7. A backup domain controller can authenticate and log on domain users.

A. True

B. False

Answer: A

8. If you do not designate a server to be a primary domain controller or backup domain controller when you install the Windows NT Server operating system, you can change your mind later and promote the server to primary domain controller or backup domain controller status.

A. True

B. False

Answer: B

9. When your Windows NT workstation joins a domain, user accounts in the local Administrators and Users groups are added to the domain Administrator group and to the domain Users group that the primary domain controller maintains.

A. True

B. False

Answer: B

10. The User Manager program that comes with Windows NT Workstation cannot administer the domain user and administrator accounts.

A. True

B. False

Answer: A

11. If no domain controller is available, you can still log on to the workstation using the domain account.

A. True

B. False

Answer: A

12. Computers running the Windows for Workgroups operating system cannot perform the function of network browsers.

    A. True

    B. False

    Answer: B

13. A Windows NT workstation will win an election between a workstation and a server, all other considerations being equal.

    A. True

    B. False

    Answer: B

14. The computer with the more recent operating system version will win an election, all other considerations being equal.

    A. True

    B. False

    Answer: A

15. A Master Browser can promote a nonbrowser to backup or potential browser.

    A. True

    B. False

    Answer: B

16. Owing to the delay between the time when a computer goes down and when the computer entry is removed from the Browse list, up to 36 minutes can elapse before the Master Browser's list reflects the computer's condition.

    A. True

    B. False

    Answer: A

17. The backup browser delay in combination with the delayed computer announcement to the Master Browser could result in a resource not being available for as long as 90 minutes while a backup browser maintains the resource in its Browse list.

    A. True

    B. False

    Answer: B

18. The Master Browser can force other domains to announce themselves.

    A. True

    B. False

    Answer: A

19. A domain or workgroup can be down for up to 45 minutes before it is removed from the Browse list.

  A. True

  B. False

  Answer: A

20. The _____ model governs the interactions of Windows 95 and Windows NT computers in a server-based network with a Windows NT Server (designated the primary domain controller) coordinating the actions of the computers on the network.

  Answer: domain

21. The controlling computer in a Windows NT domain is called the _____ _____ _____.

  Answer: primary domain controller

22. The _____ _____ _____ maintains a copy of the primary domain controller's database.

  Answer: backup domain controller

23. The network _____ maintains the list of currently available network resources for a workgroup or domain.

  Answer: browser

24. A _____ browser does not receive a copy of the browse list unless it is promoted by a Master Browser to be a backup browser.

  Answer: potential

25. A _____ does not maintain a browse list for other computers or receive a browse list from a Master Browser.

  Answer: nonbrowser

26. Microsoft networks hold _____ to determine which computer will be the Master Browser.

  Answer: elections

27. A client computer, a backup browser, or a preferred Master Browser can cause an election to occur by broadcasting a special packet called an _____ packet.

  Answer: election

28. If the Master Browser does not receive a message from the computer for longer than _____ announcement periods, it removes the computer from the Browse list.

Answer: three

29. Backup browsers poll the Master Browser at _____ minute intervals.

Answer: 15

30. The size of the browse list that the Master Browser maintains is limited to _____K.

Answer: 64

31. The _____ _____ packet requires all computers participating in the domain or workgroup to respond within 30 seconds.

Answer: Request Announcement

32. When a computer becomes the Master Browser, it broadcasts a _____ _____ message to each workgroup or domain.

Answer: domain announcement

Chapter 12

1. RAS can use more than one modem simultaneously to make a connection to a RAS host.
   A. True
   B. False

Answer: A

2. RAS allows computers to communicate over a local area network.
   A. True
   B. False

Answer: B

3. RAS allows seamless remote access by controlling the functions of the host computer from the remote client.
   A. True
   B. False

Answer: B

4. Using the RAS monitor will not slow down your RAS connection.

   A. True

   B. False

   Answer: A

5. RAS server does not support the SLIP protocol.

   A. True

   B. False

   Answer: A

6. Internet connectivity requires the TCP/IP protocol.

   A. True

   B. False

   Answer: A

7. RAS supports either hardware or software compression, but not both.

   A. True

   B. False

   Answer: B

8. RAS supports _____ Windows NT interprocess communication mechanisms.

   Answer: all

9. The RAS _____ is used to check the status of a RAS connection.

   Answer: monitor

10. RAS scripts can be debugged by enabling logging and checking the _____ file.

   Answer: device.log

11. You can use the _____ to browse the World Wide Web after establishing a remote access session with an Internet service provider.

   A. Internet Explorer

   B. Windows NT Explorer

   C. FTP

   D. telnet

   Answer: A

12. Which protocol is RAS not capable of routing?

   A. TCP/IP

   B. IPX

   C. NetBEUI

   Answer: C

13. Which of the following protocols does SLIP support?

    A. IPX

    B. NetBEUI

    C. NetBIOS

    D. TCP/IP

    Answer: D

14. RAS does not yet support which of the following WAN connections?

    A. PSTN

    B. ISDN

    C. X.25

    D. ATM

    Answer: D

15. RAS on Windows NT Workstation is limited to how many inbound connections?

    A. 1

    B. 4

    C. 10

    D. 256

    Answer: A

16. You should use the following serial protocol with RAS whenever possible:

    A. SLIP

    B. TCP/IP

    C. NetBEUI

    D. PPP

    Answer: D

17. Which transport protocol is recommended for connecting Windows NT computers via RAS?

    A. TCP/IP

    B. NWLink

    C. NetBEUI

    D. Any TDI-compliant protocol

    Answer: C

18. Which is the slowest RAS transport between Windows NT computers?

    A. NetBEUI

    B. NWLink

    C. TCP/IP

    Answer: C

19. Which authentication protocol is used by default?

    A. CHAP

    B. MS-CHAP

    C. DES

    D. MS-DES

    E. PAP

    Answer: B

20. The connection device log is cleared

    A. When the user clears it in the RAS administrator

    B. Every time a new connection is made

    C. When it hits the size limit stored in the Registry

    D. Never

    Answer: B

Chapter 13

1. In Windows terminology a printer is the physical device that produces printed pages.

    A. True

    B. False

    Answer: B

2. Some print devices are not attached to a computer, but are instead connected directly to the network.

    A. True

    B. False

    Answer: A

3. In Windows NT all printing devices print directly on paper.

    A. True

    B. False

    Answer: B

4. Every printer is connected to one and only one printing device.

    A. True

    B. False

    Answer: B

5. Windows NT Workstation can provide printing services for Windows, UNIX, Apple Macintosh, and MS-DOS computers.

   A. True
   B. False

   Answer: A

6. The GDI translates application print requests into DDI calls to the print driver.

   A. True
   B. False

   Answer: A

7. DDI calls are not specific to the drawing characteristics of a printer.

   A. True
   B. False

   Answer: B

8. A journal file print job contains DDI calls that must be made to the device driver to produce a raw print job.

   A. True
   B. False

   Answer: A

9. The GDI will produce a journal file for a print job destined for a remote printer.

   A. True
   B. False

   Answer: B

10. You must have a print driver for the type of printer your workstation is connected to when you print.

   A. True
   B. False

   Answer: A

11. Windows NT can send print jobs to HP network printers and to UNIX printers.

   A. True
   B. False

   Answer: A

12. The print provider is also known as the spooler.
   A. True
   B. False

   Answer: A

13. Windows NT does not support printing Macintosh PostScript files to non-PostScript printing devices attached to the Windows NT computer.
   A. True
   B. False

   Answer: B

14. You can schedule several times during the day when a printer is and is not available from within the printer's Properties window.
   A. True
   B. False

   Answer: B

15. The _____, in Windows terminology, is a software construct that will translate print requests from applications and forward the resulting print job to the appropriate printing device.

   Answer: printer

16. A _____ consists of several printing devices fed by one printer.

   Answer: printer pool

17. GDI stands for _____ _____ _____.

   Answer: Graphics Device Interface

18. DDI stands for _____ _____ _____.

   Answer: Device Driver Interface

19. A _____ print job contains the sequence of instructions for the printer that will produce the printed document.

   Answer: raw

20. The _____ _____ is the software component that translates the printer-generic DDI calls generated by the GDI system into the printer-specific commands that will be passed on to the actual printer.

   Answer: print driver

21. The _____ _____ performs modifications to the print job before it passes the print job to the print monitor.

Answer: print processor

22. The _____ _____ is the software component that transmits the print job (by now transformed into the language of the printer) to the printing device.

Answer: print monitor

Chapter 14

1. Running the performance monitor does not affect the performance of the computer.

A. True
B. False

Answer: B

2. The performance monitor measures system performance.

A. True
B. False

Answer: B

3. Upgrading your hardware is one way to eliminate bottlenecks.

A. True
B. False

Answer: A

4. Bottlenecks are components that are not operating at peak performance.

A. True
B. False

Answer: B

5. Even the fastest computers have bottlenecks.

A. True
B. False

Answer: A

6. Windows NT can vary priority levels up to _____ priorities higher or lower automatically.

Answer: two

7. _____ performance counters are disabled by default to increase overall operating speed.

Answer: Disk

8. _____ are the measures taken to reduce the impact of a bottleneck on performance.

Answer: Optimizations

9. _____ are the basic units of division among processors in a multiprocessing environment.

Answer: Threads

10. Windows NT supports which type of multiprocessing?
   A. Symmetrical
   B. Asymmetrical
   C. Both symmetrical and asymmetrical
   D. Neither

Answer: A

11. Windows NT provides this tool for optimizing Windows NT performance:
   A. Microsoft Diagnostic tool (WinMSD)
   B. Performance tuner
   C. Windows NT Diagnostics (NTD)
   D. Performance monitor
   E. Task Manager

Answer: D

12. Which performance optimization is not implemented in the Windows NT operating system?
   A. Symmetric multiprocessing
   B. Swapping across multiple disks to increase performance
   C. Prioritizing threads and processes
   D. Caching RAM in the external processor cache
   E. Caching disk requests

Answer: E

13. In Windows NT, memory is divided into pages of what size?

- **A.** 4KB
- **B.** 16KB
- **C.** 64KB
- **D.** 256KB

Answer: A

14. NTFS uses which type of caching to improve performance?

- **A.** Write through
- **B.** Write back
- **C.** Write now
- **D.** Write optimization
- **E.** Buffered

Answer: B

15. The biggest single bottleneck in most computers is

- **A.** The processor
- **B.** Memory
- **C.** Disks
- **D.** Networks

Answer: C

16. The best way to eliminate disks as bottlenecks is to

- **A.** Create a stripe set
- **B.** Use them as little as possible
- **C.** Install a RAID controller
- **D.** Use ultra SCSI drives and controllers

Answer: B

Chapter 15

1. Windows NT channels all graphics requests to the Win32 subsystem for presentation to the user.

- **A.** True
- **B.** False

Answer: A

2. Windows NT funnels all mouse and keyboard events back through the POSIX subsystem.

- **A.** True
- **B.** False

Answer: B

3. The DOS (VDM) subsystem gives application programmers the most flexible environment for developing Windows applications.
   A. True
   B. False

   Answer: B

4. Win32 programs are developed for 32-bit processors such as the 386, 486, Pentium, MIPS, PowerPC, and Alpha.
   A. True
   B. False

   Answer: A

5. A 32-bit processor can work directly with larger values than a 16-bit processor can.
   A. True
   B. False

   Answer: A

6. Win32 programs, like Win16 programs, can have only one thread of execution.
   A. True
   B. False

   Answer: B

7. Win32 threads are scheduled cooperatively.
   A. True
   B. False

   Answer: B

8. Win32 applications all run within one shared memory space.
   A. True
   B. False

   Answer: B

9. Each Win32 application receives its own input queue.
   A. True
   B. False

   Answer: A

10. Every DOS program executes multiple threads within a single VDM.
    A. True
    B. False

    Answer: B

11. Within a VDM, MS-DOS calls are translated into Win32 calls that are forwarded to the Win32 subsystem.
    A. True
    B. False

    Answer: A

12. Earlier implementations of Microsoft Windows were designed to run on top of MS-DOS.
    A. True
    B. False

    Answer: A

13. Each Win16 program that you run is executed in a separate VDM and WOW.
    A. True
    B. False

    Answer: B

14. Each VDM and WOW pair has one input queue for all of the Win16 applications running in that VDM and WOW.
    A. True
    B. False

    Answer: A

15. Win16 programs within a VDM and WOW multitask preemptively.
    A. True
    B. False

    Answer: B

16. The OS/2 subsystem supports many programs written for version 2 of the OS/2 operating system.
    A. True
    B. False

    Answer: B

17. The Windows NT POSIX subsystem allows you to run programs compiled for another operating system.

A. True

B. False

Answer: B

18. The POSIX.1 standard is also an ISO standard.

A. True

B. False

Answer: A

19. With case-sensitive naming, Test, test, and TEST all designate the same file.

A. True

B. False

Answer: B

20. With hard links, Test, test, and TEST could all refer to the same file.

A. True

B. False

Answer: A

21. Windows NT provides a subsystem-neutral implementation of operating system services in a part of NT called _____ _____.

Answer: Executive Services

22. The Win32 application subsystem gives each program _____ GB of continuous, unsegmented address space.

Answer: 2

23. _____ is an industry standard software interface for 2-D and 3-D graphics display.

Answer: OpenGL

24. VDM stands for _____.

Answer: virtual DOS machine

25. The hardware environment that MS-DOS programs expect is created with _____ _____ _____ (VDDs).

Answer: virtual device drivers

26. One instance of _____ runs for every OS/2 program that is executing under NT.

Answer: OS2.EXE

27. _____ programs are compiled to run under either DOS or OS/2.

Answer: Bound

28. POSIX stands for _____ _____ _____ _____ for computing environments.

Answer: Portable Open Systems Interface

Chapter 16

1. BIOS stands for built-in operating system, and refers to the operating system that is present in the computer when it is turned on.
A. True
B. False

Answer: B

2. ROM costs much less per megabyte than hard disk storage.
A. True
B. False

Answer: B

3. The BIOS provides an operating system with routines to access the computer's hardware.
A. True
B. False

Answer: A

4. The primary function of the BIOS, after it initializes the computer's hardware, is to find an operating system and then load it.
A. True
B. False

Answer: A

5. The BIOS does not know anything about file systems.

    A. True

    B. False

    Answer: A

6. PC compatible computers reserve the first block of a hard disk for the hard disk directory.

    A. True

    B. False

    Answer: B

7. The Windows NT boot loader allows you to select from several operating systems to boot.

    A. True

    B. False

    Answer: A

8. NTLDR is used by Intel-based and RISC-based computers to load the Windows NT operating system.

    A. True

    B. False

    Answer: B

9. BOOTSECT.DOS is used by the boot loader when you boot Windows NT.

    A. True

    B. False

    Answer: B

10. NTBOOTDD.SYS is used only when your workstation is booting an NT operating system residing on a SCSI partition that is connected to a SCSI controller that does not have a SCSI BIOS installed and enabled.

    A. True

    B. False

    Answer: A

11. NTOSKRNL.EXE is the Windows NT kernel on RISC-based computers.

    A. True

    B. False

    Answer: A

12. The firmware on a RISC-based computer contains much of the functionality that is found in other programs on an Intel-based computer.

  A. True
  B. False

  Answer: A

13. All drivers and services are loaded during the kernel load phase.

  A. True
  B. False

  Answer: B

14. If the operating system path in the boot.ini file points to an operating system on a SCSI disk drive, the path will start with SCSI instead of multi.

  A. True
  B. False

  Answer: B

15. The process of finding, loading, and initializing the operating system is called _____.

  Answer: booting

16. The microprocessor and the RAM are _____, which means that they loose any information stored in them whenever power is turned off.

  Answer: volatile

17. IBM PC compatible computers call the program stored in the ROM the _____.

  Answer: BIOS

18. The operating system-imposed arrangement of data on a disk is called a _____ _____.

  Answer: file system

19. In the _____ _____ phase, the HAL is loaded.

  Answer: kernel load

20. The _____ _____ phase initializes the drivers and services loaded during the kernel load phase.

  Answer: kernel initialization

21. The Session Manager is started in the _____ _____ phase.

  Answer: services load

22. The Win32 subsystem starts the windows logon process in the _____ _____ _____ phase.

Answer: Windows system start

23. The phase in which the user logs on is called the _____ _____ phase.

Answer: user logon

24. The boot loader timeout value is stored in the [_____ _____] section of the BOOT.INI file.

Answer: boot loader

25. Each operating system has an entry in the [_____ _____] section of the BOOT.INI file.

Answer: operating systems

26. The _____ boot option will cause Windows NT to load in standard VGA mode.

Answer: /BASEVIDEO

27. The _____ boot option will cause the names of the device drivers to be displayed as they are loaded.

Answer: /SOS

28. The _____ _____ conventions describe the meaning of each part of the path to the operating system in the BOOT.INI file.

Answer: ARC naming

29. If the boot configuration is incorrect, you can use the _____ boot option to implement a boot configuration that worked before.

Answer: LastKnownGood

Chapter 17

1. Release versions of Windows NT are bug free.

A. True
B. False

Answer: B

2. Windows NT runs on all computers capable of running Windows 95.

   A. True

   B. False

   Answer: B

3. Microsoft maintains all Internet troubleshooting resources for Windows NT in the Windows NT knowledge base at the Microsoft Web site.

   A. True

   B. False

   Answer: B

4. Microsoft does not certify hardware components as compatible with NT.

   A. True

   B. False

   Answer: A

5. Recent changes to your computer system are likely to be the cause of new malfunctions.

   A. True

   B. False

   Answer: A

6. If you use Windows NT, you no longer have any reason to use MS-DOS.

   A. True

   B. False

   Answer: B

7. The Microsoft knowledge base is the official repository for support information about all Microsoft products, including Windows NT.

   A. True

   B. False

   Answer: A

8. With MS-DOS, you cannot access _____ volumes.

   Answer: NTFS

9. To create an emergency repair disk, use the _____ utility.

   Answer: rdisk

10. The _____ section of the Windows NT diagnostic tool is the most useful for troubleshooting.

    Answer: Resources

11. The _____ is by far the best troubleshooting resource for any computer problem.

    Answer: Internet

12. Which of the following is not good practice when troubleshooting?
    A. Be patient.
    B. Perform easy tests first.
    C. Change only one setting at a time.
    D. Make as many changes as possible.

    Answer: D

13. The most common hardware problem in PCs is
    A. Bad memory
    B. Hardware conflicts
    C. Loose cables
    D. Power supply failure

    Answer: B

14. Which of these failures is the most damaging of all computer component failures?
    A. Processor
    B. Memory
    C. Motherboard
    D. Hard disk

    Answer: D

15. An emergency repair disk can restore
    A. Missing Windows NT system user files
    B. Damaged user files
    C. Back up tapes
    D. Registry information

    Answer: D

16. To view the Event log, use the:
    A. Event Monitor
    B. User Manager
    C. Notepad
    D. Event Viewer

    Answer: D

Glossary

Numbers and Symbols

80386

The Intel microprocessor that introduced the power of 32-bit computing to the IBM PC-compatible computer. The 80386 also introduced memory management, which allowed the use of virtual memory and hardware level multitasking, and protected mode, which increased the stability of operating systems by allowing them to restrict the activities of user-level programs. See *i486, Pentium.*

A

Access Control List (ACL)

A list of security identifiers contained by an object. Only the processes identified on the ACL with appropriate permissions can activate the services of that object. See *Object, Security Identifiers, Permissions.*

Access Tokens

Objects containing the security identifier of a running process. A process started by another process inherits the starting process's access token. The access token is checked against each object's ACL to determine whether or not appropriate permissions are granted to perform any requested service. See *Access Control List, Permissions, Object, Security Identifiers, Process.*

Accounts

Containers for security identifiers, passwords, permissions, group associations, and preferences for each user of a system. The User Manager administers accounts. See *Security Identifiers, Preferences, Permissions, Password, Groups.*

ACL

See *Access Control List.*

Adapter

Any hardware device that allows communications to occur through physically dissimilar systems. This term usually refers to peripheral cards permanently mounted inside computers that provide an interface from the computer's bus to another media such as a hard disk or a network. See *Network Interface Card, Small Computer Systems Interface.*

Address Resolution Protocol (ARP)

An Internet protocol for resolving an IP address into a Physical layer address (such as an Ethernet media access controller address). See *Physical Layer, Internet Protocol.*

Administrator Account

A special account in Windows NT that has the ultimate set of security permissions and can assign any permission to any user or group. The Administrator account is used to correct security problems. See *Permissions.*

Administrators

Users who are part of the Administrators group. This group has the ultimate set of security permissions. See *Administrator Account, Permissions, Groups.*

AltaVista

A World Wide Web indexing service operated by Digital Equipment Corporation. This service allows you to query nearly the entire set of World Wide Web pages by keyword and returns a best-match-first result. This site is located at www.altavista.digital.com.

AppleTalk

The built-in (to firmware) suite of network protocols used by Macintosh computers. Windows NT Server uses AppleTalk to service Macintosh clients by simulating an Apple server. See *Macintosh, Network Protocol.*

Application

Large software packages that perform specific functions, such as word processing, Web browsing, or database management. Applications typically consist of more than one program. See *Programs.*

Application Layer

The layer of the OSI model that interfaces with User mode applications by providing high-level network services based upon lower-level network layers. Network file systems like named pipes are an example of Application layer software. See *Named Pipes, Open Systems Interconnect Model, Application*.

ARP

See *Address Resolution Protocol*.

Asymmetrical Multiprocessing

A multiple processor architecture in which certain processors are designated to run certain threads or in which scheduling is not done on a fair-share basis. Asymmetrical multiprocessing is easier to implement than symmetrical multiprocessing, but does not scale well as processors are added. See *Microprocessor, Symmetrical Multiprocessing*.

Asynchronous Transfer Mode (ATM)

A wide area transport protocol that runs at many different speeds and supports real-time, guaranteed packet delivery in hardware, as well as lower-quality levels of service on a bandwidth-available basis. ATM will eventually replace all other wide area protocols, as most worldwide PTSN providers have declared their support for the international standard. See *Public Switched Telephone Network, Wide Area Network*.

Audit Policy

Audit policy determines which user events you wish to track for security reasons. Audit policy can track the success or failure of specified security events; it is set in the User Manager. See *Security*.

B

Back Up

The process of writing all the data contained in online mass storage devices to offline mass storage devices for the purpose of safe keeping. Backups are usually performed from hard disk drives to tape drives. Also referred to as archiving. See *Hard Disk Drive*.

Backup Browser

A computer on a Microsoft network that maintains a list of computers and services available on the network. The Master Browser supplies this list. The backup browser distributes the Browsing service load to a workgroup or domain. See *Master Browser*.

Backup Domain Controllers

Servers that contain accurate replications of the security and user databases; servers can authenticate workstations in the absence of a primary domain controller. See *Primary Domain Controller*.

Basic Input/Output System (BIOS)

A set of routines in firmware that provides the most basic software interface drivers for hardware attached to the computer. The BIOS contains the bootstrap routine. See *Boot, Driver, Firmware*.

Bindery

A NetWare structure that contains user accounts and permissions. It is analogous to the Registry in Windows NT. See *Registry*.

Binding

The process of linking network services to network service providers. The binding facility allows users to define exactly how network services operate in order to optimize the performance of the system. By default, Windows enables all possible bindings. The Network control panel is used to change bindings. See *Network Layer, Data Link Layer*.

BIOS

See *Basic Input/Output System*.

Bit

A binary digit. A numeral having only two possible values, 0 or 1. Computers represent these two values as high (voltage present) or low (no voltage present) state on a control line. Bits are accumulated in sets of certain sizes to represent higher values. See *Byte*.

Boot

The process of loading a computer's operating system. Booting usually occurs in multiple phases, each successively more complex until the entire operating system and all its services are running. Also called *bootstrap*. The computer's BIOS must contain the first level of booting. See *Basic Input/Output System*.

Bottlenecks

Components operating at their peak capacity that restrict the flow of information through a system. Used singularly, the term indicates the single, most restrictive component in a system.

Bridge

A device that connects two networks of the same data link protocol by forwarding those packets destined for computers on the other side of the bridge. See *Router, Data Link Layer*.

Browser

A computer on a Microsoft network that maintains a list of computers and services available on the network.

Browsing

The process of requesting the list of computers and services on a network from a browser.

Byte

A set of 8 bits taken as a unit that represent up to 2^8, or 256, possible values. Because bytes are convenient for storing characters such as letters or numbers, they are the baseline used to measure memory sizes. See *Bit*.

C

Caching

A speed optimization technique that keeps a copy of the most recently used data in a fast, high-cost, low-capacity storage device rather than in the device upon which the actual data resides. Caching assumes that recently used data is likely to be used again. Fetching data from the cache is faster than fetching data from the slower, larger storage device. Most caching algorithms also copy the data most likely to be used next and perform write caching to further increase speed gains. See *Write-back Caching, Write-through Caching.*

CD-ROM

See *Compact Disk-Read Only Memory.*

Central Processing Unit (CPU)

The central processing unit of a computer. In microcomputers such as IBM PC compatible machines, the CPU is the microprocessor. See *Microprocessor.*

Client

A computer on a network that subscribes to the services provided by a server. See *Server.*

Client/Server

A network architecture that dedicates certain computers called servers to act as service providers to computers called clients, which users operate to perform work. Servers can be dedicated to providing one or more network services such as file storage, shared printing, communications, e-mail service, and Web response. See *Share, Peer.*

Client/Server Applications

Applications that split large applications into two components: computer-intensive processes that run on application servers and user interfaces that run on clients. Client/server applications communicate over the network through interprocess communication mechanisms. See *Client, Server, Interprocess Communications.*

Client Services for NetWare (CSNW)

A service provided with Windows NT that connects a workstation to NetWare file servers. See *NetWare.*

Code

Synonymous with software but used when the software itself, rather than the utility it provides, is the object of discussion. See *Software.*

COM Port

Communications port. A serial hardware interface conforming to the RS-232 standard for low-speed serial communications. See *Modem, Serial*.

Compact Disk-Read Only Memory (CD-ROM)

A media for storing extremely large software packages on optical read-only discs. CD-ROM is an adaptation of the CD medium used for distributing digitized music. CD-ROM discs can hold up to 650MB of information and cost very little to produce in quantity. See *Hard Disk Drive*.

Components

Interchangeable elements of a complex software or hardware system. See *Module*.

Compression

A space optimization scheme that reduces the size (length) of a data set by exploiting the fact that most useful data contains a great deal of redundancy. Compression reduces redundancy by creating symbols smaller than the data they represent and an index that defines the value of the symbols for each compressed set of data.

Computer

A device capable of performing automatic calculations based upon lists of instructions called programs. The computer feeds the results of these calculations (output) to peripheral devices that can represent them in useful ways, such as graphics on a screen or ink on paper. See *Microprocessor*.

Control Panel

A software utility that controls the function of specific operating system services by allowing users to change default settings for the service to match their preferences. The Registry contains the Control Panel settings on a system and/or per-user basis. See *Registry, Accounts*.

Cooperative Multitasking

A multitasking scheme in which each process must voluntarily return time to a central scheduling route. If any single process fails to return to the central scheduler, the computer will lock up. Both Windows and the Macintosh operating system use this scheme. See *Preemptive Multitasking, Windows for Workgroups 3.11*.

CPU

See *Microprocessor*.

CSNW

See *Client Services for NetWare*.

D

Data Link Control (DLC)

An obsolete network transport protocol that allows PCs to connect to older IBM mainframes and HP printers. See *Transmission Control Protocol/Internet Protocol*.

Data Link Layer

In the OSI model, the layer that provides the digital interconnection of network devices and the software that directly operates these devices, such as network interface adapters. See *Physical Layer, Network Layer, Open Systems Interconnect Model*.

Database

A related set of data organized by type and purpose. The term also can include the application software that manipulates the data. The Windows NT Registry (a database itself) contains a number of utility databases such as user account and security information. See *Registry*.

DDE

See *Dynamic Data Exchange*.

Default Shares

Resources shared by default when Windows NT is installed. See *Share, Resource*.

Desktop

A directory that the background of the Windows Explorer shell represents. By default objects on the desktop contain the local storage devices and available network shares. See *Explorer, Shell*.

DHCP

See *Dynamic Host Configuration Protocol*.

Dial-Up Connections

Data Link layer digital connections made via modems over regular telephone lines. The term *dial-up* refers to temporary digital connections, as opposed to leased telephone lines, which provide permanent connections. See *Data Link Layer, Public Switched Telephone Network, Modem*.

Directories

In a file system, directories are containers that store files or other directories. Mass storage devices have a root directory that contains all other directories, thus creating a hierarchy of directories sometimes referred to as a *directory tree*. See *File, File System*.

DLC

See *Data Link Control*.

DNS

See *Domain Name Service*.

Domain

In Microsoft networks a domain is an arrangement of client and server computers referenced by a specific name that share a single security permissions database. On the Internet a domain is a named collection of hosts and subdomains registered with a unique name by the InterNIC. See *Workgroup*.

Domain Controllers

Servers that authenticate workstation network logon requests by comparing a username and password against account information stored in the user accounts database. A user cannot access a domain without authentication from a domain controller. See *Primary Domain Controller, Backup Domain Controllers, Domain*.

Domain Name Service (DNS)

The TCP/IP network service that translates textual Internet network addresses into numerical Internet network addresses. See *Transmission Control Protocol/ Internet Protocol, Internet*.

Drive

See *Hard Disk Drive*.

Drive Letters

Single letters assigned as abbreviations to the mass storage volumes available to a computer. See *Volume*.

Driver

A program that provides a software interface to a hardware device. Drivers are written for the specific device they control, but they present a common software interface to the computer's operating system, allowing all devices (of a similar type) to be controlled as if they were the same. See *Data Link Layer, Operating System*.

Dynamic Data Exchange (DDE)

A method of interprocess communication within the Microsoft Windows operating systems.

Dynamic Host Configuration Protocol (DHCP)

DHCP is a method of automatically assigning IP addresses to client computers on a network.

E

Electronic Mail (E-mail)

A type of client/server application that provides a routed, stored-message service between any two user e-mail accounts. E-mail accounts are not the same as user accounts, but a one-to-one relationship usually exists between them. Because all modern computers can attach to the Internet, users can send e-mail over the Internet to any location that has telephone or wireless digital service. See *Internet*.

Encryption

The process of obscuring information by modifying it according to a mathematical function known only to the intended recipient. Encryption secures information being transmitted over nonsecure or untrusted media. See *Security*.

Environment Variables

Variables, such as the search path, that contain information available to programs and batch files about the current operating system environment.

Ethernet

The most popular Data Link layer standard for local area networking. Ethernet implements the carrier sense multiple access with collision detection (CSMA/CD) method of arbitrating multiple computer access to the same network. This standard supports the use of Ethernet over any type of media including wireless broadcast. Standard Ethernet operates as 10 megabits per second. Fast Ethernet operates at 100 megabits per second. See *Data Link Layer*.

Exchange

Microsoft's messaging application. Exchange implements Microsoft's mail application programming interface (MAPI) as well as other messaging protocols such as POP, SNMP, and faxing to provide a flexible message composition and reception service. See *Electronic Mail, Fax Modems*.

Explorer

The default shell for Windows 95 and Windows NT 4.0. Explorer implements the more flexible desktop objects paradigm rather than the Program Manager paradigm used in earlier versions of Windows. See *Desktop*.

F

FAT

See *File Allocation Table*.

Fault Tolerance

Any method that prevents system failure by tolerating single faults, usually through hardware redundancy.

Fax Modems

Special modems that include hardware to allow the transmission and reception of facsimiles. See *Modem, Exchange*.

Fiber Distributed Data Interface (FDDI)

A Data Link layer that implements two counter-rotating token rings at 100 megabits per second. FDDI was a popular standard for interconnecting campus and metropolitan area networks because it allows distant digital connections at high speed, but ATM is replacing FDDI in many sites. See *Asynchronous Transfer Mode, Data Link Layer*.

File Allocation Table (FAT)

The file system used by MS-DOS and available to other operating systems such as Windows (all variations), OS/2, and the Macintosh. FAT has become something of a mass storage compatibility standard because of its simplicity and wide availability. FAT has few fault tolerance features and can become corrupted through normal use over time. See *File System*.

File Attributes

Bits are stored along with the name and location of a file in a directory entry to show the status of the file, such as archived, hidden, read-only, etc. Different operating systems use different file attributes to implement such services as sharing, compression, and security.

File System

A software component that manages the storage of files on a mass storage device by providing services that can create, read, write, and delete files. File systems impose an ordered database of files on the mass storage device, called volumes, that use hierarchies of directories to organize files. See *Mass Storage Device, Files, Database, Volumes, Directories*.

File Transfer Protocol (FTP)

A simple Internet protocol that transfers complete files from an FTP server to a client running the FTP client. FTP provides a simple no-overhead method of transferring files between computers but cannot perform browsing functions. You must know the URL of the FTP server to which you wish to attach. See *Internet, Uniform Resource Locator.*

Files

A set of data stored on a mass storage device identified by a directory entry containing a name, file attributes, and the physical location of the file in the volume. See *Volume, Mass Storage Device, Directories, File Attributes.*

Firmware

Software stored permanently in nonvolatile memory and built into a computer to provide its BIOS and a bootstrap routine. The entire operating system of simple computers may be built into firmware. See *Basic Input/Output System, Boot, Software.*

Floppy Disk

The first convenient removable media mass storage device. Floppy disks typically store 1.4MB of data magnetically on a thin mylar film coated with ferric particles encased in a protective plastic shell. Because floppy disks have been around longer than hard disk drives, most computers are capable of booting operating systems from a floppy disk. See *Mass Storage Device.*

Format

The process of preparing a mass storage device for use with a file system. There are actually two levels of formatting. Low-level formatting writes a structure of sectors and tracks to the disk with bits used by the mass storage controller hardware. The controller hardware requires this format, and it is independent of the file system. High-level formatting creates file system structures such as an allocation table and a root directory in a partition, thus creating a volume. See *Mass Storage Device, Volume.*

Frame

A data structure that network hardware devices use to transmit data between computers. Frames consist of the addresses of the sending and receiving computers, size information, and a check sum. Frames are envelopes around packets of data that allow them to be addressed to specific computers on a shared media network. See *Ethernet, Fiber Distributed Data Interface, Token Ring.*

FTP

See *File Transfer Protocol.*

G

Gateway

A computer that serves as a router, a format translator, or a security filter for an entire network.

Graphical Device Interface (GDI)

The programming interface and graphical services provided to Win32 for programs to interact with graphical devices such as the screen and printer. See *Programming Interfaces, Win32.*

Graphical User Interface (GUI)

A computer shell program that represents mass storage devices, directories, and files as graphical objects on a screen. A cursor driven by a pointing device such as a mouse manipulates the objects. Typically, icons that can be opened into windows that show the data contained by the object represent the objects. See *Shell, Explorer.*

Group Identifiers

Security identifiers that contain the set of permissions allowed to a group. When a user account is part of a group, the group identifier is appended to that user's security identifier, thus granting the individual user all the permissions assigned to that group. See *Security Identifiers, Accounts, Permissions.*

Groups

Security entities to which users can be assigned membership for the purpose of applying the broad set of group permissions to the user. By managing permissions for groups and assigning users to groups, rather than assigning permissions to users, security administrators can maintain control of very large security environments. See *Permissions, Accounts, Security.*

GUI

See *Graphical User Interface*.

H

HAL

See *Hardware Abstraction Layer*.

Hard Disk Drives

Hard disk drives are mass storage devices that read and write digital information that is stored on spinning disks. The spinning disks must be precisely aligned and cannot normally be removed. Hard disk drives are an inexpensive way to store gigabytes of computer data permanently. See *Mass Storage Device*.

Hardware Abstraction Layer (HAL)

A Windows NT service that provides basic input/output services such as timers, interrupts, and multiprocessor management for computer hardware. The HAL is a device driver for the motherboard circuitry that allows the Windows NT operating system to treat different families of computers the same way. See *Driver, Service, Interrupt Request*.

High Performance File System (HPFS)

The file system native to OS/2 that performs many of the same functions of NTFS when run under OS/2. See *File System, New Technology File System*.

Host

In remote access the computer providing data to the RAS client and hosting its connection to the remote network. See *Remote Access Service*.

HPFS

See *High Performance File System*.

HTML

See *Hypertext Markup Language*.

HTTP

See *Hypertext Transfer Protocol*.

Hub

An Ethernet Data Link layer device that connects point-to-point Physical layer links, such as twisted pair or fiber optic cables, into a single shared media network. See *Data Link Layer, Ethernet*.

Hypertext Markup Language (HTML)

A textual data format that identifies sections of a document as headers, lists, hypertext links, etc. HTML is the data format used on the World Wide Web for the publication of Web pages. See *Hypertext Transfer Protocol, World Wide Web*.

Hypertext Transfer Protocol (HTTP)

Hypertext transfer protocol is an Internet protocol that transfers HTML documents over the Internet and responds to context changes that happen when a user clicks on a hypertext link. See *Hypertext Markup Language, World Wide Web*.

I

I/O

Input/Output.

i486

An Intel 80386 compatible microprocessor that includes an onboard floating point unit for increased mathematical speed and operates at higher clock speeds than the 80386. See *80386, Pentium, Microprocessor*.

Icon

A graphical representation of a resource in a graphical user interface that usually takes the form of a small (32 x 32) bitmap. See *Graphical User Interface*.

IDE

A simple mass storage device interconnection bus that operates at 5 Mbps and can handle no more than two attached devices. IDE devices are similar to but less expensive than SCSI devices. See *Small Computer Systems Interface, Mass Storage Device*.

Industry Standard Architecture (ISA)

The design standard for 16-bit Intel compatible motherboards and peripheral buses. The 32/64-bit PCI bus standard is replacing the ISA standard. Adapters and interface cards must conform to the bus standard(s) used by the motherboard in order to be used with a computer.

Ink-Jet Printers

Output devices that create paper copies of computer data by squirting microscopic ink dots onto paper from a rapidly moving ink-jet nozzle. Ink-jet printers create very high quality, inexpensive documents and have replaced most forms of mechanical impact printers. See *Laser Printers, Printers*.

Integrated Services Digital Network (ISDN)

A direct, digital dial-up PSTN Data Link layer connection that operates at 64KB per channel over regular twisted pair cable between a subscriber site and a PSTN central office. ISDN provides twice the data rate of the fastest modems per channel. Up to 24 channels can be multiplexed over two twisted pairs. See *Public Switched Telephone Network, Data Link Layer, Modem*.

Intel Architecture

A family of microprocessors descended directly from the Intel 8086, itself descended from the first microprocessor, the Intel 4004. The Intel architecture is the dominant microprocessor family. It was used in the original IBM PC microcomputer adopted by the business market and later adapted for home use.

Internet

An interconnected global network of computers based upon the TCP/IP protocol suite. TCP/IP was originally developed by the U.S. Department of Defense's Advanced Research Projects Agency to facilitate the interconnection of military networks and was provided free to universities. The obvious utility of worldwide digital network connectivity and the availability of free complex networking software developed at universities doing military research attracted other universities, research institutions, private organizations, businesses, and finally the individual home user. The Internet is now available to all current commercial computing platforms. See *File Transfer Protocol, Telnet, UseNet, World Wide Web, Transmission Control Protocol/Internet Protocol.*

Internet Explorer

A World Wide Web browser produced by Microsoft and included free with Windows 95 and Windows NT 4.0. See *World Wide Web, Internet.*

Internet Protocol (IP)

The Network layer protocol upon which the Internet is based. IP provides a simple connectionless packet exchange. Other protocols such as UDP or TCP use IP to perform their connection-oriented or guaranteed delivery services. See *Transmission Control Protocol/Internet Protocol, Internet.*

Internet Service Provider (ISP)

A company that provides dial-up connections to the Internet. See *Internet.*

Internetwork Packet eXchange (IPX)

The Network and Transport layer protocol developed by Novell for its NetWare product. IPX is a routable, connection-oriented protocol similar to TCP/IP but much easier to manage and with lower communication overhead. See *Internet Protocol, NetWare, NetWare Link.*

Interprocess Communications (IPC)

A generic term describing any manner of client/server communication protocols, specifically those operating in the Application layer. Interprocess communications mechanisms provide a method for the client and server to trade information. See *Named Pipes, Remote Procedure Calls, Network Basic Input/Output System, Mailslots, Network Dynamic Data Exchange, Local Procedure Call.*

Interrupt Request (IRQ)

A hardware signal from a peripheral device to the microcomputer indicating that it has I/O traffic to send. If the microprocessor is not running a more important service, it will interrupt its current activity and handle the interrupt request. IBM

PCs have 16 levels of interrupt request lines. Under Windows NT each device must have a unique interrupt request line. See *Microprocessor, Driver, Peripheral*.

IP

See *Internet Protocol.*

IP Address

A four-byte number that uniquely identifies a computer on an IP internetwork. InterNIC assigns the first bytes of Internet IP addresses and administers them in hierarchies. Huge organizations like the government or top-level ISPs have class A addresses, large organizations and most ISPs have class B addresses, and small companies have class C addresses. In a class A address, InterNIC assigns the first byte, and the owning organization assigns the remaining three bytes. In a class B address, InterNIC or the higher level ISP assigns the first two bytes, and the organization assigns the remaining two bytes. In a class C address, InterNIC or the higher level ISP assigns the first three bytes, and the organization assigns the remaining byte. Organizations not attached to the Internet can assign IP addresses as they please. See *Internet Protocol, Internet.*

IPC

See *Interprocess Communications.*

IPX

See *Internetwork Packet eXchange.*

IRQ

See *Interrupt Request.*

ISA

See *Industry Standard Architecture.*

ISDN

See *Integrated Services Digital Network.*

ISP

See *Internet Service Provider.*

K

Kernel

The core process of a preemptive operating system, consisting of a multitasking scheduler and the basic services that provide security. Depending upon the operating system, other services such as virtual memory drivers may be built into the Kernel. The Kernel is responsible for managing the scheduling of threads and processes. See *Operating System, Driver*.

L

LAN

See *Local Area Network*.

LAN Manager

The Microsoft brand of a network product jointly developed by IBM and Microsoft that provided an early client/server environment. LAN Manager/Server was eclipsed by NetWare but was the genesis of many important protocols and IPC mechanisms used today, such as NetBIOS, named pipes, and NetBEUI. Portions of this product exist today in OS/2 Warp Server. See *Operating System 2, Interprocess Communications*.

LAN Server

The IBM brand of a network product jointly developed by IBM and Microsoft. See *LAN Manager*.

Laser Printers

Output devices that produce paper copies of computer data by creating an electrostatic charge on a metallic cylinder using a laser, which is then passed through a toner reservoir. Toner (ink) sticks to the charged areas of the drum. The toner is pressed into paper and then heat cured. Because of the fine resolution that the extremely narrow laser beam achieves, laser printers create very high quality paper documents. Laser printers are faster than many other printers but are generally more expensive.

LaserJet

The most popular brand of laser printer in the world, manufactured by Hewlett Packard. See *Laser Printers, Ink-Jet Printers*.

Local Area Network (LAN)

A network of computers operating on the same high-speed, shared media network Data Link layer. The size of a local area network is defined by the limitations of high speed shared media networks to generally less than 1 kilometer in overall span. Some LAN backbone data link protocols such as FDDI can create larger LANs called metropolitan or medium area networks (MANs). See *Wide Area Network, Data Link Layer*.

Local Procedure Call (LPC)

A mechanism that loops remote procedure calls without the presence of a network so that the client and server portion of an application can reside on the same machine. Local procedure calls look like remote procedure calls (RPCs) to the client and server sides of a distributed application. See *Remote Procedure Calls*.

Logging

The process of recording information about activities and errors in the operating system.

Login

The term used by Novell NetWare to indicate opening a session with a server by providing a valid user account name and password. See *NetWare, Logon*.

Logoff

The process of closing an open session with a server. See *Logon*.

Logon

The process of opening a network session by providing a valid authentication consisting of a user account name and a password to a domain controller. After logon, network resources are available to the user according to the user's assigned permissions. See *Domain Controllers*.

Logon Scripts

Command files that automate the logon process by performing utility functions such as attaching to additional server resources or automatically running different programs based upon the user account that established the logon. See *Logon*.

Long Filename (LFN)

A filename longer than the eight characters plus three-character extension allowed by MS-DOS. In Windows NT and Windows 95, long filenames may be up to 255 characters.

LPC

See *Local Procedure Call*.

M

Macintosh

A brand of computer manufactured by Apple. Macintosh is the only successful line of computers neither based upon the original IBM PC nor running the UNIX operating system. Windows NT Server supports Apple computers despite their use of proprietary network protocols.

MacOS

The operating system that runs on an Apple Macintosh computer. See *Macintosh*.

Mailslots

A connectionless messaging IPC mechanism that Windows NT uses for browse request and logon authentication. See *Interprocess Communications*.

Mainframes

A generic term for large powerful computers not based upon single-chip micropro-cessor technology. Mainframes usually used terminals with no computing ability for user interfaces and shared a central CPU throughout an organization. The central processing paradigm of the mainframe/terminal architecture is the antithesis of the distributed processing architecture implemented by local area networks and the client/server paradigm. Distributed processing has won the market, and mainframes are now being used as superservers. See *Client/Server, Server.*

Mass Storage Device

Any device capable of storing many megabytes of information permanently, but especially those capable of random access to any portion of the information, such as hard disk drives and CD-ROM drives. See *Small Computer Systems Interface, IDE, Hard Disk Drive.*

Master Browser

The computer on a network that maintains a list of computers and services available on the network and distributes the list to other browsers. The Master Browser may also promote potential browsers to be browsers. See *Browser, Browsing, Potential Browser, Backup Browser.*

Memory

Any device capable of storing information. This term is usually used to indicate volatile random access semiconductor memory (RAM) capable of high-speed access to any portion of the memory space, but incapable of storing information without power. See *Random Access Memory, Mass Storage Device.*

Microprocessor

An integrated semiconductor circuit designed to automatically perform lists of logical and arithmetic operations. Modern microprocessors independently manage memory pools and support multiple instruction lists called threads. Microprocessors are also capable of responding to interrupt requests from peripherals and include onboard support for complex floating point arithmetic. Microprocessors must have instructions when they are first powered on. These instructions are contained in nonvolatile firmware called a BIOS. See *Basic Input/ Output System, Operating System.*

Microsoft Disk Operating System (MS-DOS)

A 16-bit operating system designed for the 8086 chip that was used in the original IBM PC. Because IBM was unable to ship a better operating system, MS-DOS became the standard operating system used in microcomputers and is still the most widely used. MS-DOS is a simple program loader and file system that turns over complete control of the computer to the running program and provides very little service beyond file system support and that provided by the BIOS.

Modem

Modulator/demodulator. A Data Link layer device used to create an analog signal suitable for transmission over telephone lines from a digital data stream. Modern modems also include a command set for negotiating connections and data rates with remote modems and for setting their default behavior. The fastest modems run at about 33Kbps and will probably not get much faster due to the inherent physical bandwidth limitations of telephone cables. See *Data Link Layer*.

Module

A software component of a modular operating system that provides a certain defined service. Modules can be installed or removed depending upon the service requirements of the software running on the computer. Modules allow operating systems and applications to be customized to fit the needs of the user.

MS-DOS

See *Microsoft Disk Operating System*.

Multilink

A capability of RAS to combine multiple data streams into one network connection for the purpose of using more than one modem or ISDN channel in a single connection. This feature is new to Windows NT 4.0. See *Remote Access Service*.

Multiple Universal Naming Convention Provider (MUP)

A software component of Windows NT that allows two or more UNC providers, for example, for Microsoft networks and NetWare networks to exist simultaneously. The MUP determines which UNC provider will handle a particular UNC request and forwards the request to that provider. See *Universal Naming Convention, Multiprovider Router*.

Multiprocessing

Using two or more processors simultaneously to perform a computing task. Depending upon the operating system, processing may be done asymmetrically, wherein certain processors are assigned certain threads independent of the load they create, or symmetrically, wherein threads are dynamically assigned to processors according to an equitable scheduling scheme. The term usually describes a multiprocessing capacity built into the computer at a hardware level in that the computer itself supports more than one processor. However, *multiprocessing* can also be applied to network computing applications achieved through interprocess communication mechanisms. Client/server applications are, in fact, examples of multiprocessing. See *Asymmetrical Multiprocessing, Symmetrical Multiprocessing, Interprocess Communications*.

Multiprovider Router

A software component of Windows NT that allows two or more Win32 network API providers to exist simultaneously. The MUP determines which Win32 network provider handles a particular API request and forwards the request to that provider. See *Multitasking*.

Multitasking

The capacity of an operating system to rapidly switch among threads of execution. Multitasking allows processor time to be divided among threads as if each thread ran on its own slower processor. Multitasking operating systems allow two or more applications to run at the same time and can provide a greater degree of service to applications than single-tasking operating systems like MS-DOS. See *Multiprocessing*.

MUP

See *Multiple Universal Naming Connection Provider*.

N

Named Pipes

An interprocess communication mechanism that is implemented as a file system service, allowing programs to be modified to run on it without using a proprietary application programming interface. Named pipes were developed to support more robust client/ server communications than those allowed by the simpler NetBIOS. See *OS/2, File Systems, Interprocess Communications*.

NDIS

See *Network Driver Interface Specification*.

NDS

See *NetWare Directory Services*.

NetBEUI

See *NetBIOS Extended User Interface.*

NetBIOS

See *Network Basic Input/Output System.*

NetBIOS Extended User Interface (NetBEUI)

A simple Network layer transport developed to support NetBIOS installations. NetBEUI is not routable, and so it is not appropriate for larger networks. NetBEUI is the fastest transport protocol available for Windows NT.

NetBIOS Gateway

A service provided by RAS that allows NetBIOS requests to be forwarded independent of transport protocol. For example, NetBIOS requests from a remote computer connected via NetBEUI can be sent over the network via NWLink. See *Network Basic Input/Output System, NetWare Link, NetBIOS over TCP/IP, NetBEUI.*

NetBIOS over TCP/IP (NetBT)

A network service that implements the NetBIOS IPC over the TCP/IP protocol stack. See *Network Basic Input/Output System, Interprocess Communications, Transmission Control Protocol/Internet Protocol.*

NetDDE

See *Network Dynamic Data Exchange.*

NetWare

A popular network operating system developed by Novell in the early 1980s. NetWare is a cooperative, multitasking, highly optimized, dedicated-server network operating system that has client support for most major operating systems. Recent versions of NetWare include graphical client tools for management from client stations. At one time, NetWare accounted for more than 60 percent of the network operating system market. See *Windows NT, Client Services for NetWare, NetWare Link.*

NetWare Directory Services (NDS)

In NetWare, a distributed hierarchy of network services such as servers, shared volumes, and printers. NetWare implements NDS as a directory structure having elaborate security and administration mechanisms. The CSNW provided in Windows NT 4.0 supports the NDS tree. See *NetWare, Client Services for NetWare.*

NetWare Link (NWLink)

A Windows NT transport protocol that implements Novell's IPX. NWLink is useful as a general purpose transport for Windows NT and for connecting to NetWare file servers through CSNW. See *Internetwork Packet eXchange, Client Services for NetWare.*

NetWare NetBIOS Link (NWNBLink)

NetBIOS implemented over NWLink. See *Network Basic Input/Output System, NetWare Link, NetBIOS over TCP/IP.*

Network

A group of computers connected via some digital medium for the purpose of exchanging information. Networks can be based upon many types of media, such as twisted pair telephone-style cable, optical fiber, coaxial cable, radio, or infrared light. Certain computers are usually configured as service providers called *servers*. Computers that perform user tasks directly and that utilize the services of servers are called *clients*. See *Client/Server, Server, Network Operating System.*

Network Basic Input/Output System (NetBIOS)

A client/server interprocess communication service developed by IBM in the early 1980s. NetBIOS presents a relatively primitive mechanism for communication in client server/applications, but its widespread acceptance and availability across most operating systems makes it a logical choice for simple network applications. Many Windows NT network IPC mechanisms are implemented over NetBIOS. See *Interprocess Communications, Client/Server.*

Network Driver Interface Specification (NDIS)

A Microsoft specification to which network adapter drivers must conform in order to work with Microsoft network operating systems. NDIS provides a many-to-many binding between network adapter drivers and transport protocols. See *Transport Protocol*.

Network Dynamic Data Exchange (NetDDE)

An interprocess communication mechanism developed by Microsoft to support the distribution of DDE applications over a network. See *Interprocess Communications, Dynamic Data Exchange*.

Network Interface Card (NIC)

A Physical layer adapter device that allows a computer to connect to and communicate over a local area network. See *Ethernet, Token Ring, Adapter*.

Network Layer

The layer of the OSI model that creates a communication path between two computers via routed packets. Transport protocols implement both the Network layer and the Transport layer of the OSI stack. IP is a Network layer service. See *Internet Protocol, Transport Protocol, Open Systems Interconnect Model*.

Network Operating System

A computer operating system specifically designed to optimize a computer's ability to respond to service requests. Servers run network operating systems. Windows NT Server and NetWare are both network operating systems. See *Windows NT, Server, NetWare*.

New Technology File System (NTFS)

A secure, transaction-oriented file system developed for Windows NT that incorporates the Windows NT security model for assigning permissions and shares. NTFS is optimized for hard drives larger than 500MB and requires too much overhead to be used on hard disk drives smaller than 50MB.

Nonbrowser

A computer on a network that will not maintain a list of other computers and services on the network. See *Browser, Browsing*.

NTFS

See *New Technology File System*.

NWLink

See *NetWare Link, Internetwork Packet eXchange*.

NWNBLink

See *NetWare NetBIOS Link*.

O

Object

A software service provider that encapsulates both the algorithm and the data structures necessary to provide a service. Usually, objects can inherit data and functionality from their parent objects, thus allowing complex services to be constructed from simpler objects. The term *object oriented* implies a tight relationship between algorithms and data structures. See *Module*.

Object Counters

Containers built into each service object in Windows NT that store a count of the number of times an object performs its service or to what degree. You can use performance monitors to access object counters and measure how the different objects in Windows NT are operating. See *Object*.

Open Graphics Language (OpenGL)

A standard interface for the presentation of two- and three-dimensional visual data.

Open Systems Interconnect Model (OSI Model)

A model for network component interoperability developed by the International Standards Organization to promote cross-vendor compatibility of hardware and software network systems. The OSI model splits the process of networking into seven distinct services. Each layer uses the services of the layer below to provide its service to the layer above. See *Physical Layer, Data Link Layer, Network Layer, Transport Layer, Session Layer, Presentation Layer, Application Layer*.

OpenGL

See *Open Graphics Language*.

Operating System

A collection of services that form a foundation upon which applications run. Operating systems may be simple I/O service providers with a command shell, such as MS-DOS, or they may be sophisticated, preemptive, multitasking, multi-processing applications platforms like Windows NT. See *Network Operating System, Preemptive Multitasking, Kernel*.

Operating System 2 (OS/2)

A 16-bit (and later, 32-bit) operating system developed jointly by Microsoft and IBM as a successor to MS-DOS. Microsoft bowed out of the 32-bit development effort and produced its own product, Windows NT, as a competitor to OS/2. OS/2 is now a preemptive, multitasking 32-bit operating system with strong support for networking and the ability to run MS-DOS and Win16 applications, but IBM has been unable to entice a large number of developers to produce software that runs native under OS/2. See *Operating System, Preemptive Multitasking*.

Optimization

Any effort to reduce the workload on a hardware component by eliminating, obviating, or reducing the amount of work required of the hardware component through any means. For instance, file caching is an optimization that reduces the workload of a hard disk drive.

OS/2

See *Operating System 2*.

OSI Model

See *Open Systems Interconnect Model*.

P

Page File

See *Swap File*.

Partition

A section of a hard disk that can contain an independent file system volume. Partitions can be used to keep multiple operating systems and file systems on the same hard disk. See *Volume, Hard Disk Drives.*

Password

A secret code used to validate the identity of a user of a secure system. Passwords are used in tandem with account names to log on to most computer systems.

Pathworks

A version of LAN Manager for DEC computer systems running the VMS operating system and DEC Unix. See *Network Operating System.*

PC

See *Personal Computer.*

PCI

See *Peripheral Connection Interface.*

PDC

See *Primary Domain Controller.*

Peer

A networked computer that both shares resources with other computers and accesses the shared resources of other computers. A nondedicated server. See *Server, Client.*

Pentium

The fifth generation of the Intel family of microprocessors upon which PC-compatible computers are based. The Pentium includes advanced microprocessor features like parallel pipeline, out-of-order execution, large on-chip caches, built-in support for multiprocessing, and extremely fast floating point math performance.

Pentium Pro

The sixth generation of the Intel family of microprocessors, the Pentium Pro is actually a RISC microprocessor that translates Pentium op codes into multiple RISC instructions for execution. This architecture allows the Pentium Pro to take advantage of advancements in microprocessor design more efficiently than complex instruction set computers (CISC) like the Pentium can. See *Reduced Instruction Set Computer*.

Peripheral

An input/output device attached to a computer. Peripherals can be printers, hard disk drives, monitors, and so on.

Peripheral Connection Interface (PCI)

A high speed 32/64-bit bus interface developed by Intel and widely accepted as the successor to the 16-bit ISA interface. PCI devices support I/O throughput about 40 times faster than the ISA bus.

Permissions

Security constructs used to regulate access to resources by user name or group affiliation. Permissions can be assigned by administrators to allow any level of access, such as read only, read/write, delete, by controlling the ability of users to initiate object services. Security is implemented by checking the user's security identifier against each object's access control list. See *Security Identifiers, Access Control List*.

Personal Computer (PC)

A microcomputer used by one person at a time (i.e., not a multiuser computer). PCs are generally clients or peers in an networked environment. High-speed PCs are called *workstations*. Networks of PCs are called *LAN*s. The term *PC* is often used to refer to computers compatible with the IBM PC.

Physical Layer

The cables, connectors, and connection ports of a network. The passive physical components required to create a network. See *Open Systems Interconnect Model*.

Plotters

Print devices that use a numeric-control stylus to draw on paper rather than the raster print processes employed by laser and ink-jet printers. Plotters are typically used to produce large, high-resolution line art such as blueprints.

Point-to-Point Protocol (PPP)

A Network layer transport that performs over point-to-point network connections such as serial or modem lines. PPP can negotiate any transport protocol used by both systems involved in the link and can automatically assign IP, DNS, and gateway addresses when used with TCP/IP.

Policies

General controls that enhance the security of an operating environment. In Windows NT, policies affect restrictions on password use and rights assignment and determine which events will be recorded in the Security log.

POP

See *Post Office Protocol*.

Portable Open Systems Interconnect (POSIX)

A set of standards used to ensure cross-platform compatibility of client/server applications.

Post Office Protocol (POP)

An Internet protocol that manages the routing and delivery of e-mail. See *Electronic Mail*.

Potential Browser

A computer on a network that may maintain a list of other computers and services on the network if requested to do so by a Master Browser. See *Browser, Master Browser*.

PowerPC

A microprocessor family developed by IBM to compete with the Intel family of microprocessors. The PowerPC is a RISC-architecture microprocessor with many advanced features that emulate other microprocessors. PowerPCs are currently used in a line of IBM computers and in the Apple Power Macintosh. Windows NT is available for the PowerPC.

PPP

See *Point-to-Point Protocol.*

Preemptive Multitasking

A multitasking implementation in which an interrupt routine in the Kernel manages the scheduling of processor time among running threads. The threads themselves do not need to support multitasking in any way because the microprocessor will preempt the thread with an interrupt, save its state, update all thread priorities according to its scheduling algorithm, and pass control to the highest priority thread awaiting execution. Because of the preemptive nature, a thread that crashes will not affect the operation of other executing threads. See *Kernel, Thread, Operating System, Process.*

Preferences

Characteristics of user accounts, such as password, profile location, home directory, and logon script.

Presentation Layer

That layer of the OSI model that converts and translates (if necessary) information between the Session and Application layers. See *Open Systems Interconnect Model.*

Primary Domain Controller (PDC)

The domain server that contains the master copy of the security, computer, and user accounts databases and that can authenticate workstations. The primary domain controller can replicate its databases to one or more backup domain controllers and is usually also the Master Browser for the domain. See *Domain, Master Browser.*

Printers

Peripheral devices that produce paper copy of computer data. See *Laser Printers, Ink-Jet Printers, Plotters, Peripheral.*

Priority

A level of execution importance assigned to a thread. In combination with other factors, the priority level determines how often that thread will get computer time according to a scheduling algorithm. See *Preemptive Multitasking*.

Process

A running program containing one or more threads. A process encapsulates the protected memory and environment for its threads.

Processor

A circuit designed to automatically perform lists of logical and arithmetic operations. Unlike microprocessors, processors may be designed from discrete components rather than be a monolithic integrated circuit. See *Microprocessor*.

Program

A list of processor instructions designed to perform a certain function. A running program is called a process. A package of one or more programs and attendant data designed to meet a certain application is called software. See *Software, Application, Process, Microprocessor*.

Programming Interfaces

Interprocess communications mechanisms that provide certain high-level services to running processes. Programming interfaces may provide network communication, graphical presentation, or any other type of software service. See *Interprocess Communications*.

Protocol

An established communication method that the parties involved understand. Protocols provide a context in which to interpret communicated information. Computer protocols are rules used by communicating devices and software services to format data in a way that all participants understand. See *Transport Protocol*.

Public Switched Telephone Network (PSTN)

A global network of interconnected digital and analog communication links originally designed to support voice communication between any two points in the world but quickly adapted to handle digital data traffic when the computer revolution occurred. In addition to its traditional voice support role, the PSTN now functions as the Physical layer of the Internet by providing dial-up and leased lines for the interconnections. See *Internet, Modem, Physical Layer*.

R

RAID

See *Redundant Array of Inexpensive Disks*.

RAID Controllers

Hard disk drive controllers that implement RAID in hardware. See *Redundant Array of Inexpensive Disks*.

Random Access Memory (RAM)

Integrated circuits that store digital bits in massive arrays of logical gates or capacitors. RAM is the primary memory store for modern computers, storing all running software processes and contextual data. See *Microprocessor*.

RARP

See *Reverse Address Resolution Protocol*.

RAS

See *Remote Access Service*.

Real-Time Application

A process that must respond to external events at least as fast as those events can occur. Real-time threads must run at very high priorities to ensure their ability to respond in real time. See *Process*.

Redirector

A software service that redirects user file I/O requests over the network. Novell implements the Workstation and Client services for NetWare as redirectors. Redirectors allow servers to be used as mass storage devices that appear local to the user. See *Client Services for NetWare, File System*.

Reduced Instruction Set Computer (RISC)

A microprocessor technology that implements fewer and more primitive instructions than typical microprocessors and can therefore be implemented quickly with the most modern semiconductor technology and speeds. Programs written for RISC microprocessors require more instructions (longer programs) to perform the same task as a normal microprocessor but are capable of a greater degree of optimization and therefore usually run faster. See *Microprocessor*.

Redundant Array of Inexpensive Disks (RAID)

A collection of hard disk drives, coordinated by a special controller, that appears as one physical disk to a computer but stores its data across all the disks to take advantage of the speed and/or fault tolerance afforded by using more than one disk. RAID disk storage has several levels, including 0 (striping), 1 (mirroring), and 5 (striping with parity). RAID systems are typically used for very large storage volumes or to provide fault-tolerance features such as hot swapping of failed disks or automatically backing up data onto replacement disks.

Registry

A database of settings required and maintained by Windows NT and its components. The Registry stores Control Panel settings. You can use the Registry Editor to change these settings.

Remote Access Service (RAS)

A service that allows network connections to be established over PSTN lines with modems. The computer initiating the connection is called the RAS client; the answering computer is called the RAS host. See *Modem*.

Remote Procedure Calls (RPC)

A network interprocess communication mechanism that allows an application to be distributed among many computers on the same network. See *Local Procedure Call, Interprocess Communications*.

Requests for Comments (RFCs)

The set of standards defining the Internet protocols as determined by the Internet Engineering Task Force and available in the public domain on the Internet. RFCs define the functions and services provided by each of the many Internet protocols. Compliance with the RFCs guarantees cross-vendor compatibility. See *Internet*.

Resource

Any useful service, such as a shared network directory or a printer. See *Share*.

Reverse Address Resolution Protocol (RARP)

The TCP/IP protocol that allows a computer that has a Physical layer address (such as an Ethernet address) but does not have an IP address to request a numeric IP address from another computer on the network. See *Transfer Control Protocol/ Internet Protocol*.

RFC

See *Requests for Comments*.

RISC

See *Reduced Instruction Set Computer*.

Router

A Network layer device that moves packets between networks. Routers provide internetwork connectivity. See *Network Layer*.

RPC

See *Remote Procedure Calls*.

S

SAM

See *Security Accounts Manager*.

Scheduling

The process of determining which threads should be executed according to their priority and other factors. See *Preemptive Multitasking*.

SCSI

See *Small Computer Systems Interface*.

Security

Measures taken to secure a system against accidental or intentional loss, usually in the form of accountability procedures and use restriction. See *Security Identifiers, Security Accounts Manager*.

Security Accounts Manager (SAM)

The module of the Windows NT executive that authenticates a username and password against a database of accounts, generating an access token that includes the user's permissions. See *Security, Security Identifiers, Access Tokens*.

Security Identifiers

Unique codes that identify a specific user to the Windows NT security system. Security identifiers contain a complete set of permissions for that user.

Serial

A method of communication that transfers data across a medium one bit at a time, usually adding stop, start, and check bits to ensure quality transfer. See *COM Port, Modem*.

Serial Line Internet Protocol (SLIP)

An implementation of the IP protocol over serial lines. SLIP has been obviated by PPP. See *Point-to-Point Protocol, Internet Protocol*.

Server

A computer dedicated to servicing requests for resources from other computers on a network. Servers typically run network operating systems such as Windows NT Server or NetWare. See *Windows NT, NetWare, Client/Server*.

Service

A process dedicated to implementing a specific function for other processes. Most Windows NT components are services used by User-level applications.

Session Layer

The layer of the OSI model dedicated to maintaining a bidirectional communication connection between two computers. The Session layer uses the services of the Transport layer to provide this service. See *Open Systems Interconnect Model, Transport Layer.*

Share

A resource (e.g., a directory or a printer) shared by a server or a peer on a network. See *Resource, Server, Peer.*

Shell

The user interface of an operating system; the shell launches applications and manages file systems.

Simple Network Management Protocol (SNMP)

An Internet protocol that manages network hardware such as routers, switches, servers, and clients from a single client on the network. See *Internet Protocol.*

SLIP

See *Serial Line Internet Protocol.*

Small Computer Systems Interface (SCSI)

A high-speed, parallel-bus interface that connects hard disk drives, CD-ROM drives, tape drives, and many other peripherals to a computer. SCSI is the mass storage connection standard among all computers except IBM compatibles, which use either SCSI or IDE.

SNMP

See *Simple Network Management Protocol.*

Software

A suite of programs sold as a unit and dedicated to a specific application. See *Program, Application, Process.*

Spooler

A service that buffers output to a low-speed device such as a printer so the software outputting to the device is not tied up.

Stripe Set

A single volume created across multiple hard disk drives and accessed in parallel for the purpose of optimizing disk access time. NTFS can create stripe sets. See *New Technology File System, Volume, File System.*

Subdirectory

A directory contained in another directory. See *Directories.*

Subnet Mask

A number mathematically applied to Internet protocol addresses to determine which IP addresses are a part of the same subnetwork as the computer applying the subnet mask.

Swap File

The virtual memory file on a hard disk containing the memory pages that have been moved out to disk to increase available RAM. See *Virtual Memory.*

Symmetrical Multiprocessing

A multiprocessing methodology that assigns processes to processors on a fair-share basis. This method balances the processing load among processors and ensures that no processor will become a bottleneck. Symmetrical multiprocessing is more difficult to implement than asymmetrical multiprocessing, as processors must share certain hardware functions. See *Asymmetrical Multiprocessing, Multiprocessing.*

T

Task Manager

An application that manually views and closes running processes. Press Ctrl+Alt+Del to launch the Task Manager.

TCP

See *Transmission Control Protocol.*

TCP/IP

See *Transmission Control Protocol/Internet Protocol.*

TDI

See *Transport Driver Interface.*

Telnet

A terminal application that allows a user to log into a multiuser UNIX computer from any computer connected to the Internet. See *Internet.*

Thread

A list of instructions running in a computer to perform a certain task. Each thread runs in the context of a process, which embodies the protected memory space and the environment of the threads. Multithreaded processes can perform more than one task at the same time. See *Process, Preemptive Multitasking, Program.*

Throughput

The measure of information flow through a system in a specific time frame, usually one second. For instance, 28.8Kbps is the throughput of a modem: 28.8 kilobits per second can be transmitted.

Token Ring

The second most popular Data Link layer standard for local area networking. Token ring implements the token passing method of arbitrating multiple-computer access to the same network. Token ring operates at either 4 or 16Mbps. FDDI is similar to token ring and operates at 100Mbps. See *Data Link Layer.*

Transmission Control Protocol (TCP)

A transport layer protocol that implements guaranteed packet delivery using the Internet Protocol (IP). See *Transmission Control Protocol/Internet Protocol, Internet Protocol.*

Transmission Control Protocol/Internet Protocol (TCP/IP)

A suite of Internet protocols upon which the global Internet is based. TCP/IP is a general term that can refer either to the TCP and IP protocols used together or to the complete set of Internet protocols. TCP/IP is the default protocol for Windows NT.

Transport Driver Interface (TDI)

A specification to which all Window NT transport protocols must be written in order to be used by higher level services such as programming interfaces, file systems, and interprocess communications mechanisms. See *Transport Protocol*.

Transport Layer

The OSI model layer responsible for the guaranteed serial delivery of packets between two computers over an internetwork. TCP is the Transport layer protocol for the TCP/IP transport protocol.

Transport Protocol

A service that delivers discrete packets of information between any two computers in a network. Higher level connection-oriented services are built upon transport protocols. See *TCP/IP, NetWare Link, NetBIOS Extended User Interface, Transport Layer, Internet Protocol, Internet*.

U

UDP

See *User Datagram Protocol*.

UNC

See *Universal Naming Convention*.

Uniform Resource Locator (URL)

An Internet standard naming convention for identifying resources available via various TCP/IP application protocols. For example, `http://www.microsoft.com` is the URL for Microsoft's World Wide Web server site, while `ftp://gateway.dec.com` is a popular FTP site. A URL allows easy hypertext references to a particular resource from within a document or mail message. See *Hypertext Transfer Protocol, World Wide Web*.

Universal Naming Convention (UNC)

A multivendor, multiplatform convention for identifying shared resources on a network. See *multitasking*.

UNIX

A multitasking, kernel-based operating system developed at AT&T in the early 1970s and provided (originally) free to universities as a research operating system. Because of its availability and ability to scale down to microprocessor-based computers, UNIX became the standard operating system of the Internet and its attendant network protocols and is the closest approximation to a universal operating system that exists. Most computers can run some variant of the UNIX operating system. See *Multitasking, Internet*.

UseNet

A massive distributed database of news feeds and special interest groups maintained on the Internet and accessible through most Web browsers. See *Internet, World Wide Web*.

User Datagram Protocol (UDP)

A nonguaranteed network packet protocol implemented on IP that is far faster than TCP because it doesn't have flow-control overhead. UDP can be implemented as a reliable transport when some higher level protocol (such as NetBIOS) exists to make sure that required data will eventually be retransmitted in local area environments.

User Manager

A Windows NT application that administers user accounts and manages policies.

Username

A user's account name in a logon-authenticated system. See *Security*.

V

VDM

See *Virtual DOS Machine*.

VFAT

An extension of the FAT file system; VFAT allows long filenames up to 255 characters. Windows 95 and Windows NT use the VFAT file system.

Virtual DOS Machine (VDM)

The DOS environment created by Windows NT for the execution of DOS and Win16 applications. See *MS-DOS, Win16*.

Virtual Memory

A kernel service that stores memory pages not currently in use on a mass storage device to free up the memory occupied for other uses. Virtual memory hides the memory swapping process from applications and higher level services. See *Swap File, Kernel*.

Volume

A collection of data indexed by directories containing files and referred to by a drive letter. Volumes are normally contained in a single partition, but volume sets and stripe sets extend a single volume across multiple partitions.

W

Wide Area Network (WAN)

A geographically dispersed network of networks connected by routers and communication links. The Internet is the world's largest WAN. See *Internet, Local Area Network*.

Win16

The set of application services provided by the 16-bit versions of Microsoft Windows: Windows 3.0 and Windows for Workgroups 3.11.

Win32

The set of application services provided by the 32-bit versions of Microsoft Windows: Windows 95 and Windows NT.

Windows 3.11 for Workgroups

The current 16-bit version of Windows for less-powerful, Intel-based personal computers; this system includes peer networking services.

Windows 95

The current 32-bit version of Microsoft Windows for medium-range, Intel-based personal computers; this system includes peer networking services, Internet support, and strong support for older DOS applications and peripherals.

Windows Internet Name Service (WINS)

A network service for Microsoft networks that provides Windows computers with Internet numbers for specified NetBIOS names, facilitating browsing and intercommunication over TCP/IP networks.

Windows NT

The current 32-bit version of Microsoft Windows for powerful Intel, Alpha, PowerPC, or MIPS-based computers; the system includes peer networking services, server networking services, Internet client and server services, and a broad range of utilities.

Windows on Windows (WOW)

The compatibility service that allows the use of Win16 apps under Windows NT. WOW serves as a 32-bit interface shell for 16-bit applications.

Windows Sockets

An interprocess communications protocol that delivers connection-oriented data streams used by Internet software and software ported from UNIX environments. See *Interprocess Communications*.

WINS

See *Windows Internet Name Service*.

Workgroup

In Microsoft networks, a collection of related computers, such as a department, that doesn't require the uniform security and coordination of a domain. See *Domain*.

Workstation

A powerful personal computer, usually running a preemptive, multitasking operating system like UNIX or Windows NT.

World Wide Web (WWW)

A collection of Internet servers providing hypertext-formatted documents for Internet clients running Web browsers. The World Wide Web provided the first easy-to-use graphical interface for the Internet and is largely responsible for the Internet's explosive growth.

WOW

See *Windows on Windows*.

Write-back Caching

A caching optimization wherein data written to the slow store is cached until the cache is full or until a subsequent write operation overwrites the cached data. Write-back caching can significantly reduce the write operations to a slow store because many write operations are subsequently obviated by new information. Data in the write-back cache is also available for subsequent reads. If something happens to prevent the cache from writing data to the slow store, the cache data will be lost. See *Caching, Write-through Caching*.

Write-through Caching

A caching optimization wherein data written to a slow store is kept in a cache for subsequent rereading. Unlike write-back caching, write-through caching immediately writes the data to the slow store and is therefore less optimal but more secure.

WWW

See *World Wide Web*.

Index

Note to the Reader:

Note to the Reader: First level entries are in **bold**. Page numbers in **bold** indicate the principal discussion of a topic or the definition of a term. Page numbers in *italic* indicate illustrations.